CIPS Study Matters

Level 6

Graduate Diploma in Purchasing and Supply

Public Sector Stakeholders and Governance

Dr David Moore

Cranfield University

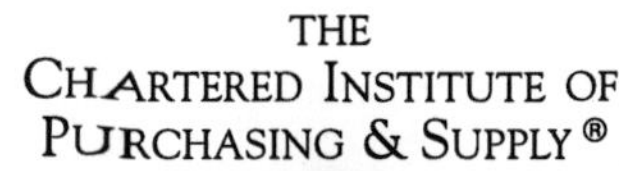

Published by

The Chartered Institute of Purchasing and Supply

Easton House, Easton on the Hill, Stamford, Lincolnshire PE9 3NZ

Tel: +44 (0) 1780 756 777

Fax: +44 (0) 1780 751 610

Email: info@cips.org

Website: www.cips.org

First published December 2008

Instructional design: Etrinsic

ISBN: 1-86124-169-0
ISBN: 978-1-86124-169-6

Contents

Introduction

This course book has been designed to assist you in studying for the CIPS Public Sector Stakeholders and Governance unit in the level 6 Graduate Diploma in Purchasing and Supply. The book covers all topics in the official CIPS unit content document.

The focus of this unit is on the strategic management of key and critical stakeholders of the public sector. This unit looks at providing tools and techniques for developing a range of relationship strategies, along with examining the significance of changing social and political agenda, such as Corporate Social Responsibility and Small Medium Enterprises agenda for procurement organisation and processes.

By the end of this unit, students should be able to demonstrate the ability to critically evaluate the above strategies and agendas, as well as to analyse governance of the procurement process and the effectiveness of financial accountability and performance evaluation arrangements.

How to use this book

The course book will take you step by step through the unit content in a series of carefully planned 'study sessions' and provides you with learning activities, self-assessment questions and revision questions to help you master the subject matter. The guide should help you organise and carry out your studies in a methodological. Logical and effective way, but if you have your own study preferences you will find it a flexible resource too.

Before you begin using this course book, make sure you are familiar with any advice provided by CIPS on such things as study skills, revision techniques or support and how to handle formal assessments.

If you are on a taught course, it will be up to your tutor to explain how to use the book – when to read the study sessions, when to tackle the activities and questions, and so on.

If you are on a self-study course, or studying independently, you can use the course book in the following way:

Scan the whole book to get a feel for the nature and content of the subject matter.

Plan your overall study schedule so that you allow enough time to complete all 20 study sessions well before your examinations – in other words, leaving plenty of time for revision.

For each session, set aside enough time for reading the text, tackling all the learning activities and self-assessment questions, and the revision question at the end of the sessions, and for the suggested further reading. Guidance on roughly how long you should set aside for studying each session is given at the beginning of the session.

Now let's take a look at the structure and content of the individual study.

Overview of the study sessions

The course book breaks the content down into .20 sessions, which vary from three to six or seven hours' duration each. However, we are not advising you to study for this sort of time without a break! The sessions are simply a convenient way of breaking the syllabus into manageable chunks. Most people would try to study one to two sessions a week, taking one or two breaks within each sessions. You will quickly find out what suits you best.

Each session begins with a brief **introduction** which sets out the areas of the syllabus being covered and explains, if necessary, how the session fits in with the topics that come before and after.

After the introduction there is a statement of the **session learning objectives**. The objectives are designed to help you understand exactly what you should be able to do after you've studied the session. You might find it helpful to tick them off as you progress through the session. You will also find them useful during revision. There is one session learning objective for each numbered subsection of the session.

After this, there is a brief section reproducing the learning objectives and indicative content from the official **unit content document**. This will help you to understand exactly which part of the syllabus you are studying in the current session.

Following this, there are **prior knowledge** and **resource** sections if necessary. These will let you know if there are any topics you need to be familiar with before tackling each particular session, or any special resources you might need, such as a calculator or graph paper.

Then the main part of the study session begins, with the first of the numbered main subsections. At regular intervals in each study session, we have provided you with **learning activities**, which are designed to get you actively involved in the learning process. You should always try to complete the activities – usually on a separate sheet of your own paper – before reading on. You will learn much more effectively if you are actively involved in doing something as you study, rather than just passively reading the text in from of you. The feedback or answers to the activities are provided at the end of the session. Do not be tempted to skip the activity.

We also provide a number of **self-assessment questions** in each study session. These are to help you to decide for yourself whether or not you have achieved the learning objectives set out at the beginning of the session. As with the activities, you should always tackle them – usually on a separate sheet of paper. Don't be tempted to skip them. The feedback or answers are again at the end of the session. If you still do not understand a topic having attempted the self-assessment question, always try to re-read the relevant passages in the textbook readings to sessions, or follow the advice on further reading at the end of the session. If this still doesn't work, you should contact the CIPS membership and Qualification Advice team.

For most of the learning activities and self-assessment questions you will need to use separate sheets of paper for your answers or responses. Some of the activities or questions require you to complete a table or form, in which case you could write your response in the study guide itself, or photocopy the page.

At the end of the session are three final sections.

The first is the **summary**. Use it to remind yourself or check off what you have just studied, or later on during revision.

Then following the **suggested further reading** section. This section, if it appears, contains recommendations for further reading which you can follow up if you would like to read alternative treatments of the topics. If for any reason you are having difficulty understanding the course book on a particular topic, try one of the alternative treatments recommended. If you are keen to read around and beyond the syllabus, to help you pick up extra points in the examination for example, you may like to try some of the additional readings recommended. If this section does not appear at the end of a session, it usually means that further reading for the session topics is not necessary.

At the end of the session we direct you to a **revision question** which you will find in a separate section at the end of the course book. Feedback on the questions is also given.

Reading lists

CIPS produces an official reading list, which recommends essential and desirable texts for augmenting your studies. This reading list is available on the CIPS website or from the CIPS Bookshop. This course book is one of the essential texts for this unit. In this section we describe the main characteristics of the other essential text for this unit, which you are strongly urged to buy and use throughout your course.

The other essential text is:

Public Management and Governance edited by Tony Bovaird and Elke Loffler, published by Routledge in 2003.

UNIT CHARACTERISTICS

The focus of this unit is on the strategic management of key and critical stakeholders of the Public Sector. This unit looks at providing tools and techniques for developing a range of relationship strategies, including:

- Communication strategies
- Collaborative strategies
- Conflict management strategies

The unit also examines the significance of changing social and political agendas, such as Corporate Social Responsibility (CSR) and the Small medium enterprises (SME) agenda, for your procurement organisation and processes.

By the end of this unit, students should be able to demonstrate the ability to critically evaluate the above strategies and agendas, as well as to analyse governance of the procurement process and the effectiveness of financial accountability and performance evaluation arrangements.

Learning Outcomes

On completion of this unit, students will be able to:

LO1 Investigate relationships with key and critical stakeholders relevant to public procurement 30%

LO2 Develop Conflict management strategies to resolve differences with stakeholders. 20%

LO3 Critically evaluate the significance of changing social and political agendas for public procurement 15%

LO4 Analyse the effectiveness of Governance and oversight arrangements for procurement. 20%

LO5 Critically evaluate methods and processes of performance evaluation of procurement 15%

1.0 Investigate relationships with key and critical stakeholders relevant to public procurement. 30%

1.1 Identify and evaluate critical internal and external stakeholders relevant to public procurement.

- rationale for distinguishing between 'internal' and 'external' stakeholders

- 'internal' stakeholders e.g. clients, budget holders, finance, audit
- 'external' stakeholders e.g. elected representatives, suppliers, trade unions, industry organisations, community groups.

1.2 Assess the role, interests and resources of internal and external stakeholders in relation to procurement generally and also in relation to specific strategic procurements.

- stakeholder identification models such as Mendelow (1991)
- stakeholder analysis methods and systems
- weighting the resources and influence of stakeholders.

1.3. Analyse strategies for influencing and managing stakeholders by engaging them at an early stage in procurement plans and specific strategic procurements.

- understand the benefits of incorporating stakeholders into the planning process at an early stage
- managing diversity amongst stakeholders
- identify project failures where stakeholders were not fully in formed.

1.4 Critically evaluate communication and collaborative strategies may be developed to improve relationships with internal and external stakeholders.

- critically evaluate theories, models, policy documents and practice in relation to communication and collaborative strategies
- explain how communication and collaborative strategies may be developed
- understand the concept of shared services in the public sector.

1.5 Critically assess the effectiveness of the purchasing organisation's internal and external communications policy and processes.

- devise and apply tests of communication effectiveness
- demonstrate the effectiveness of chosen communication policies and processes
- methods of review of communications in comparable organisations
- learning from examples of effective communications demonstrated in other sectors and industries.

1.6 Critically evaluate marketing communication methods to improve internal and external stakeholder awareness of the role and purpose of procurement organisations.

- collect and disseminate 'good news stories' about procurement success

- collect and broadcast convincing data on the importance of good procurement for organisational success
- evaluate the success of marketing activities.

1.7 Explain how partnerships with appropriate stakeholders may be developed.

- understand the nature and purpose of partnerships
- identify appropriate stakeholders with which to develop partnerships
- build partnerships with appropriate internal and external stakeholders

2.0 Justify conflict management strategies to resolve differences with stakeholders. 20%

2.1 Critically evaluate theories, models, policy documents and practice in relation to conflict management strategies.

- understand causes and types of conflict
- assess methods of handling conflict
- analyse recent examples of successful and unsuccessful conflict management in various contexts e.g. public and private sectors, central, local government and the NHS

2.2 Assess the effectiveness of procedures for resolving differences in relation to the correct application of procurement procedures with internal and external stakeholders.

- review internal procurement procedures and methods of dissemi nating changes to procedures in relation to resolving differences with stakeholders
- methods of conflict resolution in contractual and non-contractual situations
- manage procedures effectively to resolve differences with stake holders
- assess the effectiveness of procedures for resolving differences with internal stakeholders

2.3 Critically assess the effectiveness of procedures for resolving differences with external stakeholders in relation to the planning of major projects, award and delivery of contracts.

- assess the effectiveness of referring up of Management Information Systems (MIS) queries and management issues for senior level action
- analyse the 'two pyramids' of management structures within client

and contractor organisation and how to bridge them
- assess and apply lessons from experiences of the effect of high level involvement on successful projects e.g. ministers, members of parliament, industry leaders, the media.

3.0 Critically evaluate the significance of changing social and political agendas for public procurement. 15%

3.1 Critically evaluate the significance of corporate social responsibility (CSR) and 'conscience procurement' for procurement organisation, policy and procedures, internal and external stakeholders.

- understand corporate social responsibility (CSR) and 'conscience procurement'
- assess the implications of CSR and 'conscience procurement' for procurement organisation, policy and procedures
- involve internal and external stakeholders in developing policy and procedures in relation to CSR and 'conscience procurement'
- the impact of changes in policy e.g. Simms Sustainability Task Force Policy.

3.2 Critically assess the significance of the SME agenda for, procurement policy and procedures.

- assess the role and significance of SME's in the UK and international markets
- develop strategies for engaging SME's in public procurement in conjunction with internal and external stakeholders
- identify and apply methods and procedures for engaging minority owned SME's in public procurement e.g. Supply2.gov.

3.3 Explain how plans can be developed to take appropriate action to address the issues arising from the sustainability agenda together with internal and external stakeholders.

- understand the sustainability agenda and its implications for procurement
- explain how strategies may be developed for sustainable procurement in conjunction with internal and external stakeholders
- understand the differences between local, regional, and national policy agendas in relation to sustainability.

4.0 Analyse the effectiveness of Governance and oversight arrangements for procurement. 20%

4.1 Critically evaluate relevant theories, models, policy documents and practice in relation to Governance arrangements for procurement, particularly in relation to the role of elected representatives.

- understand the role of internal and external stakeholders in the governance of procurement
- assess the roles of elected representatives at national, regional and local levels in oversight arrangements for procurement
- assess the effectiveness of the provision of advice and guidance for ministers, Council leaders, key decision makers and Committee members
- analyse the effectiveness of governance arrangements for procurement

4.2 Critically evaluate the effectiveness of financial accountability arrangements for procurement.

- understand the role of finance in public sector organisations and its relationships with procurement
- analyse the procedures in place to give assurance to Permanent Secretaries and Chief Executives in their exercise of personal accountability
- assess the effectiveness of financial accountability arrangements for procurement.

4.3 Analyse the adequacy and robustness of procurement financial and management information systems.

- identify sources of procurement financial and management information
- examine the robustness of procurement financial and management information
- assess the usefulness and appropriateness of procurement financial and management information available to various levels of management and stakeholders
- propose improvements to procurement financial and management information systems to improve performance.

5.0 Critically evaluate methods and processes of performance evaluation of procurement 15%

5.1 Critically evaluate the relevance of Excellence models, in particular the Procurement Excellence Model (PEM), for providing an effective performance evaluation framework for organisations.

- understand total quality management (TQM), European Foundation for Quality Management (EFQM) and the PEM models

- secure stakeholder commitment to and involvement in the devel opment and application of performance evaluation
- compare and contrast PEM with other relevant models
- explore the value of adapting performance evaluation models to suit different organisations and types of procurement functions.

5.2 Critically evaluate the methods and outcomes of performance evaluation of procurement against appropriate models and remedy any weaknesses.

- compare models of process or outcomes
- assess data validation models for procurement effectiveness
- plan for delivering improvements to identified weaknesses
- benchmark against organisations with similar procurement functions.

5.3 Develop and apply a process with internal and external stakeholders, which incorporates their feedback on the performance of a procurement organisation.

- assess stakeholder views of procurement performance
- distinguish between more influential / significant and less influential / significant stakeholder views and react accordingly
- engage with stakeholders who are critical of procurement to understand their views and improve performance.

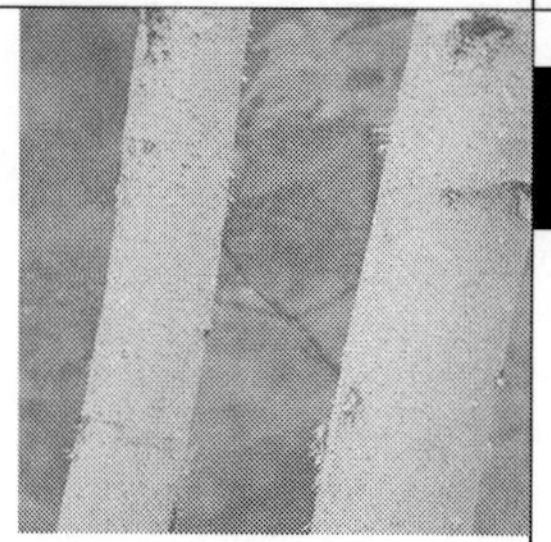

Study Session 1

"Identify and evaluate critical internal and external stakeholders relevant to public procurement"

Introduction

The public sector procurement environment has undergone considerable change over the last few decades. Much of this comes as a cumulative result of globalisation and recognition of the impact that effective procurement and supply chain management can have upon an organisation and adoption, or rather adaptation, of best practice in commercial organisations. More recently this has manifested itself in a series of initiatives and policy documents that affect all of the public sector organisations in the UK. This study session briefly sets this contextual background to the current position. It considers the nature of internal and external stakeholders, in order to develop more fully the role and impact that they may have in the subsequent study session.

Session learning objectives

After completing this session you should be able to:

discuss the contextual setting of, and background to, the public procurement environment
recognise the importance of stakeholders
utilise a rationale for distinguishing between 'internal' and 'external' stakeholders (internal examples include: clients and budget holders; external examples include: suppliers and unions)

Unit content coverage

This study session covers part of the following topic from the official CIPS unit content documents: Investigate relationships with key and critical stakeholders relevant to public procurement. Specifically, it covers: Identify and evaluate critical internal and external stakeholders relevant to public procurement.

Prior knowledge

You do not need specific knowledge prior to commencing this study session although you may find that the Units that you will have covered prior to commencing this Unit may have pertinent material.

Timing

You should take about 4 – 5 hours to read and complete this section, including learning activities, self assessment questions and the revision question.

Context / background

The UK public sector procurement environment has undergone considerable change over the past thirty years or so. The 1970's saw considerable socio-economic and political upheaval. It is hard to believe now that the early 1970's saw a three day working week and that petrol rationing coupons were issued (although not actually utilised). The late 1970's saw the 'winter of discontent' with public sector strikes and features such as rubbish not being collected from people's homes. This was followed by the election of Margaret Thatcher and, in the early 1980's, an increasing emphasis upon competition. This meant that quite a number of commercial organisations ultimately went out of business; there was the introduction of the emphasis upon the concept of value for money; a recognition that reducing costs could impact upon the bottom line for businesses just as could the increasing of sales (especially when gaining additional sales was difficult anyway!) Margaret Thatcher herself wrote the introduction to a paper on public sector procurement for the then new Central Unit on Purchasing (now evolved into the Office of Government Commerce-OGC). This highlighted how much money was spent on things within the public sector environment – "paperclips, desks, fuel and other essentials - let alone what is spent on warships and the like …" It was a time when the impact of improving purchasing performance could affect the overall profitability of commercial organisations and a similar view was taken that such approaches could apply in the public sector

As the 1980's progressed and the 1990's were entered, the public sector, just as the private sector had been for many years, was under pressure for increased efficiency. Arguably, although this also included 'effectiveness' and 'economy', it was seen by many as cost cutting. Managerial approaches that had been successful in the private sector were now being considered and applied in the public sector environment as efficiencies. During these decades, organisations that were part of the public sector were taken into the private sector. Examples include the public utilities such as gas and electricity; transport such as trains and road freight; communications such as British Telecom (originally part of the Post Office).

Remaining parts of the public sector were under increasing pressure to act in more commercial or entrepreneurial ways. In effect, trying to emulate best practice in the private sector became a driving force for the public sector generally. But who was driving this – and who were affected by it? The answer is a considerable number of people!

Learning activity 1.1

Take a short while to consider who may have been affected by such changes. List the types of people and the roles that they might have played before, and after, the changes that are indicated here. Note particularly the type of organisation for which these people worked.

You may wish to revisit (or visit if you have not undertaken) the module in Level 5 entitled Machinery of Government. Here Andrew Erridge (2007), in the study sessions 3 and 4 (pages 25 to 58) gives a clear overview of the changes that have been undertaken within public sector procurement.

Moving from the role and significance of procurement in the public sector he considers the use of the market to provide public services and comments upon outsourcing, the use of contractors and public private partnership (PPP)/private finance initiative (PFI) and concludes with the current role and significance of procurement. The reason for seeking your consideration of this is that this provides a sound contextual setting from which you can examine and assess what is now happening, in the light of what has happened in the past, in what is really a very complex environment. Decision making in respect of who gains contracts, how they are managed and thus whom is impacted upon by these contracts is considerable and not to be taken lightly. Progress through this course book will assist you in a wide perspective of the nature of and impact upon the many people who are affected by such decision making – the Stakeholders.

Self assessment question 1.1

Using a public sector organisation with which you are familiar detail people who could be considered stakeholders and how they might be affected in some way by procurement decisions.

The point of the this text so far is to identify that the public procurement sector is complex and subject to many influences and one where there can be considerable impact upon the public generally and certain groups specifically. Hence it is an environment that is subject to many initiatives and policies. Such matters can be influenced by – and affect – many differing stakeholders, therefore it is important to be aware of these initiatives – if only in overview – so that how these were received at the time may indicate the likely effect/ impact for later initiatives and/or policy changes

Stakeholders

"One should always study history – because things always repeat themselves"

Winston Churchill

It will be pertinent for you to recognise definitions of stakeholders in order to develop stakeholder managerial perspectives.

In effect, stakeholders are persons, groups, organisations, regulatory bodies or institutions with interest in procurement activities, projects or programmes. Particular definitions are:

Any group or individual who can affect or is affected by the achievement of the organisation objectives. (Freeman, 1984)

Those who have an interest in the company (so that the firm, in turn, may have an interest in satisfying their demands). (Argandona, 1998)

Everyone in the community who has a stake in what the company does. (Frederick, 1998)

Parties that have a stake in the corporation: something at risk, and therefore something to gain or lose, as a result of corporate activity. (Clarkson Centre for Business Ethics, 1999)

Whilst this takes a view on stakeholders generally, the important thing to bear in mind is that there are key stakeholders and these can be considered as those whom can significantly influence, or are important to the success of, the procurement activity, project or programme.

There are differing definitions and differing ways of categorising stakeholders and the concept has been a topic of considerable debate within academic circles. Donaldson and Preston (1995) put forward a widely accepted categorisation:

- A normative stakeholder theory - how managers should act and view the purpose of the organisation, according to some ethical principles.

- A descriptive stakeholder theory - based upon how managers and stakeholders behave and view their actions

- An instrumental stakeholder theory - how mangers should behave if they have to further their own interests or the organisations maximisation of profit / shareholder value.

Additionally, Reed (2002) noted that this allows one to recognise three stakeholder definitions:

- Normative Stakeholders – who have normative claims on the organisation

- Descriptive stakeholders – who may be affected by the organisation - /could potentially affect the organisation (the former if it is the object of the investigation is the effect of the organisation's activities and the latter if it is the decision making process of the organisation)

- Instrumental Stakeholders – defined by the need of management to take them in consideration when seeking to achieve its goals

What this does is to recognise theoretical concepts and constructs but to consider them, in due course, in a practical manner in respect of application.

Learning activity 1.2

Identify stakeholders by listing them in groups according to their relationship within and with an organisation, a) for a private sector organisation; b) for a public sector organisation.

Internal and external stakeholders

These that you have identified could be both internal and external stakeholders hence you should now briefly consider what the differences are between internal and external stakeholders.
Internal stakeholders are those stakeholders within the organisation and those who can be affected by wages and job stability such as employees, managers and owners/shareholders.
External stakeholders are those who are involved with the organisation but not employed by it such as customers, suppliers, government or society in general for example.

'Put simply, a project's stakeholders are:
The people and organisations implementing the project
The people and organisations who could be positively or negatively affected by the results of the project'

Intereg IIIB North Sea Programme

Figure 1.1 Internal / External Stakeholders

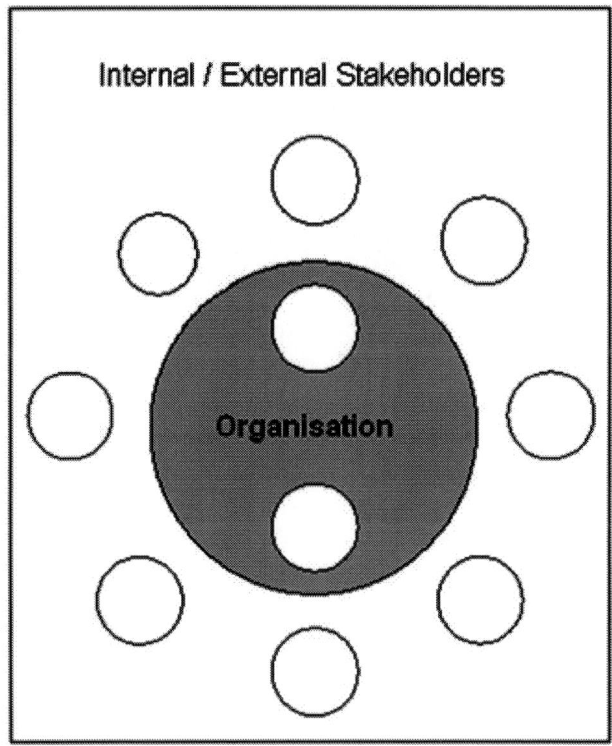

Source 12Manage.2008 *Assessing who or what really counts. Explanation of stakeholder analysis*

All those involved in business, and the public sector is an important player in this arena, have to recognise that there are interests of different people and groups to be taken into account. Organisations cannot just look to their organisation charts and consider formal structures. Whilst such formal structures may provide an indication of some of the stakeholders they do not provide a complete picture. Recalling the changes in procurement generally and public sector procurement specifically over the last decade or so one of the many features of the changes in the environment has been the move towards outsourcing – using contractors to provide services and support for activities that previously would have been undertaken in house. If this had not been developing there would anyway have been a considerable number of people or groups who would be impacted by, or have an impact upon, the activities of an organisation.

Hence there are internal (within the organisation or its immediate relationships), or external (outside the organisation or its immediate relationships), stakeholders.

Learning activity 1.3

In the following examples detail who you might consider internal and external stakeholders in the procurement of:

- a new computer system for a large school in inner London
- a new printer for all publications of the Welsh Assembly Government
- a new aircraft carrier for the Royal Navy

Thus internally you will find that, in general outline, you will have the people/ group/section/department who require the equipment or service; those who take a technical interest (such as to ensure consistency with other equipment or systems for example); those who have to enable payment; those who have to utilise what is being obtained; the people/ organisation that has to maintain/ repair equipment; audit activity to ensure rules regulations are compliant, and so on. In your detail for the activity you may have included stakeholders such as budget holders, clients, etc.

Externally you would have to consider, possible suppliers, actual suppliers, citizens affected in any way by the procurement activity either before, during or after the tender, award of contract, period of contract management and subsequent maintenance of that equipment or service (over possibly many years).

Stakeholders may be identified from many groups, for example:

- Owners or shareholders, executive management, operational management and staff of the organisation(s) who are:
  - sponsoring the procurement activity, project or programme;
  - affected by the procurement activity, project or programme;
  - responding to public sector demand;
  - creating the public sector demand.
- Customers or consumers who will be affected by the market changes;
- Internal and/or external audit;
- Political or regulatory bodies;
- The wider community such as the general public;
- Programme and Project teams.

Summary

Figure 1.2 Primary / Secondary Stakeholders

Source: Adapted from - 12Manage.2008 *Assessing who or what really counts. Explanation of stakeholder analysis*

The situation leading up to the present day situation where public procurement is affected by, and can impact upon a large number of stakeholders has its development over the past three decades when considerable changes have been made to both the private commercial sector and the public sector where procurement has generally followed the adoption of commercial best practice. This has impacted upon many individual or groups of stakeholders. Such stakeholders can now be seen as having considerable influence dependant upon the situation and the position in which they find themselves. Stakeholders can be internal or external to the organisation. Some of these have been identified in this study session. It may be that more individuals or groups may be identifiable in specific circumstances. Some individuals can be part of multiple stakeholder groups. Some stakeholders may have an explicit, formal organisation, others may not. There are Internal Stakeholders (such as employees) and External Stakeholders (such as government).
The interests of all stakeholders are closely related with the general success, wealth and well being of the organisation. However, certain stakeholders' interests are particularly important at times when certain issues must be addressed, for example:

- Customers are important when quality of products is discussed.

- Employees are important when circumstances or safety at work is discussed.
- Government is important when dealing with the environment or legislation.

We can also distinguish between Primary Stakeholders (such as shareholders) and Secondary Stakeholders (such as government). Where the line is drawn precisely, is a source of much debate.

Revision question

Discuss the changing nature of the public procurement environment noting especially the impact upon internal and external stakeholders

Feedback

Feedback on learning activity 1.1

'Take a short while to consider who may have been affected by such changes. List the types of people and the roles that they might have played before, and after, the changes that are indicated here. Note particularly the type of organisation for which these people worked.'

The period mentioned has seen considerable change – some of it uncomfortable; there will be many who worked in industrial organisations in the early 1980's who lost jobs because much of British manufacturing industry was not competitive and orders were being placed overseas. Public procurement organisations, as the 1980's moved into the 1990's, moved away from 'traditional' British companies to overseas suppliers. As an example, the Post Office, MoD and many others frequently purchased vehicles from British Leyland (later Austin Rover and then Rover).

Stakeholders in the communities at one time had many local amenities and facilities; as the 1990's progressed, best practice management concepts such as Just in Time, Total Quality Management and Lean Thinking meant that increasingly activities and services that provided employment (as an example) were being outsourced. Activities such as catering and security were amongst those to be undertaken by third parties and (even coming up to date) increasing use of contractors mean that the MoD now looks at outsourcing activities that were once procured from within the organisation or by British companies, often providing work for a local workforce. Hence, taxpayers, the general public, communities, particular work groups, trade unions, the armed forces etc have all been affected to a lesser or greater extent. In effect, all sorts of involved people and / or groups have been affected by or have an impact upon public sector procurement – and they are stakeholders.

Feedback on self assessment question 1.1

'Using a public sector organisation with which you are familiar detail people who could be considered stakeholders and how they might be affected in some way by procurement decisions.'

You have considerable scope here to take any number of organisations! You will however presumably select the one in which you operate or aspire to join. Hence selecting as an example a local authority, it may have for example:

- Local community – people with children in local schools;
- Teachers, ancillary staff at schools, the next tier of government – for example the Welsh Assembly if the school is in Wales;
- Other regional / local governments in the UK;
- Budget managers;
- Trade Unions;
- Local transport companies;
- Teaching Advisory staff;
- Local and national media;
- Suppliers;
- Procurement professionals
- etc.

This will alter and be added to depending upon the example that you have chosen and also the general and specific contextual setting – for example in times of recession there might be greater scrutiny of finances or comparative action in another area/region. Similarly, if a decision to build a new school using Private Finance Initiative (PFI)/Public Private Partnerships (PPP) principles is taken, or the catering is outsourced – or in the recent case of a meat supplier to a south Wales local authority, there is an out break of food poisoning, then there may be more stakeholders than had at first glance been the case.

Feedback on learning activity 1.2

'Identify stakeholders by listing them in groups according to their relationship within and with an organisation, a) for a private sector organisation; b) for a public sector organisation.'

a) For a private sector organisation the following could apply:

Here is a list of typical types of stakeholders:

- Owners and stockholders, investors – generally instrumental stakeholders
- Banks and creditors – generally instrumental stakeholders
- Partners (legal sense of partner) - instrumental
- Suppliers – (most probably instrumental but you will need to bear in mind priorities and strategic importance – Kraljic or a similar grid categorises suppliers and whilst most are instrumental, not all are)
- Buyers, customers and prospects – generally instrumental
- Management – most of the time normative or descriptive

- Employees, works councils and trade unions – most of the time normative or descriptive
- Competitors – often normative or descriptive but could be instrumental
- Government (local, state, national, international) and regulators mostly normative or descriptive
- Professional associations, Industry trade groups - often normative
- Media – frequently descriptive
- Non-governmental organisations – most frequently normative
- Public, social, political, environmental, religious interest groups, communities – generally descriptive

You will discern one thing from this and that is that there is no right answer! This is because it is contingent upon the situation or circumstances that pertain at any given time. For most of the time a private organisation might not be interested in, or affected by non-governmental organisations; but if for example, the company made a product that was suddenly and unexpectedly needed for humanitarian aid operations, it would take great interest in the views, opinions and observations of representatives of such organisations.

b) For a public sector organisation here is a list of typical types of stakeholders that could be applied:

- Elected members and representatives – instrumental stakeholders
- Banks and creditors – descriptive or instrumental stakeholders
- Partners (in a commercial sense example for shared services) - instrumental
- Suppliers – (most probably instrumental but you will need to bear in mind priorities and strategic importance – Kraljic or a similar grid categorises suppliers and whilst most are instrumental, not all are)
- Buyers, customers and prospects – generally instrumental
- Management – most of the time normative or descriptive
- Employees, works councils and trade unions – most of the time normative or descriptive, but could be instrumental
- Competitors (not necessarily obvious in a public sector organisation but it could occur) – often normative or descriptive

- Government (local, state, national, international) and regulators - mostly normative or descriptive but could be instrumental
- Professional associations, Industry trade groups - often normative but could be instrumental
- Media – frequently descriptive
- Non-governmental organisations – most frequently normative
- Public, social, political, environmental, religious interest groups, communities – generally descriptive but could be instrumental
- Audit activities/functions – descriptive but could be instrumental

Again there is no absolute answer and as with the private sector organisation, it all depends! However, there is a major role to play for public sector procurement, in that socio-political and economic influence can be exerted by decisions as to what contractual arrangements are made and with whom. Further, and increasingly, there is a social conscience that can be reflected in a strategy of conscience procurement and the wishes of minorities and ethical/ moral voices. This is apparent in the corporate social responsibility agenda where public sector procurement is to the fore. There is also a need to be seen to act in accordance with rules, regulations and guidelines. Hence in certain situations or scenarios, the decisions made in respect of stakeholders' interests can be considerable.

Feedback on learning activity 1.3

'In the following examples detail who you might consider internal and external stakeholders in the procurement of:

- *a new computer system for a large school in inner London*
- *a new printer for all publications of the Welsh Assembly Government*
- *a new aircraft carrier for the Royal Navy'*

There is considerable opportunity for you to develop interesting and useful if subtly different lists. Broadly this is to emphasise that whilst all organisations will have internal and external stakeholders then at any given circumstance or particular contextual setting / time there may be differences. It is all contingent upon what is happening and who is affected or involved at any given time.

For a new computer system in a large school in inner London:

- Internal stakeholders might include:
- Teachers,
- Pupils,
- Catering providers,

- Finance section / Administration,
- Governors
- Local Authority representatives
- External stakeholders might include:
- Suppliers,
- Unions,
- Central Government,
- Other local Authorities, (because they will have existing computer systems and may want a link into – or upgrade from, those systems)
- OGC
- Other public sector organisations,
- Local providers of computing services

For a new printer for all publications of the Welsh Assembly Government: Internal stakeholders might include:

- Any existing internally provided printing services
- Personnel,
- Finance Department,
- Human Resources Department,
- Elected Members of the Welsh assembly Government (AM's)
- External stakeholders might include:
- Existing and potential print organisations,
- Central Government,
- Other Regional Assemblies,
- The Welsh Language Society,
- Residents within Wales,
- Residents from other parts of the UK / EU (because, for example, they might perceive such expenditure as irrelevant in the pertaining social and economic climate)

For a new aircraft carrier for the Royal Navy, internal stakeholders might include:

- All sailors and officers within the Royal Navy,
- Ministry of Defence personnel,
- Royal Air Force and Army personnel (you may have listed these as external)
- HM Treasury (again you may have listed as external)
- External stakeholders might include:
- Suppliers of major capital equipment / assets,
- Sub contractors / suppliers of components and services,
- Education and training establishments,
- Members of Parliament (MP's)
- Inner London Schools (because they might want the relatively scarce Finance that has been allocated by the central government to war fighting equipment when education might be seen as having greater social significance / importance)
- Overseas governments and commercial organisations (because the UK is highly unlikely to purchase and operate, over many years, such a major capital equipment without impact upon or influence from such organisations).

Feedback on revision question

'Discuss the changing nature of the public procurement environment noting especially the impact upon internal and external stakeholders'
You should have briefly indicated the changing socio-political and economic context of the UK. This is detailed in the first few pages of this study session. The increased influence of Japanese approaches in respect of Supply Chain Management and Total Quality Management, the importance of competition in the early 1980's, followed by an increasing recognition of the need to work closely with certain suppliers from the early 1990's onwards and the subsequent adaptation of commercial best practice within the public sector generally should all be noted as general background to the current position. If you can detail specific examples that would be useful.

You should then consider the context of the last few years, taking into account how external factors can often influence or impact upon what an organisation generally does in response to changes, although you should identify specifically the changes in the Public sector where procurement has gained a higher profile and where it effective operation can impact favourably upon the population at large. You should think of the range of organisations within the public sector domain and how procurement that might be undertaken by such organisations could be affected by, or impact upon, a wide range of people and organisations.

This should lead you to developing the concept of stakeholders within the public sector procurement environment. There is considerable literature on stakeholders generally and you should indicate some of this (e.g. Johnson and Scholes or Reed). This should clearly state definitions and provide an indication of what such stakeholders might be considered (e.g. Normative, Descriptive or Instrumental- as per Donaldson and Preston). The OGC website contains considerable information and you should bear in mind that the OGC itself can be seen as a stakeholder. That there are both internal and external stakeholders should be brought to the fore with examples and indications of what / how they might influence or be impacted upon a public sector procurement organisation. An important point to make is that their influence or impact is contingent upon the situation at any given time.

Further Reading

Andrew Erridge, (2007) Level 5 Course Book Machinery of Government, study sessions 3 and 4 (pages 25 to 58) gives a clear overview of the changes that occurred within public sector procurement
Edward R Freeman, (1984). Strategic Management: a Stakeholder Approach
Gerry Johnson; Kevan Scholes (eds) (2001), Exploring Public Sector Strategy
Websites: http://www.12manage.com/methods_stakeholder_analysis.html

Study Session 2

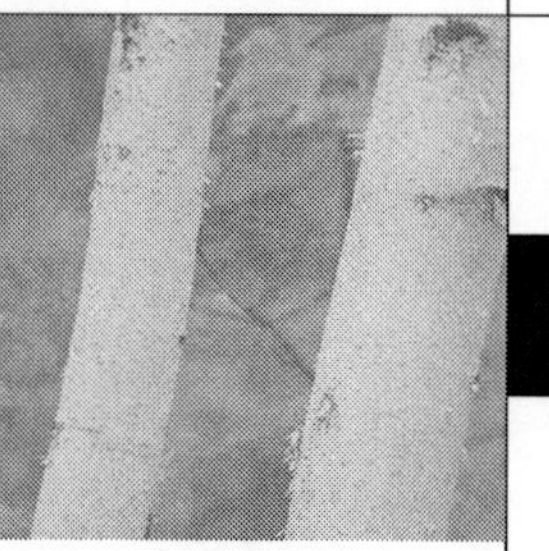

"Assess the role, interests and resources of internal and external stakeholders in relation to procurement generally and also in relation to specific strategic procurements"

Introduction

Having identified internal and external stakeholders in the previous study session, it is now necessary to consider what they may do in respect of, or how they might be affected by, procurement decision making. Thus this study session now considers the underpinning, and important strategic activity of stakeholder analysis. This requires insight into the identification of stakeholders and the use of models and methods to assist in developing effective approaches to public sector procurement.

Session learning objectives

After completing this session you should be able to:

- utilise stakeholder identification models such as Mendelow (1991)
- assess stakeholder analysis methods and systems
- consider weighting the resources and influence of stakeholders

Unit content coverage

This study session covers part of the following topic from the official CIPS unit content documents: *Investigate relationships with key and critical stakeholders relevant to public procurement*. Specifically, it covers: *Assess the role, interests and resources of internal and external stakeholders in relation to procurement generally and also in relation to specific strategic procurements.*

Prior knowledge

Prior to this study session you should have completed study session 1

Timing

You should take about 4 – 5 hours to read and complete this section, including learning activities and self assessment questions.

Stakeholder identification

The Office of Government Commerce (2006, pp.2) (OGC) defines stakeholders as 'anyone who has an interest in change and can influence or impact on the success of change.' It excludes suppliers from this analysis, but there is an imperative to recognise that suppliers (and their suppliers) are as much stakeholders as customers and managers. The OGC (2006, pp.4) sees five different types of stakeholder, each with different characteristics. These are:

(1) 'Advocates - these want change and they are prepared to drive it through. Use them as change champions and communicate often and effectively with them.

(2) Opponents - they do not agree with the project going forward and may suffer some personal loss if it goes ahead. You must discover the cause of their opprobrium and use tools and techniques to convert the opponents.

(1) Indifferent - they have no interest in the outcome. The job here is to stimulate that interest with a strong motivational communications and awareness-raising strategy.

(2) Blockers - They are pessimists who believe a project is riddled with negatives and that the business case is unachievable. Use conflict management techniques to change their negativity to positivism or, at worst, acceptance.

(3) Followers - They go with the flow, and have little real understanding of a project or its aims or objectives. Increase their understanding, keep the message positive and treat them equitably.'

OGC is referring here to specific projects, but if one replaced the noun projects with the phrase the business of procurement, these details are just as relevant.

Learning activity 2.1

Using a procurement project in which you have been involved or are familiar, specify one example from each of the above stakeholder types, their position/ interest in the project, how much influence they had in the project, and how their specific attitude affected the project.

When identifying stakeholders it is important to look beyond the formal structure of the organisation. As noted in the earlier study session, there can of course be internal and external stakeholders. However it is necessary to have a look at informal and indirect relationships too. A useful model for this purpose is to visualise the stakeholder environment as a set of inner and outer circles. Diagram 2.1 below. The inner circles stand for the most important stakeholders who have the highest influence. You should bear in mind that issues of power and influence are vital when considering stakeholders. This matter is context specific and transitory. The topic of power and influence is considered in proceeding units.

Self-assessment question 2.1

How relevant is it to identify these different stakeholder characteristics?

Diagram 2.1

This provides a general overview on possible stakeholders and their impact. In general, the formation of stakeholder groups depends on the individual situation of each organisation. Although stakeholder analysis is sometimes used as a tool for industry analysis, its true value lies in the evaluation of particular challenges for businesses and organisations. In this sense, it is also a tool for evaluating strategies and particularly useful when considering public procurement strategies

Individuals and groups may behave differently in different situations. For instance, environmental interest groups may have a low interest in staffing implications if an 'I house' service is about to be outsourced as procurement strategy; however, they may well have an extremely high impact when it comes to procurement decisions in respect of a new system for energy provision.

Identifying the impact of stakeholders

In a stakeholder analysis, impact or power of a stakeholder is defined as the extent to which they are able to persuade, induce, or coerce others into following certain courses of action. There are several ways to exert such power, for instance by direct authority, lobbying or exerting a dominant market position. The power of stakeholders can be based on various sources:

Internal Stakeholders	**External Stakeholders**
• Hierarchy (formal power) e.g. authority, senior position • Influence (informal power) e.g. leadership style • Control of strategic resources e.g. responsibility for strategic products • Possession of knowledge and skills e.g. expert knowledge that forms the organisations core competence • Control of the environment e.g. network of relationships to external stakeholders • Involvement in strategy implementation e.g. as a change agent or responsibility for strategic projects	• Control of strategic resources e.g. monopolistic supplier • Involvement in strategy implementation e.g. strategic partners in distribution channels • Possession of knowledge and skills e.g. cooperation partners, subcontractors • Through internal links e.g. networking

The power of stakeholders can grow from different sources. Therefore, it might be helpful to look out for visible signs of power. These can be some of the following indicators:

Internal Stakeholders	External Stakeholders
Status e.g. position in hierarchy, salary level, bonuses	Status e.g. speed of corporate reaction on requests
Resources e.g. budget, number of staff in department – especially in relation to other departments or the total volume of resources	Resource dependence e.g. percentage of equity stakes, credit volume, buying or purchasing volume, mutual organisational linkages and switching costs for the corporation

Representation in powerful organisations / bodies	Negotiating arrangements
e.g. membership in important project teams and commissions	e.g. fixed standard prices vs. individual price negotiations
Status symbols	Status symbols
e.g. own secretary, company car, position and equipment of office	e.g. invitations to business events, direct access to top management

No single indicator is likely to uncover the power and position of a particular stakeholder within in relation to the company. The combined evaluation of all sources and indicators of power, however, will improve general understanding of stakeholders. One that is sometimes overlooked in such a consideration of stakeholders is that of the 'gatekeeper'. Sometimes there may be an organisation, group or individual that has informant power or access to information with the ability to 'open gates' that could permit access to powerful stakeholders. Alternately they may hold some pertinent information to which others do not have access.

Analysis of interest and power

Besides the analysis of stakeholder power in terms of their ability to influence people and developments, it is also necessary to evaluate, to which extent the stakeholders will exert their power. As an example, for a commercial organisation, local authorities, for instance, can have a high impact on that organisation in certain situations. If the commercial organisation planned to move their headquarters, then local authorities would probably try to influence this decision. However, local authorities may only be interested to be aware of other important business developments for that same commercial organisation such as the introduction of new product lines or new marketing campaign, without taking any action or getting involved.

Johnson and Scholes (2001) demonstrate a fundamental tool of stakeholder mapping – the power/interest matrix first coined by Mendelow (1991). It is a template upon which the orientation of different stakeholder groupings can be mapped and through which strategic priorities can be established. The model is shown below:

Diagram 2.2 Level of interest

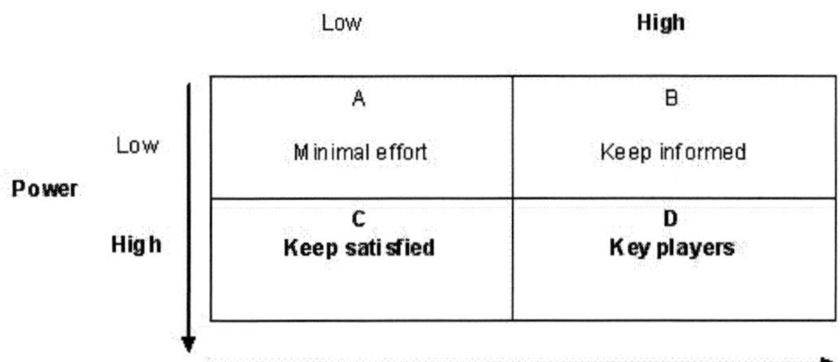

The power/interest matrix is a useful tool for evaluation the expectations and the impact of particular stakeholders. It analyses the following questions:

- How interested is each stakeholder group to impress its expectations on the organisation's decisions?

- Do they have the means to do so and do they have the power to do so?

As a result, the power/interest matrix provides valuable information on how to handle particular stakeholders and groups. It can also indicate if certain decisions will receive support or resistance, and which groups have to become included in the decision process.

Stakeholders in sector A do not have a high own interest in corporate plans nor do they have to power to exert much impact. Organisations should keep these groups informed in the necessary extent, but should not invest too much effort into them.

Stakeholders in Sector B do have a high interest in the organisation and its actions. However, they have limited means to influence things. Despite their low power, such stakeholders could be valuable allies in important decisions. Therefore, it is advisable to keep them informed about the issues in which they are interested.

The relationship with stakeholders in sector C could be difficult. In this group, you will often find institutional investors or legislative bodies. They behave passively most of the time and show a low interest in organisational, or public sector, affairs. Despite this they can exert an enormous impact on the organisation, such as when it comes to investments. It is therefore necessary to analyse potential intentions and reactions of these groups in all major developments, and to involve them according to their interests.

The most important stakeholders are those with high interests and high power, to be found in sector D. They have to be involved in all relevant developments.

All identified stakeholders should be grouped in this matrix. This can reveal the following insights:

- Recommendations for relationships to particular stakeholders

- Identification of supporters and opponents of a project.

- Necessary repositioning of stakeholders. (for example, the reduction of power of a major opponent – from D to B; increase of interest of a powerful supporter – from C to D)

- Measures to keep stakeholders in favorable positions. (for example, fulfillment of information needs in sector C)

Self-assessment question 2.2

Using your organisation as an example, draw up a power/interest matrix for stakeholders for a typical large procurement project, say a capital construction contract.

Stakeholder analysis

Stakeholder Analysis is an approach that is frequently used to identify and investigate the influence or power formed by groups or individuals who could affect or are affected by the achievement of the objectives of an organisation. Through stakeholder analysis it is possible to identify the ways in which stakeholders may influence the organisation or may be influenced by its activities, as well as their attitude towards the organisation and its targets.

Although some discussion has been made earlier in respect of stakeholder s and their role, it is pertinent to note that Freeman (1984) identifies the very purpose of the firm is to serve as a vehicle for coordinating stakeholder interests. Following Freeman's perspective, stakeholder analysis is an end in itself. However, from a public procurement perspective it is important to recognise not just who can influence decision making but also who may be affected by it. A prime example would be a case where stakeholders in an organisation are also shareholders with profit generating motives. It is also important to recognise that there are those stakeholders who may not have a voice in the larger scheme of things (because of gender, ethnic background or disability); and those within communities who may lack a collective voice but whose very standard of living may be affected by procurement decision making. Whatever the reason or contextual setting, it is an important activity that will enable enhanced understanding that can assist in developing more effective procurement decision making within the public sector.

The role of stakeholders is to ensure that all values, beliefs and interests are represented in order that efficient, effective and economic procurement strategies are formulated and implemented. Public procurement strategies should be such that decisions are made that satisfy all or most of the stakeholders, or to ensure at least that no powerful and legitimate stakeholders are excluded or at the very least are aware of what is happening and why.

Stakeholder analysis methods and systems

Learning activity 2.2

List the applications of Stakeholder Analysis.

Ricardo Ramirez (1999, pp.102) states that 'Stakeholder Analysis refers to a range of tools for the identification and description of stakeholders on the basis of their attributes, interrelationships, and interests related to a given issue or resource.

To clarify the meaning of the term, Ramirez says that it is useful to ask why stakeholder analysis is used. There are several reasons for carrying out stakeholder analysis (Grimble and Wellard 1996; Engel 1997; Röling and

Wagemakers 1998):

- Empirically to discover existing patterns of interaction;
- Analytically to improve interventions;
- As a management tool in policy-making; and
- As a tool to predict conflict.'

As Ramirez identifies, Grimble and Wellard (1996) correctly emphasise the usefulness of stakeholder analysis in understanding the issues of complexity and compatibility between stakeholders and objectives. Likewise, a key aspect of Freeman's writing is the ability of the manager to manage stakeholder relationships. "Stakeholder management" (Freeman and Gilbert, 1987) is highlighted as a conceptual framework to help managers understand the complex and often chaotic nature of the business environment. 'Hence the term "stakeholder" is often associated with corporate management.'

Ramirez (1999, pp.103) continues that 'stakeholder analysis seeks to differentiate and study stakeholders on the basis of their attributes and the criteria of the analyst or convenor appropriate to the specific situation. These may include

- The relative power and interest of each stakeholder (Freeman 1984);
- The importance and influence they have (Grimble and Wellard 1996);
- The multiple "hats" they wear; and
- The networks and coalitions to which they belong (Freeman and Gilbert 1987)'

For example, (slightly differing from the OGC model), Ramirez (1999, pp.103), referring to Susskind and Cruikshank (1987), identifies four types of stakeholders that are expected. Those with:

- Claims to legal protection
- Political 'clout',
- Power to block negotiated agreements
- Moral claims to public sympathy

'Although differentiation among stakeholders is a necessary step in stakeholder analysis, the distinction is often based on qualitative criteria that are difficult to generalise. The use of matrices is a common tool in stakeholder analysis, in which stakeholder groups appear on one axis and a list of criteria or attributes appears on the other.' Stakeholder analysis sets out to:

- 'Identify the main purpose of the analysis;
- Develop an understanding of the system and decision-makers in the system;
- Identify principal stakeholders;
- Investigate stakeholder interests, characteristics, and circumstances;
- Identify patterns and contexts of interaction between stakeholders; and
- Define options for management. '

In the article 'Stakeholder Management as a Play', Pajunen and Nasi (2004, pp. 520-533) of Tampere University of Technology put forward the whole concept of stakeholders and their analysis (and subsequent management) as a metaphorical play. They also identify two further strategies for analysing stakeholders. They are:

a) Savage et al (1991, pp.61-75) which, in a similar 2 x 2 grid to Mendelow (1991)/Johnson and Scholes (1999), posits 'stakeholders potential for cooperation with organisation' against 'stakeholders potential for threat to organisation' in order to manage stakeholders

b) Frooman (1999, pp.191-205)) who positions the question 'Is the organisation dependant on the stakeholder' against 'Is the stakeholder dependant on the organisation,' in order to analyse strategies for influencing the organisation.

Learning activity 2.3

What do you consider as the benefits of undertaking a stakeholder analysis? Do you consider that there are limitations, if so list them and comment upon them?

Self Assessment question 2.3

Outline the steps that you think would take place in the process of undertaking an analysis of stakeholders

Weighting the resources and influence of stakeholders

Stakeholders can play an important part in the success of a procurement project. Internally, the 'freeing up' of resources such as finance, facilities and personnel can impact favourably, just as could restrictions on such resources. Similarly some stakeholders, for example a national supplier in a monopsony situation, can wield considerable influence; another example of influence might be a MP representing a constituency where there is a large labour force employed by such a monopsonistic supplier.

Undertaking stakeholder relationship analysis enables an organisation or group of organisations to become aware of how to shape stakeholders to be ready, willing and able to embrace change. Taking, for example, a public sector organisation that wishes to introduce a radical new service (which impacts upon the community generally and specific internal and external stakeholders), then by understanding who the key stakeholders are across the organisation and, most importantly, beyond its boundaries, a procurement project team can be more likely to gain an optimal solution. In effect this is about providing a 'picture' of the importance of key 'players' in order to engender a 'change-ready' culture,

Stakeholders must feel equipped, motivated and confident to deal with the proposed change. Stakeholder relationship management will enable the procurement project team and key stakeholders to build relationships across the organisation and monitor those relationships throughout the procurement project/programme.

There are parallels with supplier selection techniques and supplier appraisals and vendor rating. From earlier Units you will be aware that whilst vendor rating is about assessing actual performance, supplier appraisal is about assessing potential performance. To undertake this latter activity requires a consideration of potential impacts of, and effects upon, buyers and suppliers. Hence what is useful is a mapping exercise of potential power and interest as identified in the early part of this study session. However, just like supplier assessment (which is also about stakeholders – albeit a specific category), there must be metrics applied to each axis if it is to become meaningful in assisting decision making. There are two particular challenges here. The first is that such a weighting exercise is contingent upon the circumstances prevailing at any given time (i.e. the 'value' given to a particular aspect could change over time – e.g. the financial position of local authorities before and after the 'credit crunch' of autumn 2008). The second that it is virtually impossible to be quantitatively precise in any values allocated to a particular resource or influence of a given stakeholder.

'He uses statistics as a drunken man uses a lamp post – for support rather than illumination'

Andrew Lang, attributed by Alan Mackay

Nevertheless, to undertake such a weighting of interest and power – which must include stakeholder resources and influence - is still a good way to ascertain the position of stakeholders in any given situation. The way in which influence, power and interest can be interpreted must also be considered, as often the resources possessed by a particular supplier may give it proportionately more power; however, greater exploration should be made of all stakeholder resources. It could be for example, that a particular citizen may have access to the media or that certain skills are prevalent within one stakeholders remit.

The OGC Category Management documentation provides a number of relevant approaches. One is taking into account change and trust (these are discussed in more detail in study session 7 on partnering and relationships) you could develop the stakeholder mapping tool or list the stakeholders against a number of key aspects. These are shown in grid format in the OGC document but can be weighted under the headings of 'Credibility', Intimacy', Risk' and 'Trust'. Recognising that exact values are difficult to allocate, you can rate stakeholders against each of these headings as High; Medium or Low.

Thus, a stakeholder may be Low on Credibility and High on Risk, which might mean that you adopt a particular strategy to manage and work with that stakeholder.

Summary

There is a move away from the reliance just upon a contract and the details contained therein to ensure that a procurement activity or project is successful. There has been a realisation that there is a network of stakeholders whom, if adequately involved, will enable an optimal solution that satisfies a wide spectrum of interested parties. To this end there identification of stakeholder types can provide an insight into how they could impact upon, or be affected by, the procurement activity. This study session has developed the key approach of stakeholder analysis and identification of those stakeholders who can assist or prevent satisfactory progress. In this respect, power, influence and interest have been discussed and considered. This progressed to an overview of how these could be taken into account in a seeking to adopt the optimal strategy for assessing the role and impact of stakeholders in procurement projects / activities.

The matters raised here will be referred to for the remainder of this Unit and form the basis of many of the strategies that will be developed as you work through this Unit as a whole.

Revision Question

Discuss the interests and influence of stakeholders and the means by which these could be assessed.

Feedback

Feedback on learning activity 2.1

'Using a procurement project in which you have been involved or are familiar, specify one example from each of the above stakeholder types, their position/ interest in the project, how much influence they had in the project, and how their specific attitude affected the project.'

You should be able to identify easily specimen types from each stakeholder group and apply these to a project that has been carried out in your own organisation. The following may be used as a guide:

- **Advocates –** the elected members of a public authority who want a political imperative - say a new combined heat and light scheme from landfill waste to be constructed by a council.

- **Opponents –** the landowners in the area in which the new construction is to be constructed, and the opposition elected members who are opposed to the scheme in principle.

- **Indifferent –** staff in the Environmental Services division of the Council, who will still have to lift and transport the waste to its new destination.

- **Blockers –** the environmental lobby who would rather see a materials recycling facility to intercept the waste before it is incinerated in a heat and light scheme.

- **Followers –** the citizens of the town two miles from the site who have an interest in this project but would not intend to make much of a fuss about it.

Feedback on Self assessment question 2.1

'How relevant is it to identify these different stakeholder characteristics?'

You should broadly have outlined the following aspects of the process:

- Identify stakeholders (which may be through a brainstorming activity)

- Understand stakeholder needs and interests

- Classify them into meaningful groups

- Prioritise, balance, reconcile or synthesise the stakeholders

- Integrate stakeholder needs into the procurement strategies of the organisation, in line with policy and taking into account best practice.

This is an extremely important concept for you to recognise and undertake in professional practice. A successful project depends upon a successful stakeholder engagement strategy (SES) and stakeholder engagement plan (SEP). These are part of a broader communications strategy that will form a major part of the project's outputs. You need to identify from a stakeholder map who the most important stakeholders are, and then further categorise them into stakeholder types as described in the model.

These then become the target market for stakeholder engagement and the message can be tailored precisely to reflect the importance and attitude of that stakeholder group. A completely different strategy will be required for each, and far more effort will be required to deal with opponents and blockers than with the rest.

Feedback on Self assessment question 2.2

'Using your organisation as an example, draw up a power/interest matrix for stakeholders for a typical large procurement project, say a capital construction contract.'

Level of interest

Power	Low	**High**
Low	A Minimal effort	B Keep informed
High	**C** **Keep satisfied**	**D** **Key players**

You may have included a number of stakeholders specific to your organisation and you may have more or less than is indicated on the example below. There is no 'right' answer; it is more a case of making sure that you have included all stakeholders pertinent to the particular scenario.

Feedback on learning activity 2.2

'List the applications of Stakeholder Analysis.'

There are many reasons why you should undertake such an analysis. These are some of them:

- Making a list of all stakeholders is useful to be aware of who and what stakeholders there may be in a particular procurement activity

- An analysis of the interests of the various stakeholders
- Analysing potential conflicts of interest with or between stakeholders
- The basis for further action/development, such as stakeholder mapping
- The basis of, or major influencing factor for procurement strategy formulation and ultimately decision making
- Evaluation of existing procurement strategies
- It can provide the basis for stakeholder communication
- Can also be used in programme and project management as the programme/project develops and if situations change

Feedback on learning activity 2.3

'What do you consider as the benefits of undertaking a stakeholder analysis? Do you consider that there are limitations, if so list them and comment upon them.'

The following are typically claimed benefits:

- Better insight can be obtained (in respect of each stakeholder / stakeholder group) in respect of :
    - The relationship with the stakeholder
    - Coalitions of which the stakeholder is a member
    - The significance of the stakeholder to the organisation
    - The power of the stakeholder
    - The priorities of the stakeholder
    - Associated risk areas
    - Relevant Government al policies and guidelines
- Better procurement strategies and decisions
- Better acceptance of the procurement strategy and decisions of the organisation
- Greater clarity in respect of with whom communication should be entered

The following could be typical limitations:

- Ideally, a Stakeholder Analysis should be performed regularly or even continuously, since the relevant stakeholders, their power and associations may change quickly. (i.e. it is sometimes viewed and acted upon as a one off task.
- The management of a public procurement organisation has to assess the position of each stakeholder. It is the subjective perception of management that will ultimately recommend the way in which the procurement organisation will act towards its stakeholders.
- It is normally impossible for public procurement professionals to satisfy all demands of all stakeholders completely. Therefore it becomes a balancing act or even a reconciliation or synthesising act, with the following options:
  - Focusing on one leading stakeholder group, and satisfying all others to an extent which is necessary or possible.
  - Trying to balance or reconcile or synthesize all interests according to their weight, importance or urgency

Feedback on revision question

'Discuss the interests and influence of stakeholders and the means by which these could be assessed.'

You should be able to develop a perspective that takes you from the issues covered in study session 1, concerning stakeholders generally, into recognising that not only can these be internal and external but that some may have much more influence than others. You should clearly identify the OGC view on Advocates; Opponents; those who are Indifferent; Blockers and finally those who will 'go with the flow', the Followers. Examples of how they act in particular situations would aid understanding.

This should be followed by a discussion on, and examples of, how you can consider the power and interest of stakeholders – and Mendelow, Johnson and Scholes and others could be brought to the fore with diagrams to illustrate your points. The area of stakeholder analysis has a considerable literature and a brief library or internet search will bring forth many vies, although they will all tie in with the text that you have been following. However, it is through such searches that you will find examples and these should be used (judiciously) to highlight the points that you are making.

The benefits of stakeholder analysis should be brought out and this should allow you to bring in the OGC Category Management tools where aspects such as Stakeholder relationships can be mapped and weighted in accord with the particular procurement project or activity. This identifies that the influence, power or resources of a stakeholder are often contingent upon the circumstances of the specific procurement. A final point would emphasise that the tools and techniques covered here are the basis of the strategies that will be developed to manage relationships with stakeholders.

Further Reading

Office of Government Commerce. (2006). *Category Management Toolkit: Stakeholder Management Plan*

A Mendelow,. (1991). 'Stakeholder Mapping', *Proceedings of the Second International Conference of Information Systems*

J. Frooman, (1999). 'Stakeholder influence strategies'. *Academy of Management Review.* Vol. 24, 191-205.

Ricardo Ramirez, (1999). 'Chapter 5: Stakeholder analysis and conflict management'. In Daniel Buckles ed. *Cultivating Peace: Conflict and Collaboration in Natural Resource Management*. Washington DC: International Development Research Centre. Ch.2

P Engel, (1997). *The social organization of innovation: a focus on stakeholder interaction*

Edward R. Freeman, (1984). *Strategic Management: a Stakeholder Approach*

Pajunen, Kalle; Näsi Juha. (2004). Stakeholder Management as a Play. In *The Proceedings of e-Business Research Forum 2004.*

Study session 3

"Analyse strategies for influencing and managing stakeholders by engaging them at an early stage in procurement plans and specific procurements"

Introduction

With the evolution of procurement as a major contributor to competitive strategy, and with the public sector as a major contributor to ensuring value for money (bearing in mind the need to optimise the selection of suppliers), there is also the responsibility for providing the optimal choice for communities, including those who in some way may be disadvantaged. This requires recognition of a varied range of stakeholders. It also requires careful consideration of approaches that can be undertaken for engaging with both internal and external stakeholders.

In this study session you will consider the beneficial aspects of early involvement of stakeholders especially in respect of significant procurement projects. As an element of this, insight will be gained into managing diversity and of successful and unsuccessful projects that involved stakeholders at an early stage.

Session learning objectives

After completing this session you should be able to:

- recognise the benefits of incorporating stakeholders into the planning process at an early stage
- manage diversity amongst stakeholders
- identify project failures where stakeholders were not fully informed

Unit content coverage

This study session covers part of the following topic from the official CIPS unit content documents: Investigate relationships with key and critical stakeholders relevant to public procurement. Specifically it covers: Analyse strategies for influencing and managing stakeholders by engaging them at an early stage in procurement plans and specific strategic procurements.

Prior knowledge

Prior to this study session you should have completed study sessions 1; 2.

Timing

You should take about 4 – 5 hours to read and complete this section, including learning activities and self assessment questions.

Recognise the benefits of incorporating stakeholders into the planning process at an early stage

You will recall that the OGC defines stakeholders as 'anyone who has an interest in change and can influence or impact on the success of change.' Arguably this is flawed as it does not specifically include suppliers. Nevertheless, the OGC outlines five different types of stakeholder. (At this point if you do not fully recall these types you need to revisit your work to date and generally refresh yourself on what has been covered!). You should likewise remember that each of the stakeholder types has different characteristics. To recap these are:

- **Advocates**
- **Opponents**
- **Indifferent**
- **Blockers**
- **Followers**

To be really effective in procurement, it must be considered as more than just buying. It should be considered in a 'total process' perspective that seeks an understanding of the goods/services/assets/equipment required from the concept of the requirement. This should then continue through the life of the procurement activity or project. It is in this way that the whole life costs and total costs of ownership can be fully taken into account to enable optimum value for money (i.e. over the lifetime of what is being procured).

Interestingly, HM Treasury (2007, pp.4) in the Transforming Government Procurement document acknowledges this early involvement, but only from the point that the 'procurement process formally starts'. It does however continue… 'where the need to make a purchase to deliver an objective has been identified, and its success can only ultimately be justified when the product has been used up or sold on, or the service contract has been determined in full'.

Self assessment question 3.1

Why do you think that the note refers to formally identifying the need to procure something? Would you feel that this is the first time that procurement should be involved?

Stakeholder Engagement Strategy

Best practice would dictate that a public sector organisation create a Stakeholder Engagement Strategy (SES) as part of its general procurement strategy, regardless of whether this is general practice, or appertains to a specific procurement project, though the need to get this right with regard to the latter is even more paramount than with regard to the former.

The SES should establish the objectives of stakeholder engagement and indicate how the involvement of stakeholders is achieved at each stage of the activity/project. It should indicate how the process of policy-making will be undertaken and how transparency will be achieved and continuously delivered. As part of delivering the transparency, the strategy should be made publicly available. The strategy should have at its core:

a) The vision for stakeholder engagement, and
b) Details of purpose, key players, methodology and responsibilities.

Guiding principles should include inclusiveness, transparency, appropriateness, legality, clarity and comprehensiveness.

The vision should provide an overview as to how stakeholder engagement is to be undertaken, and whether or not a participative or consultative approach will be required. This depends on the nature of the activity/project, but, in general, the more participative the stakeholder engagement, the less room there is for issues and challenges at a later date. It is at this early stage that careful and balanced consideration of stakeholder power, influence and interests should be taken into account. Time spent on this early aspect is seldom time wasted and will pay off in the long run.

"Time spent on reconnaissance is seldom time wasted"

Military adage

Following on from the SES, organisations should prepare a Stakeholder Engagement Plan (SEP), which shows in detail how the SES will be achieved. A typical SEP is outlined below:

Diagram 3.1 Stakeholder Engagement Plan

Stage	Purpose of stakeholder involvement	Stakeholders involved	Methods of achieving involvement
1 Preparation	Notify interested parties	Indicate who will be involved	Indicate initial mode of communication: e.g. letters, press adverts/ articles, newsletters, dedicated website, e-mail, stakeholder forums/workshops or other groups.
2 Information-gathering	Collect information	Identify anticipated sources of information, including that held by key stakeholders.	State how information will be gathered: questionnaires, public meetings, workshops/ forums, groups, round-table dialogue, seminars, conferences, desk research, field research, email networks. State how data will be recorded, collated and used.
3 Data review	Review by stakeholders to validate data	Identify stakeholders able to offer informed views. Different approaches may be taken with different stakeholders	State how information will be disseminated: public meetings, workshops/forums, groups, round-table dialogue, seminars, conferences, email networks.
4 Agreement	Resolve any differences and agree draft plan	This should include all stakeholders. Different groups may be informed in different ways	State how stakeholders will be informed and how they can make their views known. State how representations will be recorded, collated (e.g. use of database) and subsequently dealt with.

5 Dissemination	Ensure that all persons and organisations needing to be aware of the plan know it has been published	This should include all stakeholders and, where necessary, the general public.	Establish where the SEP will be made available and how it will be publicised. Establish whether any specific interaction with particular stakeholder groups is required for plan implementation
6 Action	Ensure that plan is fully agreed, that the data are valid, that awareness has been properly raised, that the process and decisions are transparent.	This should include all stakeholders.	State how information will be disseminated. State how responses will be made, recorded, collated and used.

Case Study: Scottish River Basin Planning Management Strategy

The European Water Framework Directive came into force in 2000 to establish new and better ways of protecting European waterways. The Directive was transposed into Scots law via the Water Environment and Water Services (Scotland) Act 2003. The Scottish Executive decided that a river basin management planning system was required, and gave SEPA (the Scottish Environmental Protection Agency – a third sector organisation) the lead role of developing, implementing and procuring the appropriate systems.

SEPA (2006, pp.13) realised that delivering the plan would require fundamental changes to working practices across a wide range of government and non-government agencies and local authorities and there was a need to engage all stakeholders at the earliest possible opportunity at the start of the project. The overriding principle in the stakeholder engagement was a spirit of openness and inclusiveness.

SEPA's structure plan project team initially held a number of stakeholder meetings to consult widely on project scope and to examine a series of options. Thus broad consensus on strategy was achieved. This took account of the need for a strategy that:

- Met European standards on water environment policy
- Ensured that sustainability objectives were met with regard to minimising water use

- Prevented deterioration of the water infrastructure
- Enhanced the status of aquatic water systems
- Passed the national and local planning and building control regulations.

SEPA (2006, pp.16) decided to create a National Advisory Group to advise the project team on implementation going forward, but, in addition, because much of the implementation work would be delivered locally, a number of sub-national groups were also created. These were to be chaired, managed and funded by SEPA. The sub-national groups were given some autonomy to deal with local issues in their own way, which gave added flexibility and ownership to their work.

SEPA and its stakeholders subsequently decided that Scotland should have one River Basin Management District covering most of Scotland, with a second covering the cross-border waterways. The national Group was headquartered in Strathclyde, and sub-national groups were set up in Orkney and Shetland, Western Highland, Moray, Argyll and Bute, Tayside, Forth and Cross-border (Scottish Borders and Dumfries & Galloway). A stakeholder communications plan was completed in the latter part of 2006.

The planning and implementation project is still ongoing and the first River Basin Management Plan is due in 2009. Procurement is represented in the project planning team. The number of external stakeholders is significant and includes, inter alia:

- The Scottish Executive (now the Scottish Government)
- The Scottish Executive Technical Advisory Group
- Various fisheries interests and lobby groups
- Flood level advisory group
- The Environment Agency
- MSPs, Scottish MPs and Scottish MEPs
- Elected members and planning officials of all 32 unitary Councils
- The European Commission and the European Parliament
- Scottish Water (the public sector water and drainage company)
- Cross-Border councils (Northumbria, Cumbria and smaller district councils such as Berwick-on-Tweed)

Learning activity 3.1

Detail the key stakeholder engagement issues which those within a senior public sector procurement position must consider.

Organisational stakeholder 'state of readiness'

You might find the following tool useful in plotting an organisation's readiness to engage with its internal and external stakeholders. This provides an excellent opportunity to plot where an organisation is in terms of its engagement with stakeholders.

Diagram 3.2 Stakeholder readiness

	Undeveloped	Developing	Mature	Best Practice
Internal stake-holders	• Lack of information on needs of internal stakeholders • Projects are generally organisation-driven • Stakeholders are generally excluded from the planning or implementation of projects.	• Building information base on internal stakeholder groups • Internal stakeholder interests are being included in project planning • Developing greater credibility with internal stakeholders	• Views of internal stake-holders rou-tinely sought in decision-making • Stakeholders represented on decision-mak-ing bodies • Stakeholders' capabilities and capacities are integrated into project planning	• High quality services to stakeholders • Stakeholders' Views paramount in policy-making, business processes, resources and services. • Top echelons of strategy delivery are client-led
External stake-holders	• Non-existent or antagonistic relationships with external stakeholders • Little or no understanding of boundaries and role with key external stakeholders	• Professional relationships evolving • Starting to form stakeholder strategy • Developing relationships with stakeholders • Developing contractual/ partnering arrangements	• Relation-ships based on regular contracts and collabo-ration • Recognition by stake-holders as credible and trustworthy organisation	• Relationships are partnership-based • Organisation key player at national and local level • Regularly and routinely engages with external stakeholders • Organisation is sought after as a model of best practice • Opinion leader • Practices followed by other organisations • Organisation can review critically in accordance with corporate vision/ mission
External public relations	• No profile outside service users • No strategy • No documentation • No professional communicators	• Poorly known outside own environment • Ad hoc PR activities • No strategy • Little access to expertise • Messages fail to support mission	• Complete picture of key audience • Developing strategies for each • Access to appropriate skills	• Clear image linked to vision/mission • Well-known by key external stakeholders • PR strategy is supported by stakeholders • Promotes organisational mission

Managing diversity

Having identified both internal and external stakeholders you will be aware that they have, for a variety of reasons, differing interests. Internally, these could be priorities, functional, staffing, objectives and so on, although there is an organisational need for unity of purpose this may not always translate uniformly amongst internal stakeholders. You will have seen from the foregoing example that there can be a wide range of external stakeholders whose interests are dependant upon the nature and extent (and potentially timing) of the specific procurement project.

Bringing together disparate views and perceptions can be challenging. However, by identifying and engaging those groups and individuals involved in major procurement projects or activities that may have significant impact them can bring benefits. At the very least all will be aware of the issues involved and if the potential conflicts of interest are managed effectively the diverse interests may all be satisfied (this will be discussed further in Unit 2). In this respect the Stakeholder Engagement Strategy, Stakeholder engagement Plan and use of the 'readiness' tool that you have just considered will be invaluable.

In a similar vein it should always be remembered that public procurement is not just about purchasing at the lowest possible price (indeed, nor is it in commercial procurement). It is about value for money and lifetime costs or total cost of ownership. In this respect those within society who may in some way be disadvantaged, or who may need assistance in some way, have to be taken into account. This could include stakeholders from ethnic minorities, disabled, particular genders, certain geographical areas or even those who wish to pursue (what might be perceived by some as costly) environmental or social policies. Such stakeholders must be given credence and engaged as soon as procurement projects or activities (that affect them or are impacted by them) are identified. (This will be discussed further in Unit 3).

Self assessment question 3.2

Take a short while to consider who might be affected by, or have an impact upon, an idea to spend public funds upon a new road crossing in a small rural village.

Successful and unsuccessful public sector procurement projects

Lancaster University (2005) analysed a successful public sector project, and published the factors of the project's success. This related to the UK motor licensing industry, which is controlled through its agencies under the Department for Transport. These agencies are in charge of all the licences issued in various categories. The Driver and Vehicle Licensing Agency (DVLA) and the Vehicle and Operator Services Agency (VOSA) are the two Government agencies responsible for issuing all motor vehicle-related licences. The DVLA has responsibility for Road Tax. VOSA provides support to delivery of a service for Traffic Commissioners, who are the regulators of the commercial vehicle industry in England, Wales and Scotland. VOSA conducted an innovative ICT project to create an internet-based real time transactional service which allows goods vehicle operators direct access to their own licence records and to input and track progress on applications.

The project was deemed to be a success if it was delivered to time and specification and brought in 5% under budget, all of which were achieved. The critical success factors that arose from the Lancaster study were:

- Appointing external consultants to articulate new vision
- A determination to seek a radical and innovative IT solution
- A major effort to manage twelve stakeholder 'bank groups.'
- Training project staff to PRINCE2 foundation standard
- Training project staff in Java applications

- Industrial collaboration to simplify and standardise IT platform and to cut costs
- Applying rigorous risk management and business continuity models.
- Substantial testing throughout the life of the project.
- Simplicity and scalability of the chosen platform
- Structural changes within the organisation
- Significant stakeholder participation
- Creation and observance of a detailed project plan
- Senior management support and 'buy-in'
- Shared vision and effective communications strategy
- Iterative software development
- The creation of a change management board

These factors would seem to be relevant (to a lesser or greater extent) with the success of any major public sector project. Procurement has a key role here, in terms of scope, specification, innovation and minimising risk.

Taking this further, OGC (2006, pp.2) defines stakeholder management as involving the 'building and maintaining the active support and commitment of these people to facilitate the timely implementation of the change of a project.' To support such tactics, organisations can compare the actual stakeholder map with a more favourable one. This allows revealing deviations. It is the basis of finding ways on how to reposition particular stakeholders. For instance, it is possible to influence the opinion of an important customer by involving him in early planning stages in order to find a solution that meets the needs of both parties. The power of a supportive department could be increased by inviting representatives from this department into project teams and planning committees.

Moreover, this type of analysis can provide insights, if it is necessary to sub-divide larger stakeholder groups into smaller groups. These sub-groups could be treated differently in order to meet their individual needs and to get their support. Such a strategy allows the formation of new alliances and to shift power into a strategic support position.

Over many years there have been some spectacular project failures. Recently, Terminal 5 at London Heathrow airport appeared to be heading for success in terms of many of the criteria of success such as time and cost. Unfortunately, as is now known, the performance, in respect of lost luggage was very poor and although now rectified, may have an effect upon the reputation of British Airways (the airline operating within Terminal 5). Arguably this was because the stakeholders' interest which is ultimately about prompt and accurate receipt and delivery of baggage was not fully appreciated, considered and adequately tested.

Case Study - Procurement of 'Warrior' in the MoD (Moore, n.d.)

This case provides an example of what is essential, following the OGC advice (noted above), in respect of supplier engagement in order to avoid failure in procurement activity. It also highlights the importance of supplier engagement in respect of the total cost of ownership.

The Warrior armoured vehicle was brought into service in the Army at the beginning of the 1990s. It is a tracked armoured fighting vehicle for the infantry, designed for fighting as well as delivering soldiers to the battle.

Warrior was procured by a team at the (then) Procurement Executive and the way in which stakeholders were engaged was a great stride forward for MoD procurement teams. As well as involving the end user at a very early stage in the design process, there was another forward-thinking move in that the repair and logistic organisations were also involved. This had not always been the case with other major equipment procurements.

At the time of design, an engine (power pack) change for all other Army armoured vehicles would take approximately 3½ hours (such as in the Challenger tank). As a result of good design, itself a result of early involvement of stakeholders such as maintenance personnel, supply and stores personnel and transport personnel as well as representatives of the personnel likely to be driving such vehicles, a Warrior power pack change took only 45 minutes under good conditions. Further, many of the minor parts such as bolts and screws were common to other vehicles already in the Army inventory, thus removing wasteful carriage of extra spares for the logisticians and enabling procurement cost reductions

From the initial in-service date, Warrior was a well respected vehicle. The soldiers who worked on it were full of praise for the ease and speed of repair. Soldiers are a critical and discerning population who were surprised that this was a vehicle that had been designed around them. Clearly Warrior went through a procurement process that considered holistically all linked and related issues from start to finish. The involvement of key stakeholders at the very start ensured an easy transition as the vehicle was brought into service. Almost 20 years later Warrior is still an excellent vehicle and for those who have to work upon it is well respected.

Learning activity 3.2

Why do you think that this case study was included in this study session?

Case Study – MoD Procurement of I.T. Equipment for Overseas (Moore, n.d.)

The sheer number of stakeholders in public organisations can hinder procurement projects. The large number of stakeholders steers those involved to committee-type decisions, even in the MoD, where one might expect commanding and authoritative decision-making. Overlaid upon this is the major stakeholder consideration of the political dimension.

The MoD also suffers from time constraints which may not be specific to that public department and is a common theme in the NHS, Police etc. An example is that of the procurement of spares, equipment and supplies for operations especially those that involve war fighting, such as in Iraq or Afghanistan.

Holding the amount of stock required, on a 'just in time' basis, ready to mount a medium scale operation at any time is so wasteful that this model is no longer followed in the MoD. Many call-off and framework agreements are in place with its industrial partners/suppliers so that stock and support can be procured just-in-time. There is however often a mismatch between the time required (or the time scale stated in contracts for suppliers to ramp up production or divert supply), and the amount of notice actually given. Until the government decides to mount an operation there can be no notice given to suppliers because of security considerations. This has in the past resulted in a lack of certain equipment and caused much frustration in the defence procurement and logistic organisations.

The tight timescales resulting from short notice deployments for overseas operations create challenges for public procurement. There is little time to decide upon a purchasing strategy and therefore what often happens is that current suppliers are approached for quotes, resulting in the awarding of contracts to suppliers simply because they are in a position to meet the urgent timescales or with whom it will be the quickest approach to get the relevant requirements. The lack of time usually means that there can be no performance incentives and no long term strategies. The MoD ends up in a very poor negotiating position and is unlikely to achieve good life time cost arrangements or set up innovative contracts.

The challenges created by short timescales are exacerbated by the situation that stakeholders have sometimes come together purely for the procurement and equipping of a deploying force and had little relationship beforehand.

As an example, in the case of a recent overseas deployment the purchase of logistic IT equipment suffered from not engaging the key stakeholders at an early stage. The central IT project team was not consulted early about what was needed for such a deployment and was handed a list of IT equipment and a budget, with instructions to procure and ship by a deadline. The list was arguably heavily over specified with some items, yet other items had been overlooked entirely. If that original list had been purchased and shipped then the entire logistic set-up would not have worked! The wrong stakeholders (in the form of a committee) had devised a set-up of equipment that was incorrect for the force it was designed to support, although this committee was unaware that their decisions were poorly informed.

The short deadlines that were inherent in this requirement created stress in the workforce and the lack of relationships between some stakeholders caused friction. The entire requirement for items to be purchased had to be re-drafted, stakeholders re-engaged and negotiated with and agreement sought and then the whole requirement had to go through the tender process, losing valuable time.

Engaging the logistic IT project team at an early stage would have meant that the correct framework of equipment would have been drafted up. In turn this would have resulted in a far quicker time between the decision to purchase and the awarding of the contract, with sufficient leeway for the MoD to be in a better negotiating position and achieve better value for money within the designated timescales. The lack of understanding on the part of the key stakeholders and the stakeholders with whom to engage almost caused a serious failure.

The point to recognise is engagement with the correct stakeholders. These must be the key stakeholders identified in the stakeholder analysis. This must be prioritised. Involving too many stakeholders in such a scenario could result in a lack of understanding and sub-optimal committee decisions. Too few may overlook important considerations in a procurement situation.

Perspective for success in procurement projects

The MoD has come in for a share of both praise and criticism for its performance in terms of procurement projects.
The measures of success are many and whilst it is possible to include certain Critical Success Factors, the nature of procurement project management is that criteria may not be mutually supportive. Often, trade offs or balancing in critical success factors is necessary. Hence, procurement projects may meet the performance criteria but may be late or over budget.
The National Audit Office (NAO) prepares many reports on procurement project performance, and many of these concern the MOD. There are a number of success and failures noted here in very comprehensive reports.
Of course, not all success or failure is due to stakeholders not being fully informed at early stages of the project. However, some do include such examples. The Apache Longbow helicopter was purchased in what at first appearance is a good (i.e. successful) project. Certainly the aircraft is now proving its worth in operations in Afghanistan. However, subsequent to its initial purchase it was realised that not all logistic support aspects had been fully considered. For example, this includes the lack of purchase of landing mats (beneficial in certain terrain and relatively easy to correct); and the lack of trained pilots (much more difficult to correct due to time, cost and availability). The NAO is particularly critical of this latter point. What seemed a well priced purchase (i.e. not over budget) actually incurred additional costs because most of the available aircraft stood unused for some time as there were no pilots to fly them. This point is particularly relevant in respect of early comments in this study session. It is not the purchase price that should be a measure of success or failure. Value for money should include the costs incurred over a lifetime. Had informal discussions taken place or wider engagement of stakeholders been entered into and subsequently managed this failure would not have occurred (or at least it could have been able to have been better managed).

Learning activity 3.3

Go to the National Audit Office web site, (http://www.nao.org.uk/publications/nao_reports/06-07/060723ies.pdf) and you will find a summary of the Major Projects Report for the MOD. Read a selection from the Summary of the Report. If you are interested then the web site provides extensive opportunity for further research and reading. You may wish to consider overall perception in terms of performance and involvement of stakeholders.

The MoD has a number of major procurement projects. They are subject to public sector rules, guidelines, procedures, policies and initiatives. Like most of the public sector, procurement projects in the MoD bring together the public and the private sectors of the economy. This is not merely on a national scale it is inevitably on an international basis, with considerable socio-political implications. It is one where there is considerable scrutiny, not just from the

NAO, but a whole range of stakeholders, not least of all the public and the media. This is amply illustrated if, unfortunately there is a loss of life, and (rightly or wrongly) it can be seen as linked to a procurement decision. Early involvement of stakeholders and co-ordination across a broad spectrum of suppliers, customers, legal, financial, political, social and assorted interested parties can assist in such co-ordination. To do this the MoD is a major subscriber to the philosophies espoused in the approach to Programme and Project management in the OGC Gateway Review and similar documents.

Summary

This study session provides insight into an important element that can lead to success in public sector procurement – that of early engagement of stakeholders. This has been undertaken through a brief revision of the nature of stakeholders and how they can assist or even block progress. Bearing this in mind, the Stakeholder Engagement Strategy provides clear direction for the way in which stakeholders can be involved. This is taken further with the Stakeholder Engagement Plan ensuring that action is taken as is deemed necessary. This can be assisted by use of the Stakeholder State of Readiness tool which can be utilised to determine where an organisation is in respect of its preparedness to engage and how that be enhanced through a development and maturity into best practice. However, there is an important reminder that in undertaking such activities one much always take into account the diversity of stakeholders and that the views of all, especially those who might in some way be disadvantaged or unable to voice opinions, are recognised and considered in procurement decision making.

A key feature in achieving success in public sector procurement is recognising not merely the price that is paid for equipment, an asset or service, but rather all the associated lifetime costs. This has been illustrated through a number of case studies.

Revision question

Critically assess the view that early involvement of stakeholders in major procurement activity/projects can bring success.

Feedback

Feedback on self assessment question 3.1

'Why do you think that the note refers to formally identifying the need to procure something? Would you feel that this is the first time that procurement should be involved?'

You could say that procurement as an activity only commences when a request for purchase (such as a requisition or other formal document), duly authorised, is received. Certainly this is the process that most public sector organisations still indicate in their procedures (e.g. Standing Orders). However, professionalism in procurement includes a need to be proactive. Assistance, advice, guidance, comments, perspectives and insights into such matters as market knowledge, current trends and initiatives, policies and best practice can be provided on an informal discussion and meetings. This cannot be undertaken for everything, and needs to be prioritised but it will assist in enabling ultimate optimal choice in terms of procurement approaches, selection of suppliers and effective engagement of stakeholders.

Feedback on learning activity 3.1

'Detail the key stakeholder engagement issues which those within a senior public sector procurement position must consider.'

The responsibility for public procurement project excellence should be owned at the highest level and procurement directors and senior managers should demonstrate a clear understanding of their roles and responsibilities. Responsibilities of stakeholders and others should be clearly communicated. Corporate philosophies, objectives, strategies and programmes must be agreed and published. Some of the key issues at corporate level are:

- Leadership
- Corporate positioning, visibility and process integration
- Philosophy and strategy
- Auditing and controls
- Degree of standardisation/simplification required
- Standards
- Environmental and CSR strategies
- Legal/regulatory framework
- Team-building
- Skills development
- Technology
- Risks
- Funding
- Resources
- Corporate identity and branding
- Performance

Feedback on self assessment question 3.2

'Take a short while to consider who might be affected by, or have an impact upon, an idea to spend public funds upon a new road crossing in a small rural village.'

This is not intended to elicit a detailed answer. It is, rather, an opportunity to explore and recognise that there are internal stakeholders such as officers, elected representatives, and departments such as legal; and a range of external stakeholders such as contractors, regulating bodies, utilities, local villagers, police, minority groups and officers for example.
You will probably identify planning departments, financial, legal and audit departments, but also the external stakeholders could include pressure groups, utilities, police, village groups, etc.

Feedback on learning activity 3.2

'Why do you think that this case study was included in this study session?'

It was included because it is a good example of how very long complex and challenging procurement processes are vastly enhanced when stakeholders are involved at an early stage. With the need to ensure success through all of the activity that contribute to the total cost of ownership, Warrior is also an indication of the advantages of involving stakeholders such as end users right at the beginning of such procurement projects / activities

There was great anticipation for the introduction of Warrior. This anticipation is common among such procurement projects; where the interest and even excitement is built up there can be a 'sting in the tail' if the end user does not get what is expected. Hence another advantage is that early stakeholder involvement will contain potential over-enthusiasm, especially in what has sometimes become a common example in public procurement, where the perfect, (often the so called 'gold-plated'), solution is rarely affordable.

Feedback on learning activity 3.3

'Go to the National Audit Office and you will find a summary of the Major Projects Report for the MOD. Read a selection from the Summary of the Report.'

The projects noted include Astute submarine, Nimrod aircraft and Trojan and Titan armoured engineering vehicles. All highlight total cost of ownership perspectives as fundamental to success and this requires early involvement of stakeholders. The MoD for some time has been emphasising this aspect but has developed the concept further as Through Life Capability Management (TLCM). It is about seeking stakeholder understanding of, and commitment to, requirements in terms of capability (subsequently this will become the specification); well before a formal request for procurement arrives.

Feedback on revision question

'Critically assess the view that early involvement of stakeholders in major procurement activity / projects can bring success.'

You should emphasise that stakeholders can affect the satisfactory outcome of a major procurement project or activity. You may wish to include examples of both internal and external stakeholders. This should be followed by a critical perspective on their early involvement. Bearing in mind that not all stakeholders may need to be involved at an early stage you will need to identify those who can have most impact / influence upon the particular procurement. This will involve use and application of the various tools and techniques that have been discussed in this study session. Effort should be made to discuss the aspects identified in these – e.g. you could discuss some of the characteristics of the 'readiness' model, noting, as an example, that in respect of a 'developing' approach to engaging with stakeholders, under the heading of 'internal stakeholders', you might examine how an organisation could build greater credibility with internal stakeholders. An example might be a 'learning event' where the procurement group outline work that they currently undertake and how best practice – taking into account lifetime costs could be enhanced with greater communication and increased contact. You should take an example from each of the headings (Undeveloped, Developing, Mature and Best Practice) to illustrate your points. Examples from differing areas of the public sector procurement environment would be beneficial. If possible a good answer would include a development of the diversity issues noted earlier, although this would not be essential.

Finally, a critical discussion on what is meant by success should be undertaken, noting that success can be defined in differing ways and mean different things to different stakeholders. Indeed stakeholders can be crucial to the long term success of a procurement project, especially if the lifetime costs are to be taken into account – i.e. a holistic perspective is taken. Such a procurement project could take years to come to fruition and hence all aspects over such a lifetime must be taken into account when considering success.

Further Reading

Office of Government Commerce. (2006). *Category Management Toolkit: Stakeholder Management Plan*

National Audit Office. (2006). *Ministry of Defence: Major Project Reports 2006*

Study Session 4

"Critically evaluate communication and collaborative strategies that may be developed to improve relationships with internal and external stakeholders"

Introduction

The study sessions thus far have emphasised the importance of internal and external stakeholders, the need to identify such stakeholders and then employ an engagement strategy. This requires a clear communication strategy. This study session will identify the relevant theory underpinning communication and consider this in a particularly complex and challenging public sector procurement project environment. Further, it will enable you to consider and apply strategies to enable communication to take place. An additional but relevant aspect is that of 'shared services' which will be considered from a general perspective but with scope for you to discuss in a number of relevant areas

Session learning objectives

After completing this session you should be able to:

- critically evaluate theories, models, policy documents and practice in relation to communication and collaborative strategies
- explain how communication and collaborative strategies may be developed
- consider the concept of shared services in the public sector

Unit content coverage

This study session covers part of the following topic from the official CIPS unit content documents: Investigate relationships with key and critical stakeholders relevant to public procurement. Specifically, it covers: Critically evaluate communication and collaborative strategies that may be developed to improve relationships with internal and external stakeholders

Prior knowledge

Prior to this study session you should have completed study sessions 1; 2; 3.

Timing

You should take about 5 – 6 hours to read and complete this section, including learning activities and self assessment questions.

Context

In any discussion on procurement there is inevitably disagreement upon the exact definition of particular words and phrases. You should not, in the context of this session be unduly concerned with semantics (although in respect of other Units and indeed study sessions in this Unit, or your existing or future employment, it could be extremely important!). This is because whether one uses the term 'procurement,' 'purchasing and supply', 'supply chain management' or even 'logistics' then (depending upon where you seek definitions), often they are very similar. This is because as the activities of recognising a need for a product or service and a specification is developed, with, in due course, tendering and contracting activities, followed by in service support and maintenance and ultimately disposal, of the product or termination of the service, there is a link between them all. Commercial best practice and the way that the public sector has responded to this (See Unit 1.1 of this course book and Erridge in the course book on Machinery of Government (2007), indicate that performance enhancements can be obtained by integration of these activities. For very simple purchases that may include a one off product or service of low value, there may be a fairly straightforward process that is followed. For many more intricate, detailed, high value or sensitive procurement actions this may involve a project or programme management approach. The OGC has produced many guides on how such activities should be managed and there are a number of relevant books. These range from a general overview such as Emmett in 'Supply Chain Management in 90 Minutes,' (2005), to more detailed project management such as Maylor's Project Management (2005).

The fundamental aspect of them all is that by taking a holistic approach to whatever products, assets, goods or services are being obtained, better performance will result. Within the public sector this may well be enhanced value for money. As discussed earlier, this must be taken as the total cost of ownership of that product, asset, goods or services over the life time of said items.

Hence the definitions or semantics are not as important in this session's context as it is the lifetime perspective that must be taken for a procurement activity or project.

Interestingly, in the MoD, a major public sector procurement 'player,' the initial approach to being more commercial and recognising numerous public sector procurement initiatives, was entitled 'Smart Procurement.' However, it was subsequently amended to 'Smart Acquisition.' This is because the former, semantically, indicated merely buying something whilst the latter recognised all of the activities mentioned earlier as elements of a 'total perspective' or holistic approach that links all activities to enable enhanced performance and value for money. This is well documented and is reflected in various policy documents.

The reason for spending some time on this aspect is that if a holistic approach is taken to procurement or project activity, there is a fundamental need for effective communication with all stakeholders involved to ensure that the best value for money and/or enhance performance will result. Hence it is essential to be aware of the nature of communication. The need for effective communication grows as a project develops and changes and amendments occur. Indeed this may necessitate negotiation to ensure that all stakeholders are in accord.

In addition to this holistic and integrated perspective, if there is to be wider recognition and use of commercial best practice and all of the initiatives

> "60% of all management problems are caused – in whole or in part – by faulty management communications"
>
> Peter F Drucker

and policy approaches are to be followed then there should be greater collaboration between stakeholders; whether customers or suppliers or indeed anyone affected by the project.

Communication

The simplest model of communication involves two people. One (the transmitter/sender) sends a message in a particular manner (the media) to the second person (the receiver). This is the basis of all communication. Unfortunately there are many aspects to even this simple model that cause challenges to the message being correctly received as the transmitter intended.

Learning activity 4.1

Indicate why a message might not accurately be received.

Diagram 4.1 Communication model

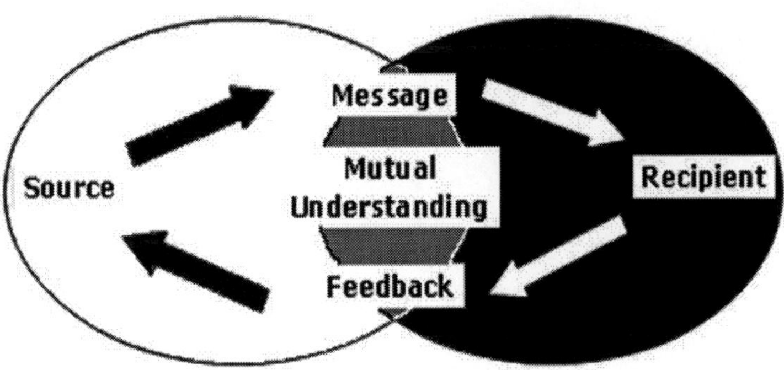

Self assessment question 4.1

Why do you think that public sector procurement might be challenging in respect of communication?

If what you have looked at earlier identified a model for communication it is important to recognise that there are barriers to communication. These may be internal or external and consideration of this will assist in developing an effective communications strategy.

The following diagram indicates some of these, which can be noted as:

- Contextual or setting (of/for the procurement project)
- Organisational
- Personal
- Cultural

Learning activity 4.2

'In seeking to recognise what might be barriers to effective communication in a procurement project, under the headings of Context/Setting; Organisation; Personal and Culture, outline examples.'

Diagram 4.2 Barriers to communication

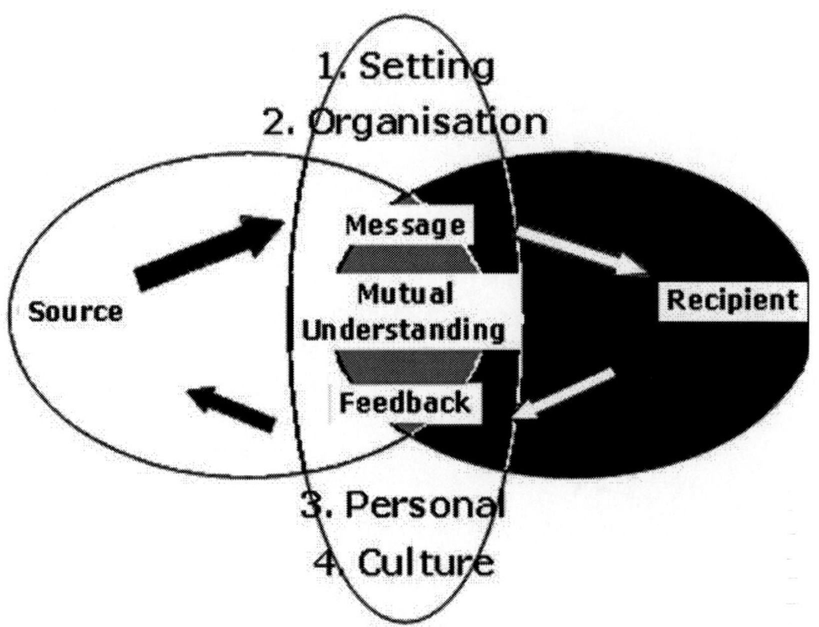

Learning activity 4.3

Go to the US Government Accounting Office (GAO) access the decision in respect of the US Air Force procurement of an aerial refuelling tanker. (Link: http://www.gao.gov/decisions/bidpro/311344.pdf) Read the conclusion and recommendations put forward by Gary L. Kepplinger at the end of the document (it is actually a long report and the summary is quite sufficient). What are your views on the way that stakeholders have influenced this particular public sector procurement project?

Communication strategy

A communication strategy is essential to ensuring the flow of information to, and from, around and between stakeholders and an organisation. Good communication will be:

- Accessible – information is readily available and presented so it is easy to understand
- Valid – accurate, informative, relevant, high quality
- Transparent – open and honest, timely
- Audience-sensitive – to suit the needs of managers, staff, suppliers, customers, users and the public

'We usually ask a question ten times and use the information once. We must learn to ask once and use the information ten times in different settings.'

Local authority chief executive
(in Bovaird and Loffler, p198)

The ODPM published an Organisational Development Resource for Local Government (2005, pp.68), within which it proposed the following elements of a communication strategy:

Diagram 4.3 Communication strategy

Heading	Content
Key principles and key aims	A statement about the outcomes of communications. How the Council wants to be experienced by staff, partners and the community
Responsibility for the communications function	Clear statements about the expectations for communications placed on all managers in the organisation. This should be reflected in job descriptions and in behaviours monitored through appraisal
The communications functions	Description of the roles played by specialists within the organisation
Internal communications	Strategy for internal communications including ways of informing and listening to staff. The key methods of communication for different purposes.
Consultation	Strategy for consulting with the public. The main methods for community engagement and the role of corporate, themed and service-based consultation
Media Relations	Guidance on dealing with the media
Corporate Identity	Covering the branding and style to be used

Engaging with the community is a prominent theme for Local Authorities but can be relevant for other sectors too, such as with the NHS. Organisations who are well engaged communicate effectively, motivate by encouraging dialogue at relevant stages, promote feedback and show that they have listened. Community engagement can:

- Enable stakeholders to participate in shaping their future
- Ensure that organisations are alive to changes in the community's views, needs and aspirations

- Unite organisations by helping members, officers and staff to understand their common purpose.

Whilst communication and feedback with external stakeholders is generally seen as a good thing, engaging with the community is not without its pitfalls. Organisations need to understand that they will be opened up to feedback and challenge, and actively anticipate the dangers of:

- Raising expectations that may not be met by the council and its partners for example
- Engaging insufficient numbers of people to legitimise a claim to be acting on the community's behalf
- Being unable to canvass views that are truly representative of the whole community
- Being unable to resolve the different needs and desires of separate sections of the community
- Over-consulting, so the procurement organisation is overwhelmed with feedback and unable to respond in a coherent way.

Communication and engagement strategies are essential for all areas and functions within a public sector organisation and should be an element within top level strategy. But what is the specific relevance to the Procurement function?

In the same way that the board of a private company is responsible to its shareholders, all public organisations are accountable to its stakeholders, all citizens who make use of and interact with the organisation. They are also ultimately responsible to central government, which gives the organisation its legitimacy. We are all individually responsible in some way to whoever gives us money to live and this is how the Procurement function is so vitally important. It is the Procurement function that has a central function in spending that money!

In a public organisation the spending of money, the allocation of resources is both challenging and supposed to be transparent. At all times the organisation is accountable to the stakeholders. Communication makes sense in order to demonstrate this accountability and to ensure good relationships. The allocation of scarce resources may be controversial or misunderstood, especially where long-term objectives are being pursued at the apparent expense of shorter-term goals. Communication to redress any misunderstanding greatly enhances the relationship between internal and external stakeholders. Understanding tends to increase support for a venture or action so when people can actively see and understand spending plans or strategies then understanding, support and cooperation usually results.

Self assessment question 4.2

Devise an outline communication strategy for a procurement project for an organisation with which you are familiar

Communication strategy and collaboration

The OGC website provides much detailed information about stakeholder issues and communication, including advice for identifying a stakeholder map at the start of any procurement project or programme. (It can be found at this web address:http://www.ogc.gov.uk/documentation_and_templates_stakeholder_issues_stakeholder_map.asp)

Developing from earlier sessions, it is possible to conceptualise views on what communication strategies should be developed as part of stakeholder management. The following indicates a broad strategy for managing stakeholders. Differing approaches would be adopted depending upon whether the stakeholder has a high or low interest in your procurement project / activity and whether the impact of your procurement project / activity had a low or high impact upon them. The resultant approaches that the procurement professionals would adopt is indicated in the relevant quadrants.

Diagram 4.4 Strategy for managing stakeholders

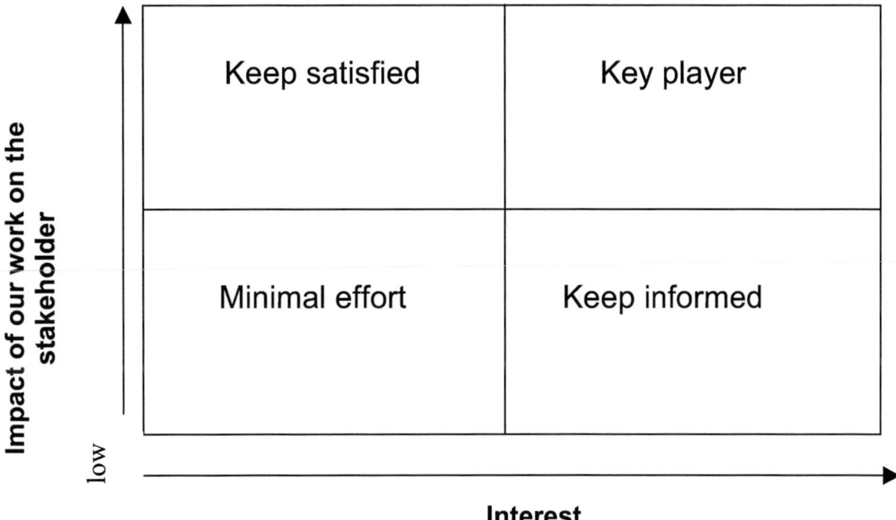

Self assessment question 4.3

Using the diagram above see if you could amend it to indicate what communication approaches you would take as providing a direction towards ensuring effective working with selected stakeholders.

Through targeted communication strategies, it should be possible to develop potential to enable savings in terms of cost and staff resources. OGC has indicated that up to £4 million could be recouped through collaboration. In this sense collaboration is underpinned by communication between procurement departments and stakeholders to seek co-operation in respect of the requirement / specification; tender and contracting processes; the delivery and installation of assets, facilities and equipment; in service support and ultimately disposal. It is in this respect that the semantics referred to earlier in this session should not be a barrier to communication and potential collaboration. Collaboration, not only saves time and effort –it should result in enhanced performance in a number of ways. This could be freeing up of procurement professionals to focus on more strategic considerations, whilst quality of service can also be improved.

Self assessment question 4.4

Briefly list means of communication with stakeholders. Consider when they could best be applied.

Collaborative Practices

"An example of a collaborative arrangement working within the region is a joint arrangement between Leicester City Council, Northamptonshire County Council and the East Midlands Regional Centre of Excellence to develop a regional framework contract for consultancy services. The aim of this was to address the need for 'tier two consultancies' (excluding construction) that can offer services at a more economically advantageous basis than those on existing framework contracts. This framework agreement is open to all of the local authorities within the East Midlands region, the Fire and Police Services and the NHS. The framework is for consultancy contracts of values less than £100,000. Within the local authorities of the East Midlands the total values of these contracts in financial year 2006/07 totalled over £71million. Even a small proportion of this amount is an attractive revenue stream for SMEs and therefore consultancies when bidding were required to demonstrate what discounts they would be prepared to make dependent on the volume of work awarded to them.

This framework went live in May 2008 and therefore it is too early to assess what the impact of it has been in financial terms. However, in providing a benchmarking tool to understand what consultancies are able to offer and to understand their individual pricing strategies it is invaluable to public sector procurers. This initiative and others like it therefore have potential to ensure that public sector procurers become more informed and that through economies of scale reasonable efficiency savings can be achieved.
The weakness with this arrangement is the potential for it to exclude organisations. The tender document extended to 130 pages and there was a requirement to submit full details on company accounts, environmental policy, health and safety policy and equal opportunities policy as well as have £10 million of public liability insurance and £5 million of professional indemnity insurance. The number of questions that were asked in response to the invitation to tender were significant and there was a general theme from sole traders / micro enterprises who questioned whether they would be expected to submit the above documentation – which of course they were required to submit although were not necessarily able to.

The other issue is for those organisations that were unaware of the opportunity to bid. This framework agreement runs for a period of 3 years with a potential for an extension of 1 year. For those consultancies that are not currently on the framework they have to wait for at least 3 years before they can access the opportunities. Information received from organisations running the tendering process was that they were surprised at the low numbers of private sector organisations who had responded to this initial opportunity. There are therefore likely to be a number of consultancies frustrated at the missed opportunity and there are also likely to be a number of public sector procurers frustrated at the paucity of competition between those organisations that successfully made it onto the framework. This is not to suggest that frameworks should include all suppliers because to do so would prove unmanageable for the public sector and unprofitable for the private sector. However frameworks should be sufficiently flexible to enable access to public sector opportunities from quality suppliers particularly if there are insufficient suppliers supporting a framework. "

Case Study - Central England Procurement Partnership

"The Central England Procurement Partnership (CEPP) was launched in 2006 and is a collaborative partnership within the housing sector. The arrangement brings together 13 housing organisations to improve the performance of the industry which collectively manage approximately 92,000 home across central England. The partnership aims to deliver quality housing for residents using modern methods of procurement and working practices while also creating an environment for learning and achieving excellence.
The savings which the partnership hopes to deliver will be re-invested to further improve the development of housing organisations and the industry, in areas of training, sustainability and business development.
One of its objectives is to "improve neighborhoods and sustainable communities, for example by incorporating effective security and environmental works on estates and local training and employment initiatives" (CEPP, 2006). Although pure cost and time savings in the construction of housing is its core goal, over £1 billion pa is to be invested in improving housing stock in the Midlands to decent homes standard by 2010 (CEPP hopes to have nearly half of this money monitored and managed by the partnership). Given such an extensive programme the CEPP has the potential to have a real impact in terms of sustainability and the local economy."

Shared Services

Shared Services refers to the provision of a service by one part of an organisation or group where that service had previously been found in more than one part of the organisation or group. Thus the funding and resourcing of the service is shared and the providing department effectively becomes an internal service provider. The key is the (rather obvious) idea of 'sharing' within an organisation or group.

Shared Services is similar to collaboration which might take place between different organisations such as a Hospital Trust or a Police Force. For example adjacent Trusts might decide to collaborate by merging their HR or IT functions.

One purpose of Shared Services is the convergence and streamlining of an organisation's functions to ensure that they deliver to the organisation the services required of them as effectively and efficiently as possible. This often involves the centralising of back office functions such as HR and Finance but can also be applied to the middle or front offices. A key advantage of this convergence is that it enables the appreciation of economies of scale within the function and can enable multi function working such as linking together HR and Finance where there is the potential to create synergies.

The 'Working paper on local authority shared services' (Department for Communities and Local Government, 2007) identifies that there has been much debate over the definition of shared services and how they differ with respect to other forms of collaborative working. In the private sector the concept of shared services means bringing back-office functions together across different business units or subsidiaries – an intra-organisation model. The concept of shared services in the public sector and in local government in particular, has come to mean inter-organisational collaboration, where entirely differing organisations share the provision of services in common. Again this often tends to be back-office functions such as HR and ICT provision.

Shared services continues to be a huge opportunity for efficiencies even between what you might call cross-functional organisations. There can be alliances between NHS bodies and local authorities to commission integrated health and social care. This 'boundary spanning' requires different thinking in respect to procurement – almost entrepreneurial albeit within the public sector context (and which could arguably therefore be called intrepreneurial).

Shared Services is different from the model of outsourcing which is where an external third party is paid to provide a service that was previously internal to the buying organisation; this typically, potentially, leading to redundancies and re-organisation. There is an on-going debate about the advantages of Shared Services over outsourcing. It is sometimes assumed that a joint venture between a government department and a commercial organisation is an example of Shared Services, but they are quite different. The joint venture involves the creation of a separate legal commercial entity (jointly owned) which provides profit to its shareholders. In this sense it is difficult to see what is being shared rather than bought. Such joint ventures could be seen as a form of outsourcing.

Precise definitions are not the issue here however. What is important is that public sector organisations are now considering wider options beyond their own boundaries as a way of enhancing performance for all stakeholders.

A key document that provides considerable detail on the concept of collaboration and shared services is published by the Department for Communities and Local Government – Rethinking Service Delivery: Volume Three – Shared Service and Public/Public Partnerships. (2006). It gives many excellent examples of every sort of collaborative procurement project.

Self assessment question 4.5

Are you aware of any examples of shared services that you could utilise to illustrate the potential benefits that can be forthcoming for stakeholders.

Case study - Shared Services in the South West Police Forces

"A plan to merge the small Police forces in England and Wales was eventually thwarted but the problem of a gap in affordable service remained, where some support services were too expensive and impractical for individual forces to fund and manage. This gap is now being closed in the South West by a shared service model. The 5 authorities and Forces of the South West Policing region have all signed up to a vision of "sharing services and operating in a consistent way (using common platforms, equipment and tactics) wherever there are demonstrable benefits from doing so".

There were already loose arrangements for joint working but there was a greater opportunity to be grasped. The 5 Forces have invested significant effort in identifying activities that would benefit from a tighter form of joint working, be this through a lead Force or a delivery vehicle owned by the 5 authorities. The range of potential activities is huge and their potential impact in aggregate is estimated to be enough to close a gap in services worth over £30 million in value.

By the end of a two year demonstrator site period, the programme expects to have delivered shared service arrangements for a number of protective service activities including Firearms, Witness Protection, Air Support, Technical Support Units, Covert Operations and more. This is not just an example of good practice at shared service – these services simply could not have been delivered by single forces acting alone."

Case study - Fire Services Act Jointly to Procure Protective Clothing

"The Integrated Clothing Project (ICP) is the first national procurement project for clothing – from station wear, sportswear through to personal Protective Equipment (PPE) for the Fire and Rescue Service. The ICP Board comprises representatives from the English fire service's nine regions, representatives from Scotland, Wales and Northern Ireland fire services together with representatives from Communities & Local Government (CLG), the Chief Fire Officers' Association (CFOA), the Fire Service College and the Ministry of Defence's fire service.

The aim of the project was to create a national identity that addresses equality and diversity issues and to deliver a standard level of appropriate protection for fire-fighters nationally. The new fire fighting kit will offer comprehensive protection in a range of hostile environments.

This procurement project saw the most rigorous and extensive research and evaluation process ever undertaken for a contract of this kind in the history of the fire and rescue service. Amongst many other activities, clothing from all bidders was put to the test over two, four week periods under strictly controlled scientific conditions at the Health & Safety Laboratories in Buxton, Derbyshire in summer 2006. Sixteen male and female volunteer fire-fighters from around the UK donned sets of protective clothing – including helmets and gloves - provided by four bidding companies and were tested for levels of heat stress, performance, comfort and durability. Rigorous physiological and ergonomic tests were undertaken to simulate physical movement, manual dexterity and hearing attenuation – all designed to gauge the relative performance of the clothing under realistic conditions.

This is a good example of stakeholders working together and all achieving their stated outcomes. As usual in many large procurement projects, the "customer" is divided between the customer who holds the money and pays and the customer who ultimately has to use the procured goods or services, in this case the fire-fighters. Add to this mix the experts, with their views – the Fire Service College – and there is huge potential for getting it wrong! In this case, giving every stakeholder a voice and giving the user the chance to be involved in the specification and testing, led to a positive outcome."

Summary

This in many ways is a fundamental study session. It builds on what you have covered thus far and adds the important element of communication. On one hand communication is something that you do all the time in your work and life generally. It is extensively written about in most procurement and management books. Yet it is also a topic that causes many problems; although if utilised well it can not only solve problems it can introduce new ways of working together to enable considerable procurement performance enhancements. Hence there are some aspects of this study session which are to some extent straight forward but where you have considerable scope to read, think and discuss more widely.

Hence having looked at aspects of communication the need to develop a suitable strategy for communication was considered. This in turn brought you to perspectives on collaboration and linked the aspect of communication to new ways of undertaking procurement that could deliver considerable benefits for stakeholders. Thus collaboration was examined with a number of examples provide, as was the notion of shared services, again with examples. There was also a reminder that you should not be too concerned about exact terminology. Semantically there are differences in many of the words, definitions and concepts put forward here – but they all impact upon performance of procurement and that impacts on stakeholders.

Revision question

Explain the concepts of collaborative procurement and shared services, indicating why communication is important in developing such approaches.

Feedback

Feedback on learning activity 4.1

'Indicate why a message might not be accurately received'

There is a very old anecdotal story of a First World War commander who sent a message back from the front line, whispered between quite a number of people, to the Headquarters. The message was 'send reinforcements, I'm going to advance.' Unfortunately, by the time it was whispered from one to another and reached headquarters the message finally delivered was 'send three and four pence, I am going to a dance.' Many will have experienced the frustration of one's message either not being fully understood or alternately, acted upon inaccurately. Even apparently straight forward statements or comments can be interpreted in different ways. For example, in respect of a public sector procurement project, a statement such as: 'We are at the early stages of the procurement project, we're looking into what is possible, but it is a big task' could be seen in two differing ways. In a positive sense, it could be seen as cautious and not raising any expectations – it is a good temporary holding statement. It should not cause concern nor frighten neutral or potential stakeholders. However, some stakeholders might see this in a negative sense. To such stakeholders, it could mean that something is being hidden or that you are doing little and getting nowhere! In essence any such statement is potentially flawed because it is extremely difficult to keep everyone happy – especially in a public sector procurement activity.

Hence it is important to remember that communication is an exchange of meaning, but that the message being sent is not always the same for each stakeholder. This is because of:

- Perception
- Interpretation
- Evaluation

Feedback on self assessment question 4.1

'Why do you think that public sector procurement might be challenging in respect of communication?'

It must always be remembered that communication is a two-way process, enabling information to be disseminated and received. Within the public sector the demands of stakeholders for information can be greater than those within private enterprises. Stakeholders can feel more attuned to the public organisation, as it is usually part of the community, delivers vital services and crucially, is paid for with public money. Procurement in the public sector has many stakeholders often with completely different perceptions and as there are socio-political and economic issues it will often be open to interpretation and differing evaluation. Because taxpayers' money is involved there are sections of the community who would, for instance, rather have money spent on education and health rather than defence. Equally for the same example there are commercial organisations who would like to gain contracts for defence work, and their workforces are taxpayers.

You can come up with many examples but also bear in mind that because it is taxpayers money that ultimately is being spent, those responsible for procurement projects in the public sector have to be seen to be making the optimal choice in line with value for money and whole life costing apart; putting values on certain aspects of procurement decision making ifs fraught with uncertainty in respect of balancing stakeholder interests.

Feedback on learning activity 4.2

'Go to the US Government Accounting Office (GAO) access the decision

in respect of the US Air Force procurement of an aerial refuelling tanker. (Link: http://www.gao.gov/decisions/bidpro/311344.pdf) Read the conclusion and recommendations put forward by Gary L. Kepplinger at the end of the document (it is actually a long report and the summary is quite sufficient). What are your views on the way that stakeholders have influenced this particular public sector procurement project?'

This is the GAO report on the US decision to award a major defence contract to what (to a major stakeholder – the existing contractor, Boeing) was in effect, a European aircraft (supplied by Airbus). Whatever the rights and wrongs of the situation, the perception of some in the US was that taxpayers' money was being given to another country and that American jobs would be lost. This is obviously an emotive issue and although it is US based it is an excellent example of stakeholder perception, interpretation and evaluation and highlights the need for careful communication. At the time of writing the decision to purchase the European aircraft had been successfully contested by Boeing, and the whole tendering process is being revisited. This also provides an insight into the power and influence of certain key stakeholders, hence the importance of stakeholder mapping (from earlier study sessions). You should note that in the US context there is a powerful lobbying ethos.

Feedback on learning activity 4.3

'In seeking to recognise what might be barriers to effective communication in a procurement project, under the headings of Context/Setting; Organisation; Personal and Culture, outline examples.'

There are many aspects, under each heading, that you might wish to take into account but the following is a brief indication of what could be outlined:

Setting:-

- Environment - is it conducive to good communication
- noise – the obvious barrier
- distance – can you see; can you hear
- contact methods – direct; indirect; telephone; video link up

Organisation:-

- management style
- functional structure
- policy and practice
- culture

Personal:-

- ego
- perception
- interest
- style

Culture:-

- nature of meetings

- policy and processes
- formality / informality

Feedback on self assessment question 4.2

'Devise an outline communication strategy for a procurement project for an organisation with which you are familiar'

The OGC advises as follows:

The stakeholder communication strategy will enable you to "document how information will be disseminated to, and received from, all stakeholders in the activity (e.g. project or programme). It identifies the means/medium and frequency of communication between the different parties. It is used to establish and manage on-going communications throughout a programme or project."

Fitness for purpose checklist:

- Has the information given to stakeholders met their requirements?
- Has the information received from stakeholders met the programme/project owner's requirements?
- Has all the necessary information been disseminated?
- Have the roles and responsibilities of the individuals involved in the communication strategy been understood by them?
- Have these roles been carried out satisfactorily?

Notes:

Suggested content:List of stakeholders and their information requirements

- Communication mechanisms to be used (such as written reports, seminars, workshops, videos, e-mails, newsletters)
- Key elements of information to be distributed by the different mechanisms - including frequency and information collection and collation
- Roles and responsibilities of key individuals responsible for ensuring communication is adequate / appropriate and timely
- Identification of how unexpected information from other parties (including stakeholders) will be handled within the scope of the activity.

Source information:

- Stakeholder Map
- Blueprint and Vision Statement
- Programme Plan

Feedback on self assessment question 4.3

'Using the diagram above see if you could amend it to indicate what communication approaches you would take as providing a direction towards ensuring effective working with selected stakeholders.'

This is intended for you to conceptualise the approaches that you think should be made (in a generic sense) towards developing a direction towards effective working with selected stakeholders. The respective quadrants indicate the broad approach to be embarked upon dependant upon the particular position on the 'impact' or 'interest' axis.

Keep these stakeholders 'on side'	Work hard to communicate (two way) with these stakeholders
Not vital but keep these stakeholders informed / 'in the loop'	Keep these stakeholders informed

Feedback on self assessment question 4.4

'Briefly list means of communication with stakeholders. Consider when they could best be applied.'

There is a considerable list to be made here but that is not the intention. Whilst a list can be made which should allow you to determine whether you are thinking along the right lines, it is also intended to encourage you to consider applications that might assist in developing collaborative approaches.

Typically, you will have said:

- Publications;
- Email;
- Scheduled reports;
- Ad hoc reports;
- Scheduled meetings;
- Websites;
- Dashboards;
- One on one sessions;
- Focus groups;
- 'Open houses';
- Town halls;
- 'Sandpits';
- Panels;
- Community Advisory Boards, etc

Always remember that communication can be formal, informal, written or oral and that it may be visual with body language indicating much more than is being said. Frequently a mix and match approach should be taken to such a communication strategy as rarely is it that 'one size fits all!' Bear in mind that to be effective communication requires not only the sender to send the message but also the receiver must clearly receive the message. Hence there is also a need for active listening!

To develop collaborative approaches will 'thinking outside the box' where procurement professionals must develop an enquiring approach that is commercial within the public sector environment or intrepreneurial in style.

Feedback on self assessment question 4.5

'Are you aware of any examples of shared services that you could utilise to illustrate the potential benefits that can be forthcoming for stakeholders.'

This is intended to encourage you to think about the large number of opportunities that exist to recoup much of the expenditure on services that is duplicated around various parts of the public sector. On one hand this should be common sense – on the other it can be seen as innovative. Two examples are given below. Many more are available quite readily as successful procurement action (innovation / creativity – or should that be professionalism?) is often communicated widely (see also study session 6)

Example 1 — 'Lichfield Council and Staffordshire Moorlands Council: Lichfield Council and Staffordshire Moorlands Councils jointly procured Serco Solutions to deliver ICT to the two councils. By joining forces, the two councils have made dramatic savings in both the procurement process and the pricing of the service. Together they procured a service delivery model and standard of service which could not have been achieved individually. The two councils shared consultancy and legal costs and managed the procurement process jointly. Each has contracted separately with Serco although the contracts are virtually identical. The contract covers all operational IT services including infrastructure, desktop management, new projects, database management and some systems development. Serco also provides remote diagnostics service and out of hours helpdesk support, something that neither council was able to provide before.

The procurement project involves another potential first in the form of a contractual commitment by both councils and the partner to achieve upper quartile performance against the industry standard indicators including a benchmark requirement.'

Example 2: Liverpool City Council and Liverpool PCTs and NHS Trust: These two partners have 'delivered an integrated health and social care public information service for children (the Integrated Children's Service) and adults (Careline). The services are accessible 24 hours per day, 7 days per week by telephone, internet and digital TV. The service has helped vulnerable people by making it easier for them to access assistance with problems such as domestic violence and homelessness. The partners have also raised efficiency gains because the service has encouraged the integration of front- and back-office operations.'

Feedback on revision question

'Explain the concepts of collaborative procurement and shared services, indicating why communication is important in developing such approaches.'

You should be able to explain that collaborative procurement s the collective purchase by several departments or groups / organisations within the public sector environment, of commonly used goods or services. OGC identifies this 'as one of the most dynamic means by which public sector funds can be freed up to be redeployed to critical front line work.'

Benefits of collaboration include: saving on staff time, cost saving, utilisation of professionals on more strategic activity, delivery of better quality products and services, uniformity and consistency between departments and regions, and greater leverage in the market place.
Shared Services refers to the provision of a service by one part of an organisation or group where that service had previously been found in more than one part of the organisation or group. Thus the funding and resourcing of the service is shared and the providing department effectively becomes an internal service provider. The key is the (rather obvious) idea of 'sharing' within an organisation or group. In this respect it is similar to collaboration which might take place between different organisations such as a Hospital Trust or a Police Force. The idea is to bring a streamlining approach through the shared service. It is an intra – organisational strategy that can provide opportunity to gain benefits. Neither of these are brand new approaches in that such concepts have appeared previously, in different guises e.g. purchasing consortia, such as Wiltshire or the Welsh Purchasing Consortium. Nevertheless they are different in that they require effective communication strategies to bring potential collaborators together and a different way of thinking in order to gain optimal benefits. This requires procurement professionals to be pro active in the way that they consider all elements of the procurement (or acquisition) process. Opportunities to work with other departments and to work across boundaries should be sought and considered. Communication in varying ways in order to enable effective linkages with relevant stakeholders will be essential.

Communication of such innovative approaches will not be easy – there are many stakeholders who are 'blockers' as you will recall. It will also require planning and preparation; the reward however can be considerable performance enhancement for stakeholders.

If possible you should include examples of such activities. You should also point out that whilst there are similarities between collaboration and shared services, outsourcing is not the same activity.

Further Reading

Andrew Erridge, (2007), *Machinery of Government*

Stuart Emmett, (2005), *Supply Chain Management in 90 Minutes*

Harvey Maylor, (2003), *Project Management* (3rd edition)

Department for Communities and Local Government, (2006), *Rethinking Service Delivery: Volume Three – Shared Service and Public/Public Partnerships*

Study session 5

"Critically assess the effectiveness of the purchasing organisation's internal and external communications policy and processes"

Introduction

The decision to embark on a promotional campaign to broadcast the activities and successes of a procurement organisation invariably implies the commitment of resources. Very few organisations, either in the public or private sectors, can make such a commitment without understanding whether or not those resources are being used to good effect. This study session therefore, whilst focusing on the measurement of internal and external communications policy, has at its core the general principles of performance measurement and management. 'You get what you measure' is a well-tried and reasonably accurate adage – just with other areas of performance management, if you choose the wrong metrics here then it is unlikely that you will ever be able to determine whether or not your communications policy is achieving the outcomes you set out to achieve.

Session learning objectives

After completing this session you should be able to:

- devise tests of communication effectiveness
- demonstrate the effectiveness of a communication campaign
- consider how best to learn lessons of both success and failure from other public and private sector organisations

Unit content coverage

This study session covers part of the following topic from the official CIPS unit content documents: Investigate relationships with key and critical stakeholders relevant to public procurement. Specifically, it covers: Critically assess the effectiveness of the purchasing organisation's internal and external communications policy and processes

Prior knowledge

Prior to this study session you should have completed study sessions 1; 2; 3; 4.

Timing

You should take about 3 - 4 hours to read and complete this section, including learning activities, self assessment questions and the revision question.

"When you can measure what you are speaking about, and express it in numbers, you know something about it…[otherwise] your knowledge is of a meagre and unsatisfactory kind……"

Lord Kelvin

Tests of Communications Effectiveness

Lord Kelvin (1883), a renowned British physicist, is reputed to have uttered the above words and the reason why they are often recited with respect to the theory and practice of communication performance management is that he strikes at the core of the issue. Managers need to know (rather than guess!) how well their organisation is doing (or is predicted to do). In the private sector they will want to make this assessment against the competition, in the public sector they are generally more concerned about understanding the performance of their organisation against some accepted benchmark.

There are in practice many reasons why procurement professionals would want to measure performance: they might consider that it is a motivator for their teams, that it can be used to identify performance shortfalls, that they can monitor the effectiveness of business improvement initiatives, that they encourage people to modify behaviours...and so on. In essence however, these reasons are likely to fall into one of three categories:

- To assess and communicate position
- To monitor and communicate progress
- To confirm and communicate priorities

Learning activity 5.1

Taking a public sector organisation with which you are familiar, identify, using the 3-way categorisation above, the primary reason why it may want to measure the effectiveness of its procurement communications activity. Try to articulate your reasoning in two or three bullet points.

In developing measurements of communication effectiveness, four key principles of an effective performance management system should be considered:

- Measure outcomes and outputs – a good measurement system should be focused on outputs and outcomes, and not the input activities that produce them. Outputs and outcomes should be measured along three dimensions: quality, timeliness and cost.
- Emphasise measures taken externally – if your customer measures your performance it is likely to be a truer reflection than if you were to second-guess their experience. This is a good way of minimising the subjectivity of quality measures.
- It almost goes without saying, but you can only measure those outputs for which a value can be established.
- Make the measurement system simple. It is generally held that the most effective measurement systems are based on six to eight indices.

Whilst in reality procurement organisations vary in the frequency and depth of measurement of their communications policies and processes, using these four principles you can now develop tests of communications effectiveness. Work through self assessment activity 5.1 below to consolidate your understanding of these principles.

Self assessment question 5.1

The central procurement organisation of a public body is planning to hold a number of events next calendar year aimed at promoting links with, and improving the effectiveness of, its supplier base. Specifically, it is seeking to inform them of the likely demands to be placed on them in the years ahead.

The events are to include a networking session to provide representatives from the top 20 construction companies in the region with guidance on the department's construction procurement strategies. This event will also facilitate informal discussion between companies on the benefits of joint venture approaches.

The organisation is also planning to hold a market information day to highlight to the construction industry the opportunities available within its new framework agreements. This event is expected to generate significant interest from industry, given the response to an earlier calling note.

A Meet the Buyer event is to be organised by the City Council to promote opportunities for small businesses in the local area.

Finally the procurement organisation will work with the local 'Business in the Community' agency to develop awareness of how to do business with the Public Sector. This event will include one-on-one meetings, the provision of sample tender documents, and advice and guidance on public procurement legislation.

The series of events is about to commence. Using the four guiding principles outlined above, how would you test whether this procurement communications campaign has achieved its required outcomes?

Demonstrating the effectiveness of a communications policy

As part of the Transforming Government Procurement initiative, the Office of Government Commerce conducts Procurement Capability Reviews (PCR) (http://www.ogc.gov.uk/ogc_-transforming_government_procurement_procurement_capability_reviews.asp). Intended to identify how and where public money is spent and how value for money is achieved, a component of the PCR is an assessment of the effectiveness of communications strategies. The OGC guidelines lay out key principles in measuring success against objectives.

- Output – has the communication been provided through effective means to stakeholders?

- Out-take – is there evidence that stakeholders have heard the message?

- Outcome – is there evidence of a desirable change in behaviour?

The Supply Chains in the 21st Century initiative (SC21) is used in other study sessions in this Unit (see 1.6 and http://www.sbac.co.uk/pages/80338686.asp). It is highlighted again here as a case study to support the second learning objective of this Session (demonstrating communications effectiveness). Briefly research the SC21 website before attempting the self assessment activity below.

Self assessment question 5.2

SC21 is a continuous improvement programme aiming to accelerate the competitiveness of the UK Defence sector through industry-wide improvements in supply chain working culture. It is run under the auspices of the Society of British Aerospace Companies, and has over 300 signatory companies of all sizes. The Ministry of Defence's procurement organisation is a signatory. A key focus of SC21's early attempts to gain national momentum was an initiative to identify development 'clusters' of key suppliers around so-called prime contractors (such as BAES, Bombardier and Augusta Westland). Whilst this proved to be a pragmatic and, as it turned out, extremely effective catalyst for progress, it had the unintended consequence of threatening to distance the remaining supplier companies that had not been selected by the primes for the initial clusters. Their nervousness over being 'left out' and therefore, in their view, suffering a potentially disadvantageous competitive position became a real concern for the SC21 project team. A concerted communications effort was deemed necessary, not only to maintain the momentum of the core programme, but also to retain the interest and progress of the other signatory companies.

Given your knowledge of the concerns of member companies, and taking note of the OGC guidance outlined above, consider the metrics you would use to determine the effectiveness of the SC21 campaign.

How best to learn lessons from the experience of others

The CBI/QinetiQ report into Innovation and Public Procurement: A New Approach to Stimulating Innovation (2006, pp.2) quoted a survey by the Engineering Employers' Federation, which found that the conduct of public procurement was more likely to be seen as negative rather than positive. Companies, it said, saw public procurement in the UK as risk averse, slow and bureaucratic. A key recommendation of the report was that public procurement organisations must 'learn and adapt', both from each other and from benchmark private sector examples. It suggested that the Ministry of Defence had the most positive lessons to share of all government departments, but that all should:

- Set up wide learning networks
- Learn from the best in the commercial work (specifically through secondments into the private sector)
- Conduct formal communications campaign evaluations

The last bullet here suggests that the formal capture of lessons is an exercise that happens at the end of a project. A more proactive approach is to establish and embed learning processes from the outset. If they exist, a review of previous lessons learned before any communications campaign commences will help to shape the intended plan. Thereafter, the regular and frequent capture of lessons as they arise provides the best chance of maximising benefit to other projects.

Setting up a central repository for all lessons will facilitate an ongoing capture process. This need not be IT/IS based; a paper system might suffice, although for more complex projects and campaigns a well-maintained and linked electronic database is usually required. The most important factor in maintaining such a repository however is the comprehensive validation of lessons prior to upload to the repository. You need to be extremely wary of taking all observations at face value. Quite often a stakeholder will report lessons in the heat of the moment and you must make every effort to corroborate an individual's perception of performance before incorporating that view formally into the lessons register.

Learning activity 5.2

There is an enormous amount of information on the web addressing lessons-learned policies and processes. Take 30 minutes to explore this information and to form your own opinion on the critical factors in establishing and exploiting lessons learned.

It is useful to be aware that organisations have given emphasis to their communications policy and processes to ensure that procurement (in its widest sense) activities, especially successes, are promulgated to stakeholders through a variety of means. The Security Industry Authority details its Stakeholder Engagement Strategy on the web and whilst there is a considerable amount of information there is emphasis upon Value for Money and obtaining relevant equipment and material. Similarly, there is a Home Office Accommodation 2005 Project Report on the National Asylum Service, whereby new contracts were designed and developed to enable improved value for money, improvements in commercial leverage and flexibility and business continuity through negotiated procurement activity. This particular success involved a range of stakeholders from central government to many ordinary citizens.

Summary

This aim of this study session was to guide you in considering how to gauge the success of a procurement organisation's communications policy. You will have established that it was necessary first to understand why you are taking measurements in the first place – is it to assess your position, to monitor progress, or to confirm priorities? Taking 'progress monitoring' one step further, you then considered four guiding principles for good performance management and applied them to a self-assessment scenario in order to establish how you would test whether or not the procurement campaign in question had achieved its required outcomes. Using the SC21 initiative as a case study you were able to go into more detail by attempting to specify metrics that would effectively indicate progress towards the campaign's objectives. Finally, you looked at the important area of lessons learned and formed your own views on how best to ensure that learning from examples of effective communications elsewhere was an intrinsic, value adding element of your own campaign.

Revision question

Assuming that you are the Procurement Director of a large public sector organisation, prepare a presentation for the elected members detailing the way that you will ensure that communication with stakeholders is effective.

Feedback on learning activity 5.1

'Taking a public sector organisation with which you are familiar, identify using the 3-way categorisation, the primary reason why it may want to measure the effectiveness of its procurement communications activity. Try to articulate your reasoning in two or three bullet points.'

This learning activity was designed to put this Study Session in a broader performance measurement context. The focus of this Session is on determining through some systematic method the effectiveness of a procurement communications campaign. Take for example London councils, which have an influential third party expenditure of around £8 billion (all 2003/4 figures). Of this, it is estimated that some 40% is on direct client facing services, such as social care and housing. For an average London Borough, third party expenditure is about £250 million per annum with an average of 7,000 suppliers. In this context the London Centre for Excellence listed a number of reasons why a council might wish to measure and manage procurement outcomes. Noted below, against the LCE list, is an attempt to categorise each bullet using the three categories:

- Identify areas for improvement, especially around cashable savings and improved quality of services [Monitor Progress]
- Ensure that procurement directly contributes to the fulfillment of the council's corporate objectives [Confirm Priorities]
- Demonstrate the value added, especially after changes (i.e. justify existence!) [Assess and Communicate Position]
- Assess the contribution to improved outcomes for the councils direct 'clients' and other stakeholders [Assess and Communicate Position]
- Support the delivery of politically related priorities such as green procurement; trading with small businesses and ethical trading [Assess and Communicate Position]
- Discharge audit obligations [Assess and Communicate Position]
- Accelerate the integration of procurement into the mainstream work of all public sector bodies (as opposed to being seen as a stand-alone administrative function) [Monitor Progress]

Feedback on self assessment question 5.1

'Using the four guiding principles…..above, how would you test whether this procurement communications campaign has achieved its required outcomes?'

It is important here to understand first why you are intending to measure communications effectiveness in this scenario. Using the 3-way categorisation you are now familiar with it would be reasonable to argue that here you are concerned with *monitoring progress*. This then will set the top-level context for the development of your measurement regime.

Now you can consider the four guiding principles of good measurement systems. Simplicity demands that at least one of the nine proposed metrics listed below is discarded. For ease of illustration, say you discard 6, 7 and 9. Of the six remaining, 8 could be discarded as arguably it is an input, not an output. 3 and 5 may also fall into this category. You might also discard 2 and 7 as they are not easily measurable, certainly in terms of output. That leaves 1 and 4. In practice it is likely you would use at least four of these metrics, but this exercise serves to illustrate how a disciplined approach to metric selection will ensure that your performance management system gives you the information you need in order to achieve your top-level objective.

1. Numbers attending events, forums, conferences and the results of feedback forms distributed at these, or face to face contact.
2. Learning from third parties as to how successful their activities have been.
3. Number and type of website enquiries.
4. Feedback forms sent on an annual basis with the subscription renewal.
5. Number of phone calls to the bookshop.
6. Feedback forms on the website.
7. Discussions with members on the phone.
8. Number of e-mails received.
9. Newsletters which also request feedback.

Self assessment question 5.2

'Given your knowledge of the concerns of member companies, and taking note of the OGC guidance outlined above, consider the metrics you would use to determine the effectiveness of the SC21 campaign.'

The OGC guidance in this area, as outlined in the main text above, provides a very useful reference point in determining communications effectiveness metrics. In the case of SC21 a range of communications methods are used. These include press releases to mainstream and specialist publications; a variety of internal communications; awareness presentations and videos; implementation guides; easy-to-follow starter parks; 'elevator briefs' and posters which are all available on the SC21 website.

In this activity you might have considered that conducting a survey of signatory companies would be an effective way of identifying what they thought of these methods (output effectiveness) and whether they had suggestions for alternatives and/or improvements. The reality however was that when the SC21 project team conducted such an exercise, only 30% of the signatory members responded. Whilst even this feedback is useful, the obvious danger is that the 70% who did not reply are those who are most in need of the communication! A reasonable conclusion to draw perhaps from the low response rate is that the communications strategy is not in fact particularly effective, and thought must be given to determining the root cause of this issue.

Despite the disappointingly low survey response, the SC21 project is able to gather evidence that some of the members, particularly those in the core programme, have heard the message (outtake effectiveness). Performance of the SC21 implementation process is tracked monthly and published on the website, and this very visual representation of progress is both a communication device in its own right, and good evidence on the pace of the initiative.

Changes in procurement behaviour (outcome effectiveness) are measured formally by recognising members who achieve pre-determined performance thresholds. From an initial baseline estimate of supply performance in the defence sector (75% on time delivery and 95% right first time), the SC21 project awards 'Silver' status to companies meeting, amongst other criteria, 97 – 99% right-first-time performance, and 'Gold' status to those with a 99 – 100% sustained delivery performance.

Feedback on revision question

'Assuming that you are the Procurement Director of a large public sector organisation, prepare a presentation for the elected members detailing the way that you will ensure that communication with stakeholders, in respect of procurement performance, is effective.'

Your report should briefly identify aspects that have been covered in earlier study sessions, notably the importance of communication and the ease with which it can be distorted if not well managed. Hence there has been a need for a clear communications strategy (utilising the headings noted in study session 4) so that stakeholders can appreciate what the vision and key objectives of that which they are being informed. This is the contextual setting for your report.

The main body of your report should now focus upon the way that you will ensure that effective communication is taking place. The key part of this is (for example) that it is about informing the stakeholders how well the particular procurement strategy is being undertaken. This is the primary reason why you are measuring communication effectiveness. You should continue by detailing the performance measures that you have (or are) utilised (utilising)
You would probably identify the OGC guidelines in respect of performance Capability Reviews. Aspects such as suitable metrics should be discussed and indicated, with proposed relevant solutions in respect of those metrics. You may also suggest comparisons or benchmarking activities. You would certainly not want this to be a 'one off' activity but rather an approach that would form the basis of continuous improvement in respect of procurement performance – and indeed the communication strategy as well!

Further Reading

CBI; QinetiQ. (2006). *Innovation and Public Procurement: A New Approach to Stimulating Innovation*

SBAC. (2006). *21st Century Supply Chains (SC21)*

Study session 6

"Critically evaluate marketing communication methods to improve internal and external stakeholder awareness of the role and purpose of procurement organisations"

6

Introduction

In marketing the activities of any procurement organisation it is essential in the first instance to understand why you might want to undertake such an activity. Engaging stakeholders properly, that is to say in an effective and focused manner, requires considerable time and resource, and it is at best wasteful at worst counter-productive to commit to such a course of action without a pre-determined idea of the beneficial outcomes required by the 'commissioning' organisation. This study session therefore will offer guidance on the types of methods that might be employed to raise both internal and external procurement awareness and, through short case studies and comment, will provide prompts to assist you in evaluating their appropriateness in different business contexts.

Session learning objectives

After completing this session you should be able to:

- understand the primary motivations behind any initiative to promote awareness about the role and purpose of procurement organisations
- determine how best to conduct quantitative and qualitative assessments of procurement performance
- consider the appropriateness of a range of promotional methods
- evaluate the success of your stakeholder engagement campaign against your pre-determined objectives

Unit content coverage

This study session covers part of the following topic from the official CIPS unit content documents: *Investigate relationships with key and critical stakeholders relevant to public procurement*. Specifically, it covers: *Critically evaluate marketing communication methods to improve internal and external stakeholder awareness of the role and purpose of procurement organisations*.

Prior knowledge

Prior to this study session you should have completed study sessions 1; 2; 3; 4; 5.

Timing

You should take about 3 hours to read and complete this section, including learning activities and self assessment questions.

Links to other study sessions in this unit

At this stage it is worth re-visiting (or visiting if you have not done so already) study session 1 in this Unit as the definition of a stakeholder, and an understanding of the subsequent principles underpinning stakeholder analysis, is an essential pre-requisite to developing communication campaigns. To recap, a stakeholder is any individual, any formal or informal grouping of individuals, or any institution which both wishes and is able to affect the future of your procurement organisation. Given this definition, it is likely that there are a considerable number of stakeholders that you will need to consider, and you must be able to focus your engagement and awareness efforts if you are to achieve your objectives in the most effective manner.

What might those objectives be? In general terms a procurement organisation might want to influence the future actions of a stakeholder for the following reasons:

- To improve effectiveness by ensuring that the right stakeholders are involved at the right stage of procurement organisation's planning and implementation cycle.
- To contribute to a wider communications and public relations exercise, either at business unit, department or enterprise level.
- To inform internal or external initiatives such as overhead reduction programs and business downsizing, functional re-structuring, (de)centralising, and service outsourcing.

These are not of course mutually exclusive. It may well be that a combination of all three needs to be factored into any stakeholder awareness campaign, but it will be very helpful in your detailed planning if you can determine the primary motivation behind your requirement to engage with the stakeholder community.

Learning activity 6.1

Using a public sector organisation with which you are familiar, identify the primary motivation behind the requirement to engage with its stakeholder community. Try to articulate your reasons for not prioritising the other motivations.

It is relevant here to recap also on the definitions of *internal* and *external* as they apply to stakeholders. Whilst all procurement organisations operate within a *traditional* business construct, that is to say they form part of an identifiable departmental entity; increasingly procurement activity is conducted as part of some form of enterprise-wide collaboration or partnering arrangement. It is quite feasible as an example for public sector procurement teams to be working closely with colleagues from private sector industry partners, having perhaps developed joint procurement strategies and ways of working. In innovative procurement scenarios such as these, the definition of 'external' and 'internal' becomes less obvious. Session 1 of this Unit makes reference to this emerging complexity. Self assessment activity 6.1 below, which is based on a real case study, will help to consider this point further in the context of communications planning and methods.

The stakeholder engagement process

Study session 2 addressed the detail of stakeholder analysis and it is not the intention of this study session to repeat that work here. It is sufficient to recall that, having determined why you might want to devote resource to a stakeholder awareness campaign, you must then undertake a systematic analysis of the stakeholder community. This analysis is but one activity in what might be viewed as the top-level stakeholder engagement process, as depicted below.

Diagram 6.1 Top-level stakeholder engagement process

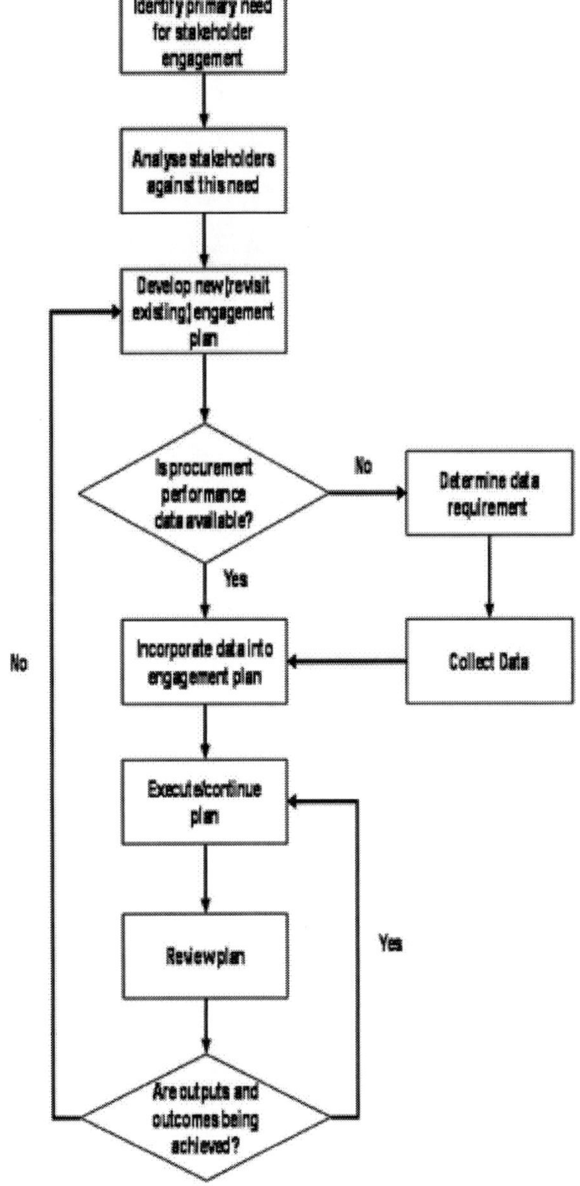

6

Self assessment question 6.1

The Ministry of Defence is embarking on a major equipment procurement programme. It has made the case, which has been accepted by its internal Investment Appraisals Board that it will partner with a number of key industry prime contractors to deliver the design, build and through-life support phases of the military platform in question. As an integral part of this joint effort, the MoD has established a collaborative supply chain and procurement group. This group has developed a procurement 'mission', which is to establish and maintain fit for purpose supply chains throughout the life of the programme. It has undertaken to determine the optimum balance between value for money procurement and sustainable risk, and it has developed a set of joint objectives and deliverables that it considers it will need to meet in order to achieve its mission.

So the MoD in this particular programme has to play a two-headed role. On the one hand it must act as the client organisation by stipulating the key legislative, security and operational constraints within which the collaborative procurement activity is conducted. It must for example ensure that the programme procures goods and services in accordance with UK and European competition law and, given the sensitive nature of the programme, is obliged to articulate to its industry partners the complex security constraints on global sourcing. On the other hand however, it must act as a fully active participant in the joint supply chain management team. Quite often, for very practical reasons, the same people are playing both roles!

The joint procurement group has decided that it is going to conduct a collaborative stakeholder communications exercise. If you were the MoD representative on the group, who would you consider to be an 'external' stakeholder from the following list, and why? Indicate where you think your industry partners may have differing views.

- The MoD's Procurement team leader
- The technical design manager (an employee of one of the prime contractors)
- The procurement departments of the prime contractors
- The MoD's central procurement strategy and policy team leader
- The programme's risk manager (a MoD employee)

Procurement performance data and information

Unless a comprehensive procurement communications exercise has been conducted in your organisation previously, it is unlikely that there is a readily available and accurate database of past procurement performance. The link between your procurement organisation's activity and the overall performance of the business is often assumed, but to make a convincing case as part of an engagement with key stakeholders, whoever they might be, it will often be necessary to back up claims with evidence of the value-adding nature of procurement activity. You must always be alive to the fact that cynicism, scepticism and in some cases active counter-briefing are not uncommonly found within business and organisational culture. One of the most effective ways to deal with these negative (and possibly uninformed) reactions is to offer up reasoned and logical argument as part of a communications plan. This section therefore deals with the middle section of the overall process, as described above in the flow diagram. It is about assessing the relevance of data sources in providing both quantitative and qualitative assessments of procurement performance.

An innovative approach to this challenge can be seen in the form of the Scottish Procurement Information Hub (RR Donnelly, 2008). Here spending analysis is undertaken at a national level and as a direct consequence opportunities for regional, national and sector procurement collaboration are being identified. Of note, communicating effectively and ensuring productive stakeholder relations is a 'core deliverable' detailed in the Scottish Best Practice study. The document goes on to identify two key measures of procurement success:

- A **supplier** satisfaction questionnaire, which seeks to determine the efficiency and effectiveness of the procurement organisation's engagement with suppliers throughout the life of a contract.

- A **customer** satisfaction questionnaire, which aims to determine how visible and helpful the procurement organisation has been to date.

In another context the emphasis may be on the collection of a more quantitative set of data. Of the three major workstreams in the NHS Procurement Review (Cabinet Office, 1998), *'Institutionalising Best Practice'* recommended that Trusts and Executives identify key performance indicators for use in monitoring procurement activity. Recommendation 5 called for a set of quantified and dated procurement efficiency targets. Recommendation 11 focused on the requirement to identify management information needs. Referring back to the flowchart above, you will note that there is an activity to 'determine data requirement' should the data required to support a communication campaign not be readily available. Use self assessment activity 6.2 below to test your understanding of the relevance of quantitative metrics.

Self assessment question 6.2

The following is a list of proposed quantitative procurement performance metrics for the Leicestershire and Rutland NHS Procurement Partnership (2008 – 2013). Firstly, identify 3 key performance indicators on the basis that you were required to provide an internal, routine procurement report to your Trust's Executive. Then identify 3 metrics you might use to input to a general publication on the Trust, which is due to be released to the press as part of a public communications exercise in 3 weeks time.

1. Savings against expenditure – savings achieved as a % of non pay expenditure
2. Electronic requisitioning - % requisitions raised from an electronic catalogue
3. Qualified staff – qualified staff as a % of all NHS procurement and supply staff
4. Studying staff – staff working towards a qualification as a % of all NHS procurement and supply staff.
5. Materials Management - % of orders raised via materials management systems & % value of orders raised via materials management systems
6. Cost of Procurement – procurement staff costs as a % of non-pay expenditure
7. Capital Contract Expenditure - % expenditure covered by competitive contractual arrangements
8. Savings against capital budget allocation – savings achieved as a % of capital budget allocation
9. Orders – value and volume of orders processed
10. Low Value Orders – volume of orders raised below £50.00
11. Number of Single Tender Approvals – single tender waivers as a % of total expenditure.

Suppliers – Number of suppliers

Question:
How do you eat an elephant?

Answer:
A slice at a time

John Gilbert
(A Slice by Slice Guide to TQM)

Broadcasting the message

You have determined the need for communicating the role and purpose of the procurement organisation, and you have gathered the supporting data that you think your target audience will want to see, understand, and indeed have the chance to question. You now need to determine how best to package this data, turn it into meaningful information, and convey it to your key stakeholders. There are a large number of ways this last element of the process, the execution of your communication plan, might be achieved. Some procurement organisations engage communications and media experts to develop and coordinate a comprehensive information campaign.

A good example of this sophisticated approach to marketing procurement activity is the *21st Century Supply Chain* initiative, or SC21 mentioned above. This is an ongoing continuous improvement programme aiming to accelerate the competitiveness of the UK Defence sector through industry-wide improvements in supply chain working culture. It is run under the auspices of the Society of British Aerospace Companies, has over 300 signatory companies of all sizes across the sector, and benefits from ministerial endorsement. The programme takes its promotional activity extremely seriously, and its media cell coordinates the following communications activity:

- Presentations and display stands at defence supply chain and logistics conferences
- Preparation and release of press statements on success stories
- Bi-monthly members meetings held around the country where the focus is on sharing and spreading best practice
- Central drafting of internal communications documents for members to adapt and use as they see fit within their own companies and departments
- A continually updated website with information on a range of subjects, from how to join, to the latest press release, and news from special interest groups.

At the other end of the *sophistication spectrum* it might be appropriate, either because of limited resources or due to the findings from the stakeholder analysis, simply to conduct a series of one-on-one briefings with key internal and external stakeholders. Both communications strategies are equally valid as long as the desired outcome of the campaign is thoroughly understood, allowing the campaign itself to be carefully focused on achieving the outcome in the most cost effective way. You should bear in mind that it is often a case of having to repeat a similar message or send segments of messages to enable successful receipt by stakeholders. The process is continual and should be seen as a 'slice by slice' approach.

Planning for communications with stakeholders

You can say that planning for such communication could be summarised in four broad steps:

- Identify procurement stakeholders
- Analyse the needs and expectations of these stakeholders in respect of communications
- Prioritise effort towards key stakeholders
- Identify existing and potential media / 'vehicles' for promulgation of required communication

  (including answers to:)
  WHOM do you wish to communicate
  WHAT do you want to communicate
  WHICH method / methods of communication
  WHEN do you wish to communicate.

Learning activity 6.2

Read 'Marketing in public sector organisations,' by Bovaird in Public Management and Governance by Bovaird and Loffler.

Note its main points and consider in the context of marketing procurement.

Summary

This aim of this study session was to help you take account of a number of critical factors when developing a campaign to promote the activities of a procurement organisation. You worked through a top-level process, which falls into 3 distinct but closely related phases. Firstly, you considered the importance of determining why you might want to engage in a communications activity in the first place. This is a most important pre-requisite for the second phase, which focuses on understanding the data and information you will need in order to support your engagement activity. Approaching key stakeholders with only a vague, unquantified view of your organisation's performance will almost certainly fail to influence them in the way you intended. Finally, having gathered the data you believe your target audience will consider important (remember not to collect data for data's sake!), then you examined a range of possible strategies through which you might conduct the engagement. It is at this stage of the process that your resourcing constraints become most evident. You might have wanted to embark on a comprehensive, professionally orchestrated campaign, but your budget might not have stretched that far! This is not the end of the world. Even in the tightest financial climate much effective work can be done, but success will depend on putting as much effort as possible into the early phases. There are unfortunately no short-cuts. Using the SC21 initiative as a case study you went into more detail by attempting to **specify** metrics that would effectively indicate progress towards the campaign's objectives. Next, you looked at the important area of lessons learned and **formed your own views** on how best to ensure that learning from examples of effective communications elsewhere was an intrinsic, value adding element of your own campaign.

Revision question

Discuss the most effective means of improving internal and external stakeholder awareness of procurement organisation's role and purpose through marketing communications.

Feedback

Feedback on learning activity 6.1

'Using a public sector organisation with which you are familiar, identify the primary motivation behind the requirement to engage with its stakeholder community. Try to articulate your reasons for ***not*** *prioritising the other motivations.'*

Clearly you have considerable scope here. If you had chosen a Police Force procurement organisation as your example, you might have considered that your contribution to the Annual Report was the overriding communications requirement. In other words, you might have felt that making a contribution to a wider communications initiative was the primary motivator. You might have argued that your communications strategy would take on an external focus in line with broader Police Authority priorities and that the other, more internally-orientated motivations, were of only secondary importance. It is very feasible that your organisation controls a significant proportion of the total annual budget (perhaps even the largest proportion outside of police and staff wages), and you will want to explain, indeed the public will expect you to explain through the Annual Report, not only how your team is organised to deliver value for money, but also how it will contribute to next year's efficiency targets.

This example highlights a more general observation; that communications strategies are by nature dynamic. Many business contexts exhibit this annual cycle and the communications strategy therefore, and the resultant methods and data employed to support it, will change in focus over time will require regular reviews. Outside the annual reporting cycle it may be that your communications strategy switches focus to informing internal efficiency reviews.

Feedback on self assessment question 6.1

'If you were the MoD representative on the collaborative procurement group, who would you consider to be an 'external' stakeholder from the following list, and why? Indicate where you think your industry partners may have differing views.

- *The MoD's Procurement team leader*
- *The technical design manager (an employee of one of the prime contractors*
- *The procurement departments of the prime contractors*

- *The MoD's central procurement strategy and policy team leader*
- *The programme's risk manager (a MoD employee)'*

Your answers to and observations on this case study activity will depend as much on how you think about the collaborative team as on how the more formal organisational structures and terms of reference describe the actual public sector/private sector interfaces. Success in partnering and alliance arrangements such as this requires an emotional attachment to the collaborative construct as well as a contractual one. In this respect if you have built up a genuine trust in, and dependency on your industry colleagues, then you might feel and act as if other MoD people working within the programme are in fact 'external' to the procurement group, and you would design your communications plan accordingly.

Unfortunately, as you have encountered elsewhere in this Unit, there are no definitive answers here! The internal team dynamics will also colour your view on the external/internal boundary. For example, the collaborative procurement group of which you are an important part, might have previously considered (as was indeed the case in the real-life example underpinning this activity) that it would have to work very closely with the programme's risk manager to ensure that what it considered to be highly important procurement-related risks, were properly recognised, costed and mitigated. This was deemed to be especially important as some of the mitigation was beyond the authority and scope of the group itself. In this respect therefore, it could be argued that the risk team were in effect an extension of the procurement group in achieving a particular outcome and that they are therefore *internal* stakeholders.

The key learning point here is that the categorisation of stakeholders, and therefore the resultant communications planning, is not a prescriptive exercise. It will be more effectively conducted in a collaborative environment however if these considerations are discussed and agreed with your partners at the outset, before the analysis work itself is conducted.

Feedback on self assessment question 6.2

*'Firstly, identify 3 **key** performance indicators on the basis that you were required to provide an internal, routine procurement report to your Trust's Executive. Then identify 3 metrics you might use to input to a general publication on the health of the Trust, which is due to be released to the press as part of a public communications exercise in 3 weeks time'*

The object of this activity is to demonstrate through practical application how different performance metrics (and therefore different underlying data) are required to satisfy different stakeholder viewpoints and perceptions. In the first instance, you were making a routine internal report and were therefore likely to want to focus the Executive's attention on operational efficiency and effectiveness. You might therefore have chosen metric 6, say, as a key indicator of efficiency and metric 8 for effectiveness. You might then consider that the Executive would be interested to set these measures in context and therefore have taken metric 9 as an indication of the 'busyness' of your operation. It might be however that you think the Executive are more interested in the up-skilling of your organisation to cope with the future complexities of NHS procurement, in which case you would have perhaps chosen metric 4.

You could reasonably argue that you would have chosen exactly the same metrics for the second scenario. That would certainly not be wrong, but you are dealing with a much broader stakeholder interest in this scenario and you would need to consider this carefully before following this line. For example, you must consider the views of the Trade Unions, who might be focused on metrics 3 and 4, the general public who are likely to be exercised by the cost efficiency metrics (1, 6 and 8), by potential suppliers who might be very interested in metrics 7 and 11, or indeed by fellow procurement professionals in other public and private sector organisations who would be interested in the more 'technical' metrics, such as 2 and 5. Given this breadth of stakeholder interest in this scenario (and remember each group could in some way have an influence on the future of your organisation) your choice of 3 **key** metrics might attempt to cover all of the efficiency, up-skilling and technical aspects of your operation.

Feedback on learning activity 6.2

'Read 'Marketing in public sector organisations,' by Bovaird in Public Management and Governance by Bovaird and Loffler.

Note its main points and consider in the context of marketing procurement.

The chapter provides an overview of marketing in the public sector generally – not procurement specifically. Nevertheless, it is a relevant insight into relevant perspectives on the contextual setting. You will note particularly the points on preparing a marketing plan, which is followed by the pertinent section on analyzing the environment with an emphasis upon stakeholders. This enlarges upon the points made in this study session. It ends with recognition of marketing limitations especially in the public sector environment.

Feedback on revision question

Discuss the most effective means of improving internal and external stakeholder awareness of procurement organisation's role and purpose through marketing communications.

This has a number of elements with which you should deal. Many of the central themes to this answer will have been covered in the earlier study sessions. Much of what can be taken into account for an answer is contingent upon the particular procurement activity or project in which one is involved. Hence it would be useful to be able to discuss a number of example procurement scenarios within the public sector context.

Recalling that the procurement process should be considered on a holistic or total process perspective, there are differing stages at which differing stakeholders could be engaged. A major procurement construction project, for example, would require extensive communication with planning departments, citizens affected by the construction and potential contractors well before any tender process commences. Indeed the consultations that would take place would almost certainly inform the tender and contract award processes. Similarly, if an environmentally friendly approach was to be taken in respect of a new transport system for the ambulance service, then the co-ordination of communication across the whole of the UK would be extensive, not least because there are different regions involved and indeed the Northern Ireland and Welsh Assemblies, the Scottish and Westminster parliaments, as well as European coordination. And this is before the consideration of whatever the actual improvement (e. g. the introduction of electric vehicles) and the impact that it might have upon the medical profession, patients, the confidence of the general public who might want a rapid service as well as those who are tax payers and might be involved in additional expenditure.

Hence it is important to clearly identify the stakeholders in terms of influence and impact, with a careful analysis of their expectations and needs. From this a prioritisation should be possible. This would be based upon the tools / models discussed in the preceding study sessions. It will then be necessary to share / impart the right information at the right time to the right audience. In doing so the optimal choice of broadcasting media / vehicle should be selected. The differing types of communication strategies should be explained and then the particular message about the role and purpose of procurement should be developed.

Often the message will be that procurement is at the centre of the organisations business. The very nature of business and trade is that of buying and selling. It is only relatively recently that the beneficial impacts that holistic (e.g. through life) approaches to procurement have been realised. For far too long, many in the public sector have not recognised anything other than a simplistic few of 'buying' as being a clerical, or at best, administrative function. Thus often the message that has to be communicated in marketing procurement to internal and external stakeholders is that the function itself is a professional activity where trained, educated and qualified professional personnel can hugely impact on the well being of the organisation for which they make decisions as well as the environment in which they function and live. Success can only be measured over time and that will come from a range of mechanisms, including general perception, questionnaires, effects on (through life) budgets, actual performance of the procured product, asset, service or goods.

You should ensure that stakeholders do not expect instant success but that a process of recognition and changing perceptions in respect of procurement's role and purpose are continually improving.

Further Reading

Marketing in public sector organisations - BOVAIRD

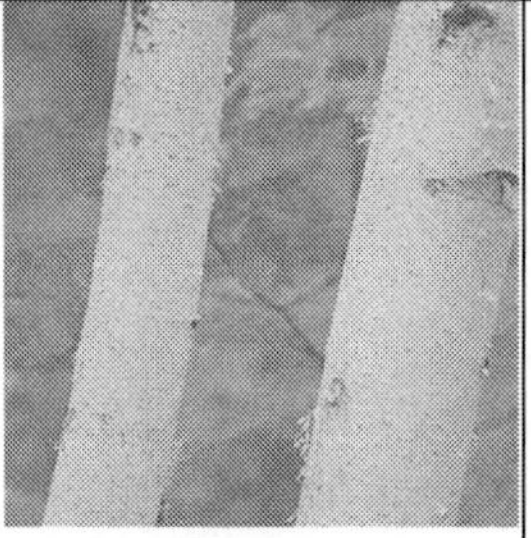

Study Session 7

"Explain how partnerships with appropriate stakeholders may be developed"

Introduction

As the first set of study sessions near a conclusion it is relevant to bring the various themes, issues and approaches discussed thus far together in order to identify how effective relationships can be formed with pertinent stakeholders. To do this will require a contextual appreciation of the nature of partnerships and then a utilisation of what has been covered to ensure that you can see when partnerships should be beneficial and how they can take place. It will also provide a relevant point from which you can progress to the following set of study sessions.

Session learning objectives

After completing this session you should be able to:

- understand the nature and purpose of partnerships
- identify appropriate stakeholders with which to develop partnerships
- build partnerships with appropriate internal and external stakeholders

Unit content coverage

This study session covers part of the following topic from the official CIPS unit content documents*: Investigate relationships with key and critical stakeholders relevant to public procurement*. Specifically, it covers: *Explain how partnerships with appropriate stakeholders may be developed.*

Timing

You should take about 4 – 5 hours to read and complete this section, including learning activities and self assessment questions.

Prior knowledge

Prior to this study session you should have completed study sessions 1; 2; 3; 4; 5; 6.

Context and background to partnerships

Study sessions from here onwards will identify approaches to working closely with stakeholders. This implicitly assumes that there are relationships to be developed in order to enhance performance (by whatever measures) in respect of procurement. This requires a brief (but important) insight into the nature of relationships. There is a strong commitment in the private sector to partnering that many policy documents indicate should be replicated in the public sector. Those in the procurement activity hold the key to this situation. It is imperative that those in public sector procurement recognise the notion not just of partnering but of the spectrum of relationships in order that they may optimise most suitable relationship strategy for their organisation.

There is a need for caution when discussing partnerships.

Learning activity 7.1

Why do you think that there is a need for caution when considering partnerships? Is there some difficulty with the topic?

For the reasons given in the feedback to this activity it will now be necessary to refer to partnering as well as partnership. (Often policies and documents do not clarify the differences, nor distinguish between the two)

The basis for considering partnering has been discussed earlier but it is predicated upon tools and strategies for differentiated approaches to procurement. Examples of these include the classic 80/20 curve (or Pareto's Law) and Kraljic's (1983, pp.109-117) 2 x 2 grid, or variations of it, as applied by a range of commercial organisations.

The 80/20 curve is produced in all Procurement and Supply Chain Management books. In effect, (as an example), a relatively small amount (approximately 20%) of inventory will be worth a relatively large amount (approximately 80%) of money or value. This, in inventory management, is the basis of an ABC classification system where different approaches to controlling inventory maybe taken. More time and effort would be spent on this relatively small quantity of stock items that have a high value or impact. Hence the 80/20 reference; it is the same principle with stakeholders; a relatively small number of stakeholders will be worth concentrating upon as their value or impact would be worth around 80% of the stakeholders views or input. This is obviously not precise and to consider this in a more accurate manner would require meaningful metrics. Inevitably however, these would probably be different for different procurement projects, although the methods identified earlier in the preceding study sessions such as stakeholder analysis and stakeholder mapping would be very useful indeed.

Self assessment question 7.1

Read a Procurement or Supply Chain Management text to see what is said concerning Pareto or the 80/20 Rule. Ensure that you comfortable with the concept.

The approach to considering strategies for purchasing and supply chain management put forward by Kraljic still holds good (even though it first appeared in 1983).

His work has been widely utilised and adapted. The following is an adaptation now commonly used by private sector companies. The public sector can utilise the same concept although the bottom line axis would probably be *value for money* or *effectiveness*. As detailed elsewhere this 2x2 grid allows strategies to be developed for undertaking procurement.

Diagram 7.1 Purchasing portfolio matrix

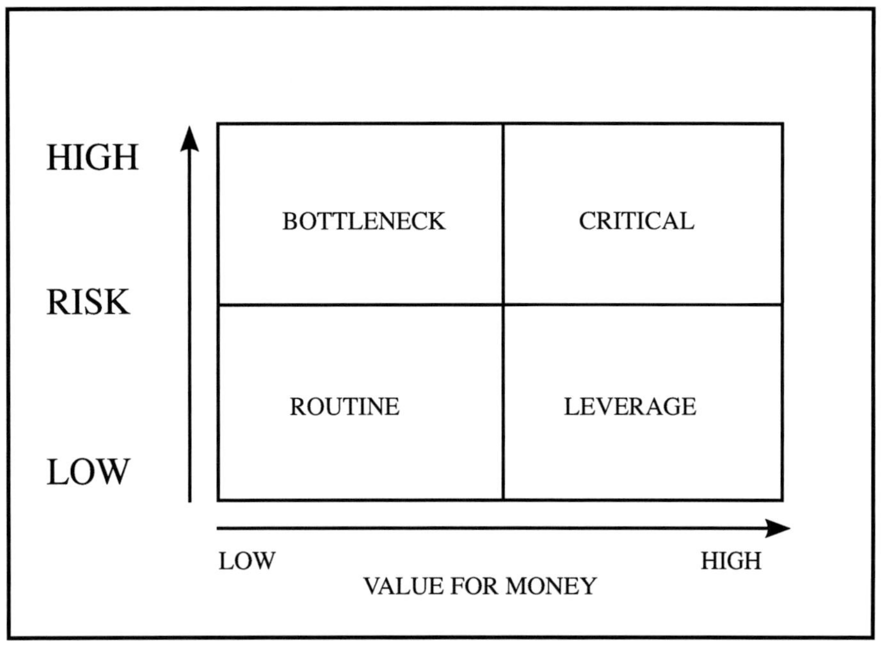

Source: adapted from Kraljic 1983

It is really about the relationship approach that the procurement organisation would take with suppliers (external stakeholders) dependant upon the asset, product, and commodity goods or services being purchased and if necessary maintained over a lifetime. For many public sector procurement organisations, there is increasingly a move towards outsourcing of activities, and, whenever possible working with other public procurement organisations to achieve maximum impact upon the supply market. This is where there is often some potential for things to go wrong. There may be considerable risk that an element of the subsequent arrangement with the contracted supplier of the service may not be able to deliver on time; or that the asset or service provided will not be as required. Against this the impact upon effectiveness or value for money may be considerable. In such a case, where there is high risk (considerable problems if something goes wrong) but considerable improvement in value for money if it can be undertaken well, the critical box in the above approach would apply. That is where a partnership/partnering arrangement should be adopted.

This is not to rule out such an approach elsewhere on the grid, but there may be such a focus on the output of the public sector procurement organisation that a plethora of partnerships/partnering arrangements would not be in the best interest of stakeholders (other than possibly suppliers) and even then not all suppliers would be content if such a universal approach to partnerships/ partnering was adopted).

Learning activity 7.2

Read 'Managing a portfolio of supplier relationships' by Professor Douglas Macbeth (2002, pp. 51-62) in the *'Handbook of Purchasing Management'*. Then in the same book read 'Purchasing in the higher education sector' by Tom Chadwick (2002, pp. 329-342).

None of this is indicating that partnership/partnering is not a valid approach; rather it is indicating that it is extremely important – in certain situations – hence the need to consider an 80/20 and Kraljic approach as well as stakeholder analysis and mapping.

In the latter piece mentioned above there is, in addition to information about purchasing consortia in higher education and national and interregional purchasing working groups, an indication of how portfolios of procurement activities can be built and utilised to enable enhanced value for money for a major public sector procurement environment of the higher education sector.

Taking an overview of the position on relationships in business, and this is relevant for overall spectrum of relationships with stakeholders, it is useful to consider the following:

Diagram 7.2 The extremes of the relationship spectrum

Relationship Spectrum of Buyers and Sellers

RELATIONSHIP SPECTRUM

Distant ⟷ **Closer**

Source Mike Fogg CIPS Course Book Managing Purchasing and Supply Relationships

Quite simply there are two extremes of relationships that can be developed and used in strategic approaches, which can be considered adversarial and co-destiny. Between these two extremes there are a wide range of relational approaches that can be taken by organisations whether in the public sector or not. The bullet points below illustrate what may be found between the extremes:

Distant ↑ … Closer ↓

- Adversarial
- Arm's length
- Transactional
- Closer tactical
- Single sourced
- Outsourcing
- Strategic alliance
- Partnership
- Co-destiny

It could be said that both extremes have not been the norm, and it is more common for relationships to be found in between. Certainly the private sector has been moving away from the adversarial end of the spectrum for some time. Such a move has not been so straight forward for the public procurement environment. There has been, and still is, the dichotomy of academic concepts, many initiatives, policy documents and commercial best practice indicating a closer relationship with suppliers whilst the pubic sector procurement environment is overseen by guidelines, rules, regulations and approaches that indicate strict propriety in dealing with suppliers. Often the result has been an interesting mix of approaches that have not always provided the most cost effective solution. In common with other departments and elements of the public sector, the MoD in adopting 'Smart Acquisition' has advocated closer relationships with suppliers, yet has, initially, undertaken a route to this through competition. It is worth noting that on Kraljic's grid the top right hand quadrant indicates partnerships as the optimal solution whilst the bottom right hand quadrant highlights competition as the optimum strategy. It is a case of trying to use partnerships/partnering but getting such an approach through a means of complying with perceptions of probity.

Learning activity 7.3

What do you think that commentators on the defence procurement scene may have had to say about this solution to utilising best practice whilst seeking to ensure probity?

Hence whilst partnerships/partnering can be extremely useful there are some limitations and background issues of which you should be aware. Much of what has been considered here is inevitably about a major group of external stakeholders - the suppliers, both potential and actual. Stakeholders, of course, can be considered more widely than just external and never more so than in the public sector. Thus it is now necessary to consider the public sector perspective in respect of partnerships more fully.

The nature and purpose of partnerships

What is partnering?

Partnering is a form of collaborative working between customers and suppliers. It can be used between public sector organisations and private sector organisations such as service providers to bring a win-win situation. It requires a recognition of shared business aims to realise mutual benefits. In contrast with traditional 'arms-length' procurement and contract management approaches, partnering is characterised by a greater degree of openness, communication, mutual trust and sharing information. The aims of partnering arrangements are often expressed in terms of business outcomes rather than specific outputs or improvements; their success is particularly dependent on the people and relationship aspects. Indeed it is recognition that it is the people within organisations who make the relationships as organisations as such are inanimate objects!

The tone of a partnering arrangement differs from a traditional contract and the behaviours of those involved are different too. The management of a partnering arrangement is usually proactive rather than reactive. Both parties work together to identify optimum solutions and to anticipate and resolve problems in a constructive, collaborative way. The arrangement needs to be based on mutual trust and openness; recognition that the relationship itself is as important as the contract; and a conviction that partnering makes good commercial sense for the particular procurement programme.

Learning activity 7.4

Why do you think that the public sector would want to consider partnering as a strategic approach?

For both the customer and supplier, shared business objectives and a collaborative approach to achieving them mean that the partnering approach offers significant strategic benefits. Partnering is about strength through collaboration. Building and maintaining a partnering arrangement will take much more effort and time than a traditional approach, not least because new attitudes and behaviours may have to be learned - and old ones unlearned.

As has already been detailed, partnering is not appropriate in every situation. It is a long term relationship, usually over five years and often much longer, where customers and providers adopt long term rather than short term views.

Partnering may be suitable where there is a need for:

- business change, especially where innovation is required and/or the future is uncertain
- using new methods of service delivery (such as providing services online)
- flexibility in constructing teams, involving specialist skills or scarce resources
- outsourcing business processes or services, perhaps to allow customer staff to concentrate on core areas.

Self assessment question 7.2

See if you can outline some situations when partnering is unlikely to be suitable. Rather than focusing solely on the benefits, costs and risks to the customer,

partnering seeks to create a mutually beneficial relationship, where both sides feel that the investments and concessions they have made, and the risks they have taken on, have helped them realise genuine gains and achieve strategic goals. For this to take place effectively there must be a greater appreciation and awareness of:

- Risk
- Trust
- Openness / transparency
- Communication

Learning activity 7.5

Using the below link, Read and summarise the main points of the document 'Managing Risks with Delivery Partners' (OGC, 2004).). (http://www.ogc.gov.uk/documents/cp0013.pdf)

Case Study - Highland Council Contract Standing Orders (2007, pp.7)

To indicate how seriously this concept is taken the following quotation provides a useful insight:

"'Partnering' means a form of collaborative working between partners and in contrast with traditional 'arms length' procurement and contract-management approaches, partnering is characterised by a greater degree of openness, communication, mutual trust and sharing information. There may often be a long-term relationship which requires clear roles and responsibilities for decision making, and effective performance reporting. Entering into such agreements is subject to the same rules of competition as other forms of agreement"

Build partnerships with appropriate internal and external stakeholders

You will recall that earlier comment was made about strategies for engaging with external stakeholders such as suppliers. Of course there are other stakeholders who are external to an organisation. Many other stakeholders will be internal to the organisation.

The approaches discussed earlier in the study sessions will assist in providing means of identifying appropriate stakeholders. However you should utilise the stakeholder relationship analysis approach as a particular and appropriate technique.

OGC identifies stakeholder relationship analysis as enabling an organisation or group of organisations to understand how to shape their people to be ready, willing and able to embrace change, for example, when introducing a new outsourced service provision or when developing working relationships, in a co-operative network, often across boundaries. By understanding who the key stakeholders are across the organisation(s) and how to engender a 'change-ready' culture, a procurement team can be successful in managing change across an organisation. Change in a collaborative environment, and associated stakeholder analysis, is potentially more challenging.

Stakeholders must feel equipped to deal with the proposed change, and as such be motivated and confident in what is to take place. Initial stakeholder analysis and then subsequent management of the resultant stakeholder relationship will enable the procurement project team and key stakeholders to build relationships across the organisation and monitor those relationships throughout the project/programme and lifecycle of the procured asset/commodity/service.

As has been noted earlier, recognising that for many stakeholders, both internal and external, change from the 'old' way of working to the 'new' can be challenging and even traumatic, OGC produces a view known as the Change Equation:

An organisation is ready for change when the three elements in the following change equation are met:

Dissatisfaction + Hope + Support = Readiness for Change

- In managing the procurement programme the project team must ensure that the Case for Change is clear. Articulation and communication of the Case for Change builds **dissatisfaction** with the current state.

- For the organisation to have hope for the future the procurement project team must build a clear and positive vision of the future so that people can make the change more tangible and look forward to change.

- Support is needed from the procurement project team for the organisation to understand how the change will be implemented; to provide confidence that the experience will be positive.

Once the procurement project team understands these key principles and focus upon them during conversations/communications/workshops etc with other stakeholders, then change planning should facilitate successful outcomes.

A key element in building relationships is that of trust. This is a topic about which it is easy to talk yet hard to practice in what can sometimes be challenging and complex circumstances.

Again OGC suggest that the trust equation should be utilised by the procurement project team to stimulate discussion on how to build relationships with key stakeholders throughout the project, with the intention of engendering confidence and support in the proposed change and individuals leading that change. It is understood that change causes stress by taking individuals outside of their comfort zones. Trust is needed to directly influence the success of any change management project, especially the way that public sector procurement is now bringing new ways of working with partners, as resistance is a natural behaviour. The trust equation is as follows:

$$\frac{\text{Credibility} + \text{Intimacy}}{\text{Risk}} = \text{Trust}$$

The project team must identify those individuals who may influence the success of the change project/programme. They can be categorised as follows:

- **Change sponsor –** Individual who legitimises the change

- **Change agent –** Individual/group who is responsible for implementing the change

- **Change target –** Individual/group who must actually change

- **Change advocate –** Individual/group who wants to achieve a change, but lacks authority to enforce

Whilst trust is a deeply embedded concept that can oft be put to the test, it is vital to at the very least appear trustworthy or progress may not be made in moving towards procurement project completion. This applies to both stakeholders (whether internal or external) and the procurement personnel/organisation/authority/department or similar.

To appear trustworthy a project member/key stakeholder must address the 3 critical factors in this equation:

1. Procurement project team leads/members must establish **Credibility** early in the project with key stakeholders who may comprise business leads, change champions across the business. Evidence of credibility may be involvement in similar successful projects, familiarity and the ability to communicate knowledge of the area of expertise/business.

2. **Intimacy** is used by people to engender trust across their personal and working lives. This may be as simple as enquiring about an individual's family.

3. The **Risk** posed by members of the project team/team lead must be low and therefore the project team/key stakeholders must work to avoid potential conflicting agendas with those whom they are trying to build trust.

Monitoring of potentially difficult relationships throughout the programme is a way of ensuring that any perceived 'lack of trust' can be addressed in order to minimise potential resistance as part of Responsible, Accountable, Consulted, Informed (RACI) analysis.

As was briefly introduced in earlier sessions, OGC recommends the use of a chart that indicate who the stakeholder is and the relevant project team/team member plus an indication of credibility, intimacy, risk and trust (each with High/Medium/Low rankings) and then most importantly a 'next steps' column. This is where, as a result of the work undertaken, action must be taken to ensure that stakeholders are fully aware of benefits, outputs, actions etc.

Summary

The whole concept of partnership / partnering is often put forward as simply working closer with suppliers. It is however much more than this – it is a concept that has its roots in the private sector, underpins philosophies such as supply chain management and in the often complex procurement project challenges that are increasingly being championed and presented in the public procurement environment, is not to be taken lightly. It involves the management of change and all of this requires careful identification of stakeholders, both internal and external, and their commitment to the procurement activity and its outcomes. Bearing in mind that for many procurement projects this entails a total (holistic) whole life or through life perspective it is actually quite a challenge to ensure long term commitment from all stakeholders. Thus, the approaches considered in this study session will hold you in good stead, as will recognition of the complexities of some of the inherent themes and issues (such as trust and risk). Like many management strategies and activities much of this is not scientific, in the sense that there is a right and a wrong answer. There is no 'do it this way and all will be well.' This is simply because the concept of partnering involves people in many differing situations and rarely do two situations unfold in exactly the same manner or result. Broad principles however can be applied and the likelihood of successful outcomes increased through use of relevant techniques tempered by a broad knowledge of the underlying issues identified in this study session.

Revision question

You have been asked to join a panel discussing challenges and opportunities in partnering. You have been asked to be the first speaker. You would have to set the scene on the nature and purpose of partnerships, followed by an insight into the challenges building such relationships in the public sector procurement environment.

You should produce bullet points to indicate what your presentation would contain.

Feedback

Feedback on learning activity 7.1

'Why do you think that there is a need for caution when considering partnerships? Is there some difficulty with the topic?'

There are two reasons for caution:
a) Firstly, partnership is a legal entity. If someone is in a partnership (from the legal perspective), they could be liable for actions (including debts) incurred by another partner.
b) Secondly, the concept of partnering is sometimes put forward especially in the public sector as a 'panacea' that can solve all problems. You must not consider it as an answer to all challenges regarding stakeholders. As has been mentioned elsewhere in this Unit there is considerable rhetoric concerning partnerships and it is important to be aware of this so that you will know where and when to utilise the philosophies inherent in the concept for optimal benefit. There is a continuum of relationships, and whilst it can be very useful and beneficial, partnership is not the only approach that may be taken.

Before continuing with this study session it is now probably best to refer to partnering rather than partnership (for the reason stated above in a). above)

Feedback on self assessment activity 7.1

'Read a Procurement or Supply Chain Management text to see what is said concerning Pareto or the 80/20 Rule. Ensure that you comfortable with the concept.'

Before you move on you should see that the concept involved is important in a range of potential applications and at the very least might be useful in thinking through how to, identify appropriate stakeholders with whom to develop partnerships. Books such as *Purchasing Principles and Management* (Baily; Farmer; Jessop; Jones and Crocker, 2008); *Supply Chain Management in 90 Minutes* (Emmett, 2005); *Gower Handbook of Purchasing Management* (Day ed., 2002) and many others, will provide the insight necessary for your thinking to evolve.

Feedback on learning activity 7.2

'Read 'Managing a portfolio of supplier relationships' by Professor Douglas Macbeth in the 'Handbook of Purchasing Management'. Then in the same book read 'Purchasing in the higher education sector' by Tom Chadwick.'

The first piece is a fairly succinct, easy to follow set of reading that will confirm and develop the concept of differentiation in purchasing and will also indicate that there is a stakeholder (as the supplier can be considered) equivalent. For example if only conceptually, but often in practice, suppliers will have a similar concept in place and if a purchasing organisation, or the asset or service that it wishes to procure is in the equivalent bottom left had quadrant, then it may well consider such a procurement organisation as a 'nuisance' and not attach much effort or support. What is required by the potential suppliers is ideally something that falls into the equivalent top right hand box. This then means that for both organisations there is the potential for a win-win situation where there is much to gain on both sides but also considerable risk for both sides.

Feedback on learning activity 7.3

'What do you think that commentators on the defence procurement scene may have had to say about this solution to utilising best practice whilst seeking to ensure probity?'
The following are quotes from two commentators who are experienced in the defence procurement area:

'Although MOD is rigorous in its policy to use competition efficiently and fairly, it cannot be denied that the intra departmental political pressure to be seen to be utilising competition can sometimes over-ride COMMON SENSE!

It is easier to put forward a procurement strategy which (it is known) will be ineffectual, than it is to apply for permission to proceed to contract with a particular company without having first run a competition.'

(Boyce 1997, pp.8)

'Competition is used too often; goes on for too long; is expensive for MOD; is more expensive for industry; results in additional costs from industry to MOD -and drives many companies out of the defence sector. It makes partnering difficult, if not impossible'

(Kincaid, 2004)

Feedback on learning activity 7.4

'Why do you think that the public sector would want to consider partnering as a strategic approach?'

OGC states that modern commercial arrangements should be based on the following principles:

- a shared understanding of what the desired outcome is and which elements are to be provided by each party
- be focused on benefits - not just on time and cost
- have a shared understanding of which party is managing particular elements of risk
- (for long term contracts) be able to cope with changing customer requirements and technology developments
- be capable of implementing efficient and effective procurement.

It goes on to say that partnering extends these principles. For the customer organisation, a good partnering arrangement offers the benefits of proactive risk allocation, technical innovation, flexibility and improved value for money. For the supplying organisation, the benefits may include more involvement in management decisions, greater freedom to suggest innovative solutions, and better insight into the customer's business (as well as, of course, commercial gain).

Feedback on self assessment activity 7.2

'See if you can outline some situations when partnering is unlikely to be suitable'

You may have referred back to Kraljic or Pareto mentioned earlier, however to summarise in a different manner, partnering is unlikely to be suitable for:

- short term requirements where there will not be time for the provider to recover initial investment costs
- projects where the customer requires complete or significant control over the specification and service delivery, with little or no flexibility for the provider to propose new ways of doing things
- contracts where there is little or no scope for continuous improvement
- contracts where the customer requires an outcome, but cannot transfer key elements of control or major risks to the provider.

Feedback on learning activity 7.5

'Go to the OGC website. Click on 'Managing Risks with Delivery Partners.' Read and summarise the main points.'

This is an excellent document which initially notes the background to partnering and then provides definitions. It quickly moves on to discuss risk as an essential feature of partnering and provides an overview of how to manage the relationship in respect of risk – which if undertaken effectively allows the relationship to build and flourish. It indicates techniques that need to be utilised and provides a number of brief examples (DTI; London Underground, DfES etc) where successful work to identity partners, especially in respect of risk, has been successful. It also provides a considerable number of references and further contact details which will be useful for your research on this topic and in the wider sense of the subject as a whole.

Revision question feedback

'You have been asked to join a panel discussing challenges and opportunities in partnering. You have been asked if be the first speaker. You would have to set the scene on the nature and purpose of partnerships, followed by an insight into the challenges building such relationships in the public sector procurement environment.'

You should produce bullet points to indicate what your presentation would contain.

The outline that you should develop for the presentation would be built around the following:

- Partnership and partnering are not the same – explain partnership is a legal entity

- Partnering is often put forward as a panacea for all procurement problems – it is not – it is one of a set of relational approaches

- It can be shown conceptually on model such as Kraljic's 1983 view – or a derivative of it. The Pareto approach indicates that there may be a small number of procurement activities / projects (in relation to the total purchase spend / procurement activity) where it is worth investing time and effort to enable a partnering arrangement

- Changing nature of contracting – a move away from confrontational (win/lose or worse lose/lose relationships to one that is intended to be win/win- i.e. mutually beneficial for all parties to the arrangement

- In certain situations, partnering would not be appropriate but in long term major / complex projects it may be suitable e.g. business change, especially where innovation is required and/ or the future is uncertain; using new methods of service delivery (such as providing services online); flexibility in constructing teams, involving specialist skills or scarce resources; outsourcing business processes or services, perhaps to allow customer staff to concentrate on core areas

- Fundamental to partnering success is the need to fully understand: risk; trust; the need for openness / transparency and effective communication

- OGC recognises the need to change perceptions and stakeholders input and effects hence promotes use of relevant tools and the trust equation

- Partnering and trust are well accepted approaches in the commercial sector but the public sector has to utilise guidelines and ensure probity and propriety. This can bring challenges whenever partnering is considered within the public sector. Public sector procurement professional seek innovative ways to maintain probity yet still bring value for money and optimise procurement strategies.

- Frequently, this is achieved by adopting a through life perspective that takes a holistic view of all of the processes involved in procurement

- Often internal stakeholders can work collaboratively to enable enhanced through life procurement. This can be an opportunity to spread the partnering message to wider internal and external stakeholder community.

Further Reading

Office of Government Commerce. (2004). *Managing Risks with Delivery Partners*
M Day, (Eds.), *Gower Handbook of Purchasing Management* (3rd Edition)
Peter Baily; David Farmer; David Jessop,; David Jones; Barry Crocker, (2008), *Procurement, Principles and Management*., 10th ed

Study session 8

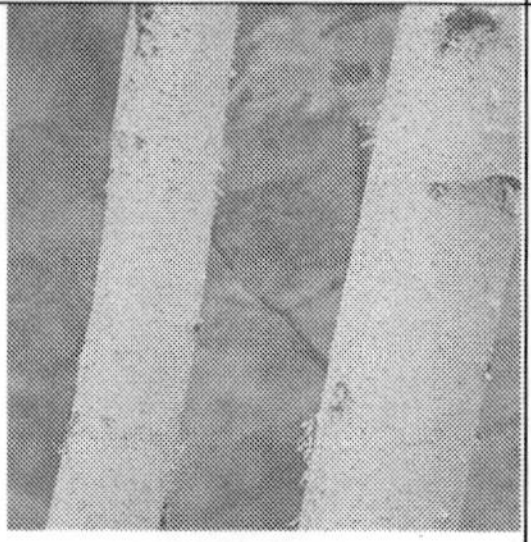

"Critically evaluate theories, models, policy documents and practice in relation to conflict management strategies"

Introduction

This study session examines strategies that can be used in management situations to deal with conflict between you and your stakeholders and your teams and subordinates and their stakeholders. Conflict is, in a latent sense, omnipresent in the procurement profession in that the profession's stock-in-trade relates to differences between negotiating parties and strategies for dealing with these differences.

Conflict within the public procurement environment can take various forms, from disputes with suppliers and internal customers via dissonance between political imperatives and legislation to disagreements with subordinates on human resource issues.

Session learning objectives

After completing this session you should be able to:

- consider causes and types of conflict
- assess methods of handling conflict
- analyse recent examples of successful and unsuccessful conflict management in various contexts, e.g. public and private sectors, central, local government and the NHS.

Unit content coverage

This study session covers part of the following topic from the official CIPS unit content documents: *Justify conflict management strategies to resolve*

differences with stakeholders. Specifically it covers; *Critically evaluate theories, models, policy documents and practice in relation to conflict management strategies*.

Prior knowledge

Study sessions 1; 2; 3; 4; 5; 6; 7.

Timing

You should take about 4-5 hours to read and complete this section, including learning activities, self-assessment questions, the suggested further reading, and the revision question.

Conflict management strategies

"Conflict is the beginning of consciousness"

M. Esther Harding – Stakeholder analysis

You will recall that in earlier study sessions consideration was given to concepts of stakeholder analysis. Use of this concept will assist in justifying conflict management strategies to resolve differences with stakeholders. This is because, as has been previously mentioned, one of the reasons for conducting stakeholder analysis is to make devising conflict management strategies easier. Recognising this in the context of stakeholder analysis is beneficial because it can be an important tool for predicting and managing conflicts and dispute resolution, as identified by Long (1992).

Learning activity 8.1

Analyse why stakeholder analysis is an important part of conflict management.

Stakeholder power/interest tool

You will also recall that you examined a basic (although effective) tool for stakeholder mapping. It is a template upon which the orientation of different stakeholder groupings can be mapped and strategic priorities established. Additionally, it can be useful for prioritising different stakeholders within conflict management strategies.

Diagram 8.1 Stakeholder power/interest tool

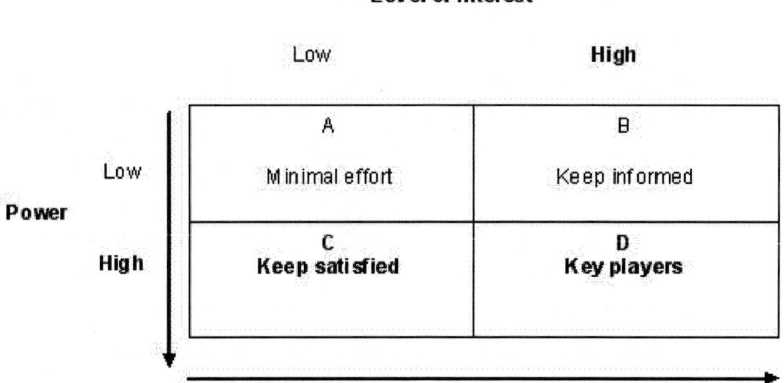

General issues around conflict

"Creativity comes from a conflict of ideas."

Donatella Versace

The following section is based on the views of Carter McNamara (2007), from his book: *Field Guide to Leadership and Supervision*.

Conflict is when two or more values, perspectives and opinions are contradictory in nature yet have not been aligned or agreed about; including:

1. Within oneself when one is not living according to one's own values;
2. When one's values and perspectives are threatened; or
3. When one experiences discomfort from fear of the unknown or from lack of fulfilment.

Conflict is inevitable and often in certain circumstances may be beneficial; for example, good teams always go through 'forming, storming, norming and performing 'phases. Within both public and private sector environments, getting the most out of diversity often means a meeting and subsequent acceptance of contradictory values, perspectives and opinions.

Conflict is often necessary. It:

1. Helps to raise and address problems.
2. Energises work to be on the most appropriate issues.
3. Helps people "be real"; for example, it motivates them to participate.
4. Helps people learn how to recognise and benefit from their differences.

Conflict is not the same as discomfort. The conflict itself is not the problem – rather it is the poor management of it.

Conflict is a problem when it:

1. Hampers productivity.
2. Lowers morale.
3. Causes more and continued conflicts.
4. Causes inappropriate behaviours.

Identification of stakeholder conflict

Stakeholders can be seen as part of a management strategy, an arbitrary concept that exists only to the extent that people can agree on its goals, boundaries, membership, and usefulness (Röling and Wagemakers, 1998). Stakeholder analysis tools tend to be straightforward: matrices or lists of criteria or attributes. Complex and ever-changing, however, are the challenges of establishing commonly agreeable definitions of issues or problem situations, defining the boundaries, and identifying the relevant stakeholders.

Procurement professionals bring different expectations, goals, values, beliefs, needs and desires to the negotiating table to those of other stakeholders. These differences invariably lead to conflict. Since conflict is inevitable, procurement professionals have to develop their understanding of conflict and their capacity and capability to manage it.

In this context, conflict may be defined as a struggle or contest between two or more parties whose needs differ and where the result cannot be predetermined.

According to the National Computing Centre (*Managing conflict in the e-world*, 2008), conflict is the process of expressing dissatisfaction, disagreement or unmet expectations by someone or some group that is unhappy with someone else or something else. 'Such dissatisfaction can result from multiple factors, differing expectations, competing goals, conflicting interests, confusing communications or unsatisfactory relationships.' The NCC says that the expression of conflict may take the form of:

- '**Sabotage**: when the stakeholder says that everything is fine and then without notice holds a press conference to announce the commencement of a lawsuit for negligence in relation to contract implementation; or internally, when innuendoes about managerial incompetence and lack of integrity begin to surface and spread.

- **Inefficiency and lack of productivity**: when a disgruntled employee refuses to participate efficiently and meaningfully as part of the team effort.

- **Low morale**: where employees weary of change or restructuring, lose energy, morale and motivation.

- **Other negative actions**: withholding knowledge, bad press or withdrawal of business.'

The NCC continues to state that, 'there are a number of conflicts which will have an impact on the efficient management of a relationship, preventing it functioning at its optimal level and, if not identified and managed at an early stage, may turn into a full-blown dispute. Examples where unmanaged conflict issues may become more severe include where IT system which does not function to expected standards; if employees are unhappy about a change in their role and function following its implementation; or if the project team is experiencing tension with external consultants. 'Disputes are simply the end point of a chain of events - the *product* of unmanaged conflict.'

From this it can be seen that the NCC thinks that, whilst the costs of *dispute* may be quantifiable as legal fees and expenses, the costs of unmanaged *conflict* as expenses of time, energy and creativity are largely hidden. Such costs can equal if not exceed those of a financial nature, and as such can prove a powerful source of competitive disadvantage. Because most people feel uncomfortable with conflict situations, the typical response is to deny or avoid it, or alternatively to attempt to control or fight it. As such the traditional approach to the management of conflict is often reactive and crisis-oriented. But this approach does not fit well with a project where the ethos is actively to manage risk and conflict.

Conflict might escalate and lead to non-cost-effective results, or it can be resolved beneficially and that can lead to a satisfactory outcome for all parties. Learning to recognise and manage conflict is integral to better procurement

Conflict risk

According to a study conducted by UK law firm Nabarro, which surveyed 100 lawyers and risk managers in 2007, only 12 per cent of risk management policies contain detailed information on how to resolve conflict, and a further 27 per cent cover the topic only superficially. The firm's *Controlling Conflict* (2008) report said that even when risk management was in place, it was often handled poorly.

Jonathan Warne, partner at Nabarro, said that conflict management had been less effective than anticipated and that almost two-thirds of organisations had no training programmes on dispute avoidance. Warne stated that even when risk management policies were in place, their implementation was not as robust as it might have been. People were not trained to handle the conflict management policy properly.

The Nabarro report also posited that commercial disputes cost UK businesses £33 billion a year. Those arising between firms and their suppliers were the third most frequent type of dispute, behind customers and employees (all potential stakeholders in a procurement contract or project). Common causes of disagreement included poorly written or non-existent contracts. The report stated that if procurement management was serious about reducing disputes then one of its first steps should be to set out clear contractual procedures.

The report found that the resolution of conflicts without resorting to legal proceedings is also becoming more popular. David Liddle, managing director of professional mediators Total Conflict Management, suggests that courts focus purely on legal or financial remedies, and as such resolution by mediation out of court is far more likely to be sustainable. Such a view has become more popular and substantiated with reviews such as that by Michael Gibbons (2007, pp.55) into the Dispute Resolutions Act 2004, and its recommendation to repeal the statutory dispute resolution procedures.

A recent study conducted by Professor Andrew Cox the University of Birmingham Business School found that over 60% of large outsourcing contracts unravel before they go the full term; the reason often being that the two parties get into protracted disputes about the rising costs of service provision. Firms need to examine how they can avoid getting into conflicts with their outsource partners and, when they do, how they can manage the conflicts efficiently. Part of the task of avoiding conflict is having realistic expectations at the outset. Birmingham Business School found that outsourcing options have to be at least 20% lower in cost to cover start-up costs and 40% lower to take full account of business risk. The importance of risk transfer in these deals cannot be under-estimated, and organisations must understand the part emotion plays in escalating disputes. They need to look at both the causes of conflict and the best strategies with which it can be managed.

Conflict management

"Well, it has some of that, but what I think also is people like to see conflict. They like to see conflict. And they also like to see it resolved."

Judge Mills Lane

Conflict is often brought about by poor communications, so procurement managers should develop communications strategies, in conjunction with their stakeholders, that minimise risk in that area. (You will recall that communication was discussed in earlier study sessions).

Conflict management operates under the principle that not all conflicts can necessarily be resolved, but learning how to manage conflict strategically can decrease the odds of non-productive and costly escalation. Conflict management involves the acquisition of skills relating to conflict resolution, self-awareness about contract 'modes', conflict communication skills and competencies and establishing a strategy for conflict management within the organisation.
According to Thomas-Kilmann (1979), typically we respond to conflict by using one of five 'modes':

- Competing
- Avoiding
- Accommodating
- Compromising
- Collaborating

The Thomas-Kilmann Conflict Mode Instrument (TKI) is a widely-used assessment tool for determining conflict modes. The model is replicated below:

Diagram 8.2 Thomas-Kilman conflict mode instrument

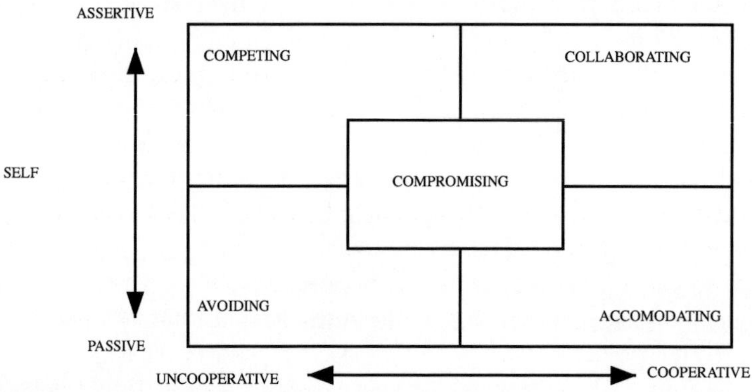

Source Thomas-Kilmann 1974

The 'competing' conflict is high assertiveness and low co-operation. This mode is necessary when quick decisions need to be made, vital issues need to be handled or the interests of the organisation need to be protected.

The 'avoiding' conflict is low assertiveness and low co-operation. Such a mode is useful when a conflict is of little value; when there is a need to reduce tensions, or when there is a need to buy time to reassess a position.

The 'accommodating' conflict mode is low assertiveness and high co-operation. It is used when one needs to show goodwill and reasonableness, to keep the peace, or the issue is of relatively minor importance.

The 'compromising' mode is moderate assertiveness and moderate co-operation. Compromise might be defined as 'settlement of dispute by mutual concession.' It is used when the power base does not favour one side, the matter is of moderate importance or there is a genuine will to settle quickly.

The 'collaborating' mode is high assertiveness and high co-operation. Collaboration can be defined as the repetition of ideas with one idea being repeatedly added on top of another so as to achieve the best solution to a conflict for all concerned. It would seem obvious that this should be the prevalent mode to resolve all disputes, but it is time-consuming and requires a lot of dedicated energy and goodwill from all parties to the conflict.

Strategically, procurement professionals should not engage in the collaboration mode unless the benefits that flow from such participation clearly outweigh the costs in terms of time and effort. These imponderables should be costed into a short business case to establish whether this approach is sensible.

Factors that affect conflict modes

- **Gender**: males taught to 'stand up for themselves.' More likely to be at the assertive end of the model's continuum.
- **Self-concept:** how we feel about ourselves. An assessment as to whether one is naturally assertive, insecure, or shy. Insecure types might be less assertive.
- **Expectations:** how people expect us to act, especially in team situations.
- **Situation:** whether the conflict is personal or professional. One must never drag a conflict down to a personal level.
- **Power:** the distribution of power within parties to a conflict is often unequal. For example, monopoly supply situations typically do not favour the buying organisation.
- **Practice:** degree of experience in using all conflict modes.
- **Strategy:** the need to define the best mode to use in any given conflict situation.
- **Communications:** the essence of conflict resolution and management is good communications. Procurement staff that use effective communications strategies will resolve conflicts more quickly and effectively.

- **Life skills:** experience, role models, deliberate attempts to change modal style, personal, professional, negativity, positivism.

Discerning how to manage conflict is important. With greater understanding, procurement professionals can make informed choices about how and when they engage in conflict.

Learning activity 8.2

Do you agree with McNamara's view that conflict in stakeholder relationships is a force for the good? Can you think of individual instances where the opposite is true?

Self-assessment question 8.1

Competing, avoiding, accommodating, compromising, and collaborating. Which of the Thomas-Kilmann styles of stakeholder conflict management do you typically adopt? Illustrate a practical example where you applied your normal style, and was that the best way to have handled the conflict given the other styles in the model?

Summary

Conflicts occur when there are fundamental and ongoing differences amongst parties concerning values and behaviours as they relate to an ongoing project situation or procurement activity. Differences between stakeholders are a key component. Stakeholders can be identified by the process known as stakeholder mapping, explained in other parts of this course book. Adverse behaviour between stakeholders can lead from mere disputes to open conflict. Such conflict may be defined as situations where people deliberately, with or without knowledge of the consequences of their actions, damage a project or business with their stance over a particular matter. A diverse range of drivers for conflict have been identified. Some latent conflicts have underlying causes such as power imbalances or unequal relationships. These emerging conflicts are potentially damaging and costly to the efficient execution of stakeholder project and have to be effectively managed. Four conflict typologies have been identified. These are:

- Conflicts of interest – i.e. one group wants one thing whilst another wants something else from the same outcome.
- Conflicts over process – these include conflict over the legal process, community processes and institutional processes.
- Structural conflicts – these refer to the way society is structured in terms of social, legal, economic and cultural arrangements.
- Inter-personal conflicts – between two or more people that relate to personality differences.

One beneficial strategy is to focus more broadly on participatory approaches and building understanding between stakeholder groups. This should ensure that relationships at all levels are improved and stakeholders feel a sense of ownership which might change their initial conflicting stance. Conflicts are usually complex and multi-layered, often making it difficult to reach the core of the conflict. People in conflict situations display different traits, or styles, and the Thomas-Kilmann model has identified these. Understanding which style each stakeholder displays will lead to the dispute-handlers to a possible early solution. If a conflict is irresolvable, it may be necessary to use a mediation service of some form.

Revision question

You are in a conflict situation with another stakeholder. Analyse the core processes in managing him or her so that the conflict has a good chance of being resolved.

Feedback

Feedback on learning activity 8.1

'Analyse why stakeholder analysis is an important part of conflict management.'

Although differentiation among stakeholders is a necessary step in stakeholder analysis, the distinction is often based on qualitative criteria that are difficult to generalise. The use of matrices is a common tool in stakeholder analysis, in which stakeholder groups appear on one axis and a list of criteria or attributes appears on the other. For each overlapping area, a qualitative description or quantitative rating is given. The following is a set of steps for conducting stakeholder analysis:

- Identify the main purpose of the analysis;
- Develop an understanding of the system and decision-makers in the system;
- Identify principal stakeholders;
- Investigate stakeholder interests, characteristics, and circumstances;
- Identify patterns and contexts of interaction between stakeholders; and
- Define options for management.

Three major phases are involved: defining the problem, analysing constraints and opportunities, and agreeing on an action plan. These phases are common to several methods that seek to engage multiple stakeholders in joint analysis and action.

Stakeholders are part of a management strategy, an arbitrary concept that exists only to the extent that people can agree on its goals, boundaries, membership, and usefulness. Stakeholder analysis tools tend to be straightforward: matrices or lists of criteria or attributes. Complex and ever-changing, however, are the challenges of establishing commonly agreeable definitions of issues or problem situations, defining the boundaries, and identifying the relevant stakeholders.

However, thorough analysis and knowledge of the stakeholder base is a vital pre-requisite of developing strategies to deal with conflict management and for minimising the impacts of those conflicts. If a project sponsor or procurement manager fails to understand the dynamics of his stakeholders, he cannot easily 'head off at the pass' disputes which might turn into full-blown conflicts without mitigating action.

Feedback on learning activity 8.2

'Do you agree with McNamara's view that conflict in stakeholder relationships is a force for the good? Can you think of individual instances where the opposite is true?'

Richard M. Marshall, a conflict management specialist in an internet article suggests the following:

"Everything from coffee-machine debate through to shouting matches at meeting-room whiteboards will help deliver better ways of doing things." He argues that there is a natural limit on these debates that, once that is exceeded, leads to 'bad conflict', which is especially harmful and injurious to a project.

He continues, the "job of project manager is to ensure the right level of conflict for a particular project, organisation, and culture. In many companies any deviation from the official line brands one with that most heinous of crimes: not being a team player. In many companies it is better for your career to let the ship sink than to point out that you're taking in water."

A team of stakeholders all thinking alike—or at least not able or willing to speak their thoughts—are not going to give the project manager optimal results. Since many team members are rather shy and awkward, they are often reluctant to speak up, particularly in a culture where conformance is highly valued.

"Most of us are conditioned to conform, and it is not by chance that artists are often less conventional, outside of the social norm. Most people like to agree, but works of art are not made by committee. Recognising this, some companies teach people to use conflict. They train their staff to speak—or shout—their minds. There are also so-called "creativity consultants" who claim to help teams unlock their latent potential. The key is granting permission to differ."

"You have to give people permission to question, permission to express their concerns and doubts, without the fear of repercussions. And "granting permission" doesn't just mean sending out a memo encouraging people to drop suggestions in the box outside the project office. It means actively encouraging debate."

"One thing to try is to join with other senior stakeholder members in reviewing work publicly. Constructive criticisms will help the more junior staff to voice their opinions. Invite comments as often as possible," and make sure that these are welcomed.

"At the other end of the scale are stakeholders who are always eager to shout out their opinion….It is, however, important to channel the energy that comes from their belief that they are right and the other team members are wrong." The project manager needs to concentrate purely on what is right and good for the project. "When he or she can do that, conflict will release a huge burst of creative energy. That energy must always be tempered with the willingness to accept other views, to admit error. The project manager should try saying "OK, I was wrong" in a meeting—it will shock the rest of the team into silence."

"Some people, however, can't tell that they are creating bad conflict. This will usually happen when they go too far, refusing to admit that they are wrong." One can always tell when something has gone too far if attention is paid to the other people in the room. Just as one is "supposed to look at people while one is presenting, one can do the same thing during a raging debate. Don't focus on the person with whom you are locking horns; watch what the rest of the group is doing."

If most of the stakeholders are "reluctant to voice their opinions in public, they are likely to crawl under the table and hide when a real debate starts. For them it would be hard enough to voice their opinion at all, let alone have some monster tell them in no uncertain terms that they are wrong. It's much easier for them to keep their thoughts to themselves."

"Every person in a stakeholder meeting should have something to contribute—or they shouldn't be there. To extract the thoughts from the silent folks, you'll have to make the loud ones back off. This will require a bit of order, something that is missing from most meetings. You need someone who can take control of the meeting—and I don't mean take it over. A meeting leader should be able to guide the meeting to get the most out of each member, whether prone to mouthing off or clamming up. He or she will be able to take discussions that are getting too heated or too long off-line, so as to avoid derailing the rest of the event."

A project manager must be aware however, "that one cannot be both a meeting leader and a contributor." He or she must "decide beforehand which role he or she will play." A project manager may find that he or she is "itching to pitch in on some technical fight, but that is not compatible with being referee. And remember: Listening and presenting are mutually incompatible; one has actively to switch between them."

"Controlled conflict works well for thorny technical issues, but it must be allowed to run on an equal footing. Constructive debate is pointless if hierarchical authority is more important than technical merit. The most junior stakeholder can provide an insight, and should be allowed to speak as much as the senior stakeholders. The project manager should ensure that his or her decision-making process is defined by who is most competent to decide, not who wears the right colour of hat."

"There are many ways to make things happen such as persuasion, leadership, teamwork. But don't forget that conflict and creativity go hand in hand. Eliminate one and you risk losing the other. Just make sure you accentuate the positive while monitoring for any excess."

In summarising Marshall's text, then, it is clear that some conflict is good, but where that leads to 'bad conflict', including personal enmity, conflict is not. Creating an atmosphere where stakeholders are all free to contribute to the ongoing debate is a job for a true leader, and the project manager must prioritise on that leadership, not on the technical nuances of the project.

Feedback on self-assessment question 8.1

'Competing, avoiding, accommodating, compromising, collaborating. Which of the Thomas-Kilmann styles of stakeholder conflict management do you typically adopt? Illustrate a practical example where you applied your normal style; and was that the best way to have handled the conflict, given the other styles in the model?'

Most experienced strategic procurement managers would tend towards the collaborative model, because that is the style that normally gains the most success in stakeholder engagement and projects in which multiple layers of stakeholders are contributing to the development of the project, against a tight timescale and budget. This is supported by a range of literature (including, for example, Cox, Erridge, Moore).

However, at times, you have to adopt different styles to suit different conflict situations. For example, you cannot be collaborative when the other party's preferred position would lead to a breach in legislation, the 'competing' style would have to be used. 'Avoiding' is not good, unless you are buying a short period of time to improve a tenuous position. Continual avoidance shows weakness and lack of assertiveness, and conflicts are not resolved by avoiding the difficulties and ambivalences that are consequently thrown up.

The style you adopt can be tempered by the relative power you have in resolving a conflict situation. It can be accepted that if someone has to keep 'referring back' to a superior because they are not empowered to make decisions that can resolve conflicts, then they will find themselves in a weaker position.

Feedback on revision question

'You are in a conflict situation with another stakeholder. Analyse the core processes in managing him or her so that the conflict has a good chance of being resolved.'

The following 11 points below have been adapted from Carter McNamara's *Field Guide to Leadership* (2007) (which has been previously mentioned) and identify several methods for managing a person during a conflict situation:

1. **Identify key traits for increasing conflict and ameliorate them**. Know what you do not like about yourself, early on in your career. We often don't like in others what we don't want to see in ourselves. Write down the key traits that really irritate you when see them in others. Be aware that these traits are your "hot buttons".

2. **Use calming tactics.** Manage yourself. If you and/or the other stakeholder are becoming heated, then manage yourself to stay calm by speaking to the other person as if he or she is not heated - this can be very effective! Avoid use of the word "you" - this avoids blaming. Nod your head to assure him or her you have heard him or her. Maintain eye contact with him or her.

3. **Seek privacy.** Move the discussion to a private area, if possible.

4. **Draw the heat by giving the other person his or her head.** Give the other person time to vent. Don't interrupt them or judge what they are saying.

5. **Verify that you are accurately hearing each other.** When they have finished speaking, ask the other person to let you rephrase (uninterrupted) what you are hearing from them to ensure you are hearing them as he or she wishes to be heard. To understand them more, ask open-ended questions. Avoid "why" questions - those questions often make people feel defensive.

6. **Ensure that your message is being understood.** Repeat the above step, this time for him or her to verify that they are hearing you. When you present your position, use "I", not "you". Talk in terms of the present as much as possible and mention your feelings.

7. **Clearly state areas of agreement and disagreement.** Acknowledge where you disagree and where you agree.

8. **De-subjectivise the conflict.** Work the issue, not the person. When they are convinced that you understand them, ask: "What can we do fix the problem?" The other party will likely begin to complain again. Then ask the same question. Focus on actions they can do, too.

9. **Seek common ground.** If possible, identify at least one action that can be done by one or both parties. Ask the other person if he or she will support that action. If they will not, then ask for a "cooling off period".

8

10. **Give credit to the other party.** Thank the person for working with you.

11. **Pass the conflict up the management chain in an orderly way.** If the situation remains in conflict, then conclude the discussions if the other person's behaviour conflicts with policies and procedures in the workplace and if so, present the issue to the relevant senior manager. Consider seeking a third party to mediate.

Suggested further reading

Tony Bovaird; Elke Loffler, (eds), (2003), *Public Management and Governance*. London: Routledge., Chapters: 1, 5, 7, 11, 12, 13, 14, 15, 17.

Gerry Johnson; Kevan Scholes, (eds), (2001), *Exploring Public Sector Strategy*. Dorchester, UK: Pearson Education Ltd., Chapters: 1, 2, 7, 8, 9, 11, 12, 13, 15, 16, 17.

N Long, (1992). 'From paradigm to lost paradigm regained?'

Carter McNamara, (2007), *Field Guide to Leadership*

National Computing Centre. N.d. *Managing Conflict in the e-world*. [online] NCC.

Kenneth W. Thomas,; Ralph H. Kilmann, , (1974), *Thomas-Kilmann Conflict MODE Instrument*, Mountain View, CA: Xicom and CPP Inc.

Websites

Chartered Institute of Personnel and Development: http://www.cipd.co.uk/

Office of Government Commerce: http://www.ogc.gov.uk/

IDeA: http://www.idea.gov.uk

The Foundation Coalition website: "Understanding conflict and conflict management": http://www.foundationcoalition.org/publications/brochures/conflict.pdf

Total Conflict Management Solutions: http://www.tcmsolutions.co.uk/

Study session 9

"Assess the effectiveness of procedures for resolving differences in relation to the correct application of procurement procedures with internal and external stakeholders"

Introduction

In this study session, you will examine the effectiveness of protocols used to resolve differences relating to the correct application of procurement procedures by procurement professionals dealing with both internal and external stakeholders. Another strand of learning will be an examination of these same protocols, only applied in the context of major procurement projects and external stakeholders, whom, from the preceding Unit, you will recall, includes suppliers, customers, the community at large and the government.

Session learning objectives

After completing this session you should be able to:

- review internal procurement procedures and methods of disseminating changes to procedures in relation to resolving differences with stakeholders
- assess methods of conflict resolution in contractual and non-contractual situations
- assess the effectiveness of procedures for resolving differences with internal stakeholders.

Unit content coverage

This study session covers part of the following topic from the official CIPS unit content documents: *Justify conflict management strategies to resolve differences with stakeholders*. Specifically, it covers: *Assess the effectiveness of procedures for resolving differences in relation to the correct application of procurement procedures with internal and external stakeholders*.

Prior knowledge

Study sessions 1; 2; 3; 4; 5; 6; 7; 8.

Timing

You should take about 4-5 hours to read and complete this section, including learning activities, self-assessment questions, the suggested further reading, and the revision question.

Role of Procurement and application of procedures

"Everything has two sides - the outside that is ridiculous, and the inside that is solemn."

Olive Schreiner

Andrew Erridge (2007) suggests that the role of procurement in the public sector has expanded from the tactical or operational level to the strategic and is now a core function of business improvement, at the heart of every corporate business decision. Procurement managers hold a core skill in enabling the acquisition of any procurement project for services or works. They especially procure strategic services under contract so that policy objectives may be attained.

This brings procurement into contact with internal and external stakeholders, which includes suppliers. Most public sector procurement departments are governed by external and internal rules. The external rules are enshrined in directives, regulations, EU, UK and Scots Law; and the internal rules are governed by standing orders, financial regulations, strategy and policy documents. These rules are often prescriptive. They do not always suit all stakeholders, who may have a different agenda to that of procurement professionals.

Conflict is created when procurement management insist on the rules being wholly and properly applied. In local authorities, if they turned a blind eye to the demands of stakeholders, they would be acting *ultra vires*, i.e. acting outside their responsibility and authority in allowing transgression of those rules.

Public sector procurement is governed by EU procurement legislation. This provides a complex set of rules, extended timelines, strict observance of procedure, and a mass of complexities and challenges for procurement professionals to overcome. The recent Aquatron case (Aquatron Breathing Air Systems v Strathclyde Fire Board [2007] CSOH 185), in which a breathing apparatus supplier successfully sued Strathclyde Fire Authority and was awarded significant damages because the authority's complacence over evaluation criteria for a framework contract, has almost sounded the death knell for the restricted procedure, because it is now just too difficult to administer. It may be that stakeholders exerted some pressure on the procurement activity to select a certain supplier, and he or she acquiesced by using evaluation sub-criteria that neither appeared in the OJ notice or the tender documents, which could potentially be seen as a breach of EU law.

It is important that procurement professionals are not persuaded by such pressure; that they get their procurement strategies right, and be prepared to report any stakeholder who is pressuring them to break the rules. The procedures should be used as a positive force, not something to be blocked or by-passed. They protect the organisation, they protect the purchasers, and they protect the stakeholders.

Learning Activity 9.1
Research the Aquatron case on the web and analyse whether there might have been any direct interference from any stakeholder. Assess how the Fire Authority should have handled the procurement project to meet EU procurement rules.

Typical procurement procedures and difficulties for stakeholders

Below is an extract from Leeds City Council's procurement policy (2008, pp.8):

"6. Pre-Procurement Procedure

6.1 Before undertaking procurement activity the Authorised Officer shall:

a) identify the need and outcomes to be achieved and fully assess all options for meeting those needs and achieving the outcomes.

b) establish a business case for the procurement, and for contracts over £100K, identify provision for resources for the management of the contract, for its entirety.

c) choose a course of action which will represent Best Value for Money to the Council giving consideration to the use of internal providers, the Strategic Design Alliance, existing Framework Agreements, Corporate Procurement Strategy, provision of shared services and the powers to trade, collaborative working and the voluntary sector.

d) establish a written specification for the procurement requirement and associated evaluation criteria and strategy which must be formally approved by the Relevant Chief Officer

e) ensure that the tender documents are available in a suitable electronic format (usually Portable Document Format (PDF)), unless there are exceptional circumstances where the use of electronic documents are not appropriate. PDF format will not be suitable for documents requiring completion or signature.

f) inform the Chief Procurement Officer prior to inviting tenders or quotations to ensure that the Transfer of Undertaking (Protection of Employment) (TUPE) issues are managed correctly where any employee either of the authority or of a Contractor may be affected by any transfer arrangement

g) form an evaluation team with responsibility for evaluating tenders where quality evaluation criteria has been set. The Authorised Officer shall invite the Chief Procurement Officer and finance Officer to form part of the evaluation team. Where appropriate, the evaluation team shall include representatives from the other professional services within the Council such as engineers/architects to ensure adequate consideration of the Best Value option. Consideration should also be given to including service users on the evaluation team where appropriate. For procurements over £100K, the evaluation team shall also carry out a risk assessment as part of its pre-qualification assessment and the evaluation process. Guidance can be sought from the Council's Risk Unit.

h) consider all aspects of the tender and contract lifecycle with reference to the checklist guidance in appendix 3 of the Contracts' Procedure Rules Code of Practice.

i) apply a gateway review process to all contracts above £100K or deemed to be high risk. This process must be applied at key stages of the procurement process in conjunction with the Chief Procurement Officer, and in line with the Council's Project Management Methodology.

6.2 Where the risk in a specific procurement is perceived to be high then that procurement shall be treated as a High Value Procurement regardless of the value of the contract.

6.3 For procurement of consultants/consultancy services of any type or value the Authorised Officer must obtain all relevant authority to proceed. The approval will be initiated by completion of the Application to Engage Consultants Form available from the Council's Resources Directorate. This requirement also applies to purchases from existing Framework Agreements."

This set of rules give procurement in Leeds far more powers over the process than in many other public sector organisations. That in itself may create stakeholder challenges, because each stakeholder has a different position and at times wishes to brook no interference from corporate procurement. The following are areas where disputes, friction and finally conflict are likely to emerge, from the procurement responsibilities shown in the Leeds model:

- Identification of need and business case management: Stakeholders might say this cannot be vested in procurement because they are only interested in the bottom-line.

- Best Value: (Again) stakeholders might say this cannot be vested in procurement because they are only interested in the bottom-line.

- Managing the scope and specification: stakeholders might argue that procurement is not innovative enough, or technically aware, to achieve the absolute best from the specification.

- TUPE: this is usually the domain of the Head of HR or the Chief Solicitor.

- Measurement of risk: Clear disputes possible here, especially in treating low-value spends as high-value because procurement classes them as too risky to buy in a more mundane fashion.

Self-assessment question 9.1

Get hold of a copy of your organisation's procurement rules and analyse any that might lead to potential conflict with internal and external stakeholders

Soft skills required for internal stakeholder conflict resolution

"You have to know when to be arrogant. You have to know when to be humble. You have to know when to be hard and you have to know when to be soft."

Talib Kweli

Daniel Goleman in 'Working with Emotional Intelligence' (1998) states that in order to be winners, all organisations must have an emphasis on 'soft' skills. Goleman suggests that there are five important areas of emotional intelligence (EQ) for an individual who is engaged in stakeholder relationships:

- **Self-awareness**: knowing one's internal states, preferences, resources and intuitions, and having the ability to recognise one's strengths and limitations.

- **Self-regulation**: managing one's internal states, impulses and resources. This requires keeping disruptive impulses and emotions in check, maintaining honesty and integrity, taking responsibility for personal performance, handling change, and being comfortable with new ideas.

- **Motivation**: emotional tendencies that guide or facilitate reaching goals. This requires striving to improve or meet a standard of excellence, aligning with goals of the group or organisation, showing readiness to act on opportunities and persistence in pursuing goals despite obstacles and setbacks.

- **Empathy**: awareness of others' feelings needs and concerns. This requires an ability to sense others' development needs and coach their abilities; anticipating, recognising and meeting customer needs; cultivating opportunities through different kinds of people and reading a group's emotional currents and power relationships.

- **Social skills**: adeptness of inducing desirable responses in others. This requires influencing skills and effective tactics for persuasion, the ability to listen openly and send convincing messages; conflict management skills for negotiating and resolving disagreements; the ability to inspire and guide individuals and groups; the ability to initiate and manage change; working with others towards shared goals, and team capabilities of being able to create group synergy in pursuing collective goals.

Wilding says that competition is not between individual companies but between the *supply chains* of which they are part. Poor relationships are also a major source of supply chain risk and can result in a loss of competitive advantage for the whole supply chain, so he advises buyers to develop the "relational skill sets" to make their organisations more resilient.

Variables for conflict engagement

According to the Foundation Coalition (2001), there is a choice as to whether to engage in conflict or not. The Coalition believes that the following six variables should be considered for anyone who is contemplating a conflict situation:

- **"Investment in the relationship**

  The importance of the working/personal relationship often dictates whether one will engage in a conflict. If one values the other party and/or the relationship, going through the process of conflict resolution is important.

- **Importance of the specific conflict issue**

  Even if the relationship is not of great value to the organisation, one must often engage in conflict if the issue is important to one of the parties. For example, if the issue is a belief, value, or regulation that one believes in or are hired to enforce, then engaging in the conflict is necessary. If the relationship and the issue are both important to one, there is an even more compelling reason to engage in the conflict.

- **Expending energy on the conflict**

  Many people say that there is insufficient time to do all that they want to do in a day. Often the issue is not how much time is available but how much energy one has for what one needs to do. Energy, not time, is being managed in these situations.

- **Awareness of the potential consequences**

  Prior to engaging in a conflict, thinking about anticipated consequences from engaging in the conflict is wise. For example, there may be a risk for one's safety, a risk of job loss, or an opportunity for a better working relationship. Many times people will engage in conflict and then be shocked by the outcome or consequence of engagement. Thoughtful reflection about the consequences, both positive and negative, is useful before engaging in or avoiding a conflict.

- **Readiness for the consequences**

  After analysing potential consequences, one must determine whether one is prepared for the consequences of engaging in the conflict. For example, one employee anticipated a job loss if she continued to engage in the conflict she was having with her line manager over a particular issue. After careful consideration the employee thought and believed strongly enough about the issue that she did engage in the conflict with her boss. Her annual contract was not renewed for the upcoming year. Because this individual had thought through the consequences of engaging in the conflict, she was prepared to be without a job for a while and able to financially and emotionally plan for this outcome. Most consequences of engaging in conflict are not this severe, but this example illustrates the value of thinking through consequences.

- **Consequences of not engaging in the conflict**

  To avoid losing a sense of 'self', there are times when one must engage in conflict. Most people have core values, ideas, beliefs, or morals. If a person is going to sacrifice one of their core beliefs by avoiding a conflict, personal loss of respect must be considered. In such cases, even if a person is not excited about confronting the conflict, one must carefully consider the consequences of its evasion. When the personal consequences of turning away from the conflict outweigh all other factors, then a person usually must take part in it."

The unreality of change: reducing unnecessary and imagined conflict between stakeholders

> "I believe strongly that we need to get beyond rhetoric, beyond industry and environmentalists fighting with each other, and seriously solve problems."
>
> **Gale Norton**

The following text represents the views of Rob Paton, Professor of Social Enterprise at the Open University Business School and is relevant in the context that it is important to understand the true rationale behind any conflict insofar as the other stakeholders are concerned. Paton says that you must understand the 'shadows' behind the conflict, and that skills must be developed to draw out these shadows and expose them. He argues that many of these shadows are fallacious for reasons such as they exist only in the imagination of the complainant, or they have been blown out of all proportion, or they are merely arguments used to ensure the continuance of an entrenched position. Only if the shadows can be brought out into the uplands where there is light will stakeholder conflict resolution be possible. The quotation is extensive but pertinent.

Learning activity 9.2

As you read through this – imagine the type of strategic procurement decision that may have been made in a public sector organisation where the following might apply: outsourcing a major service provision and using contractors for what was previously an 'in house' activity.

> "Changing ways of working is always controversial. The disagreements may turn on different values and priorities, or they may reflect conflicting narratives about why the problems have arisen and the likely effects of different choices.
>
> Arguments of this sort are practically essential for problem analysis as they test reasoning, bring additional information to the surface, highlight important risks, and provide different interpretive frames to consider ambiguous developments and possibilities.
>
> Even if the arguments do not substantially add to the analysis, they will certainly highlight issues and angles that will need to be addressed in explaining and justifying proposals.
>
> However, for anyone already convinced of the rightness of their view, or, conversely, of the foolishness of the entire exercise, or who is just in a hurry to get on with things, the careful scrutiny of possibilities can be frustrating and dispiriting. The tendency then will be either to push, or to resist, more overtly, re-emphasising the same points and staking out increasingly strong positions.
>
> Such escalation leads to a gradual polarisation around conflicting positions and values: each side sees itself as comprising the 'good and true', upholding progress or defending things everyone holds dear against the mindless damage wrought by the benighted forces ranged against them. In fact, of course, these conflicts are not cases of 'right against wrong' so much as 'right against right'.
>
> Classic fault lines lie between stakeholders, both internal and external, between managers and professionals,

between 'street-level' and senior staff, between politicians (and political advisers) and civil servants, and especially between the innovators (those involved in a pilot project, say) and those defending established practices.

Both sides base their claims on important values but, nevertheless, in no time the stereotypes are being rolled out and the splitting and projection begins. The larger the scale of the proposed changes, and the harder for those affected to engage directly with each other as people, the worse all these difficulties are. And they may be overlaid by other, social and geographical differences.

One technique for containing and working with potentially divisive polarities is to gradually bring to the surface the 'shadows' of the opposing positions. For example, when new ways of working are proposed, it is very common for the argument to take the following form.

The advocates of the changes point to various shortcomings in the current arrangements and set out an uplifting prospect of a new scheme, emphasising the benefits it will provide.

Those who identify with the old ways then raise questions about the proposed changes, suggesting various difficulties with them, and deny that the problems with the current arrangements are anything like as serious as has been presented (and if they are, this is for reasons they have often said needed to be addressed in other ways).

The interesting point about these exchanges is that they may hardly engage with each other at all. The advocates compare the way they *hope* things will be with the way (they say) things actually are, while the defenders compare the way things are currently *meant* to be with their predictions about how things would actually be. An air of unreality can permeate the whole discussion.

The table below illustrates what often goes on. The advocates contrast their 'sunny uplands' with a murky picture built up from various awkward and neglected (shadow) aspects of the current arrangements. But this feels too much like an attack on those who have invested years in making the old ways work. Their collective self-image provides not just a coherent rationale for what they do, but one that *justifies* them, locating the reason for shortcomings elsewhere.

So they present a robust defence to the implied criticism (as people always can) and, of course, since the advocates have presented a somewhat wishful or idealised sketch of their proposals, it is not difficult for the defenders to home in on important omissions, likely difficulties and major costs – while perhaps also alluding to some questionable motives underlying the proposals.

Diagram 9.1 Arguments for and against change – how much is discussable?

	The old familiar system	**The proposed or emerging arrangements**
Collective self-image(or ideology)	**The way it's meant to be** – the official line or public story. An answer for everything; explains away shortcomings (e.g. lack of resources). Emphasises staff contribution and commitment.	**Sunny uplands** – the simple, idealised system. Answers, in principle, to all major current difficulties and weaknesses.
Collective shadows(or blind spots)	**Inconvenient truths** – aspects denied, ignored or played down; undeclared personal interests and advantages in the existing arrangements.	**Awkward questions** – the gaps, ambiguities and elisions; obvious risks and unwarranted optimism about predictable pitfalls; undeclared personal interests and advantages in the proposed arrangements.

The only way to progress such discussions is to acknowledge the shadows. This may be much harder than it sounds; if the discussion has become at all adversarial, getting beyond the defences takes time. And it is not just a matter of whether people are *willing* to acknowledge certain things, but whether they are *able* to. After all, if you have been personally and publicly committed to a particular position for years, it may be painful to acknowledge that it has had major shortcomings (this can be just as true for change consultants as it is for staff in public bodies).

To the extent that each side can own its shadow, this shifts the basis of the argument from 'past bad, future good' (or vice versa) to 'past problematic, future problematic' – a much more realistic foundation (which certainly does not preclude making real improvements, of course).

Framing the differences in this way does not, in itself, resolve them. What it *can* do is one of two things. It can winch the arguments back down to earth, puncture the more high-flown and value-laden rhetoric and establish a basis around what is agreed, where the main differences and uncertainties lie and how they can be jointly investigated.

Alternatively, where 'helpfulness' or other considerations mean that disagreements are not being expressed, this approach can help to bring the difficult issues into the open."

Learning activity 9.3
Using Paton's ideas, and taking as your model the procurement of a completely new IT system to handle a council's previously manual library service, draw out some of Paton's shadows between stakeholders and suggest how these 'misconceptions' can be put right.

Self-assessment question 9.2

Do you agree with Paton's views, or in your experience, has conflict in stakeholder engagement occurred for other, perhaps more pragmatic, reasons?

Individual conflict management plan

Those involved in stakeholder engagement strategies may wish to create an individual conflict management plan. This is a thought and behaviour process that he or she can follow when he or she finds him or herself in conflict. One creates a list of steps/stages that one can follow when conflict arises, so that it can be effectively managed at each stage. There are typically three steps to creating a plan. These are:

- Write down one's physiological responses to conflict (fight or flight, heart racing, sweaty palms etc.)

- Write down one's thoughts when in conflict situations ("I want to hurt him or her badly", or "I wish I could leave the room"),

- List 6-8 steps that one can follow to help one manage your thoughts and emotions in a productive way to manage or even resolve your conflict. Refer to Algert and Watson (2002) to learn more about creating a conflict management plan. Improving listening skills is a sure-fire way to improve conflict management and resolution. Eugene Raudsepp (2002*)* in *Hone Listening Skills to Improve your Career* states that studies have shown that only about 10% of the population listens properly.

Another typical method for handling conflict is utilising a Conflict Handling Framework. This has five phases. These are:

1) **Clarify**: identify the other party's attitude and position, what he or she desires as an outcome from the conflict, and what he or she is failing to disclose, and the reasons for that failure.

2) **Identify**: establish what is the nature of the other party's claim and who has the better claim. Analyse which party has more to lose.

3) **Access**: try to identify the pressures on the other party. Examine any potential issues around the other party's self-esteem. Identify any other social or organisational pressures at play.

4) **Recognise and plan***:* identify the other party's modal strategy – identify whether he or she is accommodating, avoiding, collaborating, competing or compromising with you. Plan your strategy once you have defined the other party's strategy. Identify the correct mode to use.

5) **Implement strategy**.

Conflict Management Plus, one of the leading conflict and mediation services for the UK provides several useful case studies demonstrating effective use of conflict management skills. Below is such an example:

Case study – Sussex Ambulance Service

"Sussex Ambulance Service introduced a three-stage training programme for managers to improve their handling of conflict and to set up an internal mediation service for staff disputes. The Service wanted a process that would avoid things reaching the disciplinary stage, and wanted to introduce the concept of 'dignity at work' and place more emphasis on working with diversity. The goal was to imbue different values in people's minds, so that they could sort problems out before they got to significantly difficult areas. If a situation did reach that point, then they also needed people with the skills to turn conflicts round more positively."

"The service identified a need at a management level for about 20 staff to receive conflict management training as part of their general management development training. Of these about 12 went on to complete the full mediation skills training. They also trained 12 managers in investigation skills training, some who had also done the conflict management training and some who only take the investigator role."

Relationship Management

As you have seen, managing inter-organisation relationships is necessary but difficult, especially as inter-dependencies and risk transfer are so fluid, and vary considerably in each relationship. Cousins (2002) indicates that there are two key variables which determine the management of inter-organisational relationships, namely 'certainties' and 'dependencies'. Certainties include the need to reflect on likely levels of performance under the contract, the competencies of both parties, the goodwill shown by both parties and political imperatives driving both parties.

Dependencies, on the other hand, are things that create a reliance by either party on the other, or both parties on each other. Cousins said that there are four key dependencies: Economic, Historic, Technological (product and process) and Political. These dependencies are not mutually exclusive and not all may be in effect at any one time. The aim here is to achieve 'equilibrium of inter-dependency', in other words, ensure that no party has a comparative advantage over the other. The irony is that if that is achieved, both parties are operating 'sub-optimally', as compromise and consensus have weakened them, and, in order to be absolutely effective, one or the other should in theory exercise total control.

Mediation

As we have seen, conflict is inherent in human social organisations, particularly complex ones. Organisations need to address the root causes of their conflicts, thereby reducing recurring problems. Litigation and grievance procedures are adversarial and divisive, undermining the collegiality and collaboration necessary to manage complex organisations effectively. There is some evidence that firms are increasingly turning to mediation to resolve intractable disputes with stakeholders. However, the development of new ways of resolving such disputes needs to be carefully thought through, and all stakeholders and managers will need to understand all their options before deciding whether or not to try mediation.

When a party requests mediation or facilitation, a first step is to determine whether other parties involved are also interested in participating. Some requesting parties choose to contact the other directly; some prefer to have a chosen mediator call the other to explain the process and determine interest. Once parties have agreed to participate in a mediation or facilitation session, the mediator sets up a time for a meeting to occur. Mediations and facilitations are scheduled as soon as all parties are available to meet.

Mediation typically begins with a mediator conducting a brief overview of the process and then requesting that the parties explain the situation from their perspectives. The mediator listens to the parties' concerns and helps them communicate and engage in creative problem-solving. Through a series of joint and private meetings with the parties, the mediator helps parties to narrow and clarify issues, and, if possible, reach a mutually agreeable solution. The mediator may help to draft an agreement or design next steps.

Facilitation may begin with a facilitator talking with some or all members of a group to outline goals and design an appropriate process to reach those goals. At a group meeting, the facilitator acts as a process guide to help the parties reach their stated goals. The facilitator may help to draft an agreement or design next steps.

Summary

This study session has identified that unmanaged conflict is a powerful source of competitive disadvantage and that the costs of unmanaged conflict are the largely hidden expenses of time, energy and creativity. Thus identifying the potential for conflicts and disputes at an early stage and resolving them by simple co-operative means, rather than complex adversarial processes, reduces the cost and cycle time of conflict and helps managers to remain in control. You will have seen that creating and implementing a framework to enable effective dialogue and conflict management is so important that it should be the foundation for everything else that happens. From this, conflict can then be turned from a potentially destructive force into a creative force capable of building commitment and understanding, and of discovering and creating value out of difference.

This study session has also shown that you need to develop a range of softer skills to help you manage conflict and that you need a conflict management plan to work your way through potential conflict situations. Finally, it indicates that you need to develop an 'instinct' for discovering the rationale behind conflict and convert the conflict into 'bite-sized chunks.'

Revision question

Assess what main steps are required from the Project Board, through project governance, to ensure that stakeholder conflict is minimised.

Feedback

Feedback on learning activity 9.1

'Research the Aquatron case on the web and analyse whether there might have been any direct interference from any stakeholder. Assess how the Fire Authority should have handled the procurement project to meet EU procurement rules.'

Expert lawyers Eversheds (2007) provided the following summary on the outcome of the case:

'Strathclyde excluded Aquatron's tender from the tendering process at the first stage on the following grounds:

- Quality standards: Aquatron was said not to have supplied evidence of quality standards achieved by their workforce. This was not accepted by the court as the specification simply asked for evidence of the quality standards of the tenderer's workforce to be supplied. It did not set any minimum requirement to be met in order to proceed to full evaluation.

- Qualified staff: Aquatron was said to lack qualified staff to carry out the contract. Strathclyde incorrectly concluded that Aquatron lacked the requisite staff to carry out the contract due to Strathclyde's failure to ensure that the relevant members of the evaluation team had a copy of Aquatron's tender covering letter. Therefore, it had failed to consider a crucial part of Aquatron's tender in breach of their general obligation to treat all tenderers fairly.

- Inadequate accreditation: In evaluation, Strathclyde decided they wanted the tenderers to be accredited by a government body and not a private company as Aquatron was. This was not what the specification provided for; it merely required 'accreditation to ISO 9001:2000 issued by a recognised accreditation centre'.'

The court decided the evaluation team lacked the necessary expertise and understanding of what was required in evaluation processes. This resulted in the tenders being evaluated against criteria that were different from the published criteria.

The court was satisfied that the other tenderer was legitimately excluded due to deficiencies in its certification. The court therefore turned to the question of 'what ought to have happened if the evaluation had taken place in accordance with the regulations' to determine 'the most economically advantageous tender'.

The court concluded that, as both the winning tenderer's and Aquatron's tenders complied with the technical specifications, the only remaining criteria set out in the Official Journal of the European Union (OJEU) Notice that was of any relevance was price.

Therefore, had the criteria published in OJEU been properly applied, given that Aquatron's tender had a lower price than that of the successful tenderer, Aquatron would have been awarded the contract.

The court assessed Aquatron's loss, on the facts, to be £122,149.20 against their tender price of £222,300.

If Aquatron's tender could have been assessed using the revised evaluation criteria (rather than those published), damages would have been assessed at 50 per cent of the actual loss on the basis that the tender 'would still have stood at least an even chance of acceptance' alongside the higher priced winning tender, and therefore the claim would be for loss of chance.

As Aquatron's tender was ruled out and the deficiencies could not have been assessed, it was entitled to 100 per cent of the loss.

In assessing damages, the starting point was to assess the income generated by the contract (£222,300) plus the extra work likely to be commissioned under it (£92,550), then to consider the loss of profit. Aquatron had only claimed loss of profit on the contract sum. This was awarded together with interest at 4 per cent during the life of the contract and 8 per cent thereafter.'

Practical issues for you to consider:

'This case highlighted the failures of Strathclyde's evaluation team and identified many practical issues that evaluation teams need to keep in mind.

In relation to the tender evaluation team:

- Members must have the relevant expertise, knowledge and experience to carry out the evaluation
- Ideally the team should be consistent throughout the process (this ensures full knowledge and enables effective evaluation)
- Where team members must change throughout the procurement process, a thorough handover must take place.

In relation to the procurement process:

- Avoid presumptions/assumptions or any ambiguity by setting out requirements (including minimum requirements) in full
- Follow the process strictly as described in the tender documents and criteria published in the notice

- Take effective minutes of clarification and other meetings

- Manage documents effectively to ensure that all relevant people have access to all information relating to a tender.'

Although there is nothing in this summary that lays the blame on the stakeholders *per se*, it could arguably be seen as inconceivable that stakeholder pressure did not influence this decision. Stakeholders wanted a certain type of breathing apparatus, come what may, and it would appear that procurement heads complied with this request. You should be aware that what you write in the OJ notice and what you place in the PQQ and the invitations to tender are now absolutely critical; and you should be at pains to advise the project board and stakeholders that the 'route to market' should be planned at the very inception of the project. This would include all of the text that would populate the OJEU notice, the PQQ and the tender. It is clearly the case that the criteria for evaluation of expressions of interest in a PQQ process is entirely separate to tender evaluation criteria.

Feedback on self-assessment question 9.1

'*Get hold of a copy of your organisation's procurement rules and analyse any that might lead to potential conflict with internal and external stakeholders*'

Procurement rules and procedures take many varied forms. However, most have commonalities that can be analysed. Some of the key areas are as follows:

- Differentiation of treatment of supplies, services and works contracts
- Limits for seeking quotations
- Limits for seeking tenders
- Treatment of on-cat and off-cat procurement
- Collaborative procurement through a consortium
- Projects
- Framework arrangements
- Individual spending limits for officers
- A hierarchy of reporting arrangements
- Details of tenders and contracts and methods of their advertisement
- Details of what is placed in the public domain
- Derogations and devolved procurement facilities
- Procurement under EU legislation
- Procurement under all other EU and UK legislation
- Freedom of information
- Data protection
- Sustainability and equality
- Rules for returning PQQs and tenders
- Post-tender negotiations
- Sacking a contractor
- Rules for tender evaluation
- Performance bonds and parent company guarantees

- Partnership contracts
- Tender acceptance
- Standstill period
- Disposals of life-expired assets

Any of the above bullet-points could cause conflicts with stakeholders. Some common problems occur with the need to apply competition between suppliers, rather than procure via a 'preferred supplier' route.

Feedback on learning activity 9.2

'As you read through this – imagine the type of strategic procurement decision that may have been made in a public sector organisation where the following might apply: outsourcing a major service provision and using contractors for what was previously an 'in house' activity.'

As the public sector has sought to adopt the best practice indicated by commercial organisations, and academic theory and concepts, one of the fundamental changes in procurement activity has been the increased use of outsourcing. Theory indicates that assuming all other aspects are equal a service that was previously undertaken in house could be provided at a lower cost from an outside contractor. This approach has been extensively utilised within the public sector and examples abound, which include: the NHS, MOD, police, Welsh Assembly Government, and charity organisations.

Depending on the perception of the stakeholder, such an outsourcing approach might be beneficial or detrimental. These two extremes indicated in the article may have varying degrees between them. Depending on the example you utilise you should be able to plot them on the diagram shown earlier in the study session. For example, it may seem to an existing local authority workforce that they are in danger of losing there livelihood; the public sector financier might perceive a considerable saving on expenditure; the local residents might perceive a potential lack of quality in the service that may subsequently be delivered; potential contractors may see the opportunity to increase profitability. If the fundamental issues can be drawn out it may be that the 'landscape' can be viewed differently. Thus it may be that the work force would not loose their livelihood (albeit that they would be employed by another organisation); it may be that once a contract is in place additional costs are identified that could negate any saving; the local residence may find that the particular is undertaken on a more regular basis or more effectively than previously; it may be that it is not a profit that is the driving motivation for the potential contractor, rather it is survival and the opportunity to continue a local business.

Feedback on learning activity 9.3

'Using Paton's ideas, and taking as your model the procurement of a completely new IT system to handle a council's previously manual library service, draw out some of Paton's shadows between stakeholders and suggest how these 'misconceptions' can be put right.'

Imagination and creativity are required from you here. Libraries are widening their range of services into what they call a 'managed learning' environment.

They are looking to open infrastructure systems, such as Talis, using web browser technology, to manage both the procurement of library stock and the logistics of keeping and issuing library books. One important feature from these systems is the need for real-time information and sophisticated yet simple management information and reportage. Selling this vision to external stakeholders would undoubtedly expose the following 'shadows' from defensive stakeholders, resistant to any change:

- The system is too costly and will not achieve Best Value.
- The current system is working fine. 'If it isn't broken, don't fix it.'
- The new system will require far more resources than we have available
- Training will be too difficult and time-consuming
- The risk of service breakdown is greatly increased
- This system will not meet the needs of our customers
- There's no guarantee that the interface to the finance system for commitment accounting will work.
- The procurement module is far more labour-intensive than picking up a phone and ordering from the supplier
- "If customers can renew loans on-line, it's bound to mean staff reductions. I've no intention of losing my job to a computer."

You have to deal with each of these issues at a strategic level. Use performance indicators to show, for example, how the 'costs per click' will in fact turn out much lower than anticipated. Describe how standing still is not an option. Customers are demanding change and 24/7 access, and other library services have already embarked on these huge modernisation and change programmes. Explain that the complainant cannot have too few resources available and argue simultaneously that he is going to lose his job. Explain that because this is virtually a self-service system, training can be achieved in a much shorter time than one would expect. Say that the organisation is putting together a risk management and business continuity strategy that will minimise service disruption, and, in any case, this is an open IT system which is not generally prone to breakdown. Say that this system is in fact, the minimum that customers are demanding. Reinforce the view that the complainants should look at the bigger picture – commitment accounting is proven to work where this system has been set up elsewhere and the procurement strategy dictates use of the system for management information and accountability, rather than use of the telephone.

Feedback on self-assessment question 9.2

'Do you agree with Paton's views, or in your experience, has conflict in stakeholder engagement occurred for other, perhaps more pragmatic, reasons?'

According to the Centre for Effective Disputes Resolution (CEDR) (2006), a not-for-profit organisation that claims to be the leader in 'neutral-assisted dispute resolution,' conflict costs business £33 billion per year. If the cost of conflict to British business were a country it would have the 57th largest economy in the world.

80% of conflicts have a significant effect on the smooth running of a project. In a case that is over £1,000,000 in value, managers will spend an average of three years trying to resolve the conflict.

Many managers are frightened of addressing conflict. 35% would rather undertake a parachute jump that deal with a conflict. Only 37% of managers feel that they have had sufficient training to deal with conflict. It is surely hard to argue against Paton's logic, but there are also some pragmatic reasons why stakeholders create these dark shadows in defence of an entrenched position:

- Personal reputation
- Morale
- Empowerment and motivation
- Cynical or sceptical thinking
- Damaged relationships
- Disloyalty
- Jealousy
- Dislike of superiors and orders
- Poor experiences from previous projects
- Genuine disapproval of the way the organisation conducts its business
- Politics

Feedback on revision question

'Assess what main steps are required from the Project Board, through project governance, to ensure that stakeholder conflict is minimised.'

Objective: to achieve a through-life, evolutionary governance process to integrate the interests of all stakeholders in order to avoid any subsequent areas of conflict.

Key governance requirements:

- Set requirements in the operating context. Governance must anticipate and define the operating context and circumstances in which the capability or service must deliver

- Engage key stakeholders early. Project Board/Team must identify stakeholders right across the project. This ensures that during requirements capture the focus is not too narrow. Establish a methodology for resolving conflict between stakeholders.

- Focus on acquisition of operational capability not equipment.

- Identify and address interoperability early. Few capabilities can be effectively deployed in isolation from other capabilities. The majority need to be designed to integrate with, interoperate with, or interface with, other capabilities. The Project Board must identify and address the interoperability and integration requirements from the outset. This ensures they are built into the solution to deliver a system-of-systems solution.

- Separate Customer, Supplier and User roles clearly. The three roles require different mind-sets, competencies, values, objectives, accountabilities and working methods. Separation enables professionalism in each of the roles, and robust audit of related activities.
- Discriminate clearly between operational need and solution. The operational need and solution to that need must be defined to enable any mismatch to be measured and managed. Both definitions require their own differing taxonomies, metrics and drivers, which evolve at different paces. Real world constraints may prevent the solution from exactly meeting the operational need but the mismatch between them must be manageable and documented separately.
- Define explicit, quantified and testable requirements. If the requirement is not explicit, the supplier might not correctly interpret what was asked for, and not deliver what's needed. Upon receipt the recipient cannot know if what is received meets the identified need. If the requirement is not quantified no one will know how much is good enough. "It must be comfortable" might be a reasonable request, but cannot be contracted for. What is comfortable for one could be uncomfortable for another. If the requirement is not testable then it will be difficult to reach consensus that the solutions satisfies the requirement.
- Help to identify, analyse and select options objectively. The 'obvious' solution is not necessarily the best one. Through analysis the Board needs to convince the organisation that the solution chosen represents best value for money for performance, time and cost based on credible evidence. This requires the Board to be 'solution-independent'. To help this and to consider the widest possible range of solutions: needs must be expressed in terms of what must be delivered, not how it will be delivered. Real constraints must be identified and respected, but unjustified ones must be challenged and suppressed.
- Capture the through life perspective across the project.
- Control change. Operational need can change significantly within the life-cycle of an acquisition. The Project Board must control and manage the impact of changes to the defined operational need. Requirements drift (scope creep) should not be allowed.
- Assess achievability. The Project Board must support the continuous assessment of the intended solution - including risk and uncertainty - to ensure it is achievable and the defined requirements are satisfied.
- Help to manage risk and uncertainty. Uncertainties that arise in the system requirements can focus the attention of stakeholders on unrealistic user requirements and may highlight ambiguity and lack of consistency.

- Trade across performance, cost and time. If acquisition risk has to be reduced then either performance, cost or time have to be compromised which may impact on value-for-money. The Project Board must define the trade-space within which compromises and re-balancing can take place without recourse to higher authority. It must integrate the technical specification activities with the scheduling, budgeting and risk management activities.
- Support key decisions.
- Adapt or scale to suit. The Project Board must be adaptable to all acquisitions of both goods (including software, estates and Business Information Systems) and services, of any value and complexity.

Suggested further reading

Tony Bovaird; Elke Loffler, (eds) (2003) *Public Management and Governance* chapters. 1, 5, 7, 11, 12, 13, 14, 15, 17.

Gerry Johnson; Kevan Scholes, (eds), (2001) *Exploring Public Sector Strategy* chapters 1, 2, 7, 8, 9, 11, 12, 13, 15, 16, 17.

The Foundation Coalition, n.d. *Understanding Conflict and Conflict Management*, [Online] The Foundation Coalition

Websites

Chartered Institute of Personnel and Development - http://www.cipd.co.uk/about

Office of Government Commerce - http://www.ogc.gov.uk/

IDeA - http://www.idea.gov.uk

Institute of Conflict Management's website: www.conflictmanagement.org
www.impactfactory.com
www.c-r.org
www.mindtools.com
www.ibisassoc.co.uk
www.cedr.com

Study session 10

"Critically assess the effectiveness of procedures for resolving differences with external stakeholders in relation to the planning of major projects, award and delivery of contracts"

Introduction

As you work towards completion of the last study session in this unit you will now be able to consider the importance of sound processes that ensure senior level action in respect of procurement projects. This study session will enable you to examine the two pyramids of management structures within client and contractor organisations. It will enable you to consider how to make relationships more effective and avoid conflict. Finally it will allow you to consider lessons and experiences in respect of the governance of procurement projects in the public sector.

Session learning objectives

After completing this session you should be able to:

- assess the effectiveness of referring up of management information systems (MIS) queries and management issues for senior level action
- analyse the 'two pyramids' of management structures within client and contractor organisations and how to bridge them
- assess and apply lessons from experiences of the effect of high-level involvement on successful projects of e.g. ministers, MPs, industry leaders, the media.

Unit content coverage

This study session covers part of the following topic from the official CIPS unit content documents: *Justify conflict management strategies to resolve differences with stakeholders*, specifically *Critically assess the effectiveness of procedures for resolving differences with external stakeholders in relation to the planning of major projects, award and delivery of contracts*.

Prior knowledge

Study sessions 1; 2; 3; 4; 5; 6; 7; 8; 9.

Timing

You should take about 5 - 6 hours to read and complete this section, including learning activities, self-assessment questions, the suggested further reading, and the revision question.

Conflict in procurement projects – referring of queries and management issues for senior level action

Project management is an evolutionary process, albeit one with customers (internal or external stakeholders, or both) at the forefront. The best delivery depends on the success of human interactions. Consequently, conflicts occur. Some are minor disagreements, some threaten the continuance of the project, and might even have life-threatening consequences. The primary causes of conflicts between stakeholders are time schedules, communications, team set-up, cultural differences, project priorities, personal issues etc. Project team members come from diverse backgrounds. In a large project, they may not know each other well. A key priority for the project manager is to ensure the project team bonds well and quickly. Customer satisfaction is the top priority. An organisation has to develop a very robust project management system in order to meet growing demands from customers and other stakeholders. One of the primary methods of reducing conflict is to perform careful project planning and communicate constantly to customers and key stakeholders. The project manager is, in short, a conflict manager.

Senior level consultation in procurement projects

The following model might be useful to see how stakeholder engagement can be undertaken in any procurement project. This follows a three-pronged approach: the project board controlling the process and model, the project team (including procurement) controlling the technical and commercial input and the stakeholders feeding into the project team.

Diagram 10.1 Stakeholder engagement in any procurement project.
Source: based on the PRINCE2 model available from the OGC website

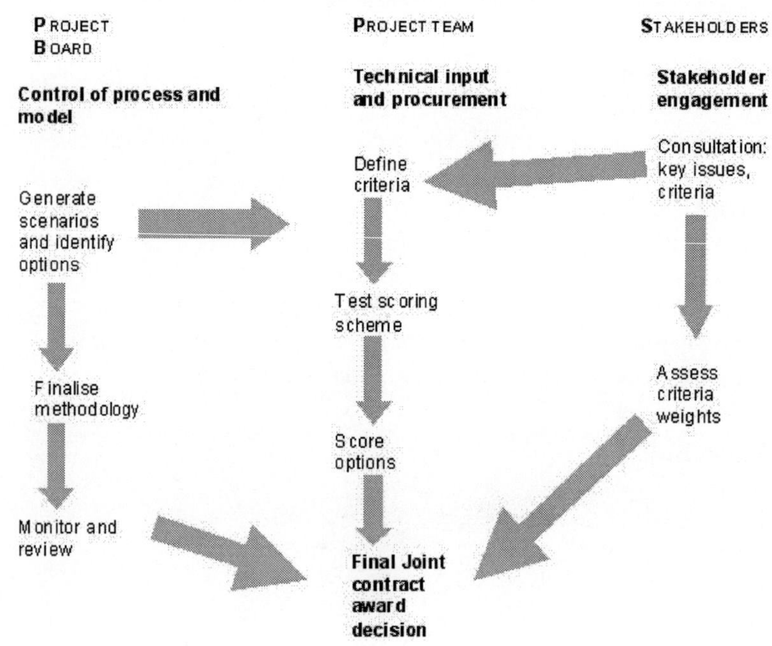

The Office of Government Commerce's PRINCE2 project management model is the generally accepted best practice model for procurement projects in the public sector. It recommends that, when setting up project controls, an organisation needs to identify all stakeholders outside the project management team and agree with them their information needs, plus any information needed from them by the project board. Furthermore, there is a need to define the communication content, the senders and recipients of the communication, the method and frequency for all these communications. It also suggests that stakeholders should receive the project brief immediately after the project initiation (start-up) stage of the project, thus engaging all stakeholders at as early a stage as possible.

Self-assessment question 10.1

How does your organisation handle major procurement projects? Does it use PRINCE2 or another variant model? Does it abide faithfully by the PRINCE2 (or equivalent) rules?

Managing 'human' risk in a project

PRINCE2 also defines the organisational and human factors that create risk in any procurement project. These are:

- Management incompetence
- Inadequate corporate policies
- Inadequate adoption of management practices
- Poor leadership
- Lack of authority of key personnel
- Poor staff selection procedures
- Lack of clarity over roles and responsibilities
- Vested interests creating conflict and compromising the overall aims
- Individual or group interests given unwarranted priority
- Personality clashes
- Indecision or inappropriate decision-making
- Lack of operational support
- Inadequate or inaccurate information
- Health and safety constraints

Learning activity 10.1

Can you give practical examples of each of the first eight 'human risk' elements outlined above, in the context of your own organisation's failure to deal with this problem in projects?

"Traditionally, most activity in managing major projects has focused on the top three levels of the pyramid. The strongest message emerging from our analysis is that it is the 'softer' factors about building and sustaining relationships upon which success is predicated."

"Successful working relationships are characterised by soft factors such as team-working, trust and honesty. When.....partners on a project display these behaviours, they are more likely to develop a common understanding of the task, the progress being made and some early warning of problems."

NAO 2005

Avoiding the 'two pyramids' of management between client and contractor as stakeholder

There are bound to be cultural differences between the management of client and contractor – after all, they have different sets of objectives and, as we have seen, a consensual approach is required to maximise benefits for both parties. These cultural differences can to an extent be overcome by careful planning and the observance of a set of behaviours which should be developed by both parties. The contract itself drives performance and due attention has to be paid to getting the contractual relationship right. The National Audit Office (2005) has laid down a set of principles that mirror best practice in this area. The key principles are:

- Open, trusting and honest relationships between client, prime contractor and supply chain. This includes a 'no blame' culture, regular and timely discussion of all matters apropos of the contract, shared ownership of the end product of the contract, clarity of purpose and common understanding at all levels throughout both organisations, treating the contract as a true strategic alliance between the parties.

- Management of the relationship, including regular independent assessments of client-contractor relationships as these develop during a project,

- Supportive and open corporate environment, including clear requirements with clear purpose, clear boundaries of authority and action, and a clear link between corporate and project governance.

- Efficient organisational structures, responsibilities and lines of authority, including pre-agreed team structures, frequency and purpose of meetings, project controls, performance measures, delegated authority, decision-making and escalation criteria, and flexibility of approach by both parties.

- Availability of skills and resources, including staff selection, skills and training structure across all areas of expertise, continuous professional development and experience and qualifications of key staff.

- Thoroughness of the review procedures, including early (pre-contract) agreement over work packages, costs, specification, risks, performance, time and boundaries, and use of subject matter experts in drawing up cost and risk models.

- Setting performance, time and cost boundaries when all risks are understood and at formal approval milestones (gateways), including projections grounded in realism and a pragmatic and achievable business case.

- Dynamic change management system, including mechanisms in place for making informed trade-offs between time, performance and cost as project progresses and delegated authority to do so.

- Transparent and accountable processes, including the use of a shared data environment and clear method for sharing information, co-location of client/contractor team and staff, suitable arrangements for access to each other's data, use of common IT where possible, commercial staff reside with project, and the contract is realistic, mutually beneficial and properly reflects the ownership of risk.

- Introduction of a peer review process and lessons learned culture, including formal and informal mechanisms for the exchange of ideas, problem-solving, sharing experience and best practice between members of staff of both parties and capturing formally all lessons learned.

- Consistent reporting system feeding into analysis for senior management, including reporting system based on the principle of 'generate once, use many times', clear purpose for the reporting system and analysis of reports by dedicated staff.

- Formalised senior management review process, including a clear information requirement and lucid and achievable benefits realisation strategy.

- Ongoing review and measurement of contractor performance, including the collection and management of relevant data, senior-level contact with contractors, analysis of trends and issues, and observance of commercial confidentiality where that is appropriate.

Learning activity 10.2

Analyse the main elements of a successful peer review process for a procurement project with both internal and external stakeholders. Use a practical example to illustrate your reasoning.

Good Practice for successful projects

"The best work is not what is most difficult for you; it is what you do best".

Jean-Paul Sartre

Neil Goodall (2004), the European MD of Tescom, and former banking programme director for the Post Office, who undertook one of the most successful national IT projects of 2003, has written that a large scale implementation project is a huge undertaking for any organisation. Within the Public Sector, when public funds are being used and the smooth running of public services is dependent on a successful outcome, implementation becomes a matter of national concern.

Goodall believes that, 'ather than just keeping the internal corporate stakeholders appraised of project progress, the external world also needs additional guarantees that projects will be delivered on time, to budget and to the required quality. If not, questions on misspending, poor decision-making and bad management cloud the picture, diverting attention from the real issue of what went wrong, and how to avoid repeating the same mistakes.'

He says that too 'many projects fail because those responsible for the project are expected to consider the work as additional to their normal roles and duties. Particularly in the public sector, where spending is tightly controlled and regulated, it can often be tricky to allocate appropriate resources outside the core team to ensure that delivery is a priority.'

'The right approach and procedures must be in place from the start if a project is to be a success, and this begins with the project proposition. Problems typically arise because of a 'requirements mismatch' – what the organisation thinks it has asked for differs from what the potential suppliers think they are being asked to bid for and supply.'

Goodall believes that it is 'also vital to involve the procurement department at an early stage. If the project specifications are to fit policy, those involved need to fully understand its purpose and requirements from the outset. Leaving procurement involvement to the contract negotiation phase or later runs the risk of highlighting potential issues late in the day, which will be time-consuming and costly to fix.'

Another vital aspect to project success is the testing regime. 'The traditional approach to this aspect of project management has either been to rely upon the suppliers to test their own solutions or else bring in testing specialists towards the end of the project. However, using testing experts and a testing strategy throughout the project lifecycle is a proven way of achieving better results.'

Case Study: A Case of Successful Complex IT Project for the VOSA

Lancaster University (2005) analysed a successful public sector project, and published the factors in the project's success. This related to the UK motor licensing industry, which is controlled through its agencies under the

Department for Transport. These agencies are in charge of all the licences issued in various categories. The Drivers and Vehicle Licensing Agency (DVLA) and the Vehicle and Operator Services Agency (VOSA) are the two Government agencies responsible for issuing all motor vehicle-related licences. The DVLA has responsibility for Road Tax. VOSA provides support to delivery of a service for Traffic Commissioners, who are the regulators of the commercial vehicle industry in England, Wales and Scotland. VOSA conducted an innovative ICT project to create an internet-based real time transactional service which allows goods vehicle operators direct access to their own licence records and to input and track progress on applications.

The project was deemed to be a success if it was delivered to time and specification and brought in 5% under budget, all of which were achieved. The critical success factors that arose from the Lancaster study were:

- Appointing external consultants to articulate new vision
- A determination to seek a radical and innovative IT solution
- A major effort to manage twelve stakeholder 'bank groups.'
- Training project staff to PRINCE2 foundation standard
- Training project staff in Java applications
- Industrial collaboration to simplify and standardise IT platform and to cut costs
- Applying rigorous risk management and business continuity models.
- Substantial testing throughout the life of the project.
- Simplicity and scaleability of the chosen platform
- Structural changes within the organisation
- Significant stakeholder participation
- Creation and observance of a detailed project plan
- Senior management support and 'buy-in'
- Shared vision and effective communications strategy
- Iterative software development
- The creation of a change management board

These factors would seem to be relevant with the success of any major public sector project. Procurement has a key role here, in terms of scope, specification, innovation and minimising risk.

Learning activity 10.3

What in your view is the significance of appointing external consultants to 'articulate the new vision' to the satisfaction of stakeholders, as an absolute pre-requisite to a successful procurement project, as the Lancaster study suggests? If you disagree with this statement, then objectively articulate the reasons for your disagreement.

Self-assessment question 10.2

Do you think stakeholders are generally adept at successfully creating change in procurement projects?

Lessons from experiences of the high-level involvement on successful projects

Case Study: "Choosing Health" project

On 18 November 2004, the Government published a white paper: *Choosing Health* (Department of Health, 2004). The three core principles of the strategy were 'informed choice', 'personal responsibility', and 'working together'. Headline issues covered a campaign to raise awareness, action on obesity, nutrition signposting on foods, further restrictions on the advertising of high-fat foods, working with industry to reduce salt and sugar in foods and nutritional standards for the public sector. The output was to be a Food and Health Action Plan and Strategy. There was to be a multi-stakeholder approach to the project, with England, Wales, Scotland and Northern Ireland, all at various stages of readiness, to be dealt with independently. Other stakeholders were the World Health Organisation, the European Commission, the Food Standards Agency, the Department of Health, the Department for Culture, Media and Sport, the Department for Education and Skills and their counterparts in the other home countries, UK Treasury, and the public sector in all four home countries. An EC Communication on Nutritional and Physical Activity was subsequently published in 2006. The key factors in the successful delivery of this project were seen to be:

- Effective vision and ambition
- Effective ownership and leadership
- Appointment of local 'champions'
- National message but local delivery in each of the home countries
- Collaborative working
- The need for high-level political involvement, at ministerial level (First Minister in Scotland)
- The need for industry leader champions to support the campaign publicly (Chairman/Chief Executive of Tesco etc).
- De-politicisation of the project, if possible
- Wide political support
- Realistic targets
- Attitude to achieving changed
- Managing expectations and 'false dawns' appropriately. Keeping up momentum.

It was recognised that other powerful potential stakeholders were global non-governmental organisations or single-issue lobbying groups who could be very organised and whose power could be usefully tapped into to promote the project. The media was also a very powerful influence if used effectively.

The preferred approach was entitled 'the four 'Ms':

- Mandate – political support, organisational support, power of consumers as citizens in achieving a public mandate
- Method – inclusive, participatory, consensus-building
- Means – resources, cash, manpower, machines
- Monitoring – evaluation and feedback, improving understanding, public disclosure to help influence.

Readers can see that these principles might apply in a good many complex and high-profile procurement projects of a deeply political nature. There was tacit agreement by the chair of the project board that the whole project would founder if it were not championed by those at the very summit of the political hegemony and also the key players in the national media.

Self-assessment question 10.3

How might your organisation best incorporate the three core strategic principles for a successful procurement project of 'informed choice', 'personal responsibility', and 'working together' in a project involving a wide variety of stakeholders?

Summary

In assessing the effectiveness of procedures for resolving differences with external stakeholders, this study session has covered several important points. Firstly it is important for your organisation to analyse its own state of readiness in term of its ability to engage with its stakeholders prior to any major procurement project. By doing so you will find yourself more prepared to defuse and resolve any differences or tensions between stakeholders in a procurement project should they manifest. The structures described in this study session will allow you to address multiple factors of concern from stakeholders, allowing you to create an effective approach to managing the issues and queries; particularly with a multi-stakeholder procurement project which needs to be related to senior management and the project board. Though learning about the key factors that influence the stakeholders and a particular procurement project, the delivery of such projects is going to become all the more effective. This has been demonstrated in this study session through the examples of best practice for the governance of public procurement projects with the case studies discussed above.

Revision Question

Discuss the challenges that may arise in managing procurement projects (for example, major construction project or procurement of capital assets) bearing in mind that you might have to accommodate two managerial structures. Utilise examples to illustrate your answer.

Feedback

Feedback on Self-assessment question 10.1

'How does your organisation handle major procurement projects? Does it use PRINCE2 or another variant model? Does it abide faithfully by the PRINCE2 (or equivalent) rules?'

This depends to an extent on how advanced the organisation is in terms of its general procurement and project management strategies. More and more public sector organisations are using PRINCE2 or Gateway reviews. Some organisations have inadequate skilled resource to handle complex procurement projects, and may buy in these skills. There is a danger that inadequate resource is attached to these projects anyway – many times full-time managers are pulled away to manage projects part time with dire results. One benefit of using PRINCE2 is that it can be scaled down for smaller projects, and some of the stages missed out. Full blown PRINCE2 is onerous, rigorous, and labour-intensive. Its great benefit is that it is disciplined, and the project can be pulled at an early stage if the costs start to outweigh the benefits.

Feedback on Learning activity 10.1

'Can you give practical examples of each of the first eight 'human risk' elements outlined above, in the context of your own organisation's failure to deal with this problem in projects?

Examples here are many and varied, and this exercise should prove useful in stretching you to think about some of them. Some immediate examples spring to mind:

- Management incompetence in starting a procurement project near the end of the financial year when there were inadequate revenue funds to pay for the important early stages, leading to poor delivery.
- Inadequate corporate policies where procurement were not part of the initial project team and inadequate supplier management processes ensued in a negotiated procedure, leading to abandonment of the project following a legal challenge by a disgruntled (and excluded) supplier.
- Inadequate adoption of management practices whereby diktats from the project board were not communicated properly, so when these reached the coal face, the message was diluted and performance and delivery were poor
- Poor leadership where the Chief Executive abrogated his responsibility as project sponsor and handed power to the director of corporate resources, who did not have the necessary support to drive the project through properly.
- Lack of authority of key personnel whereby an external consultant was hired as project manager of a large procurement project and employees refused to accept that he had the same authority as an employee of the organisation
- Poor staff selection procedures in which an engineer with no formal project management qualifications was put in charge of a flood prevention project. He had to be replaced within a few weeks.
- Lack of clarity over roles and responsibilities, in which an ICT project, developed with an outsourced IT partner, fell apart because neither the organisation nor the outsourced ICT partner understood clearly the roles and responsibilities of the other
- Vested interests in which elected members interfered in a schools PFI project which caused scope creep, extra cost and a poorer quality construction, because the politicians insisted on local labour being subcontracted for 75% of the construction works, in a market where there were insufficient ready skills.

Feedback on learning activity 10.2

'Analyse the main elements of a successful peer review process for a procurement project with both internal and external stakeholders. Use a practical example to illustrate your reasoning.'

A peer review allows a team of people who understand the pressures and challenges of running a public sector organisation project which involves a wide variety of internal and external stakeholders to review the practices of an organisation in a challenging but supportive way. This process allows a constructive discussion of the project's strengths and weaknesses and provides recommendations of how improvements can be made.

The reasons why organisations have peer reviews are many and varied, including:

- To provide a progress check against previous peer reviews
- To undertake an external stocktake for a new project sponsor or project manager
- To provide tangible evidence for the project board, the organisation and all stakeholders
- To give inspection experience/coaching for the project team or any relevant stakeholders
- To inform improvement planning or decisions on re-assessment
- To aid the continual improvement

Organisations want to make sure that they are on the right track and draw on skills of experts from outside their authority.

The chief consideration when selecting peers is who can best help an organisation's situation and requirements. For this reason peers come from local authorities, the private and not-for-profit sectors. Peers from local authorities include specialist officers, chief executives and elected members.

How peers interact with an organisation depends on the peer review and its needs. At the start of the process, your authority will agree with the reviewers precisely what the peers will do and on what they will focus.

A team of peers visits an organisation for a short period of time - usually between three to five days. They use a specifically designed diagnostic tool and, for most reviews, an established benchmark to help an organisation identify strengths and weaknesses of a procurement project. Peers will review documentation and interview senior officers, elected members, service users, stakeholders and representatives of your authority's key partners and contractors.

At the end of the process, the peers make a presentation outlining the team's key findings and recommendations based on the benchmark. For most reviews, this is followed up with a report outlining their evidence and conclusions in more details.

A useful practical example could be, say, the outsourcing of an in-house roads maintenance contract. The peer review would involve all stakeholders at an early stage in the project, perhaps after the project initiation document (PID) has been signed off, and at two or three key milestones thereafter.

Feedback on learning activity 10.3

'What in your view is the significance of appointing external consultants to 'articulate the new vision' to the satisfaction of stakeholders, as an absolute pre-requisite to a successful procurement project, as the Lancaster study suggests? If you disagree with this statement, then objectively articulate the reasons for your disagreement.'

Consultants can bring the following skills to a procurement project:

- Entrepreneurial: to ensure the most cost effective innovative solutions are chosen and promoted

- Commercial awareness: to manage the scheme budgets and resources

- Team leader or player: ability to adapt to differing cultures, and lead or work within a project group

- Project management: to manage all interfaces within the project and deliver the project on time and within budget

- Communication skills at all levels: ability to present to and, where required, manage meetings from board level through to contractor liaison meetings

- Motivational skills and influencing skills

- Understanding of Health and Safety legislation: including the employers' and employees' obligations under European legislation

- Awareness of current European and international standards and their application

- Practical knowledge of the issues surrounding the installation and integration of various systems: understanding of the system interface protocols, and physical and technical constraints of systems integration

There are various reasons as to why an end user may require the advice of an independent technical consultant. The main reasons can be categorised as follows:

- No in-house experience of technology areas
- Limited in-house technical resources which may not have relevant skill sets
- To supplement a competent in-house technical team e.g. provide additional resource
- To co-ordinate an in-house engineering team
- To carry out a feasibility study to establish and quantify the merits of the investment
- To prepare contract documentation and technical specifications
- To audit existing systems
- To review existing proposals
- To act as planning supervisor for the scheme
- To plan and manage a project.

It is worth noting that in today's 'best value' environment it may be prudent for a client to consider using an external consultant instead of in-house team, since in some cases it may be more cost effective in delivering the project. There are other benefits to this arrangement such as reduced project risk to the client organisation, design and implementation risk (contracted to the consultant) and reduced levels of internal supervision (checking/validation and project management).

'Selling the vision' is one of the core communications and motivational skills that consultants with their training can add to the project management mix. The points above relate to the appointment of external consultants to manage the project throughout its life.

Feedback on self-assessment question 10.2

'Do you think stakeholders are generally adept at successfully creating change in procurement projects?'

Change is threatening, not only to established power bases, but also to workers' views of their competencies and professional expertise. The new governance approach, which places great store in partnerships, networks, participation and common involvement, has promoted the concept that these elements empower change in the public policy system – a release from the inflexibilities of policy-driven bureaucracy. In truth, this approach has tended to expect better results from stakeholder change than have actually occurred. One of the key characteristics of this form of governance is managing change with a broad range of interdependent stakeholders. Success here depends on the way organisations set up consultation, the way stakeholders

are empowered in partnership bodies, the strategy chosen to modernise and deliver change corporately, the use of internal and external resources to deliver change, and the way in which projects are developed and planned.
If stakeholders are suitably empowered, have the passion and energy to initiate change, and are given the opportunity to contribute as fully as possible at all stages of a procurement project, they can be valuable initiators of change as well as innovation.

Feedback on self-assessment question 10.3

'How might your organisation best incorporate the three core strategic principles for a successful procurement project of 'informed choice', 'personal responsibility', and 'working together' in a project involving a wide variety of stakeholders? '

According to Loffler (2003), public agencies now no longer only have to be good at getting their internal management systems right – financial management, human resource management, ICT and performance management – but they also have to manage their most important external stakeholders well in order to achieve the desired policy outcomes and a high quality of public service. Scholes (2001) says that different stakeholders may have commonality of purpose at a very general level but have their own agendas at specific levels.

Strategic managers must understand the political context in detail to be able to develop and implement strategies that are politically viable as well as organisationally and economically rational. It will probably be necessary to adopt differing styles to different stakeholder groups even for the same strategy. Thus the concept and principle of 'informed choice' has to be tempered by the need to differentiate the communications and stakeholder engagement strategies to suit the needs of the specific stakeholder groups. Key stakeholders are powerful, which means that personal responsibility in their case needs to be better harnessed by corporate strategists than minor stakeholders.

The notion of all stakeholders taking personal responsibility for maximising the possibility of project success is almost a given, because the alternative is abrogation of responsibility by stakeholders and its adoption by a corporate caucus, which will narrow the strategic vision for the project as well as hinder its execution. If external stakeholders are to be important, then they should be allowed to take personal responsibility for the decisions they make.

The third principle, that of 'working together', can be difficult because of the diverse nature of stakeholder groups each with its own agenda. However, some key principles can help improve a team approach to working together:

- Sponsorship from the very top of the organisation
- Alliance and team-building strategy, including training and motivation
- Building on a common vision
- Reward for change/incentivisation

- Informal influence through links and networks
- Involvement in strategy implementation
- Charismatic leadership
- Possession of knowledge and skills
- Concentrating on specialisms, e.g. IT.
- Concentration on stakeholder status
- Good planning and control
- Investment in resources, both human and fiscal.

Revision feedback

'Discuss the challenges that may arise in managing procurement projects (for example, major construction project or procurement of capital assets) bearing in mind that you might have to accommodate two managerial structures. Utilise examples to illustrate your answer.'

When accommodating several management structures in a single procurement contract you will find that different stakeholders have may have varying factors that they wish taken into account. You will have to accommodate these differing concerns whilst still ensuring that the required procurement action is effectively undertaken.

Some of the major challenges you may face when accommodating multiple structures include:

- Mismatch between timescales (for example, in respect of clients budgets and contractors resources)
- Differing objectives of client and contractor
- Lack of a uniform approach to supply chain management
- Differing organisational structures and reporting mechanisms
- Lack of communication methods between client and contractor
- Insuring effective procurement project review procedures

You will find a number of examples in this study session, but can also find examples on the OGC and NHS procurement websites.

Further Reading

OGC website on Prince2 - http://www.ogc.gov.uk/methods_prince_2__overview.asp

Goodall, Niel., 2004, Best Practice for Public Sector I.T. Projects, [Online] Tescom, Available at: http://tescom-intl.com/site/en/tescom.asp?pi=61&doc_id=2005

Study session 11

"Critically evaluate the significance of CSR and 'conscience procurement' for procurement organisations, policy and procedures, internal and external stakeholders"

Introduction

This study session discusses the increasingly important area of Corporate Social Responsibility (CSR) and what that means in respect of stakeholders and then examines the ways that you can be aware of the issues and implications of CSR and 'conscience procurement'. There is then analysis of the issues around the development of policy and procedures for CSR and how you could involve stakeholders. The session ends with an insight into the Simms Task Force and what that means in terms of policy and philosophy for public procurement.

Session Learning Objectives

After completing this session you should be able to:

- consider CSR and 'conscience procurement'
- assess the implications of CSR and 'conscience procurement' for procurement organisation, policy and procedures
- involve internal and external stakeholders in developing policy and procedures in relation to CSR and 'conscience procurement'
- the impact of changes in policy e.g. Simms Sustainability Task Force Policy

Unit content coverage

This study session covers part of the following topic from the official CIPS unit documents: *Critically evaluate the significance of changing social and political agendas for public procurement*. Specifically it covers: *Critically evaluate the significance of CSR and 'conscience procurement' for procurement organisation, policy and procedures, internal and external stakeholders.*

Prior knowledge

Prior to this study session you should have completed study sessions1; 2; 3; 4; 5; 6; 7; 8; 9; 10.

Timing

You should take about 4 – 5 hours to read and complete this section, including learning activities, self assessment questions, the suggested further reading and the revision question.

Consider CSR and 'conscience procurement'

It is useful, before proceeding further, to consider the definition of Corporate Social Responsibility (CSR).

'Corporate social responsibility is the commitment of business to contribute to sustainable economic development—working with employees, their families, the local community and society at large to improve the quality of life, in ways that are both good for business and good for development.'

The World Bank

The agenda for corporate social responsibility (CSR) is founded in recognition that organisations that engage in business, particularly those of a commercial nature, are part of society, and therefore have the potential/obligation to make a positive contribution to societal goals and aspirations. CSR is at heart a process of managing the costs and benefits of business activity to internal stakeholders such as workers and shareholders, and external stakeholders such as investors, customers, suppliers, civil society, and community groups. Setting the boundaries for how those costs and benefits are managed is a balance of business policy/strategy and of public governance.

The notion of corporate social responsibility is not new, but the contemporary CSR agenda, with its origins in respect of the focus upon globalisation in the 1990s, is still relatively immature.

Business approaches to CSR can largely be understood as a response to a series of external and internal drivers that generate a 'business case' for CSR. The drivers include the pursuit of new business opportunities through social and environmental innovation; reputational risk management; campaign pressure from non governmental organisations (NGOs) or trade unions; media exposure to the practices of individual companies or sectors; regulation; and litigation. Building effective drivers of CSR is one pillar in approaches to build an optimal enabling environment for CSR or responsible business practices (World Bank, 2004).

The current definition of CSR suggests that organisations should engage with stakeholders rather than just shareholders. The stakeholder model of a firm, developed in the United States in the mid 1980's, and the current business case for CSR are fundamentally different. The stakeholder model is based on the view that stakeholders should be engaged with decisions that affect the firm as they are likely to be directly affected by the firm's activities - as Bichta (2003. pp. 8) notes. Bitcha also comments that, on the other hand, 'the business case for CSR is rooted on the (utilitarian) notion that shareholders will increase their financial interests by engaging in dialogue with other stakeholders of the firm.' Thus, 'in its conventional form corporate social responsibility is, for private sector organisations, 'profitability plus compliance plus philanthropy'.' Andriof et al (2003) puts the current meaning of corporate responsibility into context of stakeholder engagement, as the 'recognition that day to day operating practices affect stakeholders and that is in those impacts where responsibility lies, not merely in efforts to do good.'

Self assessment question 11.1

List the social issues which you think your organisation, or one with which you are familiar, would need to address when developing a procurement strategy, particularly one with a focus on including SMEs?

Learning activity 11.1

Outline the time scale during which Corporate Social Responsibility has come to the fore as a part of the changing social and political agendas.

Four central public sector roles in strengthening CSR

You will be able, however, to see that it is not just commercial organisations that would have an interest, and role to play, in respect of CSR. In a baseline study conducted by the World Bank into public sector roles in corporate social responsibility (Fox; Ward; Howard, 2002) four roles that the public sector can take in developing and encouraging CSR are highlighted. These are:

- **Mandating**
- **Facilitating**
- **Partnering**
- **Endorsing**

Learning activity 11.2

Taking an organisation with which you are familiar, consider each of the four roles that the public sector can play in respect of CSR and note examples against each of the headings.

The importance of the public sector in developing the CSR agenda should not be undervalued, as frequently through public sector procurement there has been a spread of CSR into the private sector via tender and contract terminology, plus careful supplier relationship and management development. The potential for this is noted in a World Bank report on research which was originally targeting the private sector response to the CSR agenda.

'Virtually all participants (in the World Bank–commissioned study to assess barriers to implementation of CSR codes) noted that the absence of action by local governments presented a significant barrier; not only as a barrier to the achievement of good practice generally, but also as a barrier to the implementation of codes of conduct and other critical steps taken by non-state actors. The consensus on this point was so overwhelming that it was taken into consideration despite the fact that the focus of the present study, as formulated in the Bank's Terms of Reference, was intended to be on the private sector rather than the public sector' (Jørgensen et al, 2003).

The whole approach to CSR is a global one, and there is considerable reporting available that indicates that there is growing interest around the world in respect of the roles of public sector organisations and the contributions they can make.

Emphasising the international perspective, it has been reported in research (Berman et al, 2003) that over 80% of respondent organisations, when seeking to work in other countries, look at the CSR performance of potential partners and locations before they close the deal on a new venture. More than half of the respondents reported that the review takes place while they are still looking at multiple partners and potential countries. The majority of companies reported that CSR issues are at least as influential as traditional considerations (for example, cost, quality, delivery) in new venture assessment, and that this influence has grown in the last five years.

The UK government has clearly set out its view on CSR, and its importance to the economy and its citizens, which it sees as the business contribution to sustainable development goals. It is about how business takes account of its economic, social and environmental impacts in the way it operates – maximising the benefits and minimising the downsides. Importantly, it is the voluntary actions that business can take, over and above compliance with minimum legal requirements, to address both its own competitive interests and the interests of wider society. The influence of the public sector, through potential procurement power, can encourage and foster a major move towards greater corporate social responsibility.

The implications of CSR and 'conscience procurement' for procurement organisation, policy and procedures

As the recognition of CSR and its importance for global well being grows so too does the influence of public sector procurement. This however, has implications for the way that procurement organisations and those within them are developed and organised. If an organisation is to have a collective conscience, then there are implications in respect of how that organisation deals with CSR sensitive issues. For example, there are certain points of ambiguity that might arise when a health authority wishes to purchase new waste disposal system. It may well be that this will not be the lowest cost option and that the most effective 'green' solution is the most expensive option. Arguably, this merely means that an individual buyer within the authority makes a business case/investment appraisal – based upon 'value for money' over the lifetime of the system and although it might not be the cheapest option it does meet the CSR agenda of that authority. As such it could be argued that it is becoming more necessary to measure up the benefits of a socially responsible (all be it possibly a more costly one) against more traditional measures of an organisations effectiveness such as keeping costs low. However, deciding whether to incorporate a responsible approach is not so straightforward. There will be many stakeholders, not least the general public, who whilst thinking that the CSR approach is laudable, would rather have a less expensive waste disposal system and (simply put) more patients cured for the money that is available. Hence organisationally, and/or individually, procurement may have a conscience but the wishes of stakeholders will have to be taken into account and this has an impact upon procurement organisation, policy and procedures. The more stakeholders that need to be considered the greater the variables affecting the procurement decision.

Learning activity 11.3

Taking an organisation with which you are familiar, make notes on the impact that the CSR agenda and the notion of conscience procurement can – or could have, on the following:

a) Procurement organisation;
b) Procurement policy and procedures

Sir Neville Simms (2006), who leads the UK Sustainable Procurement Task Force, has made it clear that using procurement to support wider social, economic and environmental objectives will be beneficial over the long term. He has highlighted that an organisation can achieve successful operations through sustainability procurement. Through the implementation of sustainable procurement it will also gain reputation and recognition and will, in due course, enhance performance (for an organisation, its environment, the country etc). This of course will both affect and be impacted upon by stakeholders. It will require adherence to standards and necessitate policies and procedures to be enhanced. For example, benchmarking and risk management will need to be practised to ensure effective operations. This can be illustrated by diagram 11.1.

Diagram 11.1

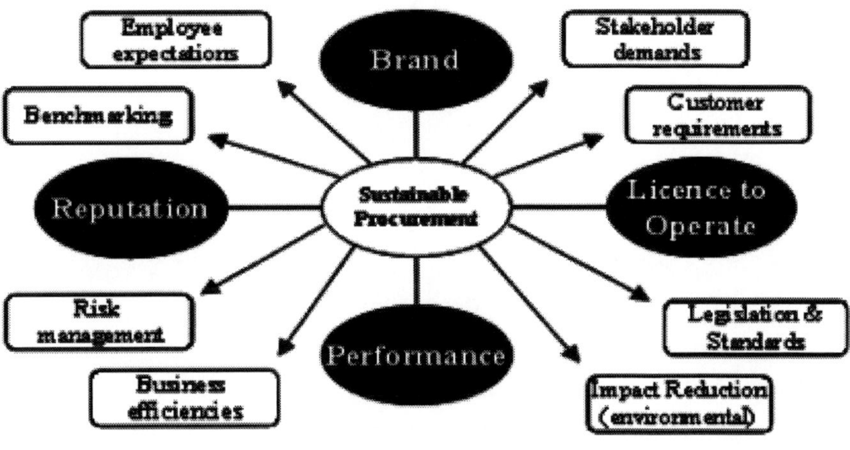

The impact of the Task Force is significant, giving credence to the topic and high profile to the aspects that affect public procurement such as legal matters, moral imperatives and ethical behaviour. Were such an approach not to be taken there would be a lack of a cohesive approach to public sector procurement in respect of CSR and 'conscience procurement', although it must be emphasised that the Task Force is not promoting government policy *per se*. Rather it is utilising the government philosophy to provide authority and impetus to the CSR agenda.

Through the tender and contracting processes, public sector procurement organisations and personnel can build into procedures, policies and decision making a requirement for sustainability. In a number of ways it is an important aspect that, as the National Audit Office (2004, pp.36) states, CSR is not incompatible with the concept of value for money – indeed the implication is that value for money assessments must be developed such that sustainability can be incorporated. The OGC produces guidance that encourages departments to incorporate sustainability. Such guidance covers among other things issues such as energy efficiency, biodegradability, and re-cyclability etc.

Sustainable procurement (SP) is about the incorporation of sustainability into the 'total process,' whole life perspective of procurement. As public sector procurement organisations emphasise corporate social responsibility as an important supplier selection criteria, it will encourage more sustainable production/procurement on the part of potential suppliers.

SP could be integrated into business processes and decision-making as an extension of lean support practices. As well as benefiting the environment and its inhabitants, timely integration of SP goals can boost business efficiency by encouraging:

- Delivery of products and outputs with less material resources and environmental impacts reduced logistics and supply chain constraints and lower support costs.
- Value for money. Sustainable alternatives are not necessarily more expensive.
- Stakeholder involvement with better informed decisions.
- Positive media coverage and public perception.

Whereas a lack of, or late, consideration of SP could lead to:

- Inability to operate equipment in future due to altering climate and fuel availability.
- Risk to reputation from public perception.
- Delay in operational capability, if objections from stakeholders impact on use of equipment or delivery of supporting estate requirements.
- Increased risk of legislative non-compliance.
- Increased through life and disposal costs.

Successful delivery relies on real, demonstrable and determined leadership with commitment and resource provision from the top down as demonstrated by the variety of Board level endorsed strategic initiatives. Within the MOD for example, the Key Supplier Reporting initiative will be one mechanism for reviewing how closely suppliers meet the sustainable procurement Flexible Framework standards (which will be covered in study session 13). Sustainability considerations should be written into tendering and contracting documents as well as ongoing supplier management frameworks. It is vital for technical, engineering and user personnel to work with procurement professionals to capture sustainable requirements at early stages in the process, as it is usually more difficult or costly to add them retrospectively. Sustainable procurement is an evolving field, and as breakthroughs continue to be made in reconciling sustainable concepts with competition and contracting law, there will be greater scope for implementation through commercial approaches. This involves communication with and consideration of stakeholder interests at all levels.

Although an important element of CSR, sustainable procurement is covered in detail in study session 13.

Self assessment question 11.2

Access the Simms Report on Sustainable Procurement (2006). As it presents a considerable step change in government policy in respect of the use of public procurement influence to achieve sustainability it is important to be aware of the impetus that this has brought to the sustainability agenda in the UK. Note its main strategic principles.

The following indicates the type of internal and external stakeholders who would need to be involved in developing policy and procedures in relation to CSR and 'conscience' procurement:

11

Figure 11.2

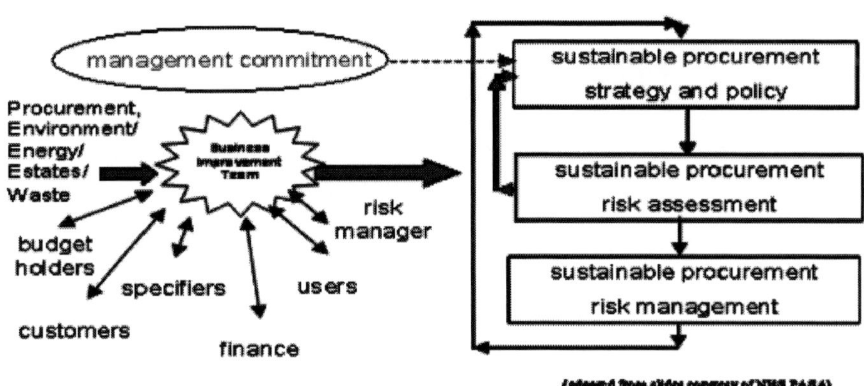

It is interesting to note that whilst the public sector leads in the area of sustainability and CSR generally, there is a mixed response from the suppliers to the whole agenda. Whilst most recognise the need for and have acceptance of the views expressed in the Simms Report, the requirement to meet shareholder expectations can sometimes have greater influence than the desire to want to serve communities and meet green targets. (This is the issue referred to by both Bitcha and Andriof noted earlier).

Further, the government itself is not necessarily consistent or coherent in its policy, documentation and various guidelines. Erridge (2007, pp.239) in the

CIPS course book on 'Machinery of Government' notes a cautionary tale from the construction industry. The Simms report (2006, pp.23) (Full title: Procuring the future, Sustainable Procurement Action Plan: Recommendations from the Sustainable Procurement Task Force) highlights Morrison Plc's view as a supplier that 'if the procurement activities of the public sector are to help deliver sustainability objectives, there needs to be a consistent and unbroken connection between the sustainability objectives expressed at the highest level in government and those expressed in the specification for the facility/service/ asset that is being procured'.

Yet, to ensure that the whole area of CSR is addressed and that the core message of Simms is taken further and acted upon, all those involved must be 'on board'. It is through the public sector leading by example (leadership) that this will happen.

All stakeholders have to ask the following questions and face up to answering them. How much longer will it be acceptable for organisations to:

- Grow their business and increase greenhouse emissions
- Send waste to landfill
- Buy from organisations with poor human rights practices
- Deplete natural resources in construction and operations
- Disrupt their neighbours

Leading experts now state that all stakeholders must take action to secure the nation's and the world's future. As former Prime Minister Tony Blair said of the Simms report and its subsequent direction, 'We have spent a long time getting to grips with the concept of sustainability. I want to declare a moratorium on further words. I want this new strategy to be a catalyst for action to secure our future'.

Learning activity 11.4

The MoD has a public sector procurement organisation that has been impacted upon by in policy terms since the Simms Sustainability Task Force was created. Discuss what you think the MoD's response to the new policy on CSR and sustainability may include?

Summary

The notion of corporate social responsibility has continued to develop as a major consideration for organisations, particularly in relation to their procurement activities. It is through public sector procurement that government policy and general response to CSR that an impact can be made. The benefits of engaging in sustainable CSR may not be compatible with traditional shareholder interests but is a necessary consideration for engaging the interests of the wider external stakeholders which can bring benefits in the long run. The recognition that CSR is increasingly of a greater concern to its stakeholders, means that organisations must do more to manage their procurement activities with the sustainability theme to the fore.

Revision question

Discuss the changing CSR agenda and consider how this impacts upon stakeholders within the public sector procurement environment.

Feedback

Feedback on self assessment question 11.1

'List the social issues which you think your organisation would need to address when developing a procurement strategy.'

The OGC document *Buy and make a difference: How to address Social Issues in Public Procurement* (2008, pp.14) contains a list of what it considers important do's and don'ts in the procurement process. (You should compare your responses against these) These are:

'Do make sure:

- Social issues addressed in procurement are relevant to the subject of the contract.
- Actions to take account of social issues are consistent with the government's value-for-money policy, taking account of whole-life costs.
- Actions to take account of social issues comply with the law, in particular, the principles of the EU Treaty, around a level playing field for suppliers from the UK and other member states, and the UK Regulations implementing the EU Public Procurement Directive(s).
- Any social benefits sought are quantified and weighed against any additional costs and potential burdens on suppliers, which are likely to be passed onto the public sector.
- Not to impose any unnecessary burdens that would seriously deter suppliers, especially small and medium sized enterprises (SMEs), from competing for contracts, which in turn would reduce the choice available and could impact on costs and service standards. The suppliers deterred could include the very ones whose participation would help to further the government's social agenda e.g. those owned by under-represented groups.
- To consider whether any social legislation, such as the public sector equality duties, are relevant to a procurement and take appropriate action to address this.

Do not:

- Act in such a way as to distort competition or discriminate against candidate suppliers from other Member States.
- Add social elements to a contract without careful evaluation and justification of any additional costs.

11

- Leave consideration of social issues until too late in the process.
- Confuse obtaining value for money, which is required, with awarding contracts on the basis of lowest initial price, which is bad practice.
- Impose contract conditions that are not relevant to the performance of the individual contract.
- As part of the procurement process, ask suppliers about their policies generally on issues which are not related to the specific contract. '

Feedback on learning activity 11.1

'Outline the time scale during which Corporate Social Responsibility has come to the fore as a part of the changing social and political agendas.'

This Corporate Social Timeline (Dougherty Centre for Corporate Social Responsibility, 2008) provides an outline of some of the events that have brought this topic to the fore in respect of both social and political agendas. It is comprehensive and indicates that there has been considerable pressure in differing ways for a greater awareness of CSR. It is only latterly, as a result of such pressure, that there has been an emphasis upon the role that public procurement can play. This list does however; indicate a considerable breadth of stakeholders within this topic area.

1982	• Business in the Community established by companies such as IBM, BP, Shell, British Steel (Industry), Marks and Spencer, Barclays Bank, W.H. Smith, ICI and Midland Bank.
1983	• 100th Local Enterprise Agency established in England
1984	• Am algamation of CBI Special Programmes Unit with BITC
1985	• Live Aid Concert
1986	• Launch of Per Cent Club by HRH the Prince of Wales and Prime Minister Margaret Thatcher • Employees Forum on Disability launched • Institute of Business Ethics launched

1987	• First One Town Partnership in Halifax • Launch of first Education Compact in East London • Brundtland Commission report on sustainable development: "our common future" • Corporate Responsibility Group starts • Montreal Protocol to protect ozone layer
1988	• "The Green Consumer Guide" • Margaret Thatcher's environmental speech: "no generation has a freehold on this earth. All we have is a life tenancy – with full repairing lease"
1989	• Business in the Environment set up at the request of HRH The Prince of Wales. • Exxon Valdez tanker runs aground in Alaska and spills 11m gallons of crude oil • The Natural Step think tank for the promotion of sustainability in core business strategy
1990	• Estimated 8 million living with HIV/AIDS worldwide • International Business Leaders Forum created after Charleston Conference; • Charles Handy's RSA Lecture: "What is a Company for?"

1991	• Launch of Opportunity 2000(Opportunity Now) with over 60 founder members • Directions for the Nineties launched with Prime Minister John Major, Charles Kennedy, Tony Blair • Coffee farmers suffer as prices fall to a 30 year low. In response CaféDirect is founded by Oxfam, Traidcraft, Equal Exchange and Twin Trading. • Formation of BSR including early members such as Ben and Jerry's and Tom's of Maine • Companies & Communities" by Fogarty & Christie: PSI • Business decide to participate for the first time in the UN Conference on Environment and Development for the first time with NGO's and Governments on a new global platform to help guide world affairs
1992	• First National Volunteering National Challenge (now Cares) with 30 corporates, 500 community challenges and the participation of more than 8000 people • Earth Summit in Rio • Britain phases out manufacture of CFCs through concerns over the ozone layer • Start of Tesco's Computers for Schools
1993	• Aim High campaign launched • First Managing Corporate Community Investment training programme
1994	• Launch of Local Investment Fund • First supplement in Financial Times on Responsible Business • Union Carbide plant in India leaks toxic gas killing 2,000 and injuring 150,000 • Sustainability coins phrase: "Triple Bottom Line"

1995	• Shell forced to back down on scrapping of Brent Spar rig through environmental pressure • Cedric Brown "fat cat" scandal • WICE merged with BCSD to form the World Business Council for Sustainable Development (WBCSD) • RSA "Tomorrow's Company" Report
1996	• BiE Index of Corporate Environmental Engagement launched – 73 FTSE 100 companies benchmark their environmental management
1997	• Kyoto Protocol • European Business Network for Social Cohesion set up (now CSR Europe); • Copenhagen Centre; • Global Reporting Initiative created • Marine Stewardship Council set up • "Cannibals with Forks" by John Elkington published
1998	• Business Action on Homelessness launched • Launch of first European Online Resource Centre on CSR
1999	• Committee of Inquiry into New Vision for Business reports – launched by Anita Roddick and Tony Blair • UK writes off £1bn of debt owing by some of the worlds poorest countries • Mass protests at the WTO meetings in Seattle • World population reaches 6 billion

2000	• Winning with Integrity' final report of Business Impact taskforce launched at CBI conference • UK appoints first CSR Minister • No Logo' by Naomi Klein published; • UN Global Compact launched at Davos by Kofi Annan • Millennium Development Goals
2001	• Development of CR Index • Establishment of the All Party Parliamentary Group • FTSE 4 Good; • First EU CSR Conference by CSR Europe; • Association of British Insurers Guidelines on Socially Responsible Investment; • Collapse of pharmaceuticals' companies court case against South African Government
2002	• CR index launched • David Varney's "A Perfect Storm" • European Commission adopts a formal CSR strategy • World Summit on Sustainable Development in Johannesburg • Enron collapse • launch EABIS; • Sarbanes Oxley Act
2003	• publication of results of first CR Index • Skills for Life • Parmalat Scandal

2004	• Launch of CSR Academy • Launch of Prison Partners • "Corporate Social Opportunity" by Grayson and Hodges • Kyoto Protocol comes into effect • Super Size Me, documentary • "Good Migrations" – study looking at impact of off-shoring of jobs – BT case-study • "The Corporation" movie
2005	• Indian Ocean earthquake causes large tsunamis • Hurricanes Katrina, Rita, and Wilma • 40 million living with HIV/AIDS • Ian Davis – The Economist: "By special invitation"
2006	• Marketplace principles launched by Business in the Community • Companies Act 2006 • Al Gore's "An Inconvenient Truth" • Michael Porter in Harvard Business Review: Strategy and Society: Competitive Advantage and Corporate Social Responsibility
2007	• Climate Change Bill • Inter-governmental panel on Climate Change • One planet Business" published by WWF • report of Tomorrow's Global Company Inquiry led by BP and Infosys • Baker Report into health and safety failings in BP North America

Feedback on learning activity 11.2

'Taking an organisation with which you are familiar, consider each of the four roles that the public sector can play in respect of CSR and note examples against each of the headings.'

Helina Ward (2004, pp.5) in a follow up study for the World Bank into public sector roles in strengthening CSR provides several examples:

- **Mandating:** This could include laws, regulations, penalties, and associated public sector institutions that relate to the control of some aspect of business investment or operations.
- **Facilitating:** This covers setting clear overall policy frameworks and positions to guide business investment in CSR, development of nonbinding guidance and labels or codes for application in the marketplace, laws and regulations that facilitate and provide incentives for business investment in CSR; by mandating transparency or disclosure on various issues, tax incentives, investment in awareness raising and research, and facilitating processes of stakeholder dialogue (though not necessarily in the lead).
- **Partnering:** Typically this should be about combining public resources with those of business and other actors to leverage complementary skills and resources to tackle issues within the CSR agenda, whether as participants, convenors, or catalysts.
- **Endorsing:** This entails showing public political support for particular kinds of CSR practice in the marketplace or for individual companies; endorsing specific award schemes or nongovernmental metrics, indicators, guidelines, and standards; and leading by example, such as through public procurement practices.

Feedback on learning activity 11.3

'Taking an organisation with which you are familiar, make notes on the impact that the CSR agenda and the notion of conscience procurement can – or could - have, on the following:

a) Procurement organisation;
b) Procurement policy and procedures'

You could identify that organisations would have to seek aggregation of requirements to optimise CSR potential. This might mean a change in organisation. A central unit might need to be set up and reporting lines developed; alternately an advice 'clearing house' could be implemented.

Clear policy guidelines must be implemented in order for all stakeholders to be clear not only on policy but exactly whom they should contact regarding procedures, queries and comments. This whole subject area may be one where education and training of personnel should be undertaken, obviously to enable optimal professionalism in public sector procurement but also to ensure effective communication to all stakeholders.

Feedback on self assessment question 11.2

'Access the Simms Report on Sustainable Procurement (2006). As it presents a considerable step change in government policy in respect of the use of public procurement influence to achieve sustainability it is important to be aware of the impetus that this brought to the sustainability agenda in the UK. Note its main strategic principles.'

The Simms Report identifies the importance of sustainability to the UK as a whole. It provides strategic direction for all organisations – especially through implication, the procurement activities – in the public sector. They apply to the UK Government, Scottish Executive, Welsh Assembly Government and the Northern Ireland Administration. For a policy to be sustainable, it must respect all five principles. We want to live within environmental limits and achieve a just society, and we will do so by means of sustainable economy, good governance, and sound science. The following diagram illustrates these principles:

Diagram 11.3

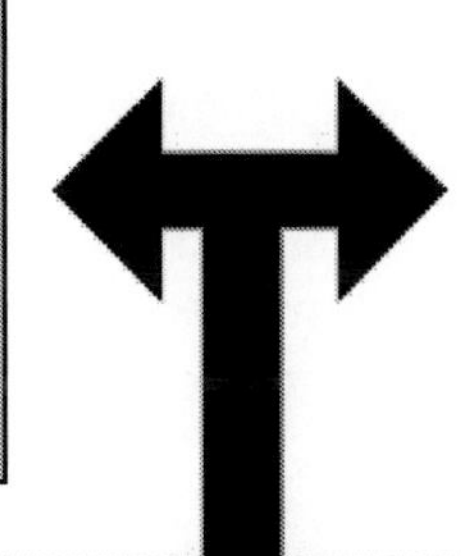

11

Feedback on learning activity 11.4

'The MoD is has is a public sector procurement organisation that has been impacted upon by in policy terms since the Simms Sustainability Task Force was created. Discuss what you think the MoD's response to the new policy on CSR and sustainability may include?'

There has been considerable impact upon the MOD policy although it is still being developed and implemented. The following is an overview of policy actions and new strategic approach being taken.

MOD's strategic approach to SP is driven by the Secretary of State for Defence in the Policy Statement on safety, health, environmental protection and Sustainable Procurement (SP)/Sustainable Development (SD) (2008).

"I expect the Ministry of Defense and the Armed Forces to ensure that MOD plays its part in leading by example to deliver SD in line with *Securing the Future (*2005)".

It also states that targets set, along with safety, environmental and SD performance, is measured, monitored and reported and, is consistent with and supports wider Government initiatives. Most relevantly it indicates that the MoD will embed SP/SD considerations into investment and spending decisions.

Sustainable Procurement (SP) in the MoD is the delivery of sustainable development objectives through specifications, contracts and management of suppliers; and it applies to equipment, commodities, estate infrastructure and services. SP will enable the MoD to procure in a way that achieves value for money on a through-life basis and benefits society and the environment, as well as the economy. Additional drivers for SP in the MoD include:

- Environmental legislation.
- UK Government's framework for National SD delivery (*Securing the Future,* 2006) and SP delivery in *Procuring the Future* (HM Government, 2005).
- Sustainable Operations on the Government Estate (SOGE) targets. These focus on performance improvement in estate-related areas, e.g. waste, water, biodiversity, and energy.
- Flexible framework which focuses on training procurement staff and recognising SD achievements; boosting policy guidance and processes; building SD into the procurement process; engaging suppliers and measuring progress.

It is fair to say that the very nature of the MoD's mission contributes strongly to SD, for example, by diffusing conflicts abroad and acting as a force for good in promoting stability and humanitarian support. Each MoD department has a role in realising that these objectives are not understated. The following are examples of where the MOD approach has yielded CSR benefits.

Area	Activity	Benefit
Defence Fuels Group	Relaxed specification for diesel and unleaded gasoline	Ability to utilise diverse fuels and biofuel additives
Utility vehicles	Car replacement policy	Smaller cleaner vehicle category
Defence Estates	New accomodation blocks	Combined heat and power plants
General spares	Timber	Use and stock of sustainable product up from 40% to 80%
Defence food services	Catering equipment	Heavy duty, long lasting, requires less servicing

Revision Question – Feedback

'Discuss the changing CSR agenda and consider how this impacts upon stakeholders within the public sector procurement environment.'

You should be able to provide in a fairly straight forward manner the main drivers behind the CSR agenda. You need only outline these –the list from the Doughty Centre is extensive although you should make sure that the Simms report and the Sustainability Task Force are noted. You should bring out that initially this was seen as a fairly simple 'green' agenda but it has gained impetus through the actions of celebrities and governments, especially in the last five years or so the UK Government. You should then make sure that you include other public sector procurement initiatives especially using examples such as the defra web site.

This should lead you to the main area that requires an extension of the issues raised in this study session. In opening this you could develop the role of government in respect of: Mandating: Facilitating: Partnering and Endorsing.

For public sector procurement there is opportunity to implement policies through mandating but it could increasingly be through facilitating. All types of public sector procurement functions can take a major role in facilitating wider understanding if issues and ensuring that supplier selection takes into account a wide range of stakeholder's views. Partnering is an area where both external and internal stakeholders could be engaged very clearly and ensure that the stakeholder input and impact is recognized and actioned. The awarding of contracts that have included CSR aspects in the requirement, specification, tendering and consideration of bids will rapidly 'send a message' that will endorse the CSR agenda.

You may wish to illustrate your answer with specific examples from a range of public procurement organisations.

Recommended Reading

Constantina Bichta,; Corporate Social Responsibility: A Role in Government Policy and Regulation [Online] University of Bath School of Management. Available at: http://bedsatbath.co.uk/cri/pubpdf/Research_Reports/16_Bichta.pdf

Tom Fox; Helina Ward; Bruce Howard, (2002) Public Sector Roles in Strengthening Corporate Social Responsibility: A Baseline Study

Helina Ward, (2004), Public Sector Roles in Strengthening Corporate Social Responsibility: Taking Stock

Sir Neville Simms, (ed.), (2006), Procuring the Future – Sustainable Procurement National Action Plan: Recommendations from Sustainable Procurement Task Force

Useful Websites On Corporate Responsibility:

Accountability: www.accountability21.net

Boston College Centre for Corporate Citizenship: www.bccc.net

Business for Social Responsibility: www.bsr.org

Business in the Community: www.bitc.org.uk

Copenhagen Centre: www.copenhagencentre.org

Corporate Citizenship Briefing: www.ccbriefing.co.uk

CSR Europe: www.csreurope.org

The CSR Initiative, Kennedy School of Government, Harvard: www.ksg.harvard.edu/m-rcbg/CSRI/

Ethical Corporation: www.ethicalcorp.com

Forum for Future: www.forumforthefuture.co.uk

Global Reporting Initiative: www.globalreporting.org

International Business Leaders Forum: www.iblf.org

Mallen Baker: www.mallenbaker.net

Sustainability: www.sustainability.com

UN Global Compact: www.unglobalcompact.org

World Business Council for Sustainable Development: www.wbcsd.org

NHS Procurement: http://www.pasa.nhs.uk/PASAWeb/NHSprocurement/

Study session 12

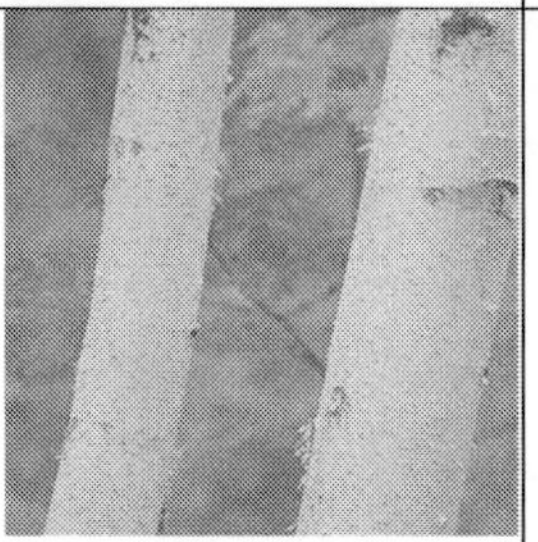

"Critically assess the significance of the SME agenda for procurement policy procedures"

Introduction

In this study session, the important place which Small and Medium Enterprises (SMEs) occupy in the UK economy is assessed. Following this is an examination of the issues involved in, and means of, engaging SMEs in public procurement. This is taken from a broad perspective allowing you to think through the internal and external stakeholder effects and impacts. To round off this session, insights are provided into the means by which SMEs (including those that are minority owned) can be engaged in the public procurement environment.

Session learning objectives

After completing this session you should be able to:

- assess the role and significance of SMEs in the UK and international markets.
- develop strategies for engaging SME's in public procurement in conjunction with internal and external stakeholders.
- identify and apply methods and procedures for engaging minority owned SMEs in public procurement e.g. Supply2.gov.uk.

Unit content coverage

This study session covers part of the following topic from the official CIPS unit content documents: *Critically evaluate the significance of CSR and 'conscience procurement' for procurement organisation, policy and procedures, internal and external stakeholders*. Specifically it covers: *Critically assess the significance of the SME agenda for procurement policy procedures*

Prior knowledge

Prior to this study session you should have completed study sessions 1; 2; 3; 4; 5; 6; 7; 8; 9; 10; 11.

Timing

You should take about 4 – 5 hours to read and complete this section, including learning activities, self assessment questions, the suggested further reading and the revision question.

The role and significance of SMEs in the UK and International Markets

SMEs

SME is the recognised abbreviation for Small and Medium Sized Enterprises. SMEs are vitally important for the UK economy as the majority of the workforce is employed by SMEs. Statistics for 2006 published by the Small Business Service (SBS) Statistics Unit show that out of 4.5 million businesses in the UK, 99.3% were small firms with fewer than 50 employees, and 0.6% were medium firms with 50-249 employees (Department for Business Enterprise and Regulatory Reform, 2007). Despite governments and many of the multinational organisations targeting this group for special financial business support, there is no single definition for a SME either nationally or internationally.

One that is generally accepted is the following:

- An SME is one that has fewer than 250 employees;
- Has either (a) an annual turnover not exceeding €50 million (approximately £24 million) or (b) an annual balance sheet total not exceeding €27 million (approximately £16 million); and
- 25% or more of the capital or the voting rights are not owned by one enterprise, or jointly by several enterprises falling outside this definition of an SME.

Learning activity 12.1

Search for differing definitions of SMEs. There are generally one or two aspects that are quite consistent.

Why contract with SMEs?

A good starting point to consider why an organisation should contract with SMEs would be to look at the abstract below from The District of Easington Corporate Procurement Manager (2006). The report concerns the district's particular public sector procurement approach and how it will engage with SMEs. Part of the report addresses why SME's should be given serious thought when it comes to procurement contracts:

"Why help small businesses?

4.1 SME's represent a powerful engine for economic growth. Small firms are a crucial part of the UK economy. At the beginning of 2002, SME's in the UK accounted for 99.8% of all businesses, 56% of employment and 52% of turnover.

4.2 There are approximately 1700 SME's operating within the District and make up 98% of the business base of the District.

4.3 The belief that small & medium sized enterprises (SME's) need to be more fully used in the public procurement process has become very topical. Given the size and significance of public procurement the question of how SME's can develop and maximise opportunities is of considerable importance for local, regional and national economies.

4.4 A number of key drivers currently exist which support the debate such as the need to achieve efficiency savings highlighted in the 'Gershon' efficiency review and the implications of the new Race Relations Act (Amendment) and Freedom of Information Acts in relation to improving transparency in public procurement. The business community itself has become more vociferous in its demands for greater transparency in the public procurement market."

The large proportion of economic activity represented by SME's, as noted above, makes a convincing case in its own right for ensuring support for these businesses. Indeed, given their preponderance in the market it may be difficult to *avoid* contracting with them. There are, however, a number of compelling reasons why SMEs must be considered as potential suppliers in the procurement process.

Firstly, SMEs represent business start-ups and such entrepreneurs often play an important role in ensuring both that overall the economy adapts quickly to new market opportunities and that niche markets can be captured. They also drive innovation through their willingness to experiment with radical new ideas, implement innovative processes and operate new business models. A procurement organisation may therefore find that an innovative solution is more easily found by contracting with a small business.

Arguably, by contracting only with large suppliers an organisation can run the risk of the market stagnating as the number of large suppliers decreases. It could be postulated that small firms are 'closer to the action', less hamstrung by large companies' rules and procedures, quicker to respond to customers, and have an increased personalised level of service. It therefore could be said, as a result, that SMEs can often represent excellent value for money. As a large customer of a small business, the procuring organisation will enjoy considerable attention and focus on the delivery of the product or service. A good business will always focus on its key accounts - more so if that business is potentially able to make a considerable impact upon the profitability and reputation of the smaller business. If the large procuring organisation is in the public sector then as a key account it could anticipate high levels of responsiveness, service and quality as one might expect, but also in respect of conformance to sustainability criteria.

SMEs do not always win large contracts but they are very often found as sub-prime or second tier suppliers. The construction industry could not operate without such SMEs, who might be teams of labourers or specialist plant and equipment for hire. Procuring organisations ignore the second tier supplier at their peril as they may find that any challenges or problems in their major contracts are as a result of activity at lower levels. Hence it makes sense to engage in a lower tier and this will often be an SME.
The sustainability agenda means that SMEs cannot be ignored. Sustainable procurement (covered in detail in study session 13) is about the long-term view; making procurement decisions that will benefit communities,

individuals and the environment in the long term. Since SMEs represent the growth stage of businesses it could be beneficial to contract with them in order to grow the economy. SME suppliers to the public sector are enjoying access to large and stable markets which will benefit them in the long term and contribute to economic sustainability.

It could be said that opening potential markets to SMEs widens the supplier base and opens up competition. Increasing the diversity of the supplier base can only be a step towards efficiency. It is argued that an increased supplier base will lead to greater competition and better value for money.

Taken internationally, SMEs can in many ways have an even more significant part to play. The Ministry of Defence spends a considerable amount of money on equipment and services. In respect of equipment, much of the defence market for major equipment procurement is with a relatively small number of large suppliers. Within this there are a very small number of major UK suppliers and a larger number of international suppliers. However, many of the lower tier suppliers to these organisations are SMEs. The Defence Industrial Strategy (MOD, 2005) clearly identified the need to work closely with all suppliers, especially in a partnering sense. It also identified that SMEs were vital to these major defence equipment organisations (even if those major organisations were not UK companies – as long as they had a UK base and that the subcontractors for equipment projects and contracts were UK based) and of course to the well being and future of the UK economy. The situation in respect of the procurement of services for the MoD is even more reliant upon SMEs. Increasingly, with Public Private Partnerships (PPP) / Private Finance Initiatives (PFI), outsourcing in general is being brought to the forefront in respect of public sector procurement. The MoD has utilised contractors to provide a plethora of services to the defence environment. These range from the short term, such as guarding of sites, catering and cleaning; to long term support of operations (in both benign and hostile environments) around the globe, such as covering transport and delivery of materials and commodities, maintenance and support of vehicles, aircraft and ships, to training and education. All of these have provided considerable potential for SME involvement, and the claimed benefit for doing so is an enhanced efficiency and effectiveness which allows the armed forces to focus upon their core activities whilst all other activities can be undertaken by contractors. Within this SMEs become a major feature of the supply chains that deliver the required service and support.

Learning activity 12.2

Recognising the importance of SMEs to the economy, what do you think the government strategy might be for assisting SMEs?
http://www.berr.gov.uk/files/file45778.doc

Strategies for engaging SMEs in public procurement in conjunction with internal and external stakeholders

Many potential suppliers that are SME's, may be discouraged from tendering for public sector contracts because of a number of real or perceived barriers:

- Not finding out about opportunities.
- Belief that the tender process will be long and/or costly.
- Public sector contracts are growing larger and longer in order to rationalise the number of suppliers; SMEs can find the resulting contracts too large for them.
- A belief that public sector procurement officers perceive a risk in contracting with SMEs and diverse forms of business such as social enterprises.

Self assessment question 12.1
In what ways do you think that public sector procurement teams are able to assist SMEs in overcoming the real or perceived barriers mentioned above?

The OGC booklet, *Smaller supplier…better value? The value for money that small firms can offer* (OGC, 2005) is an invaluable guide to explaining the challenges faced by SMEs and the benefits that can come to the public sector by contracting with them. There is a useful checklist of considerations to be followed when devising a procurement strategy or letting a contract in order to make it "SME friendly". At the back of this particular publication is a wealth of further information and contacts including the Small Business Service (SBS) and the Social Enterprise Coalition.

Another extremely useful tool is the *Supply Chain Management Wizard* also available from the OGC website. This is an interactive tool which explains in an easy step by step manner what can be achieved at each stage of the procurement lifecycle to assist SMEs into the supply chain. It is particularly informative about the use of SMEs as sub-contractors.

Both these OGC publications are essential references and tools of which you will need to be aware and be able to apply and adapt to suit the circumstances in which you operate. Engaging SMEs may not only help you in your quest for value for money per se but also will help you to achieve sustainable procurement goals.

What has been a challenge for some time is the development of strategies for engaging SMEs in public sector procurement. The 2003 OGC Report to the Chancellor of the Exchequer entitled *Increasing Competition and Improving Long-Term Capacity Planning in the Government Market Place*, approaches for developing suppliers in the government marketplace were especially put forward. These include the following (para. 35 on the role of suppliers) as stakeholders:

"Suppliers can help the taxpayer to benefit from the actions Government takes to stimulate competition and facilitate capacity planning. Good supplier practices include:

- Proactively engaging with departments to understand their needs.
- Being realistic about their capacity and capability

and neither over-promising nor bidding in hopeless circumstances.

- Being open to the creation of consortia, the use of SMEs in the supply chain, and alternative means of working with other suppliers to provide the public sector with the most effective services and products.
- Competing fairly – in particular, not under-bidding and then exploiting contract variations to recoup losses.
- Being honest and open with departments when they spot weaknesses in procurement projects" (2003, pp.14).

The same report (2003, pp.19) lays down that "there is a widely held belief, including among suppliers, that there is a link between innovation and SMEs since in many areas SMEs are an acknowledged source of new ideas and different ways of doing things. The recommendations of the May 2003 Better Regulation Task Force and Small Business Council report *Government: Supporter or Customer'* are therefore highly relevant, in particular those relating to:

- A web portal to provide information on future contract opportunities.
- Advice and training to SMEs on selling to the public sector.
- Encouraging prime contractors to provide opportunities for SMEs.
- Simplifying or standardising pre-qualification information.
- Asking departments and other public bodies to take steps to encourage SMEs to compete for their business".

12

The *Government Procurement Code of Good Practice for Customers and Suppliers* (OGC, n.d.) sets out more fully core values and behaviours for all parts of the supply chain. The challenge is to achieve wholehearted and universal application of these principles.

The OGC acts as a conduit for two-way communication between industry and Government. Through its contacts with the CBI and other industry bodies, the OGC should be able to obtain industry's views to track progress on the issues raised in this report.

Learning activity 12.3

The OGC Checklist for engaging SMEs and achieving better value for money takes into account 4 areas – Procurement Strategy, the Procurement Process, Advertising Opportunities and the Capability and Financial Assessment. With reference to one of these areas, what is your organisation doing to encourage SMEs into the markets from which you buy? What are the areas for improvement/change in your organisation?

Identify and apply methods and procedures for engaging minority owned SMEs in public procurement e.g. Supply2.gov.uk

In recognising that SMEs can beneficially impact upon public procurement (and vice versa), it is pertinent to note that there are many in society who may in some way not have all the advantages of others. This could be broadly considered under the heading of social issues. A number of public sector initiatives (including many of those mentioned in this course book) and particularly those identified in the Level 5 course book *Machinery of Government*, indicate this; however at all stages of the procurement cycle it is possible to take cognisance of those social issues and potentially open the market place to a wider supplier base by including minority owned SMEs.

A specific approach for engaging with smaller businesses and specifically minority owned SMEs

Supply2.gov.uk (Supply to Government) is a government backed internet site that can be used by the public sector to search for lower value contracts. These lower value contracts are defined as 'typically under £100,000 (in effect contracts that would not be advertised in the OJ)' (OGC, n.d. *Tendering for Public Contracts: A Guide for Small Businesses*, pp.3). All public sector organisations are encouraged by the government to publicise their contracts on the site with the aim to open up the market especially to SMEs (but to all businesses in general) and make it easier to develop a close working relationship between the public and private sectors.

Supply2.gov.uk can be used by any small business, including those that are minority owned to search for opportunities for tendering and contracting opportunities. These may be local or within a wider geographical area.

The contracts available on the site are generally for government departments, but there may be opportunities for access to research and development contracts from the Small Business Research Initiative and for Constructionline, the government's national register of prequalified construction and construction related suppliers. This is because Constructionline and Supply2.gov assist procurement professionals by providing a link between advertised contract opportunities and a list of pre-qualified construction suppliers.

Over 2100 lower value contracts were detailed on the site upon its launch in June 2006.

Self assessment activity 12.2

Why do you think that such a site would be of interest to suppliers and what information would they find there?

This is what the site says about itself: 'Supply2.gov.uk is the first portal of call to consolidate access to lower-value opportunities from across the whole of the UK public sector. Supply2.gov.uk opens up the market to all types of business including small businesses, start-up companies and social enterprises to search and view open lower-value contract opportunities, typically under £100,000, and promote themselves to the UK public sector.

Supply2.gov.uk offers public sector buyers the opportunity to post their lower-value contract opportunities and access profiles of pre-qualification information created by suppliers registering on the site.

Objectives of the portal:

- To be seen by public sector buyers and suppliers as the 'first portal of call' for those advertising or seeking below-threshold public sector contract opportunities, typically worth under £100,000.
- To provide an easy-to-use portal uniting buyers and suppliers in a single location.
- To open up the lower-value public sector contract opportunities market to as wide a range of businesses as possible.
- To enable businesses, particularly small ones, to access central and local government's below-threshold (sub-OJEU) contract opportunities, typically worth under £100,000.
- To provide public sector buyers the opportunity to identify a wider range of potential suppliers more easily, both locally and nationally.'

The public sector accounts for around 40% of the UK's Gross Domestic Product (GDP) with central civil government alone spending £15 billion per year on goods and services. This expenditure covers almost anything from food to airplanes to uniforms and as such there are numerous areas of procurement contract opportunities available.

Below is a list provided by Supply2.gov.uk of public sector bodies who let contracts:

- Principal Government Departments
- Non Departmental Public Bodies
- English Hospital Trusts
- Strategic Health Authorities
- NHS Foundation Trusts
- Primary Care Trusts
- UK Universities

- State & Independent Primary Schools
- Secondary Schools
- Police Authorities
- Ambulance Service
- Fire Brigades
- Registered Social Landlords
- Local Authority Purchasing Departments

Not only does Supply 2gov.co.uk have the rationale of having public procurement seeking to attract enquiries just from SMEs but also the minority owned businesses. Thus in addition to the advantages already noted, there can be benefits that include providing knowledge and experience of meeting the needs of particular service users, such as disabled, ethnic minorities or a particular gender if such businesses are owned or operated by such particular groups.

Another strategy for engaging SMEs is through the prime contractor. Recommendation 9 from the BRTF/SBC report *Government: Supporter or Customer?* (2003) concerning SMEs and access to the Government Marketplace highlights that where public sector procurers opt for prime contractors, they should ensure that their business case for doing so in those particular markets brings value for money. Public sector procurers should ask prime contractors during the procurement process to demonstrate their track record in achieving value for money through effective use of their supply chain - including use of small and medium-sized enterprises. This should also be examined as part of the on-going contract management. Public sector procurement professionals should ensure that prime contractors pay subcontractors on time and that when paying progress payments to prime contractors the payments flow down through the supply chain.

"In order to make subcontracting opportunities more transparent to small and medium-sized enterprises, Government Departments and local authorities should list details of prime contractors and contracts on their websites." (taken from recommendation 9 http://archive.cabinetoffice.gov.uk/brc/government_responses/smallbusinessresponse.html)

The topic is also taken further by the following, which originates from the OGC Supply Chain Wizard (OGC, pp.6):

"Not all suppliers, particularly SMEs, are in a position to be a first tier supplier, yet there are many opportunities for them to enter the supply chain as subcontractors, especially where they can offer specialist products or services. Using your website is a key way for you to display opportunities to potential suppliers improving visibility which should encourage diversity and efficiency in the supply chain that brings good value for money. The information below is to assist the procurement function within the department when drafting information to go on the public facing website."

When using websites (or any method) for engaging SMEs in an organisations procurement activity there are several details which should be included. These are listed in the table below, as well as examples of good practice for engaging SME's through the level of detail of information that is provided to ensure that the potential access to supply chain opportunities is realised:

Information to put on your website	Why?	Example website
The name and address of your larger suppliers	This will give potential subcontractors valuable information about who they can contact about subcontracting opportunities	The Department for Constitutional Affairs gives the name and address of suppliers who have been awarded contracts: http://www.dca.gov.uk/procurement/current.htm
Details of awarded contracts	Helps potential subcontractors identify where their product, skills, services could meet your requirement	The Welsh Assembly Government shows details of awarded contracts: http://www.winningourbusiness.wales.gov.uk/fe/fe_contracts/contracts_list_awarded.asp
When the contract expires	Helps potential subcontractors plan their capacity	The Environment Agency provides a PDF document listing all current contracts and when the contracts will expire: http://www.environment-agency.gov.uk/business/444217/444285/317943/
Details of upcoming contracts	Helps potential subcontractors identify where their product, skills, services could meet your requirement	The Highways Agency provides details of forthcoming contracts http://www.highways.gov.uk/business/procure/works/index.htm

12

<table>
<tr><td>A statement inviting smaller suppliers to contact your larger suppliers</td><td>Encourages potential subcontractors to contact your larger suppliers</td><td>The Department for Constitutional Affairs actively encourages SMEs to contact their larger suppliers:
http://www.dca.gov.uk/procurement/sme.htm</td></tr>
</table>

<table>
<tr><th>Making it easier to find your information</th><th>Why?</th><th>Example website</th></tr>
<tr><td>Make your procurement pages easy to access from your homepage</td><td rowspan="4">Many public sector organisations have contract information on their websites that is buried within layers of pages and not necessarily easy to find. All of these things make it easier for suppliers to find this valuable information.</td><td>The Department of Health has a "procurement and proposals" heading on the homepage:
http://www.dh.gov.uk/Home/fs/en</td></tr>
<tr><td>If possible have a direct link from your homepage to your procurement pages</td><td>The Southampton City Council has a "selling to…" heading on the homepage:
www.southampton.gov.uk</td></tr>
<tr><td>Link your procurement pages to you're A-Z listing and search engines</td><td>The Chester City Council has 'procurement' listed under 'P' of the A-Z on their homepage:
www.chester.gov.uk
Entering "Procurement" in the Durham County Council search engine takes you to their contract information:
www.durham.gov.uk
You can search for "selling to" on the Camden Council search engine to gain access to their contract information:
www.camden.gov.uk</td></tr>
<tr><td>Signpost your opportunities by using standard words and phrases, such as: "procurement", "selling to us", "contracts" "business"</td><td>The Haringey Council uses the heading of "business"
http://www.haringey.gov.uk/index.htm</td></tr>
</table>

You should recall the earlier section on stakeholder analysis, dependency analysis, and stakeholder engagement in order to ensure that you are able to develop strategies for engaging SMEs in conjunction with stakeholders.

Learning activity 12.4
Examine and compare methods and procedures for engaging minority owned SMEs in public procurement.

Summary

Although conducting business with a larger supplier may reduce the traditional concerns of a commercial organisation's shareholders through the economies of scale available, this study session has demonstrated that this is not always the optimal approach for organisations within the public sector. It is important that SMEs be considered when it comes to awarding contracts by public sector procurement professionals, for there are several benefits they can bring to the organisation and its stakeholders; advantages which larger suppliers may not be able to bring such as:

- A greater degree of innovation
- Better understanding of the local environment where the organisation may wish to operate
- A greater ability to adjust to the requirements of the contract
- By engaging with a SME the organisation may be better at applying CSR to its procurement policies

Public procurement professionals need to develop proactive procurement strategies which enable and invigorate SMEs. Such activity takes time and care. From this session and the examples and case studies used you should have a sound perspective of the approaches that your organisation can adopt in order to develop strategies that market procurement opportunities towards SME's, and allow them to compete for procurement contracts on an equal footing with larger more visible organisations.

(If you studied the level 5 book 'Machinery of Government' you may wish to revisit (or if you have not studied that Unit, then visit) pages 241 to 242 where a succinct overview of 'Involvement of SMEs in Public Procurement' can be found).

Revision question
Critically assess the importance of SMEs to the national and local economies. Indicate ways in which SMEs can be encouraged to engage with public sector organisations.

Feedback

Feedback on learning activity 12.1

'Search for differing definitions of SMEs. There are generally one or two aspects that are quite consistent'

In the UK, sections 382 and 465 of the Companies Act 2006 define a SME for the purpose of accounting requirements. According to this, a small company is one that has a turnover of not more than £5.6 million, a balance sheet total of not more than £2.8 million and not more than 50 employees. A medium-sized company has a turnover of not more than £22.8 million, a balance sheet total of not more than £11.4 million and not more than 250 employees. It is worth noting that even within the UK this definition is not universally applied.

The British Bankers Association (BBA) embeds its own definition within the introduction of its voluntary code, The Business Banking Code (BBA, 2008). Here small business customers are defined as 'sole traders, partnerships, limited liability partnerships and limited companies with an annual turnover of under £1 million, as well as associations, charities and clubs with an annual income of under £1 million.' If the concern applying for the business account is a group of businesses, the turnover threshold applies to the combined turnover of a group of limited companies and not individual companies within the group.

The European Commission adopted Recommendation 2003/361/EC on 6th May 2003, to take effect from 1st January 2005 (published in OJ L 124 of 20.5.2003, p.36). The Commission has a third category called Micro Enterprises. A micro enterprise has a headcount of less than 10, and a turnover or balance sheet total of not more than €2 million. A small enterprise has a headcount of less than 50, and a turnover or balance sheet total of not more than €10 million. A medium-sized enterprise has a headcount of less than 250 and a turnover of not more than €50 million or a balance sheet total of not more than €43 million. The Commission considers application of this definition by Member States, the European Investment bank (EIB) and the European Investment Fund (EIF) to be an aid to improving consistency and effectiveness of policies targeting SMEs. Recommendation 2003/361/EC allowed in Article 9 for the application of the definition to be reviewed March 2006. Depending on the results, the Commission may adapt it, particularly the ceilings for turnover and balance sheet totals. No proposed alterations have been published at the time of writing this book.

An example of a SME definition from a UK public sector public procurement organisation would be:

1. Enterprises which

- have fewer than 250 employees, and
- have either,
- an annual turnover not exceeding €40 million, or
- an annual balance-sheet total not exceeding €27 million,
- conform to the criterion of independence as defined in paragraph 3.

2. Where it is necessary to distinguish between small and medium-sized enterprises, the 'small enterprise' is defined as an enterprise which:

- has fewer than 50 employees and
- has either,
  - an annual turnover not exceeding €7 million, or
  - an annual balance-sheet total not exceeding €5 million,
- conforms to the criterion of independence as defined in paragraph 3.

3. Independent enterprises are those which are not owned as to 25 % or more of the capital or the voting rights by one enterprise, or jointly by several enterprises, falling outside the definitions of an SME or a small enterprise, whichever may apply. This threshold may be exceeded in the following two cases:

- if the enterprise is held by public investment corporations, venture capital companies or institutional investors, provided no control is exercised either individually or jointly,
- if the capital is spread in such a way that it is not possible to determine by whom it is held and if the enterprise declares that it can legitimately presume that it is not owned as to 25 % or more by one enterprise, or jointly by several enterprises, falling outside the definitions of an SME or a small enterprise, whichever may apply.

These are just a few examples of how SME's can be defined. What should be clear is that there is no definitive definition which can be considered the correct one, and the aspects of consistence which can be found among several definitions are considered to be the general measures which differentiate SME from larger ones; i.e. the annual turnover in an around €50 million, and never more than 250 employees.

Feedback to learning activity 12.2

'Recognising the importance of SMEs to the economy, what do you think the government strategy might be for assisting SMEs?'

In 2004, *A Government Action Plan for Small Business* was published (Department for Trade and Industry, 2004). It formalised the Government's commitment to delivering a strategic framework for a government-wide approach to helping small businesses. That approach was built around a number of strategic themes, all designed to enhance the enterprise culture and environment and provide the conditions for more successful SMEs. The Action Plan set out the evidence base for government engagement in promoting enterprise, current and future actions within that engagement, and success measures for it. The Action Plan is available at the website of the

Department for Business Enterprise and Regulatory Reform (BERR), of which the link can be found in the further reading section below.

Work in pursuit of the Action Plan has now been completed. A summary report of activity undertaken within the strategic themes, together with an assessment of the success measures assigned to those themes, is set out in the final report on the Action Plan also available at the BERR website. You should be aware of the following from the wider European perspective:

'The "Small Business Act" for Europe is the European Commission's ambitious plan to address the needs of Europe's small and medium-sized businesses. It is a major step to make Europe more entrepreneurial and help its businesses thrive as it improves framework conditions for SMEs while taking full account of their diversity.

To elaborate this plan, the Commission worked in close cooperation with all the stakeholders, SMEs representatives, Member States, regional and local authorities and SMEs. The "Small Business Act" for Europe is the result of these joint efforts.'

Feedback to self assessment question 12.1

'In what ways for you think that public sector procurement teams may be able to assist SMEs in overcoming the real or perceived barriers mentioned above?'

Public sector procurement teams may be able to assist SMEs in overcoming obstacles by:

- Being prepared to explain the tendering process and make requirements clear and unambiguous, and avoiding jargon.
- Advertising opportunities as widely as possible and ensure that advertisements are clear and concise; and by providing a full description of the goods or services sought.
- Taking into account the nature, size and risk of specific procurements, as well as any risks associated with individual suppliers.
- Being prepared to give meaningful feedback, to successful and unsuccessful bidders, ensuring that the feedback is as helpful as possible.
- Considering using Government Procurement Card and staged payments in order to assist SMEs with cash flow.

Feedback for learning activity 12.3

'The OGC Checklist for engaging SMEs and achieving better value for money takes into account 4 areas – Procurement Strategy, the Procurement Process, Advertising Opportunities and the Capability and Financial Assessment. With reference to one of these areas, what is your organisation doing to encourage SMEs into the markets from which you buy? What are the areas for improvement/change in your organisation?'

This is a highly subjective and individual learning activity. The objective is to engage you mind in considering SMEs in a way that perhaps has not been evident to you before and perhaps has not been encouraged within your organisation (or one with which you are familiar).

The following case studies are useful. The first, the NHS, explains actions have been taken to assist their SME suppliers. The second case study, the East Midlands Centre of Excellence, focuses on the benefits achieved for all parties and groups them according to the sustainability themes of social, economic and environmental benefits.

Case Study 1 – SMEs have 20% of NHS Contracts (NHS, 2005)

'Small to medium sized enterprises (SMEs) are a critical component of the NHS supply chain and a large proportion of their business is conducted with SMEs. In 2004/5, of the 5,500 or so contracts that were awarded, approximately 1,250 were to SMEs (i.e. those businesses with less than 250 employees). The value of SME contracts exceeded £1.14 billion.

Our internal contract information management system (CIMS) is now set up in such a way that all SMEs can be identified, and each year we submit data to the Small Business Service (SBS) which feeds into their annual survey of SME success.

We have a number of ongoing initiatives to engage and support SMEs, and we have reported these in previous reports. In summary they include:

- a purchasing helpdesk to ensure we deal promptly with all enquiries
- provisions of specific guidance on any aspect of selling to the NHS, including relevant quality standards, compliance with public procurement procedures where relevant, market structure, pricing and customer requirements
- stakeholder consultation groups which include supplier representatives
- meet-the-buyer events
- production of a guide called "Selling to the NHS" and a dedicated website for suppliers

In 2004/5, we participated in a NERA Economic Consulting study for the Small Business Service (SBS) of the DTI. The study examined the benefits of public sector procurement from SMEs. We submitted four cases to the study, all of which demonstrated a particular benefit to the public sector of procuring from SMEs. The report of the study is available on the SBS website.'

Case Study 2 – East Midlands Centre of Excellence encourages SMEs by standardisation practices

During 2006/7, the East Midlands Centre of Excellence facilitated a work stream to support a Standard Documents Working Group for the region. The Group consists of local government representatives from each of the five counties, ensuring county wide buy in through feedback to local procurement forums.

The terms of reference for the working group include researching, drafting and producing a standard PQQ, Invitation to Tender, Common Tender Thresholds, Terms & Conditions and other policies using best practice examples from the public sector, avoiding re-inventing the wheel where possible.

Feedback on self assessment activity 12.2

'Why do you think that such a site would be of interest to suppliers and what information would they find there?'

Each contract notice contains a work description; the date it was put on the site; the closing date for bids; details of the organisation offering the contract; a unique reference number; and the approximate value (in pounds sterling) of the contract and contact details, including a named person. It is possible for SMEs to create a profile and put this on the supplier information data base It also provides considerable information on tendering and contract processes. (Supply2.gov.uk was developed with support from the OGC. It is managed by BiP Solutions. The services are available at www.supply2.gov.uk and www. businesslink.gov.uk).

Feedback to learning activity 12.4

'Examine and compare methods and procedures for engaging minority owned SMEs in public procurement.'

There are several methods by which an organisation can engage minority owned SMEs, many of which can be found on the web. You will recall the District of Eastington Corporate Procurement Manages' report mentioned at the start of this study session. The report discusses the method chosen by the district, that of an SME Concordat. The extract below indicates how the SME Concordat can be applied in areas and way which you will find relevant. (The link for the full copy of the report can be found under the further reading heading below):

"5. What is the SME Concordat?

5.1 A Key theme of the National Procurement Strategy; Stimulating Markets and Achieving Community Benefits; sets out the strategic objectives the council should adopt:

- Engaging actively with suppliers, and
- Use procurement to help deliver corporate objectives including the economic, social and environmental objectives set out in the Council's Community Plan.

In addition, by 2005 every council should have signed up to the national concordat for SME's.

5.2 The Small Business (SME) Friendly Concordat is a voluntary, non-statutory code of practice. The Office of the Deputy Prime Minister (ODPM), the Local Government Association (LGA) and the Small Business Service (SBS) strongly encourage all authorities to sign up to the Concordat.

5.3 The purpose of the concordat is to set out what small firms and others supplying Local Government can expect when tendering for Local Authority contracts. It is not intended that smaller suppliers automatically be given a competitive advantage when tendering for local government contracts due to the Concordat, however, there are certain steps that all contracting authorities can take to ensure that suppliers of all kinds are treated equally.

5.4 The SME Concordat represents a commitment from the council to encourage and develop appropriate levels of competition in local government markets in order to increase value for money and foster innovation, particularly from those businesses/ suppliers who may find it difficult to break into this market. These may include the following:

- ME's
- Ethnic & minority owned businesses
- Woman-owned businesses
- Social Enterprises
- Voluntary & Community organisations
- Suppliers who prefer not to use e-procurement on religious or other grounds

5.5 The National Procurement Strategy recognises that small businesses can provide best value in procurement. The Strategy therefore recommends that authorities develop diverse and competitive sources of supply and this is consistent with the spirit of Best Value legislation, which encourages authorities to develop a mixed economy of service provision. Getting the balance right is what strategic procurement is all about. The key is for the council to establish an organisational culture that exposes current service delivery models and practices to challenge."

Another good method is provided in the document *How to address Social Issues in Public Procurement'*. Within this is a diagram which summaries well the approach to engaging minority owned SMEs in public procurement and it is reproduced here:

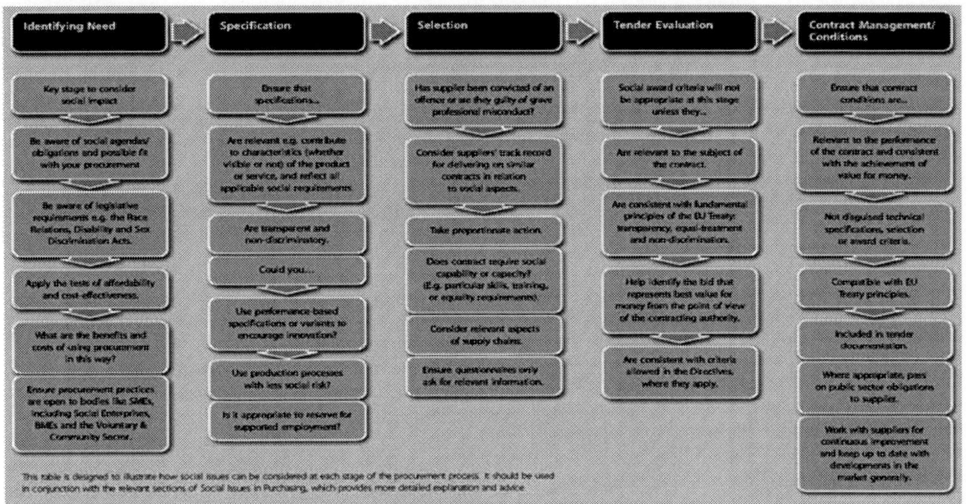

Diagram 12.1

Feedback to revision question

'Critically assess the importance of SMEs to the national and local economies. Indicate ways in which SMEs can be encouraged to engage with public sector organisations.'

There is considerable opportunity here for you to discuss the role that SMEs can play within national and local economies. You should commence by identifying the nature of SMEs and that they account for the vast majority of organisations in the UK. You should then indicate that they occupy an important position in the supply chain for many major organisations in respect of capital assets, commodities, products and services. It would be useful to provide a number of examples of each of these against a number of different public sector procurement organisations.

You should identify the importance that the government has placed on SMEs and utilised some of the information that is contained on websites such as the OGC and SBS. You should also access and refer to the UK Government's Response to the European Commission's Consultation (2008) on the EU Small Business Act (2008) which includes guidance as to how government organisations should address SMEs in its procurement strategies. These need to be balanced against a spectrum of value for money considerations that may only be possible from larger organisations. You should recall that all stakeholders need to be considered when making procurement decisions and a large organisation may be able to benefit a larger proportion of society. (As discussed earlier this is a matter of prioritisation and balance).

The methods discussed in this session, e.g. Supply2.gov.uk, the SME Condordat, and the supply chain wizard, all demonstrate what is essential to encourage an SME to engage with public sector organisations; visibility of potential procurement contracts for the SME, and visibility of the SME for the organisation. In effect it is seeking to make it easier and less daunting for SMEs to become involved in public sector procurement.

Recommended further reading

Improvement and Development Agency, (2003), Local Government Sustainable Procurement Strategy

Office of Government Commerce, (2006), Supply Chain Management Wizard

Office of Government Commerce. (2005). Smaller Supplier…Better Value? The Value of Money that Small Firms Can Offer.,

Department for Business Enterprise and Regulatory Reform (BERR): www.berr.gov.uk

SBS website: www.sbs.gov.uk

Supply2.gov.uk: www.Supply2.gov.uk

The OGC website: http://www.ogc.gov.uk/

Study session 13

"Explain how plans can be developed to take appropriate action to address the issues arising from the sustainability agenda together with internal and external stakeholders"

Introduction

This study session allows you to consider the sustainability agenda. In doing so there is opportunity to develop views on its implications for public procurement and from that how to enable effective procurement strategies in line with internal and external stakeholders. This will be considered briefly through national, regional and local agendas with opportunity for you to take into account your own position on this topic area.

Session Learning Objectives

After completing this session you should be able to:

- consider the sustainability agenda and its implications for procurement
- explain how strategies may be developed for sustainable procurement in conjunction with internal and external stakeholders
- explain the differences between local, regional and national policy agendas in relation to sustainability

Unit content coverage

This study session covers part of the following topic from the official CIPS unit documents. *'Critically evaluate the significance of CSR and 'conscience procurement' for procurement organisation, policy and procedures, internal and external stakeholders.'* Specifically, it covers: *Explain how plans can be developed to take appropriate action to address the issues arising from the sustainability agenda together with internal and external stakeholders.*

Previous Reading

Prior to this study session you should have completed study sessions 1; 2; 3; 4; 5; 6; 7; 8; 9; 10; 11.

Timing

You should take about 4 – 5 hours to read and complete this section, including learning activities, self assessment questions, the suggested further reading and the revision question.

Understand the sustainability agenda and its implications for procurement

Sustainable procurement defined

Sustainable procurement (SP) can be defined as the embedding of sustainable development (SD) considerations into public sector spending and investment decisions. SD is best described as "meeting the needs of the present without compromising the ability of future generations to meet their own needs" (UN General Assembly, 1987); with the needs being social, economic and environmental.

SP then is a process whereby organisations meet their needs for goods, assets, services, works and utilities in a way that achieves value for money on a whole life basis; whilst generating benefits not only to the organisation, but also to society and the economy, at the same time minimising damage to the environment.

Organisations which are deemed to engage in successful sustainable procurement are those which address one or all of the areas stated above. A good example can be found with an insight into Northampton County Council's standardisation of a prequalification questionnaire for conducting its procurement activity. It was found was that the standardisation had the following benefits for the community:

- Economic
  - a standard template available to all local authorities creates resource efficiencies for the authority
  - a judgement of risk and value in creating questionnaires encourages SMEs to tender and diversifies the supply base
  - reduced costs for bidders to complete questionnaires
  - a real contract opportunity for SMEs and their sub contractors
  - spin off marketing opportunities for SMEs

- Social
  - encourages organisations with social objectives
  - gives more time to prepare any supporting documentation by not asking for documentation straight away

- Environmental
  - electronic format reduces print and postage costs to authority
  - electronic submission further reduces costs of paper resources for suppliers
  - reduces storage and recycling headache for submitted prequalification questionnaires at the local authority (Sustainable Procurement Cupboard)

Considering the growing importance of the notion of corporate social responsibility (discussed earlier in study session 11) it is important that all organisations, particularly those from the public sector, engage in sustainable procurement.

Implications for procurement

The notion of sustainability in procurement was cemented as a public sector consideration with the government document, *Securing the Future* (HM Government, 2005). This paper set the ambitious goal to make the UK a leader in the EU in sustainable procurement by 2009. It created a business led task force of 33 members in 2005 with a remit to focus on environmental and sustainability dimensions of procurement and develop a National Action Plan. This was introduced earlier in study session 11 as the Simms Report. The following is the driving statement that gives direction and impetus to the sustainability agenda:

"To ensure we make rapid progress in the most effective way, the Government will appoint in Spring 2005 a business-led Sustainable Procurement Task Force to develop a national action plan for Sustainable Procurement across the public sector by April 2006. The Task Force will build on the work of other bodies active in this field, including the Sustainable Development Commission, the Sustainable Procurement Group and the Strategic Supply Chain Group" (HM Government, pp.55).

Key drivers to embed Sustainable Procurement in the public sector in particular are:

- Avoiding adverse environmental impacts arising on the government estate and supply chain
- Making more efficient use of public resources
- Stimulating the market to innovate/produce cost effective and sustainable options for all
- Demonstrating that government and the public sector is serious about sustainable development.

This will mean that public sector procurement organisations and the professionals within them, must ensure not only that these philosophies are put into effective operation within their normal activities, but also that such personnel must 'think differently' in the way that procurement is undertaken. This will necessitate advanced skill and competency. Processes and procedures must take these philosophies into account and enable optimal decision making in line with these processes and procedures, in respect of the sustainability agenda for both external and internal stakeholders.

Explain how strategies may be developed for sustainable procurement in conjunction with internal and external stakeholders

Sustainability can be incorporated into the all of the elements of the holistic (total process) view of the procurement process: defining the need, evaluating options, design and specifying, supplier selection, tender evaluation, post-contract management and supplier development; logistic support; and by utilising a through life basis of that which has been procured. This application of a 'through life' lens through which effective sustainable procurement can be optimised is fundamental to development of appropriate action plans.

Before going on to discuss the National Action Plan as the key 'driver' document for developing sustainable procurement in the public sector, it is necessary to note that what underpins the successful development and implementation of sustainable procurement strategies is the degree to which the sustainability agenda is conveyed to all stakeholders; both internal and external. Internal stakeholders will include finance and audit personnel who must recognise that value for money within the sustainability agenda may necessitate increased expenditure at various points in the decision making process. External stakeholders such as citizens must be kept informed of decisions and why certain procurement decisions are being made on their behalf especially if there may be a majority who do not necessarily agree with elements of the sustainability agenda. What will be seen is that the strategies discussed below all address the way in which the sustainable message is conveyed within the procurement environment.

In terms of public sector procurement, the National Action Plan (the production of which was a key task for the Sustainable Procurement Task Force as mentioned above) provides the best starting point for discussion for sustainable procurement strategies for it contains the recommendations through which the public sector should apply sustainability to its procurement activity. The policies and strategies discussed in the National Action Plan (and which will be discussed below) formed the basis for subsequent regional and local strategies.

It provided six recommendations (OGC, 2006 pp.26-59) which formed the philosophy behind public sector sustainable procurement. The six recommendations are:

- Lead by example
- Set clear priorities
- Raise the bar
- Build capacity
- Remove barriers
- Capture opportunities

Learning activity 13.1

Examine the Action Plan to ascertain what the OGC details as strategic approaches to be taken with each of the six recommendations listed above.

The six recommendations which make up the National Strategies philosophy are underpinned by three building blocks which were intended to provide the means to assist public sector procurement organisations make rapid progress towards introduction of the philosophy.

The 'building blocks' that have been identified can be summarised as:

a) Flexible Framework allowing assessment of the quality of procurement activity and a clear route map to better performance

b) Prioritisation of spend, utilising risk based methodology for identifying areas of spend to focus attention

c) Toolkits for delivering SP. In addition a clear identify owner for SP delivery team and the development of specialist advice and support to public sector procurers.

d) Flexible framework

The first of these building blocks is the development of a flexible framework as a roadmap to better performance. Diagram 13.1 below shows what the National Action Strategy considers the five levels of strategic procurement, measured against time and ambition:

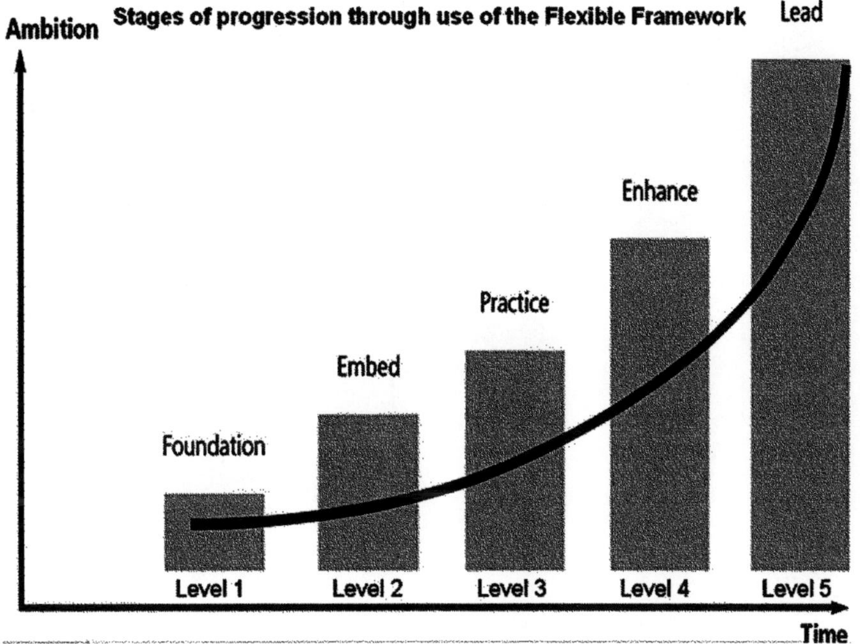

Diagram 13.1 Simms, Sir Neville (ed.), 2006, Procuring the Future – Sustainable Procurement National Action Plan: Recommendations from Sustainable Procurement Task Force

In order to develop an effective sustainable procurement strategy there are five key areas which must be address at each level. These are:

1. People
2. Policy
3. Strategy
4. Communications and procurement process and
5. engaging suppliers/measurement and results

A successful sustainable procurement strategy requires that these be addressed at each level in relation to the procurements emphasis on sustainability, with the relevant issues addressed and questions answered at each level - e.g. against 'People' in Level 1 have staff been trained in SP, or indeed is it embedded in the culture and processes etc. This structure can be scaled to a

13

particular project or procurement activity, and it allows consideration of who the stakeholders might be at each stage of the procurement process – that is of course in addition to the holistic perspective of stakeholders in the particular aim or outcome of the project or procurement activity.

Diagram 13.2 is an example of how local governments at the regional level have envisaged their flexible framework:

The Flexible Framework	Foundation – Level 1	Embedded – Level 2	Practice – Level 3	Enhanced – Level 4	Lead – Level 5
People	SP champion identified. Key procurement staffs received basic training in SP principles. SP is included as part of a key employee indication programme.	All procurement staff received basic training in SP principles. Key staff received advanced training on SP principles.	Targeted refresher training on latest SP principles. Performance objectives and appraisal include SP factors. Simple incentive programme in place.	SP included in competencies and selection criteria. SP is included as part of employee induction programme.	Achievements publicised and used to attract procurement professionals. Internal and external awards received for achievements. Focus is on benefits achieved. Good practice shared with other organisations.
Policy, Strategy and Communications	Agree overarching sustainability objectives. Simple SP policy in place endorsed by CEO. Communicate to staff and key suppliers.	Review and enhance SP policy, in particular consider supplier engagement. Ensure it is part of a wider SD strategy. Communicate to staff, suppliers and key stakeholders.	Augment the SP policy into a strategy covering risk, process integration, marketing, supplier engagement, measurement and a review process. Strategy endorsed by CEO.	Review and enhance the SP strategy, in particular recognising the potential of new Technologies. Try to link strategy to EMS and include in overall corporate strategy.	Strategy is: reviewed regularly, externally scrutinised and directly linked to organisation's EMS. The SP strategy recognised by political leaders, is communicated widely. A detailed review is undertaken to determine future priorities and a new strategy is produced beyond this framework.

Procurement Process	Expenditure analysis undertaken and key sustainability impacts identified. Key contracts start to include general sustainability criteria. Contracts awarded on the basis of value-for-money, not lowest price. Procurers adopt Quick Wins.	Detailed expenditure analysis undertaken, key sustainability risks assessed and used for prioritisation. Sustainability is considered at an early stage in the procurement process of most contracts. Whole-life-cost analysis adopted.	All contracts are assessed for general sustainability risks and management actions identified. Risks managed throughout all stages of the procurement process. Targets to improve sustainability are agreed with key suppliers.	Detailed sustainability risks assessed for high impact contracts. Project/contract sustainability governance is in place. A life-cycle approach to cost/impact assessment is applied.	Life-cycle analysis has been undertaken for key commodity areas. Sustainability KPI agreed with key suppliers. Progress is rewarded or penalised based on performance. Barriers to sustainable procurement have been removed. Best practice shared with other organisations.
Engaging Suppliers	Key supplier spend analysis undertaken and high sustainability impact suppliers identified. Key suppliers targeted for engagement and views on procurement policy sought.	Detailed supplier spend analysis undertaken. General programme of supplier engagement initiated, with senior manager involved.	Targeted supplier engagement programme in place, promoting continual sustainability improvement. Two way communication between procurer and supplier exists with incentives. Supply chains for key spend areas have been mapped.	Key suppliers targeted for intensive development. Sustainability audits and supply chain improvement programmes in place. Achievements are formally recorded. CEO involved in the supplier engagement programme.	Suppliers recognised as essential to delivery of organisation's sustainable procurement strategy. CEO engages with suppliers. Best practice shared with other/peer organisations. Suppliers recognise they must continually improve their sustainability profile to keep the clients business.

Measurement and Results	Key sustainability impacts of procurement activity have been identified.	Detailed appraisal of the sustainability impacts of the procurement activity has been undertaken. Measures implemented to manage the identified high risk impact areas.	Sustainability measures refined from general departmental measures to include individual procurers and are linked to development objectives.	Measures are integrated into a balanced score card approach reflecting both input and output. Comparison is made with peer organisations. Benefit statements have been produced.	Measures used to drive organisational SD strategy direction. Progress formally benchmarked with peer organisations. Benefits from SP are clearly evidenced. Independent audit reports available in the public domain.

Diagram 13.2 Simms, Sir Neville (ed.), 2006, Procuring the Future – Sustainable

Procurement National Action Plan: Recommendations from Sustainable Procurement Task Force

What is shown in the table is how at each stage the sustainability agenda is included into the procurement cycle via targeting the key areas so as to make the most of the potential benefits of engaging in sustainable procurement; many of which are identified in the far right column. This is by no means a definitive framework for conveying a sustainable agenda in procurement, but it is a model which has been adopted by public sector organisations at the local level. For example, the University of Gloucestershire (2006) has recently used just such a table as the basis for the implementation of their own procurement strategy.

13

The flexible framework approach also demonstrates the fundamental need to take a whole life perspective. It is an essential feature that very early consideration is made of factors that may affect the equipment or service being procured (or the stakeholders involved) many years after the actual tender and contract process. Taking action later in the product/service life cycle may be possible but if so, inevitably, it will carry very high additional costs, whether financial – which stakeholders were not expecting – or in actual SP performance, which would defeat the whole concept.

Learning activity 13.2

Analyse an organisation with which you are familiar to consider the approach that is being taken for Sustainable Procurement in conjunction with internal and external stakeholders.

b.) Prioritisation of spend

The prioritisation of spend is the second building block which the National Action Plan considers important for the implementation of effective sustainable procurement strategies. Prioritisation of spend essentially looks to determine where the money available for necessary procurement activities is best spent and in what sequence. It does this through the utilisation of the same risk based methodology (discussed in previous study sessions) which would be applicable to any procurement activity. There is a need to prioritise areas of spend (once defined) so that the organisations resources are allocated appropriately on the procurement strategies which best contribute the sustainable objective and the stakeholders involved.

The Task Force identified 10 key areas for spend:

1) Construction (building and refit, highways and local roads, operations and maintenance)
2) Health and social work (operating costs of hospitals, care homes, social care provision)
3) Food
4) Uniforms, clothing and other textiles
5) Waste
6) Pulp, paper and printing
7) Energy
8) Consumable – office machinery and computers
9) Furniture
10) Transport (business travel, motor vehicles).

These obviously represent the prioritisation of spend at the national level. Regional and local prioritisations will vary due to the differing scopes at which their procurement activities will operate.

There are several ways in which spend can be prioritised, and numerous variables to consider. As such several models have been developed, such as the sustainable procurement risk matrix (Improvement and development agency, *Sustainability and Local Government Improvement*, pp.28), although this only accommodates environmental concerns. A simple approach to prioritisation of spend could be to look at it through its risk utilisation grounding. Kraljic's 2x2 grid model for risk assessment (discussed in earlier sessions) can be used as a simple means to quickly prioritise risk as shown below in diagram 13.3:

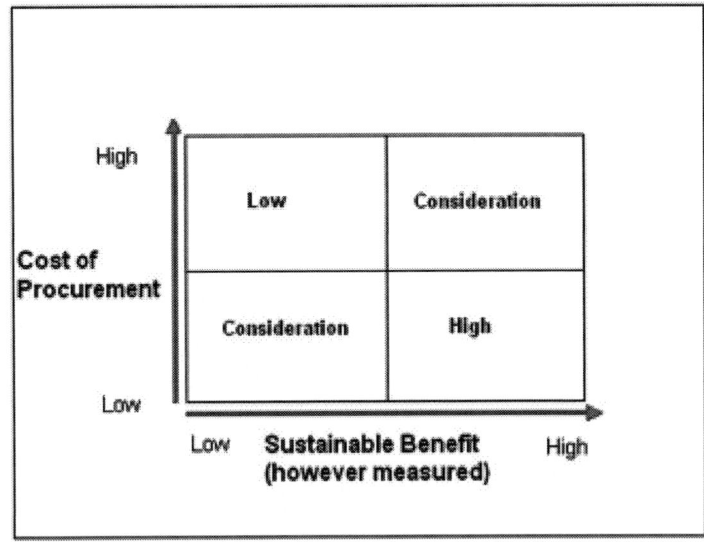

Diagram 13.3 Sustainable Benefit Davies, J; Cranfield University

Here the potential procurements can be prioritised based on their costs versus the sustainable benefit which has been chosen to measure it against, e.g. CO2 emissions, jobs created, publicity, charity's provided for etc. Though it is all well and good to measure procurements against a single benefit it is often the case that possible procurements may have different sustainable benefits to consider, and though the cost may remain the same, the potential sustainable benefit may differ depending on that which is being measured. As such a single procurement can be measured against several benefits on several graphs; and by superimposing one on top of the other a general sustainable benefit may be viewed through assessment of the correlation. This can then be compared to other procurements for a general prioritisation of spend and stakeholders. Those procurement areas of spend which fall towards the bottom right, where sustainable benefits are high against lower costs, should be a higher priority; where as those which fall closer to the top left, where costs are high and benefits low should be of lower priority.

It is easy to measure quantitative benefits on the grid, but less easy to measure qualitative benefits. As mentioned above, the grid only represents a simple conceptual means to quickly prioritise sustainable procurement spend, allowing for identification of the key stakeholders who should be of primary concern from a sustainable aspect. It must be pointed out that an area of spend should not be judged solely from the sustainable benefit derived, for there are many other variables to consider. The nature of procurement is that the organisation is essentially trying to satisfy a current or perceived future requirement, and as such the degree of urgency may take precedent.

Self assessment question 13.1

Why do you think public sector organisations should make the case for making procurement spends more sustainable?

c.) Developing toolkits to deliver sustainable procurement

The third 'building block' to consider is the means by which a more strategic approach is developed, through the development of the specific tools used by the organisation to support sustainable procurement throughout the flexible framework delivery stages. The emphasis is upon providing tools to deliver behavioural changes of the stakeholders involved in procurement to encourage a more sustainable focus; specifically the procurers, managers, specifiers and suppliers. Such toolkits will more often that not be the way in which the sustainable agenda is delivered within the flexible framework to the stakeholders. These will include training programmes, manuals and documents of guidance.

These tools will look to identify the sustainability impact of procurement activities and projects and help frame the stakeholders' requirements in a way that encourages innovative solutions into the public sector marketplace. The tools coupled with specification guidance for each priority expenditure area, delivered with training and supplemented tools will create the optimal environment for sustainable procurement to flourish within the public sector, and therefore help attain the goals for 2009 set out in the National Procurement Strategy.

At the national level many examples of toolkits and guidance have been released, though the degree of relevance to stakeholders of specific toolkits at regional and local levels will have to be assessed in respect of the contextual environment. As such individual toolkits will need to be developed along the lines of the guidance given in the National Action Plan containing:

- Getting started (using the Flexible Framework)
- Policy, strategy, targets and support systems
- Prioritisation of expenditure, risk and effort
- Promoting sustainability in specifications and tenders
- Evaluating and valuing more sustainable tenders from suppliers
- Supplier engagement, promoting sustainability in the supply chain
- Contract management and measures, ensuring sustainable outcomes are delivered

The National Action Plan (2006, pp.73-74) has identified that in order to meet its goal of the UK leading the way in sustainable procurement, then hands on support, training and advice is needed to develop teams in the centre and in regions to encourage the development of strategic toolkits to achieve national goals.

A good example of such pilot work, the tools being developed and the challenges that arise can be found with the OpenStrategy® for sustainable procurement, which addresses all of the bullet points detailed above. The *Pilot OpenStrategy® for Sustainable Procurement in the North West - Final Project Report to Defra Sustainable Procurement Task Force Secretariat* (Matthew Wilson) concluded that given insufficient time allowed and resources spent on the Pilot, the OS as the basis for the procurement strategy for the North West Region offered several benefits as a toolkit, but only if managed efficiently. As many within public sector organisations are aware, cultural change is not easy and a clear set of tools may not be enough in themselves to deliver such change for sustainable procurement.

Explain the difference between local, regional and national policy agendas in relation to sustainability

What has been discussed thus far is the approach given at the National level through the National Action Plan, although indications of how this can be applied regionally have been identified. It has already been mentioned that the purpose of the National Action Plan was to provide guidance on how sustainable procurement could be implemented throughout the whole of the public sector, with the national goals set impacting on the desired sustainable outcome related to procurement projects. In addition it was noted that the development of toolkits, whilst expecting them to be similar in many respects, will have to be tailored to reflect the conditions surrounding the individual public sector organisation; for the National Action Plan did not, nor seek to, provide a uniform strategy which could be applied across all public sector organisations.

Hence there can be a difference between local, regional and national policy agendas when it comes to sustainability which is reflected in the strategies being developed and the procurement projects being undertaken. Although subject to many variables which may create differences in sustainable procurement policy, the main reason for a noticeable change between these levels is the scope and scale of the organisations' procurement activity.

Procurements at the national (or international) level, such as that conducted by the MoD have to have policies which reflect this due to the scope and scale inherent in the type of procurement project. National level procurements have the greatest area of affect, and the sustainable benefits and detriments are felt across a greater area. As such it means that there are more stakeholders to consider, a greater degree of impact and they are of increased subjection to national and international laws.

Regional level sustainable procurement policies are likewise reflected in their scope of activity. Sustainable procurement activities at the local public sector level are subordinate to the sustainability requirement set for them to follow by their national and regional superiors. Procurement activities here may have less national impact and so there are often many less stakeholders to consider (nevertheless, at a local level the need to include stakeholder consideration, consultations and involvement may be more immediate and the effect proportionately greater). There is also a greater ability to engage with SMEs due to the reduced scale of procurement. This scale means that the benefits achieved from sustainable procurement activity is likewise reduced and the impact of individual procurements to achieve sustainability targets set diminished. All these factors can be seen to influence policies. For example, the Wealdern District Council's policy on sustainable procurement follows many of the policies set out in the national action plan, but with a greater emphasis placed on collaboration with other councils to increase the impact of its sustainable procurement activity to achieve its targets. (Sustainable Procurement Policy, pp.5)

Self assessment activity 13.2

Go on the internet and search for an example of where the considerations of the National Procurement Strategy have been implemented by a public sector organisation at the local level. How have the considerations been taken account of to attain the benefits achieved? Can you identify what such benefits were?

Learning activity 13.3

There are many examples to be found online which reflect the differing scopes of procurement activities that exist between the regional, local and national levels. Go online and see if you can find such examples.

Summary

With increasing global concerns over sustainable development a public sector procurement organisation must place greater emphasis on the sustainability agenda and its implications for its procurement activity and stakeholders. This is particularly important given the increasing focus on CSR as a whole. From studying this session you should recognise that when developing a strategy for your organisation to incorporate sustainability into its procurement process it is essential that the agenda be conveyed to as many internal stakeholders as possible, with the relevant training and guidance given; as well as actively engaging external stakeholders so that they acknowledge sustainability as an issue and can themselves adapt in line with changing requirements.

Revision Question

Discuss the nature of sustainability and its impact upon public sector procurement. Explain how relevant strategies for sustainability can be developed and provide examples of approaches to sustainable procurement at local, regional and national levels.

Feedback on learning activity 13.1

'Examine the Action Plan to ascertain what the OGC details as strategic approaches to be taken with each of the six recommendations listed above.'

'Leading by example' had the following:

- Public sector consumption
- Procurement practices can play a key role in stimulating markets
- Changing behaviour across Whitehall
- Government policies and practices
- Unfavourable or inconsistent policy signals can undermine the best efforts of Government

'Set clear priorities' had the following:

- Task Force – footprint reduction carbon, water and waste (food and timber)
- Move towards a carbon neutral, low water use, zero waste public sector
- Emissions from the production and transportation of construction materials
- Examination of supply chain

'Raise the bar':

- Government must create knowledge base on products and services
- Government must engage internationally with key markets
- Government must set mandatory minimum product/service standards for sustainable procurement
- Public and private sector industries must work together

'Build capacity' had the following:

- The benefits of this approach will be seen in better spending decisions and better procurement practice
- Benefits will accrue in government operations as well as directly through procurement

'Remove barriers' had the following:

- Create a framework to enable whole life costing
- It will lead to reduced whole life costs across the entire public sector

- Better value for money for the public purse
- Complementary rather than competing

'Capture opportunities':

- Encourage local economies and competitive advantage within the community
- Delivery to suit consumer needs
- Better performing products
- Smarter procurement leads to enhanced credibility of public sector procurement
- Opportunities for innovation and stimulation of investment in R&D

Feedback on learning activity 13.2

'Analyse an organisation with which you are familiar to consider the approach that is being taken for Sustainable Procurement in conjunction with internal and external stakeholders.'

The MoD is not necessarily the organisation that might spring to mind taking account what might have to be undertaken in respect of sustainability especially in a hostile war fighting scenario! Nevertheless, as has been noted earlier, it has a very important role as a major public sector procurement activity. For some considerable time the MoD has recognised the need to management procurement of both equipment and services on a Through Life basis. An underlying concept for consideration of this is the CADMID or CADMIT cycle. The first recognises that any equipment procurement goes through a cycle that commences with the Concept, followed by Assessment, Development, Manufacture, In service support and ultimately Disposal. The second acronym covers similar approaches with Concept, Assessment Development, followed (possibly) by Migration (from for example, in house service to outsourced contractor), In service activity, and again ultimately Termination. This type of approach is similar to many procurement organisations or activities when large complex procurement projects are being undertaken in order to enable a whole life or through life view.

If this through life view is not taken in respect of SP then success will be difficult to come by in the longer term. A feature of professionalism in public sector procurement must be the whole life perspective (arguably, this is the very essence of Value for Money considerations).

As an example of the MOD's emerging approach to SP the following bullet points are summarised from a recent (2008) presentation by Cranfield University's Dr Julieanna Powell-Turner:

- SP applies to the whole of the defence undertaking (e.g. estates, premises as well as equipment)
- MOD makes a major contribution to the UK economy through the procurement of equipment, construction, goods and services (£16 billion approximately per annum)
- The scale and manner in which the MOD undertakes procurement has an impact on its business as well as the environment

- Design and purchasing = significant influence on SP
- Considering transit of goods
- Addressing labour standards and production methods
- Reducing the use of scarce, hazardous and non renewable materials
- Specifying more efficient, waste minimising and recycling techniques
- Mechanisms for integrating the environmental purchasing policy, and other relevant SD policy requirements
- Introduce supply chain management programmes with suppliers
- Mechanisms for measuring and reporting on progress
- Commitment to undertake environmental risk assessments of contracting activity

The approach being taken details key activities, then identifies the 'owner' of those activities followed by the other stakeholders and then what actions are necessary to involve them in the key activity. This is to be undertaken for the project overall (i.e. outcomes/deliverables) and at each stage of the CADMID/ CADMIT cycle.

The MoD is committed to SP and, as indicators, would highlight as examples the following commitments: Communication Strategy to publicise SP; The creation of a sustainable procurement unit; Integrating SP policy into MoD processes; SP working group; Training and awareness of SP; Develop/ Implement environmental supply chain management programme.

Feedback to self assessment question 13.1

Why do you think public sector organisations should make the case for making procurement spends more sustainable?

The Improvement and Development Agency, in conjunction with Local Government Association and Centre of Excellence: North East in 2007 released a follow-up document to the Report of the Sustainable Procurement Task Force and the Action Plan which incorporated the Local Government Response to these documents.

In terms of local government it argues there is a compelling case for making procurement spends more sustainable:

1. The financial benefits to the council – 'where savings can be realised through the design and construction of buildings with lower through life costs, better management of demand (including re-use, recycling and standardisation) and the acquisition of products that are more efficient in there use of energy, water and mineral resources'
2. The environmental imperative – particularly in reducing CO2 emissions and the reduction of landfill waste
3. The socio-economic benefits – ranging 'from the creation of employment and training opportunities for the long term unemployed and people with disabilities to the elimination of child labour'

4. Better co-ordination of demand across local government and the wider public sector, and engagement of key suppliers at a strategic level, public purchasing power can be harnessed to stimulate product and process innovations that deliver improved environmental performance and further savings
5. Intelligent public procurement can also capture innovation from small businesses (SMEs) and third sector organisations (TSOs) while realising wider benefits for local communities. This includes the engagement of SMEs and smaller TSOs in consortium arrangements and in the supply chains for major projects. (I&DeA, 2007, Local Government Sustainable Procurement Strategy, pp.6 http://www.idea.gov.uk/idk/aio/7643299)

Feedback to learning activity 13.3

'There are many examples to be found online which reflect the differing scopes of procurement activities that exist between the regional, local and national levels. Go online and see if you can find such examples.'

The three case studies below illustrate how sustainable procurement policies have different priorities of concern given the scope to which the organization operates and the procurement covers. All the case studies below are courtesy of Department for Environment, Food and Rural Affairs (http://www.defra.gov.uk/farm/policy/sustain/procurement/casestudies/index.htm) and all concern sustainable procurement of food.

a) National level case study:

Sustainable Food Procurement Initiative - MoD increases purchase of UK meat

Case Study: MoD - increased purchase of UK meat

Region: National

Organisations: MoD's Defence Catering Group, now known as the Defence Food Services Integrated Project Team (DFS IPT) with Meat and Livestock Commission (MLC) and Purple Foodservice Solutions (PFS)

Description:
The Ministry's non-operational food supply contract is subject to the EU Public Procurement Regulations, which require advertising in the Official Journal of the European Union.

The terms of the Ministry's current food supply contract mandate PFS to give full consideration to the supply of British products where they meet the necessary contract quality specifications provide best value for money and meet the requirements for overseas supply.

The Ministry continues to work with the MLC and the Red Meat Industry

Forum to maximise the amount of British meat that can be supplied competitively. Non-UK EU pork can be up to 10 per cent cheaper than UK pork (although the price fluctuates significantly with market demand). Against an annual spend of some £2 million, savings could be realised from the purchase of non-UK pork; however, the Ministry considered the purchase of UK pork to represent better long term value because of the following points:

Benefits

- The product meets the EU processing specifications.
- The product meets the requirements necessary to export the product.
- The UK has outlawed the use of tethering stalls for sows, meeting stricter animal welfare standards.
- The security and reliability of surge supply was better guaranteed by purchasing the product for UK forces from the UK

Lessons learned during implementation

- It has been necessary to look at the long-term benefits of buying British pork over Non-UK EU pork relating to both quality and availability.
- As a result of frequent meetings between DFS IPT, the MLC and the food supply contractor, British lamb shoulder and thick rib beef have been added to a "core" list of products available to the Armed Forces.

Future developments

DSF IPT will continue to work in partnership with their food supply contractor to explore ways to increase the proportion of British meat that is supplied to UK Armed Forces. Both the Ministry and PFS remain committed to buying meat from UK sources wherever they are competitive and meet the MOD quality requirements.

What you will notice from this case study is that at the national level, there is a much greater concern over abiding by various laws and regulations due to the scale at which the sustainable procurement activity is being conducted. Due to the national scale of the procurement, the MOD is unlikely to deal with the primary suppliers or SMEs and instead the deal contract is developed with another large organisation who will deal with the primary suppliers themselves. Given the scale of the procurement, the sustainable benefits achieved from the procurement activity age going to have national implications, and as such affect a greater amount of stakeholders who may or may not have direct involvement in the deciding the procurement contract. Likewise it will be the case that there will be a greater number of variables to consider, and the implications of its procurement actions having a greater area of affect compared to regional or local level procurement activities. The scale of the procurement means that the procurement policy will reflect closely upon the strategy devised in the National Action Plan.

b) Regional level case study:

"Sustainable Food Procurement Initiative - NHS Food for Cornwall project

Case Study: NHS Food for Cornwall Project

Region: Cornwall

Organisation: NHS Trust

Description

The NHS Trusts in Cornwall have recently sanctioned a Community Food Manufacturing Study carried out by the catering team at Royal Cornwall Hospital in conjunction with Objective One. The study examined work practices, possible benefits to Cornwall and the positive impact such a scheme would have upon the social, physical and economical health of the region. The conclusion is that the long-term requirement of NHS catering within the county requires a sustainable approach to procurement and that a shared Cornwall Food Production Unit (CPFU) in a central location will assist this goal. Projects enabling sustainable development can apply for up to 50% of investment costs, providing the opportunity to establish Cornwall as an innovator and leader within the NHS.

Project time-scales

Setting-up the CFPU should take 15 months. Next is Phase Two, the capital build stage, where it is anticipated that construction will last nine months. The CFPU should be operational by September 2005, if funding is obtained. The Local Procurement model will take two years to set up, but there is an ongoing need for sustainable development and health education and the project will continue to develop, meeting the needs of future generations.

Benefits

- Maximise food quality and choice for every patient in every Cornish Healthcare property, ensuring compliance with the NHS National Plan and the Better Hospital Food initiative.

- Control food sourcing, quality and the price of our meals, enabling us to provide cheaper meals than those nationally supplied as we are a not for profit organisation.

- Reduce and recycle waste, saving money and reducing environmental damage. CFPU will also investigate new innovations, e.g. turning waste cooking oil into Bio Diesel.

- Provide a career infrastructure and development path for NHS staff, mirroring, in a small way, the 'Eden' effect, which has seen massive support for the rural economy.

- Create a positive impact on the health of the local community by providing a tailored service that caters for the personal demands of the patients.

Lessons learned during implementation

This project has yet to be implemented. A brief summary of the aims of the project are as follows:

- to work in partnership with local producers, suppliers and distributors to purchase and process a much greater percentage of our food stocks within Cornwall, for use in patient, visitor and staff meals. We recognise the synergy between the NHS and the Health Community and by aiding in the creation of a sustainable economy for Cornwall, our Trusts can have a direct impact on the social and physical well being of the clients they serve, thereby reducing patient care costs.

- to provide skilled jobs in areas of need, both in the NHS and private enterprise,;

- to encourage sustainable methods of farming and food processing, thereby safeguarding the environment. "Our Trusts recognise the importance of efficiency of procurement but are also keen to encourage local suppliers to 'bid' to supply goods and services, promoting the use of local business where this proves to be cost effective" (Royal Cornwall Hospitals NHS Trust Supply Strategy 2000).

Future developments

- Provide an Internet database of goods that the NHS uses and is interested in using. Local suppliers will be able to access this database, enabling them to compete with national contracts.

- Formulate a local procurement policy, both for ourselves and for potential suppliers. The NHS can deal with individual suppliers, but not with the small individual firm that is not able to keep pace with demand. So our policy will encourage them to join local food supply groups or co-operatives, set up by government agencies. We will share these groups and all best practice methods with other public-sector organisations, such as schools and Cornwall County Council and perhaps The Eden Project.

- Set up a Green Box Scheme for patients, visitors and staff, offering a long list of local products, such as fruit, vegetables, dairy, meat and organic produce. This aftercare service could reduce some in-patient figures and help recovery time for others.

- The local health authority or perhaps a food supply group will run the GBS, enabling the latter to sell their products directly to the consumer, having a direct and far reaching impact on the local economy."

The regional level seems to be a medium, where national sustainability policy and issues is still of concern, through there is a greater freedom to engage with SME's.

c) Local level case study:

Though when talking about sustainability the environment is usually the main reference (as will be evident from many of the case studies on the internet), the definition of sustainable procurement used at the beginning of this study session emphasises that the environmental sustainability is not the only concern. This case study (courtesy of the Department for Environment, Food and Rural Affairs, 2005) is an example of procurement at the local level address a social, economical and environmental sustainability issue. When reading the case study you should note the case study addresses issues at an individual, relatively more personal level. This reflects the scope of the procurement activity which allows for a reduced number of sustainability concerns relative to the procurement activity.

"Case Study: North Cerney Primary School

Region: Gloucestershire

Organisation: School and local Pub/Restaurant

Description: The governors of North Cerney Primary School decided in October 2004 to opt out of the LEA lunches contract and 'go it alone'. They approached the Bathurst Arms, the highly acclaimed public house and restaurant in the same village, about working with the school to improve the pupils' lunchtime experience.

Headteacher, Bridget Goodrich, says, "lunchtime is an opportunity for the children to experience a family meal with healthy 'home' cooked food. We want this part of the day to be as meaningful as the rest of the curriculum. The Bathurst Arms have designed a tasty menu, based around simple, locally produced food. We will extend the range of dishes as the pupils' tastes grow and change. We hope that the enjoyment of eating freshly prepared, healthy food will stay with them into secondary school and on into adulthood."

Benefits

- Fresh local produce is used wherever possible, helping to support the local economy
- The children are being involved and educated in the daily preparation of food
- The lunchtime experience is now part of the curriculum
- The children are becoming more aware of the benefits of eating a healthy and nutritionally balanced diet which it is hoped they will carry through into adulthood

- Pupils enjoy eating their lunch in a family environment, which builds on the strong sense of community that already exists within the school.

Lessons learned during implementation

This exciting new venture shows what can be done by governors and heads with the support of parents and pupils.

The enthusiastic approach to the project has worked, all school lunches are now prepared by the Bathurst Arms, using fresh locally sourced produce as much as possible. And all at no extra cost!

Future developments

In addition to the new lunches it is also hoped that the children will be able to see for themselves how the food is produced and to practice preparing their own lunch in a professional kitchen at least once every term.

The local level of the public organisation allows the procurement activity to engage more easily with SMEs (discussed in study session 12) which because of their small scale operation often allow for a more sustainable operation through being more in tune with the area and local sustainability issues. Local authorities are less likely to be subject to legal challenges than by their regional and national counterparts (particularly given the filtration of leadership.

Self assessment activity 13.2

'Go on the internet and search for an example of where the considerations of the National Procurement Strategy have been implemented by a public sector organisation at the local level. How have the considerations been taken account of to attain the benefits achieved? Can you identify what such benefits were?'

There are many examples to be found on the internet. One such example is the Brighton and Hove City Council procurement of 'the bike's the business'.

The following is a good example of public sector procurement project acting inline with the recommendations set out by the National Action Plan. Brighton and Hove City Council operates an in-house currier and postal service. In 2005 a vacancy arose where the council decided to procure the services of 'the bike's the business', a local business co-operative which provided pedal based bike couriers across the city. Procuring these services provided several sustainable development benefits:

- Reduced CO2 emissions – pedal bikes create no C02 emissions, and further helped reduce congestion on the roads
- Supported the development of a small, local, environmentally friendly business – contract allowed the business to expand, taking on a further 6 contracts
- Showed the council demonstrating community leadership – the nature of the service is highly visible to the constituents of the council, something not lost on its leader.

Procuring this contract helped assist the council meet the sustainable development targets identified in the National Procurement Strategy of 2006. http://www.sd-commission.org.uk/communitiessummit/show_case_study.php/00194.html . This is a good example of the national and regional strategies being applied at the local level.

Feedback to revision question

'Discuss the nature of sustainability and its impact upon public sector procurement. Explain how relevant strategies for sustainability can be developed and provide examples of approaches to sustainable procurement at local, regional and national levels.'

This is a rapidly developing topic area so you should be sure to keep yourself up to date. Initially you should develop a discussion around key points of: socio-economic and environmental benefits of sustainability; the adverse effects of not adopting sustainable procurement; stimulation of the marketplace for sustainable options / products / services; demonstrable commitment from all sectors of government to sustainable development. This means that procurement professionals will have to 'think differently' about their skills and approaches to decision making, centred upon a holistic 'through life' approach to procurement. In turn this will require action against the six recommendations of:

- Lead by example
- Clear priorities
- Raising the bar
- Building capacity
- Remove barriers
- Capture opportunities

This should be followed by the three 'building blocks' of 'Flexible frameworks; Prioritising spend; Toolkits for delivery of sustainable procurement. This latter point is particularly relevant because there is a danger of much rhetoric and little action if organisations are not motivated.

There is considerable scope to explain the details of (e.g.) the National Action Plan and to provide practical examples of the areas for prioritisation such as construction, health and social work, food etc. From here you should be able to provide a number of examples at local, regional and national level of plans for developing appropriate action in respect of SP. The text here both in the main body of study session 13 and in the feedback to activities and questions will provide a range of good examples (e.g. north west region – defra; Wealdren District Council; MOD; Welsh Assembly Government; Cornwall NHS Trust; Gloucester Local Education Authority etc) although you should also examine the web in order to keep up to date with developments.

Recommended further reading

HM Government., 2005, Securing the Future: The UK Government Sustainable Development Strategy, (Cm. 6467) London: HMSO

Simms, Sir Neville (ed.), 2006, Procuring the Future – Sustainable Procurement National Action Plan: Recommendations from Sustainable Procurement Task Force [Online] Department for the Environment, Food and Rural Affairs. Available at: http://www.defra.gov.u k/sustainable/government/publications/procurement-action-plan/documents/full-document.pdf

Office of the Deputy Prime Minister., 2003, National Procurement Strategy For Local Government. [Online] ODPM, Available at: http://www.rce.gov.uk/rce/aio/10209

Study session 14

"Critically evaluate relevant theories, models, policy documents and practice in relation to Governance arrangements for procurement, particularly in relation to the role of elected representatives"

Introduction

In this study session, you will examine the key themes around the topic of governance in the public domain and apply the principles within a procurement context. Public 'Governance' is different from 'Public Management' and this distinction will be documented here. Strong democratic public governance and accountability are increasingly important. Procurement itself has also gained much in profile and importance over the past few years, albeit more on the grounds of cost reduction and benefits realisation especially in respect of relationships between buying and supplying organisations. It is therefore important to take a fresh look at the interaction between public accountability, democracy, governance and the practice of procurement in public sector organisations.

Session learning objectives

After completing this session you should be able to:

- define governance
- analyse the nature of a typical governance structure in a large public sector organisation
- assess the role of internal and external stakeholders in the governance of procurement

Unit content coverage

This study session covers part of the following topic from the official CIPS unit content documents: *Analyse the effectiveness of Governance and oversight arrangements for procurement*. Specifically it covers the first element of: *Critically evaluate relevant theories, models, policy documents and practice in relation to Governance arrangements for procurement, particularly in relation to the role of elected representatives.*

Prior knowledge

Prior to this study session you should have completed study sessions 1; 2; 3; 4; 5; 6; 7; 8; 9; 10; 11; 12; 13.

Timing

You should take about 4 – 5 hours to read and complete this section, including learning activities, self-assessment questions, the suggested further reading, and the revision question.

Definition of governance

A particularly useful text in respect of governance is *Public Management and Governance* (2003) edited by Tony Bovaird and Elke Loffler. You should read this book thoroughly, as it is relevant and addresses all elements of this study session . Bovaird and Loffler (2003, pp.6) offer up a number of definitions of 'governance'. One of these that would fit into the context of this course book is: Governance is "the way in which stakeholders interact with each other in order to influence the outcomes of policies".

> "It is time for the world, the hemisphere and the region to make sure that relevant institutions of civil society and relevant laws are embedded in the mechanisms of governance."
>
> **Baldwin Spencer**

This is a reasonable definition, but it does not convey any form of formal structure to the governance – in fact, it seems to suggest an informal, almost unstructured approach which is not how governance evolves. Governance is not *government*, so that distinction needs to be clearly made.

It might be more useful to adopt as standard the definition of the British Council, which also emphasises that "governance" is a broader notion than government (and for that matter also related concepts like the state, good government and regime), and goes on to posit: "Governance involves interaction between the formal institutions and those in civil society. Governance refers to a process whereby elements in society wield power, authority and influence and enact policies and decisions concerning public life and social upliftment" (Quotation was taken from the British Council Website: www.britcoun.org/governance/ukpgov.html, before it was redesigned to http://www.britishcouncil.org/new/).

This seems to be a more structured definition, and allows for some sort of hierarchical approach to delivering governance, rather that it purely being a case of happenstance.

Neither is governance public management, which Bovaird and Loffler (2003, pp.5) clearly differentiate. They define public management as "an approach which uses managerial techniques (often originating in the private sector) to increase value for money achieved by public services." The two obviously inter-relate, and it would seem logical to presuppose that governance would drive public management, not the other way round.

Terms of reference for the governance of a typical public sector organisation

Below are the terms of reference of the Board of the West Midlands Police Authority (2008). The Board is made up of elected members from all of the authorities in the Force's operational area. It is a good and practical example of the governance arrangements for a large emergency service.

- "To monitor and review the financial strategies for the force and Authority

- To monitor and review the force strategies and major projects for ICT
- To ensure that the Authority's Standing Orders relating to controls and financial regulations are followed
- To oversee value for money and use of resources issues, including activity based costing and activity analysis
- To monitor and review income generation and sponsorship
- To recommend revisions to the approved capital budget and programme to the Authority
- To monitor revenue budgets both corporate and devolved
- To monitor and review the provision of corporate services other than those falling within the terms of reference of the Personnel Committee
- To monitor revenue and capital expenditure, including:
- Oversight of the estates/property strategy
- ICT projects
- Oversight of procurement
- To monitor the implementation of the efficiency plan
- To monitor e-government issues
- To have due regard, in exercising its responsibilities, to equal opportunities generally and the requirements of all equalities and anti-discrimination legislation, including implementation of the equalities schemes of both the Authority and force
- To have due regard, in exercising its responsibilities, to risk issues generally and the specific risk issues contained within the force and Authority risk registers
- To consider any other matters deemed relevant to these terms of reference"

You can see how great a responsibility it is for elected members to execute these tasks efficiently, and how heavily they rely on the Chief Constable and his or her senior management team for accurate information and recommendations to govern efficiently and effectively.

Learning activity 14.1
Using your own organisation as the example, identify from the above terms of reference the six most important governance activities and explain why you think these so important.

Self-assessment question 14.1

Can you think of any other governance activities undertaken in your own organisation (or one with which you are familiar) that are missing from the West Midlands Police Authority's Terms of Reference list of activities?

The need for strong governance for procurement

"Make yourself an honest man, and then you may be sure there is one less rascal in the world."

Thomas Carlyle

Consider the following article, which appeared in a Public Service bulletin on 18 April 2008:

"Councils were in on the con, says bidder *Friday, April 18, 2008*

Rather than being tricked by construction companies into spending more public money than necessary, local authorities have actually been involved in rigging bids, according to one company which the Office of Fair Trading had named as an offender.

The company said public and private buyers of their services had wanted to pretend that competitive bidding had taken place when in fact there was nothing of the sort.

Admitting that contractors colluded, one company representative said: "Clients like to see a few names in the frame when a project comes up. You'd chat with another bidder, find out what it was pricing at, and go in far enough over the top to make sure you didn't win."

But Mark Denman of T Denman & Sons (Melton Mowbray) said the direction often came from the buyer: "Clients (including those in the public sector) have been known to specifically request a cover price where their initial inquiries had produced insufficient response, in their own attempt to show competition. Our company, and indeed the majority of those affected by this investigation, has simply engaged in what was accepted as standard industry practice." Denman claimed that when he realised what was happening was illegal, his company stopped doing it.

The Construction Confederation's Stephen Ratcliffe defended the construction companies, saying: "The only motive was to avoid doing the work but stay on tender lists and there was no intention to make a single penny at the taxpayers' expense."

But the chairman of the Local Government Association Sir Simon Milton, said there were no excuses for collusion, bid

> rigging or cover pricing.
>
> "It will come as a shock to residents that some construction companies have rigged bids for contracts at the taxpayers' cost," he said. "Local authorities strive to ensure that any new building which they pay for is delivered at the best value for the taxpayer, but it appears that some firms have failed to abide by the law. Firms that are found to have colluded to inflate prices should not only have to apologise to the public but also should consider giving money back to local areas where this alleged activity has taken place."

Stephen Ratcliffe is surely defending the indefensible when he comments that "The only motive was to avoid doing the work but stay on tender lists and there was no intention to make a single penny at the taxpayers' expense." It could be said to be unusual, if not even bizarre, to go through a costly tendering process in order to bid so high that one has no chance of being awarded a contract.

A firm surely then gains for itself the unenviable reputation of being rather too expensive to be awarded work, and that might well mitigate against its chances of success in the future. His whole stance has a hollow ring about it, and the Office of Fair Trading is currently investigating dozens of blue-chip construction firms over allegations of collusion and price-fixing.

What is worse is that there appears to be some evidence that public sector buyers are 'conniving' with the price-fixing rings to accept higher prices. This can be seen as considerable abuse of their positions of trust and power, and likely to lead to fraud charges and perhaps even a 'spell behind bars'! Courts do not like buyers in the public sector abusing their power.

One has to ask the questions: What happened to the governance of those contracting authorities that enabled public sector buyers to collude in the first place? Where were the controls? Where were the checks and balances? The audit reviews? The reportage?

This is why, apart from giving leadership and strategic direction, strong governance is essential; to assist in eradicating fraud and sharp practices from both buyers and suppliers.

Learning activity 14.2

What are the main obstacles to achieving good procurement governance in a public sector organisation?

Self-assessment question 14.2

How do the governance arrangements in your organisation (or one with which you are familiar) ensure that procurement staff are prevented from engaging in collusive arrangements with suppliers?

Role of internal and external stakeholders in governance

"Laws control the lesser man... Right conduct controls the greater one."

Mark Twain

This is suitably explained by means of Diagram 14.1, which has been published by Cornwall County Council, but is typical of many progressive (in terms of procurement) public sector organisations:

PROCUREMENT GOVERNANCE

ELECTED MEMBERS

Procurement champion
Executive
Policy Development and Scrutiny

- Approve corporate procurement strategy
- Approve communications strategy
- Agree performance indicators

PROCUREMENT BOARD
(clearing-house for procurement decision-making)

Chaired by Chief Executive

Member Procurement Champion

Chief Officer with responsibility for procurement

Chief Officers

Head of Procurement

Head of Legal Services

- Agree corporate procurement strategy
- Set performance indicators
- Agree work programmes
- Accountable for delivery
- Agree communications strategy
- Ensure procurement capacity and capability
- Set standards for procurement
- Consider gateway reviews

PROCUREMENT PROJECT TEAM

Chaired by Senior Procurement Officer

Lead departmental procurement officers

Cross-departmental and stakeholder representatives

- Devise specific cross-functional comms and training strategy
- Agree individual procurements over specified value
- Consider project initiation documents
- Monitor programme delivery

Figure 14.1 Cornwall County Council, 2005, Corporate Procurement Strategy 2005-2008, pp.16

The Cornwall model is a practical one, and you can clearly see the hierarchical structure of the governance arrangements. At the top is the Cabinet, the ruling cabal of elected members, normally all from the ruling party (except in Scotland, where proportional representation has created a number of previously thought unlikely alliances, such as the Liberal Democrat/SNP alliance in Edinburgh, with the Liberal Democrat Lord Provost having the casting vote in a 'hung' council).

One of the members is a procurement 'champion' – he or she has the cabinet responsibility for procurement strategy. There is a scrutiny process in place here, at which opposition councillors can scrutinise decisions of the Executive and perhaps have some of the detail (though not key imperatives) changed.

The procurement board is chaired by the Chief Executive, which gives corporate 'buy-in' at the very top of the organisation and the Board is bolstered by the attendance of the Member champion, who can represent the Board's views to the Executive.

Increasingly, the status of the procurement manager is vested at a chief officer level and the term 'Head of Procurement' is now commonplace, identifying his or her strategic, rather than tactical, role in the organisation.

Under the Board is a procurement project team, and this is interesting. It is responsible for deciding 'the route to market' for every framework contract and procurement project over a certain value (perhaps the EU threshold over which the full rigour of the EU regulations will apply).

The 'objectives' boxes on the right of the chart also delineate the hierarchical importance of the tasks, from the approval of the procurement strategy at Cabinet level to the workaday monitoring of the delivery of the work programme at project team level.

This model will be familiar to procurement professionals working in the NHS, in central government and in many local authorities. It is certainly the aspirational model for those public sector organisations that have no clearly defined procurement governance structure, such as many in the third sector.

It remains to be seen how the latest category management models, which place category managers at the head of all expenditure relating to the category each commands, will sit with procurement governance structures. (This is increasingly being adopted within the Ministry of Defence for example, which is taking a careful integration of all activities involved in ensuring optimal procurement decision making in line with good governance philosophies). There is however a discussion within local authority procurement functions as to whether a general set of governance rules and obligations can be applies universally. The Cornwall model shows only a few of the Board's main responsibilities. Others are:

- Ensure effective corporate contract planning and timetabling
- Provide a challenge mechanism at the very start of a procurement process
- Consider business cases, 'route to market' strategies, budgets and resources, prior to tendering
- Supervise and sign off all contract award reportage
- Gate-keep all contracting activities
- Improve corporate procurement
- Provide a networking opportunity on procurement issues, sharing ideologies
- Facilitate the development of policy
- Monitor legality and probity of contracts
- Act as the lead for integrated procurement (and P2P) processes across the council.

Learning activity 14.3

What in your opinion are the key areas of skills and knowledge which need to be developed by those in charge of governance arrangements for procurement?

Self-assessment question 14.3

Create your own model for procurement governance in your own organisation or another with which you are familiar. Try and stay as close to the Cornwall paradigm as possible and put in the same information as is contained in that model. Do not simply replicate the Cornwall model. Outline the reasons behind the differences between your model and that of Cornwall.

Summary

From this study session you should have a clear idea of the difference between public governance and public management. In looking at the difference it should be clear that there is a need for strong governance when it comes to procurement activities, especially in key areas of resource and supplier management. Despite the need for strong governance, it is evident that some government arrangements still do not capture and root out collusion between buyers and suppliers. Methods such as dedicating a specific 'procurement champion' will help to encourage good governance and alleviate potential problem areas before and as they arise. It is much easier to identify such problems, and those stakeholders responsible for them (e.g. the board) through the use of models that display the roles and activities of internal and external stakeholders in terms of procurement governance such as in the large public sector organisation example used above.

Revision question

Assess the political and economic importance of effective procurement governance in the public sector in terms of its value and contribution to an organisation's corporate objectives.

Feedback

Feedback on learning activity 14.1

'Using your own organisation as the example, identify from the above terms of reference the six most important governance activities and explain why you think these so important.'

There are no 'right' and 'wrong' answers here, because all of these activities are important. However, those that have corporate strategy at its core, or the use and allocation of resources, might be deemed to be more important than those that do not. Where to place procurement governance? Procurement is about handling resources effectively and efficiently, so that you might consider that to be important enough to be in your top six. Enforcing standing orders on the other hand, whilst important, is operational rather than strategic and perhaps should be left to officers and senior managements to handle, rather than those at the head of governance, so perhaps that would not make your top six. One way of rationalising your approach would be to build a simple matrix, outline each activity and rank it 'high', 'medium' or 'low' in terms of its importance to the achievement of Best Value and corporate strategic objectives. If you finish with eight 'highs', say, compare and contrast them and decide which is of greater importance to get your number down to six.

Feedback on self-assessment question 14.1

'Can you think of any other governance activities undertaken in your own organisation (or one with which you are familiar) that are missing from the West Midlands Police Authority's Terms of Reference list of activities?'

You have a wide choice here. Many organisations post their terms of reference on their website, so they can be viewed by stakeholders and customers alike. The West Midlands Police model is a fairly simple one. Some are more complex and are laid out differently, such as the example below which is divided into nine sections:

1. Introduction
2. Interpretation
3. Membership and attendance of Board
4. Frequency of Meetings
5. Authority
6. Duties
7. Reporting arrangements
8. Review procedures for terms of reference
9. Items not covered

You should easily be able to select a range of terms of reference and compare them with the Police model.

Feedback on learning activity 14.2

'What are the main obstacles to achieving good procurement governance in a public sector organisation?'

The bullet-points below describe some of the key factors:

- Lack of executive sponsorship from key stakeholders and managers
- Resistance from suppliers
- Non co-operation from departments
- Poor ICT systems and use of ICT for management information
- Lack of integration between e-procurement systems and legacy systems leading to information gaps and inefficiencies
- Lack of technology support from IT department/provider
- Lack of ability to provide useful analytical information
- Poor quality of data
- Lack of employee training/motivation

- Lack of clarity in governance model
- Lack of resources/time pressures to incorporate all governance requirements
- Fragmentation of procurement process leading to split responsibilities and buck-passing
- Complexity of procurement function and the governance arrangements.

Feedback on self-assessment question 14.2

'How do the governance arrangements in your organisation (or one with which you are familiar) ensure that procurement staff are prevented from engaging in collusive arrangements with suppliers?'

The following is from a report by HM Treasury into *Managing the Risk of Fraud* (2003, pp10):

'Collusion in procurement is just one of many risks an organisation faces. Risk, in the context of managing collusion risk in procurement, is the vulnerability or exposure an organisation has towards collusion and irregularity. It combines the probability of collusion in procurement occurring and the corresponding impact measured in monetary terms. Preventive controls and the right type of corporate culture will tend to reduce the likelihood of collusion occurring while detective controls and effective contingency planning will reduce the size of any losses.'

'In organisations where the risk of collusion is known to be high, a separate specific collusion risk assessment may be appropriate. Where the risk of collusion is considered to be low, a specific collusion risk assessment may be not be necessary, with any risks being considered instead as part of the organisation's overall assessment of risk.'

'A risk-based approach enables organisations to target their resources, both for improving controls and for pro-active detection in vulnerable areas. Managing the risk of collusion should be embedded in the entirety of an organisation's risk, control and governance procedures.

In broad terms managing the risk of collusion in procurement involves:

- Assessing the organisation's overall vulnerability to collusion;
- Identifying the areas most vulnerable to collusion;
- Assigning ownership or allocating responsibility for the overall management of collusion risk and the management of anti-collusion activities;
- Evaluating the scale of collusion risk;
- Responding to the risk of collusion; and
- Measuring the effectiveness of the collusion risk strategy.'

Feedback on learning activity 14.3

'What in your opinion are the key areas of skills and knowledge which need to be developed by those in charge of governance arrangements for procurement?'

The following are some of the key skills, knowledge and competencies required by those in charge of procurement governance:

- Technical aspects of procurement: sourcing and procurement strategies;
- Management of supplier relationships, programmes and projects;
- Customer services;
- Quality management, assurance, standards and compliance;
- Health and safety assessment;
- Asset management;
- IT systems, emerging technologies, architecture; IT co-ordination;
- Client services management (commercial management);
- Professional development;
- Resourcing;
- Financial management;
- Change management;
- Organisational behaviours;
- Business analysis;
- Communications strategy;
- Risk assessment and risk management;
- Business continuity management

The list is not exhaustive and you should spend time defining other key skills and competencies.

Feedback on self-assessment question 14.3

'Create your own model for procurement governance in your own organisation or another with which you are familiar. Try and stay as close to the Cornwall paradigm as possible and put in the same information as is contained in that model. Do not simply replicate the Cornwall model. Outline the reasons behind the differences between your model and that of Cornwall.'

It should be easy to find other examples of procurement governance models. They all share the same key characteristics, but some are laid out in a slightly more complicated way than Cornwall's model. Please bear in mind that such a governance model can also be used for one-off capital projects which still require governance. The following characteristics are somewhat different to the Cornwall model:

- At the highest level, the board of governance and their responsibilities
- Role of the chief executive or project sponsor
- Transformation board, if one is required
- Status and role of 'senior responsible owner' or project manager
- Any scrutiny arrangements (a scrutiny panel)
- Stakeholder groups, internal and external
- Stakeholder advisory board, if one exists
- Governance team
- Internal and external advisors
- Peer review arrangements (if necessary)

Feedback on revision question

'Assess the political and economic importance of effective procurement governance in the public sector in terms of its value and contribution to an organisation's corporate objectives.'

This is a wide-ranging question and you can introduce quite a few concepts into your answer. The political and economic impact of sound procurement governance might be defined in terms of contribution to the achievement of corporate strategy and policy, as well as broader goals of service improvement, innovation of business processes, benefits realisation, procurement cost reductions, sustainability (in its broadest sense, not just environmental sustainability) efficiency and effectiveness of procurement. Political impact may additionally be defined in terms of increased involvement of procurement with elected representatives on developing and implementing corporate policy and strategy.

Suggested further reading

Tony Bovaird, and Elke Loffler, Public Management and Governance (eds), (2003), ch. 1, 2. 5, 7, 8, 9, 10, 11, 12, 13, 14, 15, 17.

Gerry Johnson, and Kevan Scholes, (eds) (2001), Exploring Public Sector Strategy, ch. 1, 7, 11, 12, 13, 16, 17.

Cabinet Office e-government 2005 conference papers http://archive.cabinetoffice.gov.uk/egov2005conference/documents/proceedings/pdf/051125ps7_public_sector_procurement.pdf

Cornwall County Council Procurement Governance model http://www.cornwall.gov.uk/index.cfm?articleid=14109

HM Treasury., 2003., Managing the Risk of Fraud: A Guide for Managers,. [Online] HM Treasury., Available at: http://64.233.183.104/search?q=cache:oNfbAOIHKNUJ:www.hm-treasury.gov.uk/media/2/8/Managing_the_risk_fraud.pdf+A+risk-based+approach+enables+organisations+to+target+their+resources,+both+for+improving+controls+and+for+pro-active&hl=en&ct=clnk&cd=1&gl=uk

North East Essex NHS Primary Care Trust Procurement Policy

Study session 15

"Critically evaluate the effectiveness of the provision of financial accountability arrangements for procurement"

Introduction

In this study session, you will examine the role of elected (rather than appointed) representatives, which are a key catalyst of governance as they are at the forefront of political decision-making and governance, and their decisions affect significantly the procurement process. Especially in local authorities, elected members (councillors) are often 'bothered and bewildered' about the approaches to procurement and their political imperatives do not necessarily follow the path of procurement best practice. You will learn that a rigorous set of standing orders in any public sector organisation, especially local government, is a pre-requisite and that suppliers are becoming ever bolder under the 'Alcatel' ruling (ECJ, 1999) in challenging contract award decisions because contracting authorities have not applied the principles of EU procurement legislation to the letter.

Session learning objectives

After completing this session you should be able to:

- assess the roles of elected representatives at national, regional and local levels in oversight arrangements for procurement
- assess the effectiveness of the provision of advice and guidance for ministers, council leaders, key decision-makers and committee members
- analyse the effectiveness of governance arrangements for procurement
- consider and demonstrate the impact on a public sector body of poor governance in regard to contract award decisions.

Unit content coverage

This study session covers part of the following topic from the official CIPS unit content documents: *Analyse the effectiveness of Governance and oversight arrangements for procurement*. Specifically it covers the remaining elements of: *Critically evaluate relevant theories, models, policy documents and practice in relation to Governance arrangements for procurement, particularly in relation to the role of elected representatives*.

Prior knowledge

Prior to this study session you should have completed study sessions1; 2; 3; 4; 5; 6; 7; 8; 9; 10; 11; 12; 13; 14.

Timing

You should take about 5 hours to read and complete this section, including learning activities, self-assessment questions, the suggested further reading, and the revision question.

The role of elected representatives in governance

"Public service must be more than doing a job efficiently and honestly. It must be a complete dedication to the people and to the nation."

Margaret Chase Smith

As governance becomes increasingly complex, elected officials are confronted with challenging issues relating to the financial stability, health, and welfare of their communities. Learning to govern efficiently, ethically, and wisely requires considerable time, effort, and education on their part. Andrew Erridge (2007), says that the 'political process is a representative democracy, based upon the role of elected representatives, in particular MP's (and MSP's in Scotland and AM's in Wales) and elected members.'

Erridge believes that the emergence of best value as a legislative requirement on councils makes it ever more important that the governance process is subject to 'enhanced democratic oversight of procurement,' which places the spotlight fairly and squarely on elected representatives at all levels. He refers to the 'seven principles of public life' (Nolan, 1995) which he describes as directly relevant to procurement. They are:

- **Selflessness** (decisions taken purely in the public interest)
- **Integrity** (no obligation to any outside individual or organisation)
- **Objectivity** (making choices purely on merit)
- **Accountability** (subject to public scrutiny)
- **Openness** (Giving reasons for all decisions)
- **Honesty** (avoidance of conflicts of interest and declarations of private interests).
- **Leadership** (promote these principles by example).

Refusal to accept the corporate decision might lead to his or her expulsion from the party, or the loss of an influential cabinet post which means that the elected member cannot influence for the good in the future a raft of other major political procurement decisions. It is difficult to qualify 'honesty', but there must be some degrees of it, or party political life is impossible.

Learning Activity 15.1

Can you identify any projects in which elected leaders have failed to achieve the Nolan ideal? Discuss which of the seven principles were lacking.

Effectiveness of advice to procurement leaders in the public sector

During 2006, the celebrated former civil servant Sir Michael Bichard, gave a speech to the Centre for Excellence in Leadership which gave pertinent advice on the effectiveness, or otherwise, of the public sector in engaging with its leaders and ensuring that there was a two-way flow of dialogue, between leader and those being led, that ensured optimal delivery of whatever project was the subject of the dialogue.

Self-assessment question 15.1

Examine Nolan's 'seven principles' and see where these might militate against the achievement of Best Value in procurement contracts.

Sir Michael highlighted a few key areas where improvements needed to be made, both at the leadership end of the spectrum and the organisational end. He spoke about the need for 'a single unified public service' but realised that such a feat was impossible. He therefore argued that the direction of travel should be towards a single public service, which would include the civil service and all public sector organisations.

Sir Michael (2006, pp.2) railed against some public sector organisations (and their political leaders) because they 'work against the interests of consumers because they exist to protect the interests of their members and fail to redesign services to meet the real needs of clients.' This could be seen as a damning indictment, and by definition, procurement must be implicated here, because, in Sir Michael's view, it is failing to pass on to the leaders innovative ideas and practices which could transform an organisation's service to customers. In a way, procurement is 'the eyes and ears of the business' because it has such a wide role to play in moving the business forward, so it is perhaps concomitant on procurement to be the 'dynamic for change.'

Sir Michael was also scathing in his condemnation of the hubris of the civil service, and on the public sector's predilection for long and meaningless meetings that do nothing to improve the outputs of the organisation as far as its stakeholders are concerned. He criticised political leaders for failing to engage with front-line service providers, so that the Minister for Education, say, never bothered to canvas the views of a teacher working in a classroom, even though a communication ('out of the mouths of babes and fools') might bring a gem of an idea that might spark radical improvement.

He condemned individual leaders for working in isolation when many of the issues surrounding public services would be solved better by collaboration and integration. He outlined a list of attributes that should be routinely accepted by leaders and those who they lead, who are advising and guiding them at a local, regional and national level. Among the key attributes of the advice-givers were:

- “Comfortable with greater external accountability and transparency
- Effectively delivering results/outcomes
- Skilled in procurement and supplier management as the delivery of ‘the business’ is increasingly on a contractual basis
- Politically aware, sensitive, empathetic but not designed
- Focused explicitly on issues rather than departments and on clients rather than process and on value rather than cost.
- Imaginative in the use of e-government to deliver services
- Creative, innovative and energised” (2006, pp.3)

On the other hand, the attributes the leaders (advice-takers) must develop were:

- Ability to create and obtain ownership for a clear vision, set of values and strategy
- Consistency, integrity and trust
- Communication, presentational and listening skills
- Building and sustaining partnerships in a fragmented environment
- Negotiating and influencing skills
- Capacity to refresh and redesign
- Enhancing energy and creativity

Sir Michael highlighted the negativity, sarcasm, sullenness and indifference that mars much of ‘the public service’ and called for a radical new approach to creating services for the 21st century; with the leaders and the led finding a common purpose and the political will to deliver change and continuous improvement for the benefit of stakeholders, clients and the community at large. He wryly concluded by saying that an awful lot of people would have to be replaced to make that happen to his satisfaction.

The following article appeared in ‘IT Week’ on 25 September 2006. It sums up quite neatly some of the problems that Sir Michael identified and points to some of the reasons why so many Government ICT projects have failed so dismally.

“Report labels public-sector IT chiefs “reckless”

Think-tank The Work Foundation says a gung-ho attitude is to blame for public-sector IT problems

James Murray, IT Week, 25 Sep 2006

The government's chequered history with IT projects came under fire again in September as a new report argued its Transformational Government agenda to deliver more integrated IT systems across the public sector was being jeopardised by many civil servants' "gung-ho" attitude to IT projects.

Entitled 'Where Next for Transformational Government', the report from not-for-profit think-tank the Work Foundation involved interviews with 500 frontline public-sector staff and 25 senior managers. It argued that, contrary to stereotype, public-sector managers often have a "reckless streak" that has resulted in them frequently embarking on over-complex technology projects that have been insufficiently piloted.

Alexandra Jones, associate director at The Work Foundation and co-author of the report, argued in a statement that the high proportion of failed public-sector IT projects is often due to civil servants being "dazzled by the potential of the technology and losing sight of what is practically deliverable".

"Government should not be about cutting edge innovation – it should be about serving citizens well and efficiently," she added. "If someone gets their benefit late due to computer failure, it matters in a way that it simply doesn't when private-sector ICT projects fail. The private sector can afford the luxuries of innovating; in the public sector, ICT needs to work".

The report recommended public-sector IT chiefs should look to deploy simpler IT systems; insist on more comprehensive pilot projects; resist revisions to project parameters that lead to "scope creep"; work closer with those who will use new IT products; and invest more in the process changes that accompany new systems.

Ian Cockerill, practice manager for government at Adobe Systems, which sponsored the research, suggested public-sector IT chiefs should also look to exploit existing IT assets more effectively rather than embark on major new investments". IT Directors should really asses the goals of the project coupled with the current systems that they have that are working," he added. "Often it will be easier to join the existing systems together rather then starting from scratch".

However, Alan Rodger of analyst Butler Group argued that while there may have been "over enthusiasm" amongst some public-sector IT managers, much of the blame for government IT failures also has to lie with the politicians who develop the initial strategy. "Public-sector managers haven't made these [IT project] decisions off their own back," he commented. "A lot of them have been foisted on managers by government."

The recommendations come just weeks after reports revealed the government is looking to simplify its controversial ID card programme, which has been repeatedly criticised for being too ambitious. According to reports in IT Week's sister publication Computing, the Home Office is undertaking proof of concept studies to see if it could use existing systems, such as Department for Work and Pensions databases, to underpin the new ID card technology".

You can see that the guidance and advice has arguably been flawed, with the politicians guilty of allowing politics to impede sensible business decisions, and organisations being seduced by the promises of consultants (as is often noted by many experienced procurement professionals – 'beware the snake oil salesman'). Again, the procurement activity has to be held to account here, for is it not its job to ensure that the solution proposed offers best value to the organisation and, more importantly (to paraphrase a well known television advertisement), 'does what it says on the tin?'.

The effectiveness of governance arrangements for procurement

"Democracy, good governance and modernity cannot be imported or imposed from outside a country".

Emile Lahud

The National Procurement Strategy for Local Government, published by the then Office of the Deputy Prime Minister (ODPM, 2003) contained a vision for councils which included six key principles:

- Better quality services through sustainable partnerships
- A mixed economy of service provision with ready access to a diverse and competitive range of suppliers
- Achieving continuous improvement by collaborating with partners
- Greater value from a corporate procurement strategy
- Realising community benefits
- Stimulating markets and driving innovation in the design, construction and delivery of services.

Implicit in the need to achieve greater value from a corporate procurement strategy (bullet-point 4 above) was the need to establish rigorous governance models around procurement and represent these in the corporate procurement strategy of an organisation.

There is a clear need to review procurement governance structures in organisations to ensure that governance is sufficiently robust. The complexities of managing multiple stakeholders and partnerships in public sector organisations may mean that traditional procurement governance structures could be seen as inadequate.

Public sector procurement professionals are in the public eye because of the tremendous impact that public procurement has on so many aspects of the social and business cultures of the UK. They must continually be aware of the impact of their actions and the responsibility they have to uphold the good name of the public sector and the communities they serve. However, if the governance framework that gives direction to those buyers is inadequate to support honest and fair procurement methods, it is unsurprising that some buyers may find themselves in a difficult position and act improperly ('putting themselves on the other side of the line').

The rules of procurement governance must ensure that public sector procurement professionals are accountable for the effectiveness, efficiency, legal and ethical manner in which they conduct procurements. Buyers should be empowered to use personal initiative and sound business judgment in their day-to-day work. They should also employ their specialist knowledge of markets, industry, commerce, trading principles, practices and business processes in an ethical manner to help set the tone of undertaking business with the UK public sector.

To obtain best value, quality and service, it is good procurement policy for an organisation to have:

- Procedures which are fair, non-discriminatory and transparent
- Requirements which are clear – using outcomes-based and standard specifications wherever possible
- Standard terms and conditions of contract
- Adherence to legal and regulatory obligations: e.g. the prompt payment of suppliers' invoices
- Good working relationships and trust with suppliers
- A culture which places equal competition at the head of its procurement agenda.
- Strong controls and audit checks on procurement
- A regime of performance management and continuous improvement
- Professional training and standing of procurement staff
- Efficient challenge and review systems
- A code of ethics binding on procurement professionals (CIPS Code of Ethics or equivalent).

It is the job of public sector buyers to uphold practices, policies, processes and procedures around those principles. You might find it useful to study and remember the governance framework model below:

Governance framework for a typical public sector organisation

Key elements	Control mechanisms
Regulatory	Criminal law, public procurement law, government regulations, standing orders, financial regulations, codes of practice, codes of ethics
Checks and Balances	Internal and external auditors, whistle-blowers, freedom of information, financial disclosure, reports in public domain, supplier complaints/challenges, other external oversight, professional diligence
Correction	Implementation of law and regulation, protest resolution, management action, continuous improvement, self-regulation
Prevention	• Professional independence: empowerment and business judgment • Professional standing and training: CIPS qualification, NVQ/SVQ, CPD systems, e-learning • Challenge and Review systems: creating a challenge culture from inception of need to award of contract and downstream contract management • Quality control and review systems: internal and external controls and process evaluation on the procurement process. • System management: Maintaining the procurement infrastructure and keeping in permanent contact with operational offiials

Diagram 15.1

Learning Activity 15.2

Apply the table above to your own organisation, and describe which control mechanisms apply to each key element insofar as your organisation is concerned. Make sure you describe adequately the reasons why each control mechanism is important in your organisation's case.

Typical procurement and contract standing orders

A local authority model has been selected here for illustration, but all public sector organisations will have similar rules. This is an extract from Hampshire County Council's contracts standing orders (2008):

"Contract Standing Orders

1.1 By law, the County Council must make standing orders with respect to contracts for the supply of goods or materials or for the execution of works which provide for:

- securing competition
- regulating the manner in which tenders are invited.

1.2 These Contract Standing Orders (CSOs) form part of the County Council's Constitution. Compliance by all staff is therefore mandatory and contravention is a serious matter. They set out the administrative procedure that must be followed in seeking tenders and letting contracts for the supply of services and works*.

1.3 These CSOs have three main purposes:

- to ensure that the County Council obtains Best Value in the way it spends money, so that in turn it may offer Best Value services to the public
- to comply with the laws that govern the spending of public money; and
- to protect individuals from undue criticism or allegation of wrongdoing.

1.4 The County Treasurer and Head of Corporate and Legal Services are the joint custodians of these CSOs and are responsible for keeping them under review. If the European Union (EU) Directives or any other law is changed in a way that affects these CSOs then that change must be observed until the CSOs can be revised. If the CSOs appear to conflict with EU Directives or any other legislation then the legislation takes precedence.

1.5 It is the role of the Director of Property, Business and Regulatory Services to achieve Best Value for the County Council by establishing and maintaining a purchasing network for the County Council and to have responsibility for managing a range of common use contracts.

1.6 These CSOs should be read in conjunction with the detailed practice notes provided by the Head of Corporate and Legal Services to explain how the regulations will be implemented.

1.7 These CSOs apply to all contracts for supplies, services and works entered into by staff, with some exceptions. (Examples of these exceptions are listed in paragraph 13)

1.8 Throughout these CSOs, 'Chief Officer' is a general term covering principal chief officers, heads of department and principal officers and where applicable heads of schools with delegated budgets and heads of business units.

1.9 Where the word "Executive" is used throughout these CSOs the words "governing body" are deemed to be the equivalent in schools holding delegated budgets.

Pre-contract procedures

Before starting a procurement process Best Value legislation requires that the following steps must be carried out:

- identify the need for change or improvement in service delivery
- use a formal evidence based analysis to consider the options for delivery
- evaluate those options and identify a preferred option
- ensure that sufficient budget is available and that authority has been obtained to spend it on the preferred option, in accordance with financial regulations and financial procedures.

The following CSOs apply where as a result of carrying out this process the preferred option includes entering into a contractual agreement for the provision of supplies, services or works.

2 Rules for all contracts

Aggregation

1.1 Purchases must be aggregated whenever possible. On no account should any requirement be split in an attempt to avoid using the proper procedure under these CSOs or EU procurement rules.

1.2 For aggregated requirements with an estimated annual value over the current EU threshold, Chief Officers must ensure that a Prior Indicative Notice (PIN) is placed in the Supplement to the Official Journal of the European Communities (OJEC) each year.

Contractor quality

1.3 For all contracts regardless of value, a contractor must be selected who:

- can confirm a business contact address and telephone number
- has an acceptable level of public liability insurance
- is registered for tax and holds a valid certificate (where appropriate)
- is able to provide two independent referees from whom reference may be sought for contracts completed within the last three years

1.4 The Director of Property, Business and Regulatory Services and the Director of Environment will keep registers of contractors who, following limited financial and other checks, are deemed suitable for consideration as contractors for construction, buildings' repairs and maintenance and highway works. There are also other registers available from other sources such as government and local government consortia (eg G-Cat). Budget holders should note, however, that the inclusion of a contractor on these registers is no guarantee of its quality or suitability for any particular project. Advice should be sought from the keepers of the registers on suitable contractors for specific works.

Call-off and framework contracts

1.5 Call-off or framework contracts for supplies and services should be used where they exist, regardless of value. Countywide arrangements for routine supplies and services and department-specific contracts, eg "framework agreements" for electrical appliance testing, "block contracts" placed by Social Services with care providers and "term tenders" for highways maintenance all fall into these definitions.

Contents of orders and contracts

1.6 Every order and contract must clearly and carefully specify the supplies, services or works to be supplied, the agreed programme for delivery and the price and terms for payment together with all other terms and conditions that are agreed.

3 Registers of contractors

1.1 A register of contractors is a list of contractors or suppliers qualified for invitation to tender for works or services. The purpose of registers is to provide the names of contractors or suppliers who have been checked for their competence and to invite only those firms on the list to tender. This prevents the need to advertise each contract and investigate each tenderer in what is frequently a short space of time.

1.2 For supplies and services (including consultancy services), a register should be used to invite tenders without advertising if the pre-estimated aggregate annual value of contracts is at or below the current EU threshold. Where the total is expected to exceed this amount, tenders may be invited using the register but each requirement must also be advertised under the EU Directives.

1.3 When contracts for supplies, services or works are advertised, the criteria for selecting tenderers and the contract award criteria must be the same for those who respond to the advertisement as for those on the register.

1.4 Registers of contractors must:

- be compiled and maintained by the appropriate Chief Officer or by his/her named delegate
- be approved by the Chief Officer in consultation with the County Treasurer and the Head of Corporate and Legal Services; and
- indicate, for each entrant, the categories of supplies, services or works and any maximum contract values for which approval has been given.

1.5 At least four weeks before such a register is first compiled, and thereafter every three years, an advertisement inviting applications for inclusion in the list should be published in either the local or national press and/or trade journals in order to target the appropriate market. At the time of re-advertisement existing entrants should also be required to reapply for inclusion in the register.

1.6 Where the number of contractors on a list is at a level agreed by the County Treasurer and the Head of Corporate and Legal Services, the formal review may be carried out every five years.

1.7 Sustainable development is an important element of corporate strategy. Contractors and suppliers should, therefore, be able to contribute significantly to meeting the County Council's sustainable development strategy and objectives. This should be considered when deciding criteria for admission to registers and the eventual awarding of contracts.

1.8 Once the register is established, invitations to tender for a contract should be sent to entrants by means of the application of pre-determined and objective selection criteria.

1.9 Chief Officers should continuously monitor the performance of entrants but must obtain approval of the Head of Corporate and Legal Services before taking measures to remove any contractor from the register who is not consistently meeting minimum performance criteria.

4 Thresholds

4.1 Thresholds are set for different values of transactions:

Below £25,000	Obtain three quotations
£25,000 or above but below £100,000	Three tenders required through formal procedures
£100,000 or above but below EU threshold	Five tenders required through formal tender procedures
Above EU procurement levels	Compliance with EU procurement directives

5 Low-value transactions

1.1 For contracts valued below £25,000, tenders are not required but the principles of Best Value apply and the selection process should be documented. Wherever possible three competitive quotations should be obtained. If the contract is then awarded to any other than the lowest tenderer then the reasons for doing so should be justified and recorded in writing.

6 Intermediate transactions

1.1 For transactions valued £25,000 or above or below £100,000 at least three tenders must be invited. Either a formal contract must be entered into or a formal purchase order issued as appropriate, specifying the supplies, services or works and setting out prices, terms and conditions of contract and terms of payment. Tendering procedures should be similar to those carried out for transactions valued at £100,000 (outlined below in 7 and following) except that Chief Officer should be substituted for Head of Corporate and Legal Services throughout.

7 Full tender procedures for higher value transactions

1.1 For transactions valued £100,000 or above a formal tender process must be conducted in the manner outlined below.

1.2 One of three tender procedures; Open, Restricted or Negotiated should be selected as the most appropriate for the transaction. These are designed to be essentially the same as the procedures described in EU Directives in order to provide consistency."

It is clear that compliance with some of these standing orders will be extremely difficult to monitor, and the role of internal and external auditors is important here to ensure that the necessary checks and balances are in place to measure compliance, and ensure continuous improvement and best practice. If an organisation operates 'self-service' procurement backed by a corporate core at the centre, chief officers, chief departmental procurement officers or category managers must be held responsible for compliance in their departments. It is concomitant upon the most senior officers in an organisation, from the chief executive down, to ensure that strict adherence to the governance rules is embedded into the organisation's corporate culture.

15.2 Self-assessment question

Assess which of the standing orders above are the most difficult to monitor and control effectively and suggest what steps could be taken to improve matters.

Governance and EU legislation

> "We are half ruined by conformity, but we should be wholly ruined without it."
> **Charles Dudley Warner**

Hampshire's standing orders also address, inter alia, tendering under EU rules, tender receipting procedures, contract award procedures and terms and conditions of contract.

It is now clear that the rules of governance have to ensure that contract award criteria are absolutely watertight or, under EU rules, contracting authorities will increasingly face successful legal challenges. A recent example of this is in the case of Lettings International Limited v London Borough of Newham (2008). The expert EU procurement lawyers Maclay Murray Spens (2008) have written that the Court of Appeal has upheld an interim injunction of the High Court preventing Newham from entering into any contract or framework agreement relating to a tender for leased, private-sector accommodation. The lawyers have said this:

> "As is increasingly the case in procurement actions, Lettings International's arguments focused on the award criteria used by Newham. In particular, it alleged that by having five undisclosed sub-criteria relating to the award criterion "compliance with specification", Newham had breached its obligations of transparency. Lettings International also alleged that Newham had breached the transparency principle by failing to make clear that compliance with specification would not attract the highest possible score, but that additional marks were available for exceeding the requirement. The Court of Appeal decided that the interim injunction should be upheld. The loss of a significant chance to win a contract was enough to found a claim. The five sub-criteria and their use by Newham was a serious issue to be tried and it was accepted that Lettings' arguments around the marking/specification raised a separate serious issue.
>
> In considering whether to uphold the injunction, the adequacy of damages as a remedy and the balance of convenience were considered. The court accepted that the fact that the action concerned the award of a framework contract led to difficulties in assessing possible loss for Lettings International as the number of contracts to be placed under the framework was uncertain.
>
> It considered that there was at least some commercial value in being permitted the opportunity to take part in a fair tendering process. Conversely, possible inconvenience to Newham from the injunction was considered, as was the expense which it would incur if the tender process was to be rerun. Nevertheless, the court considered that the balance of convenience lay with maintaining the injunction" (MMS, 2008).

This case, and other recent cases like it, is extremely significant to public sector procurement professionals for a number of reasons. The decision that the loss by Lettings International of the opportunity to participate in a fair tender was enough to found a claim is significant. So too is the weighting of the balance of convenience in favour of the aggrieved bidder, given that there were acknowledged potential inconveniences for both sides. Finally, the case provides a valuable insight into how the courts may treat tenders for framework agreements as opposed to traditional contracts.

Learning activity 15.3

List a minimum of six objective award criteria and two sub-criteria for each criterion that it would be acceptable to use in awarding a public sector tender following an open procedure, provided those criteria and sub-criteria had been published in the OJ notice or the tender documents (open procedure).

Self-assessment question 15.3

To what extent is the governance of a public sector body's procurement dictated by EU procurement legislation?

Summary

The study session has focused on examining the role of elected representatives in the effective governance of organisations. You should have identified the increasingly difficult nature of such a role with the growing complexity of organisations and governance structures, as well as the rapid changes in legislation and organisational behaviours. These make elected members all the more necessary. However, as you should now be aware elected members need to subjugate themselves to the people they serve, being consciously aware of possible conflicts of interest; take into account of Nolan's 'seven principles of public life', and the political pressures that they face to give up their selfless objectives to accord with party politics. The nature of the system of governance brings its own difficulties from the UK Government down through the civil service with the relentless reliance on bureaucracy and form-filling. Likewise you should be able to identify other areas of governance which can provide difficulties, such as the lack of communications and connectivity at a customer level blighting efficient governance; the number of failures of procurement projects which foundered on ignorance and lofty ideals; lack of 'nous' about the needs of the *realpolitik*; and the continuing failure to embed innovation into all aspects of governance.

For elected members to govern efficiently they must have several considerations which must be addressed when it comes to procurement, such as the effectiveness of procurement governance arrangements; the need for integrity and accountability of procurement decisions; the main elements of, and controls to, ensure good governance; an examination of standing orders; and the importance of using objective criteria when awarding procurement contracts.

Revision question

Assess the importance of elected members to the governance of an organisation, and analyse the difficulties they face in adopting a truly independent approach concerning the governance of any organisation of which they are in charge.

Feedback

Feedback on learning activity 15.1

'Can you identify any projects in which elected leaders have failed to achieve the Nolan ideal? Discuss which of the seven principles were lacking.'

The controversial contract, driven by politicians in Northern Ireland, is still being considered by the High Court. It relates to a security licensing breach by a firm that guards Northern Ireland's courts. A rival security firm took the NIO to court over a decision to award a £25m contract to firm A when that company did not have a valid security licence. The contract award was withdrawn after the NIO took legal advice about the matter. The rival company, firm B, argued that it should have received the contract. It was seeking a court order to halt a new tendering process for a five-year contract.

Firm B finished second in the aborted contract process. Firm A, which was the extant supplier, was discovered to be operating without a licence when the tendering process for a new five-year contract began. A previous licence had lapsed, although the firm had not revealed the length of time that it operated without one.

The NIO issued Firm A with a new licence days later and accepted its tender for the multi-million pound contract. The NIO refused to answer questions about whether the licensing process was fast-tracked. Police have also investigated the licensing breach, since security firms are required under anti-terrorism laws to renew their licence annually. A PSNI file on the matter has been passed to the prosecution service.

The NIO took over the tendering procedure for the courts because police were also investigating the circumstances of another contract award to Firm A, when the company was under different ownership. Court officials were entertained on a yacht belonging to the previous owner, who sold the company last year.

15

The new court action, by Firm B, was brought against the NIO Central Procurement Unit under the Public Contract Regulations 2006.
Firm B's managing director stated in papers lodged in court that his concern was how Firm A was short-listed by the Northern Ireland Office when it did not have a valid licence at the time of tender submission. Furthermore, no tender should have been evaluated when the mandatory requirements of the tender included the possession of a licence which Firm A failed to produce.

Firm B's affidavit also challenged the Procurement Unit's evaluation of the respective tenders - 812 out of 1,000 for it and 920 for Firm B.

The case is ongoing, but if the courts find for firm B, there are implications for the politicians who allowed this to happen. You would ask questions such as:

- What were the rules of governance that allowed this to happen?
- Where were the checks and balances that prevented this from happening?
- Did the politicians who approved the award act with selflessness and integrity?

- Did they challenge the rationale behind the decision?
- Were they even involved in the process?
- What was objective about the decision? What were the evaluation criteria? Did the politicians challenge them?
- What were the de-briefing arrangements?
- How could this situation be an example of good leadership?

Feedback on self-assessment question 15.1

'Examine Nolan's 'seven principles' and see where these might militate against the achievement of Best Value in procurement contracts.'

Best value might be compromised by poor performance in each, or any of Nolan's principles. Examples might be as follows:

- **Selflessness**: failure to establish the overall strategic direction of the organisation within the policy and resources framework agreed by funders by approving expenditure over and above the agreed amount
- **Integrity**: failing to ensure that high standards of corporate governance are observed at all times
- **Objectivity**: failing to insist that the organisation includes sound environmental policies and practices in its tendering processes and failing to ensure that properly weighted objective criteria are used in contract award processes
- **Accountability:** failing to oversee the delivery of planned results by monitoring performance against agreed strategic objectives and targets
- **Openness**: failure to ensure the organisation follows the principles of openness, which include giving prompt responses to public requests for information
- **Honesty**: in reaching decisions, ensuring that the organisation has taken into account any guidance issued by funding partners and other stakeholders.
- **Leadership**: failing to ensure the organisation operates within the limits of its statutory authority; within the limits of its delegated authority or in accordance with any other conditions relating to the use of public funds.

The list is not exhaustive and you can substitute your own examples from your own research or knowledge.

Feedback on learning activity 15.2

'Apply the table above to your own organisation, and describe which control mechanisms apply to each key element insofar as your organisation is concerned. Make sure you describe adequately the reasons why each control mechanism is important in your organisation's case.'

Under 'regulatory', you should point to all relevant legislation and regulation that governs your organisation. You could include best value legislation, EU procurement legislation, fraud (criminal), freedom of information, data protection. You could also include your code of ethics, code of best practice, standing orders and financial regulations. You would write a sentence about how your organisation has put specific controls into place to deal with each of these.

Under 'checks and balances' you could describe your 'whistleblowers' charter and the roles of external and internal auditors. You could explain how you deal with placing procurement contracts in the public domain, whether your organisation is willing to disclose information that is 'commercial in confidence' and the like.

Under 'correction', you could describe the strategy your organisation has adopted to put matters right; supporting whistleblowers, disciplining miscreants, improving self-regulation, strengthening external scrutiny.

Under 'prevention' you could outline what your organisation has done to mitigate risk in this area – better training, organisational structures, staff appraisal, performance measurement, review processes, lessons learned, a challenge culture, more power for procurement and empowered staff generally.

Feedback on self-assessment question 15.2

'Assess which of the standing orders above are the most difficult to monitor and control effectively and suggest what steps could be taken to improve matters.'

The question is about management control, senior buy-in and the rigor of review and monitoring, both internally and externally. The less corporate procurement has control over the business processes, the worse the performance will be, and as such it will be more difficult to enforce standing orders at a departmental level. In this case the looser the controls, the worse the problem. Hampshire says that 'contravention is a serious matter' but the author has yet to see many councils take draconian disciplinary action against any staff member breaching standing orders say, by doing a spot of maverick purchasing.

There may well also be errors in the standing orders that make them unenforceable. For example, Hampshire's 2.2 talks about a 'PIN each year'. This is not necessary, unless the frameworks are only one year's duration, which is unlikely. A large county council will typically let framework contracts for 3 or even 4 years, and the PIN would be required only once, to presage the original long-term contract.

2.3 might be discriminatory and therefore unlawful, as it precludes any firm who cannot provide two referees for contracts placed within the previous three years, regardless as to whether the references relate to any relevant contract. This is the principle of 'proportionality' and you need to be careful you 'make the punishment fit the crime.' Section 3 (and 5) might be challengeable too, because the assumption here is that no action need be taken on EU contracts below the threshold. This is an erroneous assumption to make, because the principles of the Treaty of Rome (stimulation of competition etc) apply to contracts worth £1 upwards. There is a need to advertise low-value contracts in a suitable medium accessible to all member states. Hampshire might have to review section 3 of its standing orders.

The complex process for renewing standing lists in section 3 might be difficult to achieve. The author has known councils that find it too onerous to go out to competition to renew their standing lists every three years, and end up simply adding new firms until the register is inundated with suppliers who never get any business.

Hampshire's standing orders are by no means the worst, but the principle here is that they should be completely reviewed and overhauled to meet changing needs, probably every couple of years.

Feedback on learning activity 15.3

'List a minimum of six objective award criteria and two sub-criteria for each criterion that it would be acceptable to use in awarding a public sector tender following an open procedure, provided those criteria and sub-criteria had been published in the OJ notice or the tender documents (open procedure).'

Firstly, contract award criteria are entirely different from the criteria laid down in Articles 23-26 of the Public Contracts Regulations 2006 for the selection of those firms that will subsequently be invited to tender. **The same criteria cannot be used twice.** Six suitable tender evaluation criteria with two underpinning sub-criteria for each might be:

1. **Quality of the tender**
   Closeness of the tender to the outcomes specified
   Risk management strategy
2. **Quality of staff assigned to the contract**
   Qualifications of management and staff
   Facilities for research and development
3. **Cost**
   Willingness to engage in open-book accounting
   Incentivisation in the contract
4. **Environmental characteristics**
   Environmental friendliness of the proposal
   Ability to pay SME sub-contractors within 30 days
5. **Innovation**
   Innovative use of resources to accomplish contract
   Investment in state-of-the-art IT to offer best-in-class business processes
6. **Sustainability (of the solution)**
   Ability of the service to migrate to new generation technology at cessation of contract
   Ability of the service/solution to be prepared for competition at the next tender round.

There are many variations on these themes and it is useful for you to articulate as many of these as you can, not only for accuracy of governance relating to this unit of study, but other units in the syllabus.

Feedback on self-assessment question 15.3

'To what extent is the governance of a public sector body's procurement dictated by EU procurement legislation?'

EU legislation is almost paramount in public sector procurement, and buyers have to become experts in interpretation of EU law, or know where, in their organisations, they seek the appropriate advice. The thresholds for supplies and services contracts are very low, and the requirement to treat below-the-threshold contracts in a specific way that meets Treaty of Rome principles means that few procurement contracts will escape altogether. The following elements of procurement are directly affected by EU rules:

- Competition
- Communications and media
- Advertising tenders
- Procedure
- Prescribed timescales
- Technical and qualitative specifications
- Technical standards
- Variants
- PQQs
- Tender Evaluation
- Award criteria
- Contract award and the right to challenge decisions
- Supplier de-briefing
- Post-tender negotiation
- Framework agreements
- E-procurement
- Reverse e-auctions
- Dynamic purchasing systems
- Reportage and statistical data
- Consortia
- Standing lists
- Concessions

Feedback on revision question

'Assess the importance of elected members to the governance of an organisation and analyse the difficulties they face in adopting a truly independent approach concerning the governance of any organisation of which they are in charge.'

People stand for election as councilors because they have a commitment to local government and because they want to make a difference to their community. Whether they are promoting the well-being of their area or taking part in committee or board meetings, they are giving of their time and their energy. This is the strength of local government and the public sector generally

Elected members now face significant changes to the way their organisations work. These changes are modernising local government so that it can play a key role in leading their communities going forward. They are about local government working constructively with others to deliver excellence in the service for which it is responsible. They are about local government engaging with local people in new ways. They are about the future of local government itself. Working together, central and local government can make a real difference to quality of life.

Members also need to consider the options for change and to lead their councils through them, each making their own particular contribution to success. Even longstanding members will need to learn new skills and acquire additional knowledge. That is why training and development for members is essential.

It is an exciting time to be at the centre of local government. The new political management arrangements described in the Local Government Act have brought new roles and responsibilities, and have transformed working arrangements. Through new scrutiny activity; through being fully involved in best value; through creating a new dialogue with local people; members have found their new roles have offered them new opportunities for them to be effective and influential.

Change is always difficult. And it affects elected members as much as other stakeholders and the general public. Indeed it will not succeed if members do not lead from the front. Local people look to their elected members for a lead, and they are right to do so. If that means challenging the party line and taking decisions on the basis of one's conscience than on the basis of political pressure, then that is a constructive route for elected members to take. However, members do face immense pressure from the political machine and a consensual approach is quite often considered necessary, which probably dilutes the delivery of the project or service.

Suggested further reading

Tony Bovaird, and Elke Loffler, (eds), (2003), Public Management and Governance (2003), ch. 1, 2, 5, 10,12, 14

Gerry Johnson, and Kevan Scholes, (eds) (2001), Exploring Public Sector Strategy ch. 1, 4, 7, 13, 17

Cornwall County Council Procurement Governance model - http://www.cornwall.gov.uk/index.cfm?articleid=14109.

Hampshire County Council contract standing orders - http://www.hampshire.gov.uk/

Study session 16

"Critically evaluate the effectiveness of financial accountability arrangements for procurement"

Introduction

In this study session, you will examine the key themes around the topic of financial accountability arrangements in typical public sector organisations; how finance and procurement interact and the influences of each on each other; and you will apply the principles you learn to your own organisation or organisations with which you are familiar.

Session learning objectives

After completing this session you should be able to:

- assess the role of finance in the public sector and its relationships with procurement.
- analyse the procedures in place to give assurance to Permanent Secretaries and Chief Executives in their exercise of personal accountability.
- assess the effectiveness of financial accountability arrangements as they relate to procurement.
- consider the role of, and the need for, standing orders and financial regulations as they apply to typical public sector organisations.
- analyse the reasons why a procurement policy document, linked to financial regulations, standing orders, governance and staff responsibilities, is necessary in every public sector organisation.

Unit content coverage

This study session covers part of the following topic from the official CIPS unit content documents: *Analyse the adequacy and robustness of procurement financial and management information systems*. Specifically, it covers: *Critically evaluate the effectiveness of financial accountability arrangements for procurement*.

Prior knowledge

Prior to this study session you should have completed study sessions 1; 2; 3; 4; 5; 6; 7; 8; 9; 10; 11; 12; 13; 14; 15.

Timing

You should take about 4-5 hours to read and complete this section, including learning activities, self-assessment questions, the suggested further reading, and the revision question.

Public finance management

"Finance is, as it were, the stomach of the country, from which all the other organs take their tone"

WE Gladstone

PFM concerns the effective management of the collection and expenditure of funds by governments. Societal needs are inevitably greater than resources available to government; therefore all public resources must be used as efficiently as possible with minimum government wastage.

According to the Office of Government Commerce (OGC), PFM is a core part of strategic public sector management, which is defined as a dynamic process of aligning strategies, performance and business results. It is all about people, leadership, technology and processes. Effective combination of these elements will help with strategic direction and successful service delivery. It is a continuous activity of setting and maintaining the strategic direction of the organisation and its business, and making decisions on a day-to-day basis to deal with changing circumstances and the challenges of the business environment.

As part of an organisation's strategic thinking about advancing the business, it (and its partners) will have set a course for a particular direction, but subsequent policy drivers (such as new performance targets) or business drivers (such as increased demand for services) could take the organisation in quite a different direction. There could be implications for accountability when an organisation decides whether to take corrective action to get back on course or to go with the new direction. Similarly, there could be implications for governance if relationships with partners change.

Underpinning all this is the need for strong public finance management. We have all read recent stories of public sector organisations failing to live within their means, perhaps bowing to socio-political imperatives without taking a hard look at how these are going to be financed sustainably. Two examples of this could be: a Scottish Council overspending its revenue budget to the extent that it all but wipes out its reserves, so if there is to be a natural disaster, say a flood, there would be no money to have paid for alleviating action. Another would be a UK council devising a scheme for putting a laptop on every pupil's desk without the cash to replace the laptops in due course when they become worn out. Due to short-term budgeting, when an organisation is planning only a short period ahead, such unsustainable decisions are all too common.

Learning Activity 16.1

Research resources, documents, press and media articles, the web, and examine at least three examples of allegedly poor financial management by public sector organisations.

Self-assessment question 16.1

How might these examples of poor financial management be improved?

CIPFA and the Improvement Network

The Chartered Institute of Public Finance And Accountancy (CIPFA) is one of the leading professional accountancy bodies in the UK and the only one which specialises in the public sector. It is responsible for the education and training of professional accountants and for their regulation through the setting and monitoring of professional standards. It also has responsibility for setting accounting standards for local government. Students should familiarise themselves with its work and key objectives.

The Improvement Network was established in November 2004 by the Audit Commission, CIPFA, the Employers' Organisation and the Improvement and Development Agency. In April 2006, the Leadership Centre for Local Government replaced the Employers' Organisation as a sponsor of the Network. It gave the following practical definition and overview of public finance management and, although it was concentrating purely on local government, these remarks are relevant right across the public sector:

"Financial Management is a core part of successful management. It is essential to the effective corporate governance of a local authority and fundamental to achieving an authority's objectives and improving its services.

High-performing organisations and those with a track record of improving services consistently demonstrate strengths in leadership, performance management and financial management.

Financial management is a key management discipline. It is something for which all non-executives and managers within a local authority are responsible, individually and collectively. It is not just the job of the chief finance officer and his or her staff."

"Service users are the ones who will suffer most from poor financial management as limited resources are deployed ineffectively. Strong management should lead to a local authority's money being spent appropriately and in a way that is focused on local and national priorities.

Financial management encompasses all the activities within an organisation that are concerned with the use of resources and that have a financial impact. CIPFA has defined financial management for public bodies as:

'Financial management is the system by which the financial aspects of a public body's business are directed and controlled to support the delivery of the organisation's goals.'

Financial management is central to every organisation's decision-making process. It is an essential part of the corporate governance and thereby the overall performance management of every organisation. The financial management arrangements within public sector organisations provide information that is used to:Direct the activities of the organisation

- Control the activities of the organisation
- Report and discharge accountability
- Utilise resources efficiently and effectively

Financial management is not just the responsibility of finance staff. It is the responsibility of everyone in that organisation. Every member and officer has a role to play in effective financial management whether they have responsibility for:

- Planning
- Managing services and budgets
- Ordering stock
- Authorising expenditure
- Consuming resources." (Improvement Network, n.d.)

Public Finance Management Models

James L Chan in Bovaird and Loffler (2006, pp.101-112) details the traditional Public Finance Management Model and compares and contrasts it with the newer Barnard-Simon Governance model and Public Management Model (NPM). It is useful for you to be able to assess the difference between the three and you should read chapter eight of Bovaird and Loffler. The PFM model requires that government (and by definition public sector) should 'balance its budgets' and 'should not overspend its appropriations.' These principles are enshrined in legislation.

Chan states (2003, pp.102) that PFM is 'often described in terms of revenue collection and spending,' but that there is 'no general agreement about the scope of financial management.' He says that PFM is often seen as 'an invisible bureaucratic function uninvolved in policy decisions and largely unaffected by budgeting approaches.' There is the comfort, though, that PFM 'ensures organisational stability and continuity by following standard operating procedures'.

Barnard-Simon recognised that Government was 'coalition of stakeholders' and that only a small proportion of public spending was undertaken by Government itself. The model is predicated on the point that this coalition of stakeholders came about by means of a series of complicated contractual and pseudo-contractual arrangements, all of which have financial implications which have to be assessed and managed by financial managers.

NPM, on the other hand, is 'performance-driven' and mirrors accounting principles applied in the private sector, such as double-entry accounting and accruals budgeting (one difficulty is that public organisations are unable to carry forward much in the way of unspent revenue expenditure year-on-year

Learning activity 16.2

Find a copy of the annual report and accounts of your local authority (could be available on-line). Try to find within it the following data:

- the overall value of assets of the Council
- The proportion of costs of: (i) leisure and cultural services (ii) social services that are recovered by fees and charges
- The level of locally-raised taxes as a proportion of total local revenue expenditure

What do the answers tell you about (i) potential changes in local financial policy; (ii) the level of transparency in local financial management?

The CIPFA Financial Management (FM) Model

CIPFA has created its own Financial Management Model to assist public sector organisations. FM is a series of good practice statements for public service bodies, where excellent financial management can contribute to robust organisational performance. The model invites organisations to test themselves on the effectiveness of their own financial management in support of their business objectives, and to consider whether the style and contribution of financial management supports or conflicts with their organisation's strategic direction.

Organisations can choose to apply the model in several ways:

Use	Impact
To determine the current level of financial management within an organisation	•To decide upon future actions needed •As a source of evidence for external inspection

To measure the impact on financial management of a significant change programme	• To determine any positive or negative financial management outcomes of change
To communicate with stakeholders	• To determine the perception of financial management within and outside an organisation
As a reference tool for best practice	• The Model provides a quick method of accessing best practice principles

The model is contained in a secure website (CIPFA). There are 37 best practice statements to which an organisation must aspire. The evidence is collected by means of document and business process reviews, reports, surveys, interviews and workshops. The end result is a series of scores against the 37 best practice statements which will indicate how robust is an organisation's financial management arrangements. To take an example from the good practice matrix, questions that the model would ask in order to ascertain the extent to which managers are accountable for managing their budgets would be:

1. "Are revenue and capital budgets assigned to individual managers? (note: capital expenditure is expenditure incurred on the purchase or improvement of significant assets including land, buildings and equipment, which will be of use or benefit in providing services for more than one financial year. Revenue expenditure relates to the routine regular cost of providing council services).
2. Are financial and managerial responsibilities aligned?
3. Is there a formal scheme of budget delegation?
4. Are budget-holders involved in setting their own budgets and do they take ownership?
5. Are all budgets notified to managers before the start of the financial year?
6. Are the responsibilities of budget-holders clearly documented?
7. Is there formal guidance for budget mangers?
8. Are budget-holders aware of their responsibilities?
9. Are budget-holders aware of the impact of their decisions within the overall budgetary position?
10. Are budget-holders able to explain how they manage their budgets?
11. Are budget-holders held accountable for any deviations from budget?
12. Is this included in their performance assessment?"

Self-assessment question 16.2

Answer the twelve questions above with regard to your own organisation, or an organisation with which you are familiar. Write a paragraph in justification of each of your answers.

Public Finance – Is transformation required?

"It is essential that policy instruments be developed that would firmly establish democratisation on the basis of social consensus and enable transformation on stable grounds."

Recep Tayipp Erdogan

CIPFA suggests that the current environment for public financial management is complex for the following reasons:

- Financial management responsibility is often dispersed
- Many financial constraints
- Trade-offs and rationing
- Many stakeholders claiming rights of influence
- Cost reduction pressures
- IT required to drive down costs and streamline back office functions
- Increasing political and business risks

Public sector organisations are engaged in hugely challenging change programmes (Gershon, Byatt, and McClelland in Scotland etc). The UK is seeking to improve its front-line services in education, health, social care and the emergency services. The emphasis is on continuous improvement, despite public sector bodies operating within an uncertain financial framework, with governments demanding massive efficiency savings in spite of the costs of change. The current economic climate dictates that years of largesse are about to dry up in a spectacular way. Food and fuel costs continue to spiral upwards, and yet fixed sums of money are disbursed for budgetary purposes, which take little heed of huge rises in costs. The whole process is short-term, with funds decided annually and subject to instant fluctuations, reductions, lateness of delivery, ring-fencing and other political vagaries.

Public sector accountants have a key role in trying to manage these budget pressures. Finance, like procurement, is multi-dimensional, and cross-functional. It is connected to most, if not all, business processes in an organisation. It drives the stewardship and control systems; it ensures accountability; it keeps budget-holders in line. It wires money from one budget to another to meet short-run needs, and it seeks to root out over-spending and waste. It ensures that the organisation is running its business in a financially legal, viable and appropriate fashion.

Finance checks continually that the foundations for the financial infrastructure are based on solid rock and not shifting sands. It ensures value-for-money, provides information and analysis for department heads, managers and stakeholders. It helps the organisation understand better its own performance. It is not about 'how much have we spent?' and 'how much have we left to spend?' which might be the way that some would consider the typical bureaucratic approach in the halcyon days, before the times of momentous change that were noted in section 1 of this course book.

By helping the organisation make better decisions, the accountants can help the public sector to embrace change in a positive and dynamic way, which delivers increased value for the taxpayer's 'buck'. It can help incentivise progress and ensure that change is sustainable in the long-run, by providing a solid financial bedrock as the change programme moves towards implementation and execution. Finance is at the heart of public sector change and reform, as this drawing illustrates:

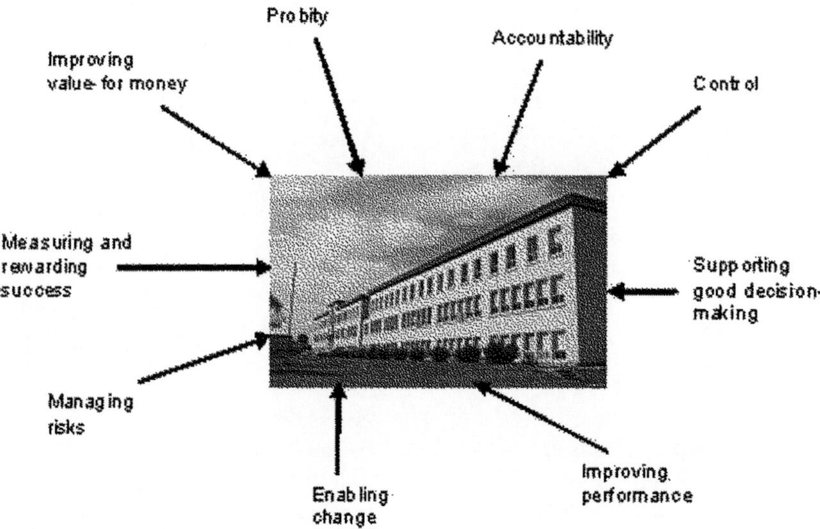

Diagram 16.1

The definition of financial management is a much broader one than simply covering the activities of the finance department. It embraces a great many of the actions and decisions which are taken by senior managers right across the range of public services. It is not about whether information and data are prepared for managers on time, it is whether the managers know what to do with the information once they have been presented with it. The organisation needs to make good decisions from the good information that finance delivers.

This is particularly challenging in large, multi-functional public service bodies. Teachers, doctors and nurses didn't enter their profession because they anticipated having to become finance managers, but they need a level of efficiency in terms of understanding and using financial data as a tool for strategic decision making to improve their core activity. Head Teachers for example, despite what they think (and might even have been told), can no longer restrict their world to the school gates; they have to see the bigger corporate picture. Accountants have to support the service managers and success hinges on the nature of those relationships.

Traditionally, finance departments were part of the corporate centre, handing out lofty diktats of 'Thou shalt not spend' to those trying manfully to provide a service to clients. Finance staff were, in such cases often remote and rarely saw their customers and stakeholders. This centralised approach is starting to change significantly. We now see accountants whose role is focused purely on supporting the front-line troops, and many are located in the trenches alongside the service providers. There are often tensions between these officials in the front-line and the corporate accountants, and there is perhaps ambivalence in the attitude of the service accountants caught between a rock and a hard place, wondering whether to support the offering different objectives of the service departments or the corporate centre.

The complexity of public sector strategy now, with its emphasis on strategic alliances and partnerships means that a solely centralised, corporatist approach will not work, and arguably more accountants are required at the rim rather than the hub of the parent organisation. The accent in public service these days is very definitely on providing services at a local level and the necessary financial infrastructure has to be put in place locally to enable that to happen. Devolved budgets are now *de rigueur* rather than *de trop*. The effect of that upon procurement professionals will be considered a little further on in the text.

You have seen that best practice dictates that finance should be underpinning the stability of an organisation by developing strong financial processes to ensure sustainability, accountability and probity; and at the same time driving performance, improvement and change. Accountants should be supporting the leadership of the organisation and the development of corporate strategy and at the same time should be part of front-line service delivery, supporting innovative practices and solutions at the front end.

Stewardship, performance and transformation models in financial management

Learning activity 16.3

Assess the role of the finance function in your own organisation and define whether, and how, it has been geared to offer proper governance and meet changing stakeholder expectations

According to Steve Freer (2002), a CIPFA accountant, in a paper he wrote entitled *Keeping up with the Pace: an Analysis of the Changing Role of the Public Sector Financial Accountant*, public sector organisations are at one of three stages of readiness with regards to their financial management structure. The first operates a 'stewardship' model. This places emphasis on achieving compliance with rules or regulations laid on the organisation by, say, an Act of Parliament, European legislation, internal audit controls, or establishing disciplinary procedures.

The second model Freer describes is a 'performance' model. This aligns the financial model more to the organisations strategic objectives. It puts emphasis on providing the right information at the right time to service managers to help them make better decisions about their services.

The third model describes a 'transformational' style. This positions finance as a key player in the leadership of the organisation's strategic agenda. It supports the work to re-engineer the organisation to operate in a completely different way and to make step-changes in performance, as well as helping shape new strategies, structures, and systems. It also seeks actively to manage and influence the organisation's culture.

The three models are not mutually exclusive. There are risks attaching to each of the models unless certain elements of the other models are included. For example, it is highly risky to operate a transformational model with no stewardship model.

Organisations need to decide which model best fits their needs. This, to an extent, depends on the age of the organisation. If it is new, it needs the fundamentals first. If it is long-established, it probably needs transformation. Organisations need to be able to measure their path along the journey from stewardship to transformational.

Analysis of financial procedures for procurement

Most public sector organisations have rules of governance that link financial limits with procurement policy. These might be enshrined in procurement strategy or policy documents, or in contract standing orders or financial regulations. The rules govern all areas of spend, including goods and general services, consultancy services and capital expenditure. The policy is reviewed regularly and normally approved by a board, committee, or full Council.
"Purchasing power is a license to purchase power".

Raoul Vaneigem

A typical policy document might contain the following sections:

- A link to standing orders
- The need to achieve Best Value (a legislative requirement).The UK Government defines Best Value as 'a duty to deliver services to clear standards – covering both cost and quality – by the most effective, economic and efficient means available.' (Modern Local Government: In Touch with the People, 1998)
- Procurement procedures. These would include financial thresholds for aspects of spend (enquiries, tenders, one-off project purchases) and limits on financial responsibilities for individual procurement officers. This section would explain the various EU procurement thresholds for supplies, services, works, and, if appropriate, utilities. This section might stress the requirement for competition, and the minimum number of lower-value quotations and tenders might be sought. There may be details of where low-value tenders are advertised, perhaps a dedicated website, or one of the generic ones, such as Supply2.gov. The EC has clarified that the Treaty of Rome applies in principle to all contracts, not just EU contracts over the threshold, provided these are substantial enough to interest other member states. The figure of £20,000 has been bandied about as a suitable sum, but there is no legislation to support this. This section might also describe the Pre-Qualification and Contract award in a two-stage restricted procedure process.
- An ethical code of practice – perhaps the CIPS Code of Ethics or a derivative thereof

- A list of other procurement legislation/regulations binding on procurement
- Ordering, requisitioning, receipting and invoice payment procedures – the 'requisition – to - cheque' continuum.

Public sector organisations are often challenged by non-compliance with the procurement policy by departmental or service staff, and that is one reason why benefits are so difficult to achieve. This tendency towards 'maverick' procurement proliferates in areas where there is little management responsibility or control over off-contract or off-catalogue spending. Anecdotal evidence notes a local authority which integrated holistic e-procurement, but allowed any purchase order valued at up to £2,500 to be accepted by the system, provided the supplier was already 'on the system'. As the vendor file numbered 19,000 suppliers, this was literally a 'licence for mavericks'. The result of this was that on an anticipated i-catalogue spend of £50 million per annum, the first year's authorised i-catalogue throughput was a mere £4 million. When one considers that the Council still had to employ two staff whose sole job it was to maintain the i-catalogue in the system (price and spec changes etc), the true cost of such approaches can be seen.

Self-assessment question 16.3

Seek out a copy of your organisation's procurement policy document and examine whether it meets the good practice model described here. Highlight deficiencies in your policy and explain what would need to be done to bring the policy up to an acceptable standard. If your policy is already an example of good practice, analyse whether your organisation applies its principles to the letter.

Internal financial management from the Chief Executive or Permanent Secretary down

The UK Treasury (2007) has published some very practical guidance on governance as it applies to central government and the public sector. One document relates to internal management and you would be well advised to read the text in full, as it gives a practical model of the need for sound practices and procedures in this regard. The link can be found in the further reading section.

The document stresses the need for public sector organisations to define their own standards of governance appropriate to the service activity each undertakes, with openness and accountability at the forefront of these standards.

HM Treasury has identified a checklist of key governing body decisions, which are the responsibility of the chief executive or permanent secretary. These are:

- The body's roles and responsibilities
- Its remit and objectives
- The scope of its delegations
- Its procedures and processes
- Arrangements for monitoring, performance and reportage

- Control and management of relationships with partners and stakeholders
- The organisation's 'risk appetite' (i.e. its degree of inclination to take risks) and risk control procedures
- How it should account for its decisions and actions – to ministers, staff and the wider community at large
- How and how often it should review its working practices

The Treasury considers it good practice to document the chain of responsibilities and processes by which communications and sign-off about these decisions will be delivered. There is a causal link between the chief executive or permanent secretary as decision-maker-in-chief and the procurement professional, especially in terms of procedures, processes, stakeholders, reportage, performance measurement, risk and accountability.

The document points out that a key joint responsibility between decision-makers for the governing body and procurement professionals is the need to achieve value for money in the deployment of public resources, including procurement; asset management; disposals; business processes; and financial arrangements such as leases and PFI contracts. This joint responsibility is to find solutions which achieve the best mix of quality and effectiveness for the least outlay. This does not mean the cheapest option.

Procurement professionals have a duty regularly to provide chief executives with accurate and high-level information about expenditure, demand trends, market behaviour, performance against objectives and evolution of procurement risk.

The Treasury has documented the essentials of effective internal decision-making. The main essentials are:

- Active management of risks and opportunities
- Appraisal of alternative courses of action
- Use of pilot schemes to provide evidence on which to make decisions about projects
- Active steering of initiatives, using Gateway reviews to help establish criticality in projects.
- Effective empowerment of staff
- Regular and meaningful management information on costs, efficiency, quality and performance
- Flexibility of business processes
- Regular reviews of decisions taken
- Systematic iterative examination of risk
- Applying lessons learned

The Treasury believes that all public sector organisations should operate as openly as is compatible with the requirements of their business. They should embrace the spirit of Freedom of Information Legislation (2000), Data Protection Legislation (1998), Environmental Information Regulations (2004) and Public Sector Information Regulations (2005). They should place in the public domain on a regular basis information about their services, standards performance, and use of public resources.

Self-assessment question 16.4

The First Minister in Scotland announced in April 2008 (The Glasgow Herald, 2008) his decision to build a new £842 million hospital in Glasgow purely from public funds, rather than using a PFI route. In terms of public finance management, this is perhaps a surprising development in view of typical construction projects. Explore and describe the possible motives as to why such a decision has been taken.

Learning activity 16.4

Identify the advantages and disadvantages of the Treasury's model for effective internal decision-making, especially its insistence that an organisation must conduct 'Gateway' reviews during a procurement project.

Summary

This study session has focused on the interaction between procurement and finance, and how finance should be accounted for within procurement. You should be able to articulate the need for strong, robust and accurate public sector finance management, as organisations have to 'live within their means'. This requires interfaces and inter-dependencies between the procurement and finance functions. There are professional bodies which are responsible for setting standards and developing models to assist in public finance management, and you should be able to identify several of these, as well as their relative advantages and disadvantages. From studying these models and the case studies you should have an insight as to whether future transformation is required to bring public finance management up-to-date. Though the analysis in this study session you should now be able to demonstrate the route towards good practice in public finance management, and the typical constituents of an effective procurement policy document, with its links to good practice finance management, regulation and governance.

Feedback

Feedback on learning activity 16.1

'Research resources, documents, press and media articles, the web, and examine at least three examples of allegedly poor financial management by public sector organisations.'

It is important that you understand how important proper public finance management is to good governance and how stakeholders need to receive accurate data and advice upon which to base strategic decisions on the direction of travel in an organisation.

Revision question

A health service trust operates an alcohol clinic and support centre. The centre's costs of occupancy are paid by the local council. However, its services are financed by central NHS grants. The Council wants to reduce the budget by 15% and the NHS wants to cut the centre's grant by 20%. Advise the executive director what to do and how to go about it.

One classic example must be the National Health Service. The current dissatisfaction of the health service workforce seems to be due in part to the way that change has been implemented, in part to its pace and scale, and in part to the lack of strong public legitimacy for the objectives. For example, by 2005 there were over 10,000 more hospital doctors than that which had been projected by HM Treasury in 2002 (*Opportunity and Security for All*, Chapter 7). This access supply of labour means that junior doctors have been faced with the same uncertainty in regards to finding jobs which is shared with many other professionals; but had previously been unknown within the health service. As Brooks (2007) points out in his analysis of the situation, 'One of the lessons of the past ten years is that it is possible to increase the pay of public service employees dramatically and still lose their support'.

There are questions here about the suitability of the PFM path chosen as well as engagement with the stakeholders (what was the consultation process, for example, and was this strategy derived purely from knee-jerk politics?). The over-riding thought that seems to arise is that this strategic decision was not sustainable in the long-run, so should this spending plan ever have been put into train, and which PFM model allowed this to happen?

Feedback on self-assessment question 16.1

'How might these examples of poor financial management be improved?'

You need to think in terms of how you prevent these decisions being taken in the first place. What were the governance and stakeholder engagement processes? How was risk managed? Was a gateway approach used as the particular project developed? Were a range of possible alternatives examined before the preferred model was adopted? How reliable was the management and financial management information? How was the project scoped and did the final result reflect the original vision and scope? Were staff empowered or simply lackeys of the Board? Was the outcome legal? Has it transgressed the organisational Code of Ethics?

Feedback on learning activity 16.2

'Find a copy of the annual report and accounts of your local authority (could be available on-line). Try to find within it the following data:

- *the overall value of assets of the Council*
- *The proportion of costs of: (i) leisure and cultural services (ii) social services that are recovered by fees and charges*
- *The level of locally-raised taxes as a proportion of total local revenue expenditure*

What do the answers tell you about (i) potential changes in local financial policy; (ii) the level of transparency in local financial management?'

This is a practical exercise, designed to test your interpretation of a set of Council revenue accounts and balance sheet. One area that is often neglected in an academic view of PFM is an organisation's ability to raise income through fees and charges to its customers. It would be useful to compare the ratio of culture and leisure income to expenditure ratios, to see which organisation gained more from income.

The principle here might be that the organisation that gains more from income has deliberately set out a strategy that maximises income, rather than one that reduces expenditure. That brings in useful concepts about the price a market is willing to pay for an organisation's culture and leisure services, and gives an interesting insight into how political decisions impact upon financial performance.

Feedback on self-assessment question 16.2

'Answer the twelve questions above with regard to your own organisation, or an organisation with which you are familiar. Write a paragraph in justification of each of your answers.'

This is testing your grasp of interpreting financial information in your own organisation. Questions such as the alignment of financial and managerial responsibilities are interesting, in that there are plenty of managers with big budgets but less responsibility and plenty with limited budgets and huge responsibility. Look at the corporate procurement team, for example. The Head of Procurement in a large local authority, may have a staff budget of only around £1.5 million (revenue), but be responsible for bringing £4 million of purchase cost reductions each year, or influencing a non-labour spend of hundreds of millions of pounds.

Questions about budget-holders are probing, because there are many public sector organisations where the budget-holder relies absolutely on corporate finance to interpret budgets for him and to suggest to him where reductions and changes need to be made.

Feedback on learning activity 16.3

'Assess the role of the finance function in your own organisation and define whether, and how, it has been geared to offer proper governance and meet changing stakeholder expectations'

Despite evidence of a very positive and dynamic role played by finance in some organisations, there remains a strong culture of risk avoidance in the public sector. We have learned that decision-makers and stakeholders are presiding over massive cultural and organisational change in the public sector just now, and organisations simply cannot afford to have a finance function that seeks to avoid risk, even if that leads to adverse public comment.

Financial information needs to be presented in such a way that it is possible to make sound strategic decisions on a range of options, and forecasting and modelling are becoming a much more critical part of the accountant's armoury. These data must be robust, and subject to 'reality testing'.

In some organisations, finance has been relegated to the role of mere book-keepers, whilst in others finance is so mighty all other departments tremble before it. A balance has to be struck: finance serves the business; the business does not service finance.

Feedback on self-assessment question 16.3

'Seek out a copy of your organisation's procurement policy document and examine whether it meets the good practice model described here. Highlight deficiencies in your policy and explain what would need to be done to bring the policy up to an acceptable standard. If your policy is already an example of good practice, analyse whether your organisation applies its principles to the letter.'

A typical procurement policy document sits below the corporate strategy and the corporate procurement strategy. It has links to standing orders and financial regulations, and describes a set of behaviours binding on procurement staff, both in a corporate procurement and self-service procurement environment. It espouses good practice, and has links to the formal documentation of all procurement or P2P business processes. It ensures that a standard model is used right across the organisation.

You should be aware that poor procurement policies give, for example, too much autonomy to a department head, say, in buying in consultancy services or business travel.

Every organisation should have a formal procurement policy or, if not, should create one. There is an argument that it should be possible to have one over-arching public sector procurement policy in the same way as there could be a national pre-qualification policy for suppliers. However, each organisation has, for example, its own thresholds for spending etc, so that view has never found favour.

16

The existence of a procurement policy isn't a guarantee that everyone will abide by it, and reference should be made here that buy-in from the very top of the organisation is required, as well as mention of the checks and balances that should be in place to ensure compliance and the roles of internal and external audit in 'policing the policy.'

Feedback on Learning Activity 16.4

'Identify the advantages and disadvantages of the Treasury's model for effective internal decision-making, especially its insistence that an organisation must conduct 'Gateway' reviews during a procurement project.'

The Treasury model deals heavily with governance and suggests an almost hierarchical approach to structuring internal decision-making. It suggests a proactive approach to risk management as a counter to a risk-averse culture. It demands that organisations examine a suite of options on an objective basis, rather than declaring early for any solution. It posits the view that if staff are not empowered, then decisions will be flawed as the decision-makers are not receiving the correct advice. It is at pains to stress the need for meaningful and clean information to aid the decision-making process and a requirement to build in flexibility at each stage of a process. The model offers a mechanism for continuous improvement by means of regular reviews and lessons learned.

The model also suggests the use of a gateway process in making any decisions about any project, whether that be a procurement project or some change in a business process or corporate direction. Gateway processes minimise risk, but are labour-intensive, time-consuming and unwieldy; PRINCE2 especially so. They also provide the temptation of early abandonment because progress is not as the project dictates, whereas an intuitive decision may, in fact, be the correct one.

Feedback on self-assessment question 16.4

'The First Minister in Scotland announced in April 2008 his decision to build a new £842 million hospital in Glasgow purely from public funds, rather than using a PFI route. In terms of public finance management, this is perhaps a surprising development in view of typical construction projects. Explore and describe the possible motives as to why such a decision has been taken.'

This is a topical and highly contentious issue. It has political undertones. Many politicos are trying to discredit the PFI model, asking how it is possible that such a system can possibly achieve best value, and also that standards and quality are much poorer because organisations hand over control of design and build to the contractor. There is also the question of what will the maintenance/refurbishment costs be when the building is handed back after 30 years and, if the contract provides for said refurbishment before the handover, how that will be priced into the contract, the implication being that the organisation pays each year for something that is not going to happen for 30 years.

There are also questions about the procurement arrangements. These contracts are typically negotiated procedure contracts, which may be seen as stifling competition. As some key firms in the construction industry are now alleged to have colluded with each other (and their clients!) in price-fixing in construction contracts, PFI is a questionable approach in some quarters. However, PFI means an organisation can build something that it hasn't the capital to pay for (the principle of 'jam tomorrow') so PFI is here to stay.

The relevance of the question in this context is around how the First Minister's decision was made and the Public Finance Model that was used to arrive at it. The question opens up the role of stakeholders here (NHS trusts, local authorities, the NHS as a body corporate, AM's, MSP's, MPs, staff, Trades Unions, lobbying bodies etc) – how well were they engaged?

Feedback on revision question

'A health service trust operates an alcohol clinic and support centre. The centre's costs of occupancy are paid by the local council. However, its services are financed by central NHS grants. The Council wants to reduce the budget by 15% and the NHS wants to cut the centre's grant by 20%. Advise the

executive director what to do and how to go about it.'

This is a wide-ranging question that embraces the whole topic. The following points are key:

- This is a change project and should be treated as a gateway project, with stages to be completed before final completion
- Stakeholders' interests have to be taken into account
- Alternative options need to be examined. Can this service be carried out in some equally effective alternative way?
- Increases in income might offset cuts of the type envisaged
- Can the money be transferred from another project which is under budget?
- Can efficiency savings be found that might deliver against the double whammy of budget and grant reductions?
- Can the centre reduce the space it occupies, thus reducing occupancy costs?
- Is there the possibility of collaboration with another agency to share costs and agglomerate service delivery?
- Can labour costs be kept down by using more volunteer labour in the centre?
- Is there a need to offer the full range of services that have been offered hitherto?
- How does the unit actually perform? Do we have any key performance indicators (KPI's) that show that it is under-performing, which means we can transform it and get more for less?
- What are the key risks in acceding to the double whammy? Is there the chance that the council and the NHS will back down if press coverage is adversarial?
- Can stakeholder champions be found to fight our cause against the cuts?
- Can cuts be recommended elsewhere that will have the same effect on the accounts but less damage to vulnerable people?
- Can the quality/quantity of the service be reduced to lower costs yet keep the service at an acceptable level for clients?

The list is not exhaustive.

Suggested further reading

Tony Bovaird, and Elke Loffler (eds), (2003), Public Management and Governance ch. 7, 8

Sir Peter Gershon, (2004), *Releasing Resources to the Front Line: Independent Review of Public Sector Efficiency*

CIPFA, (2004), Improving financial management and effectiveness in the public service: the CIPFA FM Model

CIPFA, (2004), The CIPFA FM Model: Statements of good practice in Public financial management: getting started

CIPFA, (2006), Topical Briefing – good governance for the public services

North-East Essex NHS Primary Care Trust, (2007), Report: Procurement policy: non-clinical policy

HM Treasury, Managing Public Money, (2006), section 4, Internal management

http://documents.treasury.gov.uk/mpm/mpm_whole.pdf

Study session 17

"Analyse the adequacy and robustness of procurement financial and management information systems"

Introduction

In this study session, you will assess the veracity and use of financial and procurement management information, and apply the principles you examine to your own organisation or organisations with which you are familiar.

Session learning objectives

After completing this session you should be able to:

- identify sources of procurement financial and management information
- examine the robustness, usefulness and appropriateness of procurement management information to senior managers and other stakeholders
- assess the usefulness and appropriateness of procurement financial and management information available to various levels of management and
- propose improvements to procurement financial and management information systems to improve performance

Unit content coverage

This study session covers part of the following topic from the official CIPS unit content documents: *Analyse the effectiveness of Governance and oversight arrangements for procurement*. Specifically, it covers: *Analyse the adequacy and robustness of procurement financial and management information systems*.

Prior knowledge

Prior to this study session you should have completed study sessions1; 2; 3; 4; 5; 6; 7; 8; 9; 10; 11; 12; 13; 14; 15; 16.

Timing

You should take about 5-6 hours to read and complete this section, including learning activities, self-assessment questions, suggested further reading, and the revision question.

"There is no substitute for accurate knowledge. Know yourself, know your business, know your men."

Lee Iacocca

Sources of procurement financial and management information

The profile of procurement in public sector organisations is on the increase. Some of the most valuable assets the procurement team can add to an organisation's business are the brigading of procurement and financial information, and their application in a format that can enable the business to make strategic decisions continually to improve its output and performance. This applies to all aspects of the business of procurement, including:

- Current state analysis of the procurement function - necessary if continuing improvements are to be made to the service
- Future state of the function moving forward - a prerequisite of dynamic change within an organisation
- Customer needs and requirements - the bedrock of assessing optimal service delivery
- Expenditure analysis (historical demand, forecast demand, new project requirements) - important to develop sound strategic sourcing and category management strategies
- Supplier data - necessary for vendor assessment, and supplier relationship management
- Transaction cost analysis - vital to test the efficiency of the corporate (and self-service) procurement function
- Criticality/risk assessment and costing models - necessary for developing a proper approach to project management
- Market trends/cost 'hot-spots' (fuel, food, energy etc) - vital for budgetary forecasting purposes and the redistribution of an organisation's revenue expenditure, as well as cost avoidance/ damage limitation procurement strategies
- Market capability/capacity - vital to understand the best 'route to market'
- Market oligopolies/competition - necessary to gauge the strength of the contracting organisations bargaining power and alternative sourcing strategy
- Individual market-place performance by category/commodity - necessary to make the most out of category management
- Supply chain costs - to define the likes of inventory strategy, lean and agile etc
- Engagement in CSR policies - vital to support political imperatives
- Degree of business given to local supply markets and SME's
- Expenditure by supplier - necessary to assist in a supplier rationalisation strategy

- Expenditure patterns by category, product, service, supplier and business unit - important to apprise relevant parts of the organisation (and the powers at its summit) of inefficient practices and the need for different approaches, as well as highlighting areas where greater benefits are possible

- Historical performance of suppliers - necessary for awarding future contracts to these suppliers and engendering a model of continuous improvement in their outputs

- Price patterns, past and future, in order to discover vagaries in pricing policies and possible future variations (both up and down) in pricing models

- Innovation analysis - a measure such as this will identify whether procurement embraces innovation or not. If not, steps will have to be taken to improve procurement performance in this regard

- Alternative specification analysis - information here will show whether procurement really challenges 'the business' by examining a range of variants to existing specifications; and whether it encourages suppliers to offer innovative, outcomes-based solutions which improve the product or service and drive down costs across the business

- Benefits realisation modelling - benefits tracking should be at the very core of procurement intelligence-gathering. Year-on-year 'hard' (procurement cost reductions) and 'soft' (internal efficiency savings) benefits, typically in excess of the operational cost of corporate procurement, are the bedrock of the measurement of the performance of corporate procurement. CIPS stresses that all procurement departments should be assessed on the basis of the benefits that they have actually achieved, compared with what they were expected (or promised) to achieve. That can only be done if there is sufficient 'clean' procurement management information available to allow such conclusions to be drawn after the event, as it were

- Variety reduction and standardisation - data here should show that procurement tries as a matter of course to simplify and standardise outputs, both in terms of setting specifications and also business process throughout the procurement function, from requisitioning to BACS transfer to the supplier, and beyond, to the remainder of the supply chain

Learning activity 17.1

Apply each of these information types to your own organisation, or any organisation with which you are familiar. In which of these areas is your own organisation under-performing in terms of the information it is gathering and using?

Self-assessment question 17.1

Identify how the interpretation of procurement management information could aid innovation, either for procurement itself or for the organisation as a whole.

Not in the Top Ten?

The Local Government Task Force published (2007) a monograph entitled 'Ten Top Tips for a Successful Procurement Process'. These were the ten top tips:

1. Spend time planning
2. Establish roles and responsibilities
3. Ensure transparency of proceedings
4. Observe legalities
5. Accommodate innovation and secure Best Value
6. Prepare sound and complete tender documents
7. Consider monitoring and payment arrangements at the start
8. Ensure procedures provide for probity and accountability
9. Think before you act
10. Learn from the process

Nowhere in that list is one of the most fundamental principles, which would be something along the lines of 'operate with the most accurate, up-to-date, wide-ranging procurement management information.' The whole lifeblood of the procurement function is wrapped around the assimilation of clean data in order for it to make the correct strategic sourcing decisions and obtain Best Value for the organisation. The top ten tips list is, arguably, therefore fundamentally flawed.

"There does seem to be a very poor level of accounting and management information…I think the Chair has already touched on the idea that it is only a very small minority of governing bodies that have efficiency savings reported to them."

The Hon. Iain Wright, MP, questioning Mr Mark Haysom, Chief Executive of the Learning and Skills Council, at a Public Accounts Select Committee hearing on 18 April 2007

Robustness, usefulness and appropriateness of procurement management information to senior managers and other stakeholders

Dr Gordon Murray, of the IdEA, suggests that there is a responsibility on key decision-makers to take ownership of strategic procurement decisions using the medium of scrutiny (link: www.idea.gov.uk/idk/aio/1701470). Murray states that the four principles of scrutiny are:

- Critical friendship
- Engaging the public
- Owning the process
- Making an impact

Scrutinisers need to know where procurement stands in the context of exposure to risk on its portfolio of spend. Murray posits a simple map, highlighting degrees of risk:

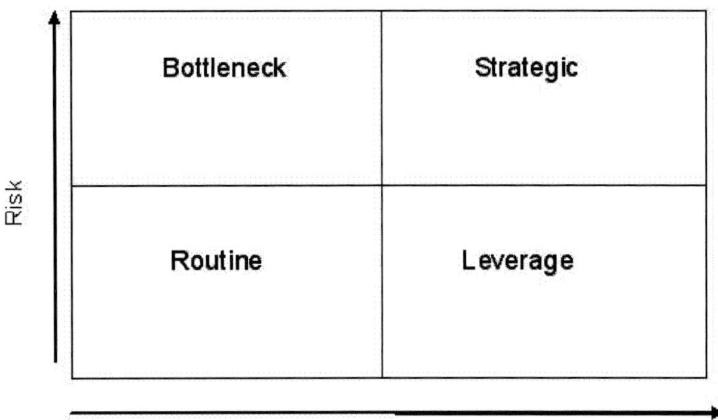

Diagram 17.1 Murray, Gordan., n.d. ...*In the Spotlight: Scrutinising Strategic Procurement*., pp.2

Bottleneck procurement categories are high-risk, and procurement departments should have significant business continuity arrangements to ensure there are alternative sourcing strategies in place. Quite often, there are a limited number of suppliers in bottleneck markets.

Strategic procurement categories assume significant investment in strategic alliances, collaboration, partnerships which are high-risk by definition. Risk management must be embedded into every element of these procurements and care taken that there is no falling-out between the partners, as alternative supply options might be very limited.

Leverage procurement categories are fairly low-risk. The supply markets are competitive and there is plenty of choice. The leverage might come from aggregation, consolidated procurement or collaboration/consortia purchasing. *Routine* procurements are extremely low-risk and should not be unduly engaging those involved in developing strategic procurement. The emphasis here is on reducing transactional costs.

This mapping exercise is very useful for those engaged in scrutinising and developing procurement strategy. If an organisation finds itself towards the apex of the map, firmly entrenched in the bottleneck/strategic areas, it needs a vastly different strategy to those comfortably occupying the lower echelons. The required skills and resources are different, for a start. This is a good example of how procurement management information can be fashioned to inform procurement strategy going forward and those at the top of an organisation (perhaps a chief executive chairing a strategic procurement board) need to be party to clear and accurate information about his or her organisation's place on the map. For example, by taking management action to move a clutch of suppliers from 'bottleneck' to 'leverage' will realise significant value savings.

Murray also outlines a list of key questions that the scrutinisers at the head of an organisation need to ask procurement staff in order that they might jointly develop new models of service delivery; review areas of high spend to identify areas for improving value-for-money; challenge the progress of major improvements; review the performance of strategic alliances and ensure that lessons are learned from strategic procurement projects and activities. Many of these require accurate and clear procurement management information, so it is worth summarising them in tabular form. Murray presents them in a phased format, moving through the stages of a project. He calls these 'gates.' Many of the questions are just as relevant in the context of 'complete procurement', not just random procurement projects, although Murray is more concerned with projects than the improvement of a procurement service as a project in itself.

Gate 0	Gate 1	Gate 2	Gate 3	Gate 4	Gate 5
Has the need been clearly articulated?	Is the high-level business case complete?	Are there suppliers that can do this?	Are supplier selection criteria objective?	Is the business case still valid?	Were the defined outcomes achieved?
What outcomes are to be achieved?	What budget is available?	Is the spec clear enough to deliver the best outcome?	Have we complied with all internal and external regulations?	Is the original outcome still valid?	What worked well?
Are these outcomes aligned to corporate objectives?	Have all possible options been considered?	What service standards are we setting?	Are sufficient resources available to ensure that outcomes are met?	Are key performance indicators being met?	How good a client were we from a supplier and stakeholder perspective?
Can the outcomes be measured in a different way?	Could the money be better spent?	What will be the benefits for the wider community?	What incentive is there for suppliers to perform well?	How will we capture the lessons learned?	What could we do better if we started over again?
What measures can be taken to demonstrate that outcomes have been met?	Have we considered all costs and benefits?	How are we addressing equalities?	What is the downstream performance measurement regime on the successful contractor?		How will the lessons learned be captured and communicated as a council asset?
How have we considered lessons learned from similar projects?	Is the timetable realistic?	Have we built in Health and Safety safeguards?	Have we got the cash?		
Can we afford it?	Have we got the people to do this?	Will we meet our CSR and sustainability objectives?			

17

	Does this project affect anything else we are doing?	Have staff been fully engaged and consulted?			
	Have all the alternative options been considered?	How will we control ongoing risk?			
	Have all risks been identified?	Are the award criteria linked to the needs of the contract?			
	Has a feasibility study been completed?	Is the procurement strategy legal and comprehensible to suppliers?			

Learning activity 17.2

Describe how Dr Murray's 'gate' model could be adapted for use as a model to review an organisation's procurement function in the round, rather than simply to deal with a specific project, and list any other questions that are missing from the table that would have to be added if one was reviewing procurement *in total*.

Self-assessment question 17.2

Thinking about your own organisation, or another with which you are familiar, identify at least five categories of spend that would fit into each of the four areas in the category map illustrated earlier, making a total of twenty categories in all.

Improvements to procurement financial and management information

"Industry leaders have used best practices and supporting technologies to reduce supply costs, mitigate risk, and gain comparative advantage. New techniques and technology approaches make these practices and results accessible to a broader number of organisations".

Tim Minahan

Anecdotally, the main source of procurement information for a particular local authority senior procurement executive prior to embracing e-procurement in 2005 would have emanated from suppliers, as there were no management information systems from which to make strategic sourcing decisions. There was budget information about staff, but nothing about levels of expenditure, rate of 'maverick' purchasing, or anything that could lead to any meaningful key performance indicators. As for measuring year-on-year procurement benefits, it could be said that, 'one might as well have tossed a straw from a bridge into the river's current' to see where that led. Some public sector organisations are still in that position today, although most are embracing some form of e-procurement, driven by national strategies and the need to drive down costs.

Many public sector organisations have utilised proprietary systems such as Oracle e-business suite or SAP, major Enterprise Resource Planning (ERP) systems which in due course can transform the procurement and finance operations; allowing for the rapid integration of procurement and payments, and ensuring a seamless transition from the manual past to the electronic present (and future). Oracle and SAP are only two of a diverse range of ERP systems in use, and without investment in an e-procurement and financial flow system of some sort, it is difficult to see how any public sector organisation can get the best from its procurement, either in terms of strategy, or benefits realisation.

E-procurement touches every aspect of the procurement business, from requisitioning, the i-catalogue, tendering, reverse auctions, through to the accounts payable regime via cheque, BACS and CHAPS payments, and the associated financial flow process via the General Ledger. Other modules of the ERP systems deal with project management, inventory control, human resources, customer relationship management, and in fact every business process that is undertaken by the organisation. In this way, there is a single platform, a 'one-stop-shop' if you like, which gives a standard data repository from which the various processes can be enacted.

The information flowing from there, governed by a vast array of reporting possibilities, is accurate, reliable, and can freely be used to improve the business, to cut costs, and to identify areas of under-performance, both in procurement, finance and elsewhere. The data can be used to develop procurement strategy to streamline and rationalise the function; to improve supplier relationships; to advise and inform stakeholders, customers and senior decision-makers; to root out inefficiencies; to aid collaboration; to direct staff into areas of greatest need or benefit; to move products and services from bottleneck to leverage categories; to aid in category management; to rationalise the supplier base; to direct more business towards SMEs; and a whole panoply of other initiatives.

Learning Activity 17.3

Describe how the information from at least different six procurement management information reports that could be generated from a typical e-procurement system could help significantly improve the procurement service at your own, or a typical public sector organisation.

Self-assessment question 17.3

Describe the key informational/reportage requirements that would be contained in a high-level business case for the implementation of an e-procurement system that would be necessary to receive business case sign-off from the project sponsor.

Summary

Accurate and robust procurement financial and management information are an absolute prerequisite of business improvement and hence procurement activity. The types of information required and available are many and diverse, and touch every element of the procurement process. It is important that decision-makers at the head of an organisation use a structured approach, such as Gordon Murray's 'Gate' model, to ensure that information is used correctly with the context of structured questions around the transformation/ improvement of the function. Stakeholders, whether internal or external may require input to, or be impacted upon by decisions and they will wish to be assured that such decision making was based upon accurate details. You should now be aware of the usefulness of mapping categories of spend in order to concentrate on 'strategic' and 'bottleneck' categories on the map, and use management information and action to move these to 'leverage' or even 'routine' categories. The incorporation of new technology and e-procurement systems will help you transform the provision and accuracy of procurement and financial management information. Committing to an Enterprise Resource Planning (ERP) system means that an organisation will have a single common platform which will drive all of its business processes, thus ensuring efficiency and effectiveness.

Revision question

Assess the types of procurement financial and management information that a chief executive might need to make informed strategic decisions about transforming a public sector organisation's business.

Feedback

Feedback on learning activity 17.1

'Apply each of these information types to your own organisation, or any organisation with which you are familiar. In which of these areas is your own organisation under-performing in terms of the information it is gathering and using?'

The list of relevant management information is laid out in the main text, so all you have to do is provide an example against each type. The list is not exhaustive, so if you think of any other types of information, feel free to express your views. If you thought, for example, that your organisation did not conduct current or future state analysis before a review of procurement, then you might take the view that an adequate review was impossible. 'Future state' in this context means asking the business (i.e. its stakeholders and customers) where it needs to be post-implementation of the transformed procurement function. Another critical area is market trends. If your organisation gets that wrong, then the costs can be alarming. If you sign up to a fixed two-year energy contract at the wrong time, such as when prices are peaking, then that is a fault probably caused partly by poor management information which should have highlighted the relevant price trends over time. You would make the point here, though, that accurate forecasting is equally vital. That is why more and more organisations are hiring energy consultants to assist them in making the correct decision.

Feedback on self-assessment question 17.1

'Identify how the interpretation of procurement management information could aid innovation, either for procurement itself or for the organisation as a whole.'

This is trickier, because innovation as a term is ephemeral, shifting. It need not be innovation as in the delivery of a brand-new radical product; instead it could be an innovative business process or an innovative change in business or procurement objectives. You might want to have a look at some innovative procurement case studies, easily available from the world-wide web, and see how procurement management information contributed to the innovation. A simple example concerns the Gloucester College of Art and Technology, the Board of which used procurement's own market intelligence information to authorise the procurement of an innovative satellite navigation van that was capable of connecting to the internet via a GPS from any location. This replaced an outreach van service that had been ferrying laptops out to various fixed community locations for years. However, these locations were often hard to reach for people living in remote parts of the Cotswolds, or who were elderly or couldn't afford the trip to the village halls and community centres. Laptops were able to connect to the sat-van via wireless broadband connectivity and they were taken to, for example, a sheltered housing community which did not have wireless broadband itself and, on one occasion, a village inn!

Feedback on learning activity 17.2

'Describe how Dr Murray's 'gate' model could be adapted for use as a model to review an organisation's procurement function in the round, rather than simply to deal with a specific project, and list any other questions that are missing from the table that would have to be added if one was reviewing procurement in total.'

The 'Gate' model is based around management information appertaining to procurement projects, but could be used to review a corporate procurement function. The question here is at what stage would each of the questions need to be asked? How many stages are there? Are the bulk of the questions asked at the inception of the review? How many of the questions are irrelevant? How many are missing? Try to visualise how these questions might apply to your own organisation and write down for which of them sufficient procurement and financial management information currently exists to enable solid decisions to be made about procurement transformation.

Feedback on self-assessment question 17.2

'Thinking about your own organisation, or another with which you are familiar, identify at least five categories of spend that would fit into each of the four areas in the category map illustrated earlier, making a total of twenty categories in all.'

This depends upon the type of organisation and its pattern of spend. If you are in a social work department commissioning services for the elderly, you might find more spend categories are in the 'bottleneck' or 'strategic' parts of the map. However, you are still likely to find 'leverage' or 'routine' items such as food, transportation, temporary agency staff etc. On the other hand, if you are in a third sector social enterprise that purely buys spare parts to refurbish donated pc's and laptops, almost all of the components on your map would be 'routine' or 'leverage.' You need to stress the importance of reducing as many 'bottleneck' categories on the map to 'leverage' or 'routine' as you can.

Feedback on learning activity 17.3

'Describe how the information from at least different six procurement management information reports that could be generated from a typical e-procurement system could help significantly improve the procurement service at your own, or a typical public sector organisation.'

Oracle provides over 100 reports in its core applications suite alone. The addition of an electronic data warehouse with some reporting software such as 'Discoverer' multiplies that fivefold. You will be looking here for management information that really makes a difference to the business, say in the area of benefits realisation modelling or performance indicators. You can explore every element of the P2P business to select key information upon which to report.

Feedback on self-assessment question 17.3

'Describe the key informational/reportage requirements that would be contained in a high-level business case for the implementation of an e-procurement system that would be necessary to receive business case sign-off from the project sponsor.'

Imagine, say, you are head of procurement in a registered social landlord organisation (third sector) and the board of your organisation is in talks about absorbing another RSL in the geographical area. The benefits seem to be obvious (synergy, efficiency savings, lower procurement costs, etc) but what key procurement management information would you need to release to the Board in order to help it make decisions about future strategy? What procurement/financial information would you need from the other merging organisation? If you deal with this question in that practical type of context, several interesting possibilities emerge. You don't have to confine yourself to the example the author has given. Again, supply markets, vendor positioning, category mapping, stakeholder mapping and some of the other information which can readily be assimilated are vitally important in this context.

Feedback on revision question

'Assess the types of procurement financial and management information that a chief executive might need to make informed strategic decisions about transforming a public sector organisation's business.'

Your answer should start by your identification of as many of the different types of procurement and financial management information that you can recall. If you wish to concentrate on transformation of a procurement service, you will need to stress the need for thorough current state and future state analyses and measurement of the strategic gaps between them and how those gaps may be made up. The future state can only be accomplished following significant consultation with stakeholders, customers and staff.

You will need to position your answer within the context of the business; the chief executive's role; the corporate objectives of the business; the systems and business processes it operates; who its market is; and who are the stakeholders influencing the direction of travel. You could explain a few of the procurement models that find approbation these days: category management, self-service procurement, the Centre-Led Action Network Model (CLAN), wholly corporate procurement, major user procurement and so on.

You could mention the desire of forward-thinking organisations to integrate procurement and payments and operate a seamless 'req-to-cheque' process, and the type of management information that would be required for that. Transactional costs in this context would be P2P, not just procurement. In that way, you could address the fact that the payments side would probably add much more cost than the procurement side, even with e-procurement systems (truly electronic self-billing is still in its infancy in the public sector).

You need to clearly point out the relationship between procurement and finance, which is a close one. Many heads of procurement report to the director of finance, and general ledger information can be modified to suit the needs of procurement professionals if they don't have their own suite of procurement management information. The two professions are to a degree inter-dependent and both should be sending out the same message on efficiency, effectiveness, best value and cost-reduction.

You might conclude by pointing out that many organisations do not have decent management information systems and, in such cases, transformation without investment in IT and e-procurement will not be possible. You might also wish to say that in these times of straitened budgets, getting past the feasibility study, never mind the business case, is not nearly so easy as it has been.

Suggested further reading

Tony Bovaird, and Elke Loffler, (eds), (2003), Public Management and Governance ch. 8, 10, 11, 12, 18.

Gerry Johnson, and Kevan Scholes, (eds) (2001), *Exploring Public Sector Strategy* ch. 15

Study Session 18

"Critically evaluate the relevance of Excellence models, in particular the Procurement Excellence Model (PEM), for providing an effective performance evaluation framework for organisations"

Introduction

This study session considers the key features of approaches to the evaluation of procurement performance. An insight will be given into the essential aspect of total quality management which should be the basis of all professional procurement activities. This is followed by consideration of models that have developed and one that is specifically adapted for procurement (and all related aspects of procurement when considered on a whole life/life cycle basis). This is the Procurement Excellence Model and it will be discussed in the context of providing an effective framework for organisations in the public procurement environment.

Session Learning Objectives

After completing this session you should be able to:

- assess Total Quality Management (TQM), European Foundation for Quality Management (EFQM) and the Procurement Excellence Model (PEM)
- secure stakeholder commitment to, and involvement in, the development and application of performance evaluation
- compare and contrast Procurement Excellence Model (PEM) with other relevant models
- explore the value of adapting performance evaluation models to suit different organisations and types of procurement functions

Unit content coverage

This study session covers part of the following topic from the official CIPS unit content documents: *Critically evaluate methods and processes of performance evaluation of procurement* and specifically: *Critically evaluate the relevance of Excellence models, in particular the Procurement Excellence Model (PEM), for providing an effective performance evaluation framework for organisations.*

Prior knowledge

Prior to this study session you should have completed study sessions 1; 2; 3; 4; 5; 6; 7; 8; 9; 10; 11; 12; 13; 14; 15; 16; 17.

Timing

You should take about 4-5hrs to read and complete this section, including learning activities, self assessment questions, the suggested further reading and the revision question.

Background and context

Two main aspects provide the background to this topic:

Firstly, the growth of Japanese manufacturing from the 1950's on a national level and then the domination of the Japanese in their approach to manufacturing business internationally. These led to the demise of many, previously dominant western manufacturing entities. Examples include automobiles, white goods, motor cycles, televisions and video etc. By the early 1980's the Japanese approach to manufacturing was being adopted as much as possible in the western world. To be successful organisations had to recognise and learn of the approaches that were necessary to bring success or in many cases to enable survival. In due course the management techniques were modified and adapted and utilised not just in manufacturing and production but in service environments and non-manufacturing arenas. One of these approaches, Total Quality Management (TQM), has at its heart the recognition of a chain of customers and suppliers – and these may not necessarily be external to the organisation. This is analogous to Supply Chain Management (SCM), which has a similar origin and a similar underpinning ethos; a chain of customers and suppliers (again not necessarily external and even if so then they are considered as a part of an 'extended enterprise' with common goals and objectives).

The second is that at the core of both TQM and SCM is the increased recognition of the impact that effective procurement can have upon an organisation. This has manifested itself in enhanced status for purchasing and supply chain management, in respect of both personnel and organisation structure. Integration of activities around the procurement function has seen considerable benefits to commercial organisations and this is being repeated across the public sector. As integration takes place and benefits are realised, the activities that might have once been disparate are now managed in a more holistic sense. This is particularly so when considering a major asset procurement (e.g. buildings) or outsourcing of a previously 'in house' activity (e.g. maintenance of vehicles). Such activities have a potential long lifetime. A contract for outsourcing of training provision may be for as long as twenty plus years, for example, Cranfield University providing academic service to the MOD; or a partnering arrangement such as Somerset County Council and Taunton Dene Borough Council working with IBM for a ten year period. When a major weapon platform is procured for the MOD it is likely that the equipment will be in service for many years (major ships such as an aircraft carrier will probably be in use for thirty to forty years) and similarly with major civil engineering construction projects such as schools and hospitals or roads.

Hence not only has procurement itself gained recognition but as integration of related activities grows, the opportunities for further enhancement of performance, based on procurement and a chain of integrated activities or processes across organisational boundaries grows even further.

Total Quality Management (TQM)

"If you don't measure it, it will not improve. If you don't monitor it, it will get worse"

Authur Schneiderman

Total Quality Management (TQM) was borne out of the requirement for quality control in manufacturing. The fewer rejects that came off the production line, the better the financial position. As the Japanese built up their manufacturing industry in the 1950s, quality management became a major theme, resulting in a huge expansion of exports to Europe by the 1970s due to superior quality and cheaper goods. By the early 1980s it was realised that quality was the key to competitive production in worldwide markets. Since then the drive for quality has grown beyond manufacturing to encompass all processes in organisations and the ISO 9000 standard was developed. This specifies requirements for documentation, implementation and maintenance of a quality system.

> "The totality of features and characteristics of a product or service that bear on its ability to satisfy stated or implied needs"
>
> ISO 8402-1986

However, TQM is an approach focused upon managing for the future, and is far wider in its application than just assuring product or service quality – it is a way of managing people and business processes to ensure complete customer satisfaction at every stage, both internally and externally. TQM, when combined with effective leadership, results in an organisation doing the right things right, first time.

Learning activity 18.1

Seek definitions of quality from any textbooks with which you are familiar or from the World Wide Web. Definitions often vary depending on the source. You should however note some consistencies between them.

TQM is not about paying a higher price for a luxury product. It is about a philosophy of working that ensure customers are always delighted with the service or product they receive, fully meeting their expectations every time. In each organisation there are a series of 'quality chains', a series of customers, suppliers and interfaces, whether these customers are internal or external. At any stage these quality chains can be broken and faults tend to multiply all the way along. Given that the principle is to give each customer what he/she wants, then even an internal problem or misunderstanding will have a detrimental effect on the external customer at the end of the quality chain. You can see that a quality chain is not so very different from a supply chain. Indeed, arguably to be most effective, supply chains and quality chains should be synonymous.

At the heart of TQM is the customer/supplier relationship along each chain. At each interface are processes. Within the organisations along each chain or network, there must be commitment to quality, communication of the quality ethos and the willingness to change organisational culture to support TQM working. People, processes and systems therefore support TQM. These are the management activities necessary for effective operations. All must be supported by leadership. This is leadership to detect and force out waste and focus on prevention of problems. Hence, TQM starts at the top of an organisation in order to initiate change and is required to involve every individual in order to be successful.

Once the strategic direction for an organisation has been set by implementing a TQM system, it needs *Performance Measures* to ensure that the organisation remains on track and that standards are being achieved. (this is detailed in the following study session)

Self assessment question 18.1

Go to the Business Enterprise and Regulatory Reform (BERR) website (www.berr.gov.uk) or any other resource to find out more about the performance management aspect of TQM. What are its limitations?

European Foundation for Quality Management (EFQM)

As the TQM model gained credence in Europe, it was realised that this was the way to improve manufacturing in order to compete with competitors from the East, who were producing quality goods at competitive prices.

In 1988 The Presidents of 14 European companies came together to create the European Foundation for Quality Management. EFQM is a not-for-profit membership foundation focused on serving its members' information and networking needs.

Its mission is,"to be the driving force for sustainable excellence in organisations in Europe." (EFQM, n.d.)

The EFQM is best know for the Excellence Model it has developed and has come to be used by many organisations as a means of performance evaluation.

Developed in the beginning of 1992, the EFQM Excellence Model was an essential framework for assessing organisations for the European Quality Award. Currently it is the most widely used organisational framework in Europe and is the basis for a large majority of national and regional Quality Awards.

The EFQM Excellence Model

The EFQM Excellence Model, which recognises there are many approaches to achieving sustainable excellence in all aspects of performance, is based on the premise that:

> 'Excellent results with respect to Performance, Customers, People and Society are achieved through Leadership driving Policy and Strategy that is delivered through People, Partnerships and Resources, and Processes.' (EFQM)

The fundamental concept behind the model is that of 'excellence'. By excellent it is meant than an organisation will display all of the following criteria:

- Results Orientation: achieving results that delight all the organisation's stakeholders.
- Customer Focus: creating sustainable customer value.
- Leadership and Constancy of Purpose: visionary and inspirational leadership, coupled with constancy of purpose.
- Management by Processes and Facts: managing the organisation through a set of interdependent and interrelated systems, processes and facts.
- People Development and Involvement: maximising the contribution of employees through their development and involvement.
- Continuous Learning, Innovation and Improvement: challenging the status quo and effecting change by utilising learning to create innovation and improvement opportunities.
- Partnership Development: developing and maintaining value-adding partnerships.
- Corporate Social Responsibility: exceeding the minimum regulatory framework in which the organisation operates and striving to understand and respond to the expectations of their stakeholders in society

Regardless of sector, size, structure or maturity; to be successful, organisations need to establish an appropriate management framework. As a structure for an organisation's management system the EFQM Excellence Model shares with TQM the requirement for absolute understanding and commitment from the highest levels of leadership within an organisation in order to be effective.'

One of the get advantages of the EFQM Excellence Model is that it can be used in a number of different ways:

- 'As a tool for Self-Assessment
- As a way to Benchmark with other organisations
- As a guide to identify areas for Improvement

- As the basis for a common Vocabulary and a way of thinking

- As a Structure for the organisation's management system' (EFQM)

Many organisations use the model as a tool for self assessment with the aim to meet the above criteria that are seen as defining excellence. The EFQM Excellence Model allows organisations to do this through its non-prescriptive framework allowing the ability to grade themselves against detailed criteria separated under the nine headings. Five of these are 'Enablers' and four are 'Results'.

The 'Enabler' criteria cover what an organisation does.

The 'Results' criteria cover what an organisation achieves.

You should note that 'Results' are caused by 'Enablers' and 'Enablers' are improved using feedback from 'Results'.

The EFQM Model is presented in diagrammatic form below. The arrows emphasise the dynamic nature of the Model. They show innovation and learning helping to improve enablers that in turn lead to improved results.'

Diagram 18.1 The EFQM Model

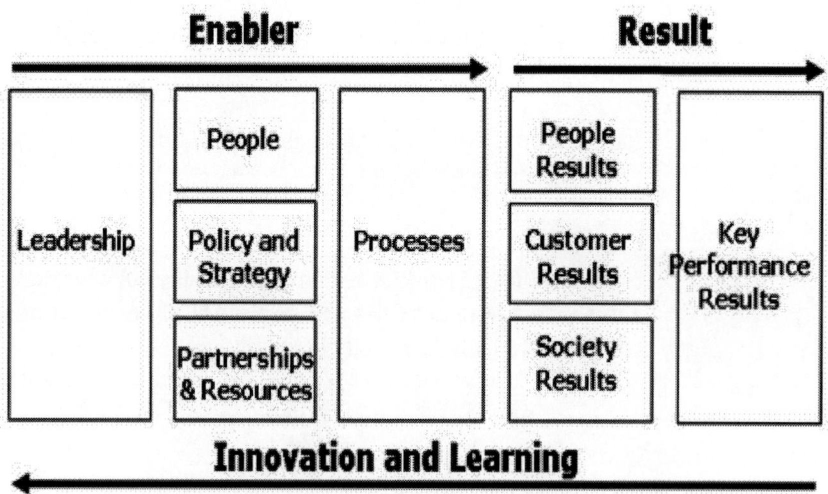

Source M. Jenkins, Cranfield University

The Criteria for the EFQM Excellence Model

The Model's 9 boxes represent the criteria against which to assess an organisation's progress towards Excellence. Each of the nine criteria has a definition, which explains the high level meaning of that criterion.

- **Leadership**
- **Policy and Strategy**
- **People**
- **Partnerships and Resources**
- **Processes**
- **Customer Results**
- **People Results**
- **Society Results**
- **Key Performance Results**

(EFQM., n.d., pp.13-15)

Learning activity 18.2
What do you think the definition would be against each of the nine headings (above) of the EFQM Excellence Model?

Benefits of using the EFQM Excellence Model

Self assessment via the EFQM Excellence Model allows organisations to identify areas of opportunity for improvement to which they can develop and implement targeted improvement plans. Likewise, because the Excellence Model identifies areas of strength it allows the organisation to further identify why it is an area of strength and what it is that makes it so effective. Such aspects could be transferred to other areas in order to improve them. Through such measures an organisation may enhance its growth and improve its performance.

Over the years a number of research studies have investigated the correlation between the adoption of holistic Models (such as the EFQM Excellence Model) and improved organisational results. The majority of such studies show a positive linkage. (For more information on the EFQM see further reading).

The advantages of the EFQM model over TQM (in its purest sense) is that it takes into account the many stakeholders which are present in a public sector organisation notably Customer and Society Results. Thus the sustainability agenda and other political goals can be incorporated into the organisation's vision of excellence.

The EFQM Excellence Model applied to procurement: The Procurement Excellence Model (PEM)

The Procurement Excellence Model (PEM), (available on the OGC website) provides a guide to applying the EFQM excellence model to procurement activities so as to identify areas of strength upon which to build, and opportunities for development. OGC states that the guide 'provides procurement related comment and interpretation to each of the main criteria in order to give emphasis and direction when applying the Excellence Model' to the Procurement function. (OGC). What is meant by this is that each of the nine criteria of the EFQM excellence model are put into context in terms of the organisations procurement activities by identifying the key performance indicators, other areas to address, procurement good practices, and possible measures for improvement.

There are three versions of guidance available on the website:

- The Procurement Excellence Pilot
- The Procurement Excellence Guide
- Local Authority Procurement Excellence Guide

The first of these is The Procurement Excellence Pilot, where the described intent is to 'provide a quick and easy method of assessing the health of your procurement operation' to meet the aims of identifying areas of strength and where improvement may be required. It is essentially a simplified form of The Procurement Excellence Guide and as such is not as 'comprehensive or rigorous as the full Excellence Model' (OGC, 1999) but it still covers the same topics and provides a good starting point via the sample model provided for those wishing to apply the PEM to their organisation's procurement activity. This is undertaken through the provision of a simplified template and scorecard against which an organisation may rate itself.

This simplified form may be sufficient for many organisation's needs but if areas need examining in greater depth then the second title – *The Procurement Excellence Guide* – should be used due to the greater depth of detail in relating the nine criteria of excellence (discussed above) to procurement. Rather that providing a set template greater emphasis is placed on the types of issues which should be addressed under the headings, allowing for the development of a model more specific to an individual organisation.

Whereas the latter two versions can be applicable to any organisation through generalisation the third version, as indicated by the title, has more criteria relevant to local authorities within the context of the same template system demonstrated in the Procurement Excellence Pilot for quick reference and use.

As mentioned above, another use for the Excellence Model may be to benchmark your organisation against others to determine whether performance is above or below comparable organisations – but this should not be seen as an 'end state' activity. It is a tool that allows an indication of progress/decline against others. Comparing the excellence of other organisations against areas that are weak in your own organisation will allow potential identification of opportunities and provide a focus for action. From this there can be an identification of the reasons for that organisation achieving a high score. In turn this will permit consideration of how these skills or attributes can be transferred into your own organisation.

Self assessment question 18.2
Go to the OGC website. Using the templates and scorecards found in the Procurement Excellence Pilot, score the procurement performance of your organisation or one you are familiar with. What are the areas for improvement?

Fundamental to the use of these models is a recognition that these have emerged from a methodology for improving production through a series of evolution and development into a range of initiatives and approaches, which have now become *de rigour* in the public sector generally and procurement specifically (e.g. Six Sigma). You may recall that in the first study section this was referred to and some indication of how that has manifested itself was given.

The Balanced Scorecard

Another model which can be used to measure and improve an organisation's performance is with the Balanced Scorecard.

The first Balanced Scorecards were devised by Robert Kaplan and David Norton (1992) for financially driven private sector organisations and were based on research from the late 1980s. What they showed was that:

- "Less than 10% of effectively formulated strategies are executed effectively"
- "In 90% of failures the real problem isn't the strategy, it is bad execution"

They found that traditional measures of evaluation focused on 'where are we', whereas successful organisations asked 'where are we going'. What typically distinguished successful organisations were:

- They managed performance as well as measured it
- Strategic direction was provided at Board level
- There was a corporate 'no blame' culture
- Performance was everyone's responsibility
- They used a range of financial and non-financial performance measures
- There was clear visibility of performance throughout the organisation

18

A balanced scorecard represents the translation of an organisation's strategy into a linked set of measures that define the long-term strategic objectives, as well as provide a mechanism for obtaining feedback on progress and a means to monitor performance. It uses integral performance measurement to track and adjust business strategy. In addition to the usual financial perspective, it includes a customer perspective, operations (processes) and the ability of the organisation to innovate and learn. The scorecard requires the organisation to ask four questions:

- What is important to our shareholders (stakeholders)?
- How are we perceived by our customers?
- Which internal processes can add value?
- Are we innovative and ready for the future?

Below is an example of a balanced scorecard in which the four questions can be seen to be addressed:

Diagram 18.2 Balanced scorecard

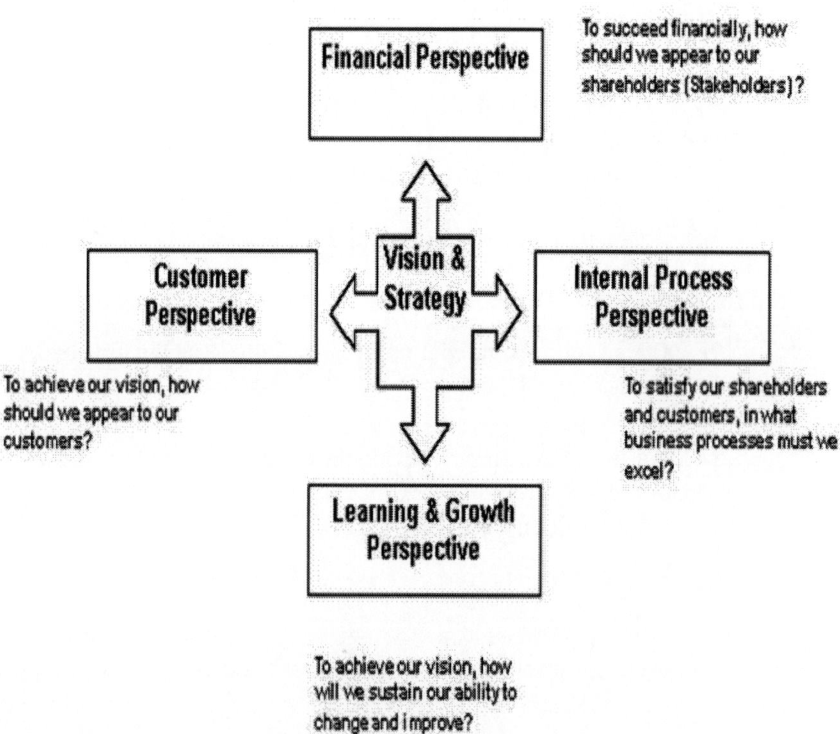

Source M. Jenkins, Cranfield University

Comparing and contrasting the models; adapting models

Each model has its own strengths and weaknesses and will not necessarily suit all organisations.

TQM is very focused on measurements in order to ensure that what is actually happening is what was originally specified in order to uphold standards. Where there is a gap, then this is an area for improvement actions. Many differing diagnostic tools (e.g. Isikawa's 'fishbone' diagram for cause and effect analysis) can be utilised within the concept when relevant.

The EFQM Excellence Model is more of a diagnostic tool that gives a holistic view of 'where we are now', hence its use as an evaluation tool for an award system. Obviously it does flag up the areas where improvement is needed and is vital for this element alone. The PEM applies this model to Procurement specifically and is therefore extremely useful for those in the

Procurement function – half the work is completed already, hence no need to attempt to relate the criteria yourself.

Diagram 18.3 PEM Model

The Defence Balanced Scorecard for 2007-08 is shown below. The objectives that form the Defence Plan are shown in italics and are described in detail in subsequent pages.

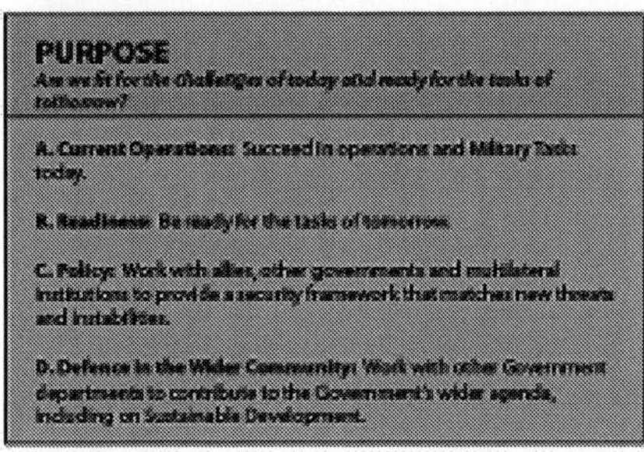

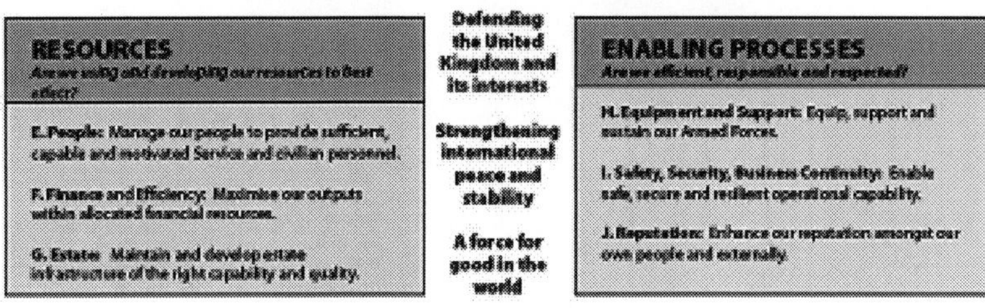

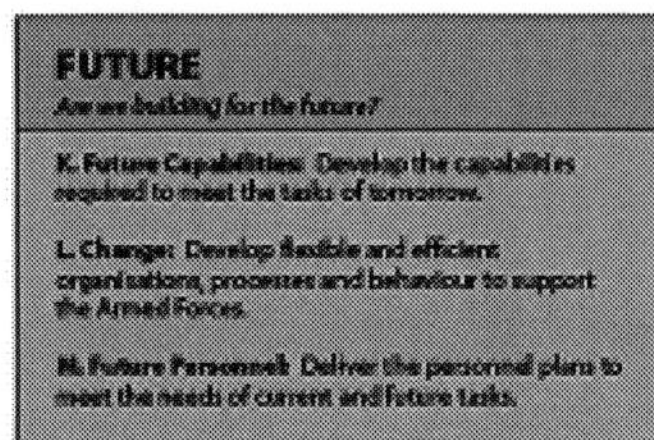

Source MOD, 2007, *Ministry of Defence Plan 2007.*, pp.10

The Balanced Scorecard is another method of evaluating the organisation with a slightly different angle from EFQM. EFQM is still valuable in this context however as it could provide the input for the Learning & Growth Perspective of the Balanced Scorecard. The Balanced Scorecard places vision and strategy at the heart of the organisation and its performance evaluation and is therefore more flexible than EFQM and more future orientated. It can be adapted to the organisation's needs if the broad outline and sense is applied. For example the MoD, as a major public sector based procurement organisation uses the Balanced Scorecard with the following 4 elements:

- Purpose (Outputs)
- Resources
- Enabling Processes
- Future Capabilities (MoD, 2005)

From this it could be identified that the PEM (in any of its guises) would be the most beneficial for a public sector organisation. This however is not necessarily the case. Depending upon where a procurement organisation is in its own development, variations on the model, or changes in emphasis might be necessary. It may even be that a model that has a wider perspective is important.

To illustrate this it is worth considering the case of the MOD.

The Defence Balanced Scorecard is measured at the very top level management board and underpinned by scorecards at lower levels across the Department. At the very centre of this contextual setting is the Vision of the MOD. Around this are the four key elements to be considered, namely:

- Purpose (Outputs);
- Resources;
- Enabling Processes;
- Future Capabilities.

Against each of these is a key question which has to be answered. In respect to each of the four elements above they are:

- Are we fit for today's challenges and ready for tomorrow's tasks?
- Are we using our resources to best effect?
- Are we a high performing organisation?
- Are we building for future success?

This is a version of the Balanced Scorecard that has been adapted for use within the MOD. It takes a high level view, although this could be developed to take into account any areas that those stakeholders within the MOD procurement environment felt were pertinent. Thus any of the subheadings shown in the diagram above could be adapted to suit procurement focussed aspects that would be measured

Taking existing models and utilising them without any consideration of the contextual setting of a particular public sector organisation can ruin any benefit that could be gained from an adaptation (as opposed to adoption) of the particular approach. Further to gain maximum benefit in terms of actual performance enhancement (why measure performance if it is not ultimately to enhance performance!), more potential opportunities will be highlighted if measurement is across the spectrum of procurement activities to gain a holistic perspective and thus organisation wide benefit. This is necessary in order to avoid sub-optimisation. The MOD utilises the term Acquisition to cover the whole life perspective and hence a wider cross boundary perspective is obtained through the measurement activity. Prior to this the MOD was open to criticism that it operated in 'silos' reflecting the old fashioned/traditional view of purchasing as a reactive function. Boundary spanning measurements can reinforce a modern proactive view of procurement – especially in the contextual setting of the (apparently bureaucratic) public sector.

In general, there is concern amongst many that quantitative measures, rather than qualitative measures, are being utilised by many organisations. For example, newspapers and media reports frequently highlight that the police are improving arrest figures by working to a set of performance measurement criteria that does not adequately distinguish between types of crime/ offence. Similarly in public procurement there are many who perceive that performance is about meeting financial targets without taking into account quality of service provided. This may or may not be the case, but is a feature that has to be taken into account when discussing, and more importantly applying measures to different contexts.

Summary

The purpose of this section has been to identify several of the most popular models currently used by organisations, and their purpose in evaluation as a means towards improvement through performance management. You will have noted that these allow opportunity to measure various aspects of a procurement organisation's activities. Underpinning all of these is the concept of TQM and the important link between customer and supplier throughout the supply chain.

To some extent you can adapt these approaches to measurement to suit your organisation and an example was given where the balanced scorecard was shown in a specific public sector context.

Revision Question

Assume that you are the head of a procurement department in a large public sector organisation (not a local authority). Examine considerations for what you would take into account when developing a relevant performance evaluation of the department.

Feedback

Feedback on learning activity 18.1

'Seek definitions of quality from any textbooks with which you are familiar or from the World Wide Web. Definitions often vary depending on the source. You should however note some consistencies between them.'

The American Society for Quality in their glossary cite quality as having two technical meanings: '1. the characteristics of a product or service that bear on its ability to satisfy stated or implied needs; 2. a product or service free of deficiencies.' (ASQ)

Philip B. Crosby (1983, pp.8) stated that 'quality is conformance to requirements' arguing it is precisely measurable. The challenge with this definition is that the customer and the producer may not have the same notion of requirements.

Peter F. Drucker (2007, pp.206) in contrast states that 'Quality in a product or service is not what the supplier puts in. It is what the customer gets out and is willing to pay for'. This puts the emphasis on defining quality towards the customer; something evident in the greater majority of definitions such as, Noriaki Kano's 'quality must be quality' (1984, pp.39-48) and Joseph M. Juran's (1992) view of quality as something the customer determines as fit for use.

Any definition of quality is undoubtedly going to be subjective, with each person or sector conforming to an individual definition. There seems to be two main camps of opinion when it comes to defining quality. This is whether quality is defined by the producer or the consumer.

When it comes to procurement performance management however emphasis should be on ensuring an effective linkage of processes that extend throughout the supply chain, or within a holistic perspective of procurement. i.e. from identification of requirement through all activities if necessary to disposal of equipment or asset; or termination of service. IN this sense, quality is perceived as fitness for purpose at every linkage between customer and supplier.

Feedback to self assessment question 18.1

'Go to the Business Enterprise and Regulatory Reform (BERR) website www.berr.gov.uk or any other resource to find out more about the performance management aspect of TQM. What are its limitations?'

The TQM performance management model was originally focused on numerical outputs. This was particularly knows as statistical process control and was developed in the manufacturing business where this is very relevant to production quality control. It is of course more difficult to determine numerical measurements for qualitative objectives such as "staff satisfaction." Although metrics can be defined such as "staff turnover," which may give indications, results will often be skewed. In this example consider the effect of high local unemployment on such a metric – staff turnover is likely to be low whether the staff are content or not. Its other drawback is that metrics can indicate short term improvements/changes as long-term strategies are often more qualitative. Particularly in local government, decisions based on securing sustainable growth can indicate poorly on performance metrics alone.

Feedback to Self Assessment question 18.2

'Go to the OGC website. Using the templates and scorecards found in the Procurement Excellence Pilot, score the procurement performance of your organisation or one you are familiar with. What are the areas for improvement?'

By scoring your organisation you should have been able to get a grasp of its relative strengths and weaknesses, and thus the areas for improvement. What these areas for improvement actually are is going to differ depending on your individual organisations procurement strategy.

A good example of a public sector organisation using the Procurement Excellence Model as a means of identifying and engaging in the required areas of improvement is Pembroke County Council when devising its *Procurement Strategy: 2006-2011* (Pembroke County Council., n.d.). The council conducts annual assessments using the PEM provided by the OGC, and then uses the results to identify its current performance against a number of objectives laid out in the strategy, allowing improvement targets to be developed.

Feedback on Learning activity 18.2

'What do you think the definition would be against each of the nine headings (above) of the EFQM Excellence Model?'

The following are the criteria against each of the nine headings:

- **Leadership**
  'Excellent Leaders develop and facilitate the achievement of the mission and vision. They develop organisational values and systems required for sustainable success and implement these via their actions and behaviours. During periods of change they retain a constancy of purpose. Where required, such leaders are able to change direction of the organisation and inspire others to follow.'

- **Policy and Strategy**
  'Excellent organisations implement their mission and vision by developing a stakeholder focused strategy that takes account of the market and sector in which it operates. Policies, plans, objectives and processes are developed and deployed to deliver strategy.'

- **People**
  'Excellent organisations manage, develop and release the full potential of their people at an individual, team-based and organisational level. They promote fairness and equality and involve and empower their people. They care for, communicate,

reward and recognise, in a way that motivates staff and builds commitment to using their skills and knowledge for the benefit of the organisation.'

- **Partnerships and Resources**
  'Excellent organisations plan to manage external partnerships, suppliers and internal resources in order to support policy and strategy and the effective operation of processes. During planning and whilst managing partnerships and resources, they balance the current and future needs of the organisation, the community, and the environment.'

- **Processes**
  'Excellent organisations design, manage and improve processes in order to fully satisfy, and generate increasing value for, customers and other stakeholders.'

- **Customer Results**
  'Excellent organisations comprehensively measure and achieve outstanding results with respect to their customers.'

- **People Results**
  'Excellent organisations comprehensively measure and achieve outstanding results with respect to their people.'

- **Society Results**
  'Excellent organisations comprehensively measure and achieve outstanding results with respect to society.'

- **Key Performance Results**
  'Excellent organisations comprehensively measure and achieve outstanding results with respect to the key element of their policy and strategy.' (EFQM pp.13-15)

Feedback to revision question

'Assume that you are the head of a procurement department in a large public sector organisation (not a local authority). Examine considerations for what you would take into account when developing a relevant performance evaluation of the department.'

Before commencing you might find it useful to revisit the study session 5 which discussed what it is you wish to measure, why it is relevant, and to whom it is you are disseminating the information. With this in mind, approaches to ensuring a customer focus in any evaluation should be to the fore in your thinking. IN particular you should talk about TQM, EFQN and PQM. Underpinning this is the philosophy inherent in TQM. The customer ethos here should be paramount, although arguably this should extend to the range of stakeholders that has been discussed in earlier study sessions.

EFQN brings a more process led view of performance with its focus being upon excellence in a number of specific areas. You should note and comment upon all of these areas, for example leadership, people, etc. It is important to note that you can adapt these to suit the circumstances of your particular organisation. It may be for example that you wish to emphasise your response to a particular national policy such as professionalisation of your staff, and here you could emphasise the training programmes or educational courses that are being attended; and the impact upon the team, organisation and society in general. If need be, you could also talk about the balanced scorecard, noting that that approach can also be adapted to suit particular situations.

All the approaches have strengths, but in your particular organisation you should focus upon the PEM, as it is grounded in procurement and you could utilise to ensure that you send pertinent information to the right audience. Additionally, this is an activity which must not be seen as a one off; it is a continuing activity that can be used as a benchmark against other organisations, and also to record progress against relevant criteria (or to highlight where action needs to be taken if there is any detrimental response).

Suggested Further Reading

Audit Commission & Improvement and Development Agency (2006) *A Manager's Guide to Performance Management* (2nd edn)

M. Bourne, P. Bourne. (2000) *Understanding the Balanced Scorecard in a Week.*

N. Olve, J. RoyM. Wetter, (1999) *Performance Drivers: a practical guide to using the Balanced Scorecard.*

J.J. Coyle; E.J Bardi; & C.J Langley; (2003) *The Management Of Business Logistics – A Supply Chain Perspective.*

H. de Bruijn (2002) *Managing Performance in the Public Sector.*

The Office of Government Commerce Successful Delivery Toolkit Ver 5.0 -
http://www.ogc.go.uk/Resources_Toolkit_resources_for_all.asp
www.efqm.org

Study session 19

"Critically evaluate the methods and outcomes of performance evaluation of procurement against appropriate models and remedy any weaknesses"

Introduction

It is relevant to take into account not just the models and approaches for performance measurement but how applicable they are to differing approaches to procurement and whether the information that is gathered is valid and can be generalised. By this it is meant whether it can be applied across a whole range of procurement scenarios, or instead is specific to certain situations. You will also have opportunity to utilise work that you have undertaken for other study sessions by examining the processes that will identify the need to make improvements and how to make them; as well as revisit the topic of benchmarking and what it entails along with its application within the context of public sector procurement.

Session Learning Objectives

After completing this session you should be able to:

- compare models of processes or outcomes
- assess validation models for procurement effectiveness
- plan for delivering improvements to identified weaknesses
- benchmark against organisations with similar procurement functions

Unit content coverage

This study session covers part of the following topic from the official CIPS unit content documents: *Critically evaluate methods and processes of performance evaluation of procurement* and specifically: *Critically evaluate the methods and outcomes of performance evaluation of procurement against appropriate models and remedy any weaknesses.*

Prior Knowledge

Prior to this study session you should have completed study sessions 1; 2; 3; 4; 5; 6; 7; 8; 9; 10; 11; 12; 13; 14; 15; 16; 17; 18.

Timing

You should take about 5 - 6hrs to read and complete this section, including learning activities, self assessment questions, the suggested further reading and the revision question.

Compare models of process or outcomes

"What gets measured gets done"

Kath Ringwald

Traditional measures of performance focused upon a simplistic counting of actions or activities. Thus, for example, measurement would be based on the number of requisitions cleared within a certain period of time; the number of purchased orders places, or the value of contracts placed. To be meaningful the measures must be relevant not only in terms of what is being measured but to whom the measures are being reported. Once meaningful measures can be made, then it is possible to manage performance. Performance evaluation is concerned with the measurement of output, the consideration of actual achievement against goals that have been set previously. Evaluation on its own, however, is meaningless unless it is used in an intelligent way. Knowing that a target has or has not been achieved is just one more piece of management information gathered. To take this information and transform it into meaningful knowledge is what is really required, and to use that knowledge to inform future performance. This requires acknowledgement of what went wrong, and what went right, where weaknesses are that need to be overcome, where there is a need for greater resources, etc - those are the real aims of performance evaluation – i.e. to shape the future. And for this reason it is beneficial to think in terms of performance management rather than measurement and evaluation.

The Office of Government Commerce (OGC) is charged with providing a range of guidance on best practice and the approach that should be adopted by Government departments; this includes very clear direction on performance management. The following, taken from the OGC website (Resources for all) is typical of the many definitions that exist for performance management:

> "Performance management is the activity of tracking performance against targets and identifying opportunities for improvement – but not just looking back at past performance. The focus of performance management is the future – what do you need to be able to do and how can you do things better?" - Managing performance is about managing for results.'

The Modernising Government agenda sets challenging new performance objectives and all public organisations are continually striving to deliver high quality services that meet the needs of their customers and stakeholders:

- achieve more within the constraints of available resources;
- meet ever more challenging government targets; and
- achieve continuous improvement in how the organisation itself operates.

The evaluation of performance underpins the operations and processes within a strategic change programme framework such as when a major procurement project/activity is being undertaken. Sound practices and targets, which are both flexible and reactive to change, are needed to achieve performance improvement.

Issues of transparency in, and accountability for, the delivery of public services provide a clear rationale for the use of performance measurement and evaluation and associated targets in the public sector. Since the 1970's private sector organisations have increasingly utilised a number of approaches to enable (initially measurement and then) management of performance. From the manufacturing management approaches such as Just in Time (JIT), came other philosophies that were to enable leading edge companies to become more effective. It was a similar situation with Total Quality Management. These all concern an examination of processes. At the heart of these approaches were the processes which linked one 'customer' with another. One acts as a customer receiving the work of another, whom at that time is acting as a supplier. What emerges from this focus upon processes is a chain of customers and suppliers – whether internal or external. This chain has resonance with supply chains, value chains, support chains etc. These in themselves developed into more complex approaches and are still, arguably, evolving; for example in 'Lean' and 'Streamlining' in the MOD. These are all predicated upon examination of processes. Yet the outcomes must be taken into account or the process improvements may not contribute to the outcomes that the organisation has to achieve. As an example, consider the case of the MoD. It must deliver armed forces to a location somewhere in the world and engage with and defeat an enemy force. All the process improvements in respect of each element of procurement – in the widest holistic sense – such as understanding the capability required, as well as contracting, logistic support, maintenance etc. will count for nought if that ultimate outcome is not achieved. Of course, it might be less dramatic if a road is not completed on schedule but outcomes such as in respect of health care, education or social issues must be seen as the ultimate outcome. Nevertheless, performance evaluation may often have to be in respect of process improvements as step changes.

Learning activity 19.1

Read the first chapter of *How to Eat an Elephant* (Gilbert, 2004 3rd ed.). Note the comments in respect of process step improvements.

Self assessment question 19.1

Draw the basic construct of a simple system showing input, process and output. This is important because it is the basis of consideration of process evaluation.

It is pertinent now, in respect of process evaluation, to asses the key approaches that can be utilised within the public sector.

Process led performance evaluation with TQM

In the TQM model there are 4 key steps in the performance management framework:

1. Strategic objectives of the organisation are converted into desired standards of performance, ensuring they are SMART goals (i.e. they are Specific, Measurable, Achievable, Relevant and Time-bound)

2. Metrics are developed to compare the desired performance with actual achieved standards

3. Gaps between actual measurements and desired outcomes are identified

4. Improvement actions are developed and initiated

This is a continuous cycle of review and improvement. For far too long organisations took action almost as a one off basis – but this will not lead to sustained performance improvement and, within the public sector where short termism (allied to budgets) is rife, there is a need to ensure that a continuous approach is taken to TQM. It is important to avoid the rhetoric associated with TQM and to genuinely embody the philosophy in the way that all stakeholders undertake their responsibilities and activities.

It is a very useful model for process change and improvement but requires strong leadership and complete commitment from the entire organisation to yield benefits.

Process led performance evaluation through lean thinking

The book *The Machine that Changed the World* (Womack, Jones and Roos, 2007) identified the importance of considering processes and examining the activities for anything that did not add value. By eliminating the non value adding activities (if possible) the authors highlighted how the automobile industry had been radically changed in terms of enhanced performance - i.e. outcome of production equalled a lower cost car of higher quality. This was based upon the concept of being lean. The whole concept has been taken further since then with not only production and manufacturing environments being enhanced through the application of lean but also managerial situations and processes. The book *Lean Thinking* (Womack and Jones, 2003) emphasises this and the concept has become one that is about thinking in a more holistic way about a series of linked processes as would be found in a supply chain/value chain or chain of customers; even if they are internal. To be really effective in a public sector procurement environment such processes should include all stakeholders as customers or suppliers with an influence or impact upon not just processes, but also final outcomes of a procurement project.

The principles of Lean Thinking (which have been covered in detail in the compulsory unit on *Strategic Supply Chain Management*) are:

- Specify value
- Identify the Value Stream
- Flow
- Pull
- Perfection

In a recent article for the Harvard Business Review on Lean Consumption, Womack and Jones (2005) have set out six additional principles of what they call lean consumption that that correspond closely with those of lean production:

- Solve the customer's problem completely by ensuring that all the goods and services work, and work together
- Don't waste the customer's time
- Provide exactly what the customer wants
- Provide what's wanted exactly where it's wanted
- Provide what's wanted where it's wanted exactly when it's wanted
- Continually aggregate solutions to reduce the customer's time and hassle.

These principles recast traditional lean thinking principles in order to bring a customer focus to the public sector service provision generally, and procurement fits particularly well in this construct.

Outcome led performance evaluation using the EFQM approach

Learning activity 19.2

Go to the CIPFA website for the article *Introduction to Lean Thinking* (McCarron, 2006). Examine the views on Lean in Public Sector services.

The EFQM model allows not merely processes to be considered and enhanced but builds into the perspective the broad outcomes upon certain areas. This in turn allows action to be taken within specific named areas (which you should recall from study session 18):

- Leadership;
- Policy and strategy;
- People;

- Partnership and Resources;
- Processes;
- Customer results;
- People results;
- Society results, and ultimately
- Key Performance Results.

There is nothing wrong with the TQM approach and indeed it is still valid, however, the EFQM approach is more holistic and includes stakeholders who may not be considered in a pure TQM approach. What the EFQM does is to provide a more focused model through its adaptation into the Procurement Excellence Model.

There was a time (not that long ago) when any reference to procurement performance evaluation centred upon fairly simplistic approaches and methods. It should be taken into account that any measure is better than none. Indeed as approaches such as TQM and Lean developed; sophistication in approaches to the evaluation of procurement performance became more pertinent. The development of an Excellence model was a considerable step forward and allowed a focus upon issues that affect on one hand elements of procurement, and on the other hand an overall perspective of the impact upon integrated procurement performance.

Assess data validation models for procurement effectiveness

The development of the EFQM Excellence Model into the Procurement Excellent model has allowed a greater focus on procurement. This is achieved via procurement specific questions being addressed under each of the nine headings. The answers have to be elicited from those who are utilising the procurement activity or are associated with its activities. It should therefore include internal and external stakeholders.

Below is a page taken from the OGC *Procurement Excellence Pilot*, which lists under the heading of leadership a number or relevant procurement questions against which stakeholders associated with procurement should complete. These questions may not be relevant to every public sector procurement organisation, put provide a good example. The *Procurement Excellence Guide*, provides more information of the context and context of the questions to be asked.

Diagram 19.1 Procurement excellence guide

	Do Managers demonstrate the role and importance of Procurement and lead by example?	0 Don't know	1 No – this doesn't happen	2 This happens occasionally but there is no consistency	3 Yes this usually happens but it could be improved	4 Yes this is recognised as the way we do business and we achieve real benefits	5 This is an integral part of our culture and operation and can be regarded as best practice	Evidence to support marking
1.1	Has your Department's Management Board or Committee clearly defined the role and strategic objectives for your Procurement Organisation and the values by which you should operate?							
1.2	Is your Procurement Organisation always involved in the overall Department's strategic planning and use of outside resources?							
1.3	Do Managers outside your immediate Procurement Organisation understand and actively support the requirements for effective procurement?							
1.4	Do Managers throughout your Department act as role models in promoting and using your Procurement Organisation?							
1.5	Are your Procurement Organisation Managers personally involved in the way that your organisation operates and continually trying to make improvements?							

Source OGC, Procurement Excellence Pilot, pp.8

Self assessment question 19.2

Go to the OGC website and look at the Procurement Excellence Pilot, the Procurement Excellence Model and the Procurement Excellence Guide. Why do you think that there are three of these – why not just one?

All of the questions under each of the headings listed earlier have 6 gradings. These range from 0 to 5 and are categorised as follows:

0 – Don't know

1 – No – this does not happen

2 – This happens occasionally but there is no consistency

3 – Yes this usually happens but it could be improved

4 – Yes this is recognised as the way we do business, and we achieve real benefits

5 – This is an integral part of our culture and operation and can be regarded as best practice

There is then against each of these questions and gradings an opportunity to provide evidence supporting the grading/marking.

Thus against each of the 'Excellence' areas and then through a range of pertinent questions there is an assessment of how the organisation is performing in respect of particular areas and importantly overall in terms of ultimate outcome in input to overall operational/organisational performance.

Thus far the discussion of these models has been within a general context, and it is worth bearing in mind that they can be designed to meet organisations specific requirements. For example, Warwick Business School has developed a tool that could be used for analysing procurement performance, with particular emphasis placed on working with stakeholders.

The Gateway Review

As has been noted in earlier study sessions there is a process know as the Gateway Review. This is intended for specific projects and allows a control over activities and processes commencing with a strategic overview, moving on to a sound business case and in due course running through all the necessary elements of project and programme management. Within this there is continual emphasis upon performance although this may take several formats and is generally outcome based. Pertinent questions have to be asked of those involved in the procurement project and there are specific roles for the Senior Responsible Office (SRO) and indeed the counterpart Senior Industry Executive (SIE).

Variations on this process of checks and control over performance are available from OGC including an extremely useful document on performance within construction projects. These are broadly based upon keeping projects to time and cost whilst ensuring that the procured equipment or asset is able to perform as required. Hence measurement/evaluation of performance is in a different data set to that which seeks to determine the specific processes and procedures or the general 'health' of a procurement organisation. That is not to say that the Procurement Excellence model for example could not be applied to a programme based procurement organisation.

Similar documents have been developed for specific areas within the public sector environment although they generally do not contain the detailed questionnaire approach noted for the PEM. In addition for many years most organisations have undertaken an appraisal of suppliers (both potential and actual) and this tends to be a mix of both qualitative and quantitative data.

The models which have been considered thus far contain either qualitative or quantitative data. You should bear in mind that there may be different perceptions of these two types of data.

Learning activity 19.3

What do you think is the difference between qualitative and quantitative data in the context of procurement performance evaluation? Does it make a difference to the perspective of stakeholders or the governance of the procurement activity?

Plan for delivering improvements to identified weaknesses

From performance evaluation models such as those discussed above, strengths and weaknesses should become evident. Strengths should be built upon, and weaknesses addressed.

Improvements to performance can be made once weaknesses or costs (no matter how defined, but examples would include eliminating waste through lean approaches) are recognised and acknowledged.

Before that can happen there is a requirement to reconsider the simple system diagram. With the addition of a 'feedback loop', mechanism is provided (at least conceptually) for action to be taken to remedy weaknesses.

This can be shown as follows:

Diagram 19.2 Process diagram with feedback loop for measurement of performance

Simple system - a Process diagram with feedback loop for measurement of performance

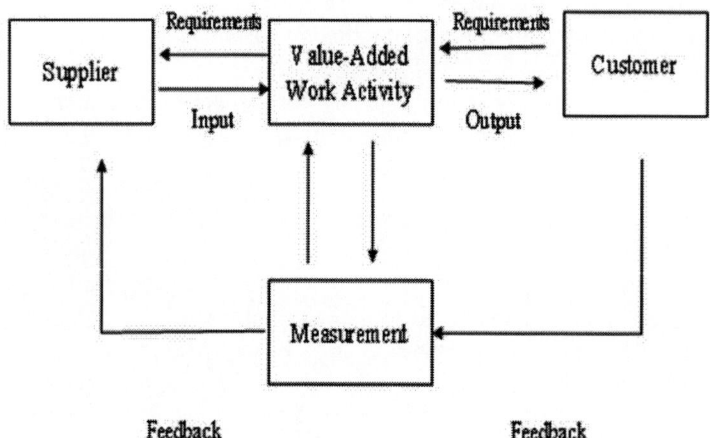

Action to be taken will depend upon exactly what the weakness is and the stage at which the procurement activity is in terms of its development towards becoming an excellent – best in class – type of organisation.

The following provides an overview of what should take place (in a generic procurement sense) to ensure that there is suitable measurement and action ultimately to correct any weaknesses:

- Origins (what would constitute success)
- Building a performance framework
- Select performance evaluation measures
- Select targets for procurement performance evaluation
- Define procurement processes
- Performance monitoring and measurement
- Utilise performance information/take remedial action
- Review

Considerations when designing procurement performance evaluation methods

From the foregoing, you will see that it is important to carefully select the measure that you intend to use in order to enable effective evaluation in line with an organisations specific procurement activity. The following provides the characteristics of good measures which should be taken into account when designing/adapting your organisations procurement performance evaluation methods:

Self assessment question 19.3

The OGC guide on *Improving Performance: Project Evaluation and Benchmarking – Achieving Excellence in Construction Procurement Guide* (OGC, 2007) provides an interesting insight into a specific area that could be applicable in a range of public sector procurement organisations. Read and note key points in respect of performance and identifying areas for improvement.

Characteristics of Good Measures	
Measure	**Description**
Quantitative	The measure can be expressed as an objective value
Qualitative	The measure is an interpretation of phenomena
Is easy to understand	The measure conveys at a glance what is measuring, and how it is derived
Encourages appropriate behaviour	The measure is balanced to reward productive behaviour and discourage 'game playing'
Is visible	The effects of the measure are readily apparent to all involved in the process being measured
Is defined and mutually understood	The measure has been defined by and/or agreed to by all key process being measured (internally and externally)
Encompasses both outputs and inputs	The measure integrates factors from all aspects of the process measured
Measures only what is important	The measure focuses on a key performance indicator that is of real value to managing the process
Is multidimensional	The measure is properly balanced between utilisation, productivity and performance, and shows the trade-offs
Uses economies of effort	The benefits of measure outweigh the cost of collection and analysis
Facilitates trust	The measure validates the participation among the various parties

Benchmarking against organisations with similar procurement functions

In general terms benchmarking is a management technique that can be used by an organisation in order to improve performance through comparison with similar organisations, or the performance of different suppliers within the same sector. In terms of procurement, benchmarking as a tool allows a public sector organisation to compare and contrast its procurement functions against other organisations procurement activity to assess its relative performance; and note areas of strengths and weakness in comparison.

There are several benefits which benchmarking can bring. The OGC in a guide on achieving excellence in construction (*Improving Performance – Project Evaluation and Benchmarking*, 2007) identified that benchmarking had the following benefits for public organisations within that sector:

- assess performance objectively
- expose areas where improvement is needed
- identify other organisations with processes resulting in superior performance, with a view to
- their adoption
- test whether improvement programmes have been successful.

Though benefits of benchmarking for construction, they could apply to the procurement activities of all public sector organisations.

There are a number of different benchmarking systems which have been developed. They do however follow essentially the same process which comprises of four basic stages listed below:

1 Planning: –
    - “assess performance objectively
    - within that process, defining the activity to be benchmarked
    - confirming the key performance measures or indicators to measure the performance in carrying out
    - the activity
    - documenting the existing way in which the activity is carried out
    - drawing up a preliminary list of potential benchmarking partners with whom to exchange information
    - identifying possible sources of information and methods of collection to confirm the suitability of potential partners”

2 Analysis:-
    - “collecting information to identify the most likely potential benchmarking partner to contact
    - confirming the best potential benchmarking partner and making a preliminary assessment of the performance gap

- contacting and visiting them, if appropriate, to validate and substantiate the information
- comparing the existing process with that of the benchmarking partner to identify differences and innovations
- agreeing targets for improvements that are expected as a result of adopting the benchmarking
- partner's way of doing things."

3 Action: -

- "communicating the results of the study throughout the relevant parts of the organisation and to the benchmarking partner
- planning how to achieve the improvements
- implementing the improvement plan, monitoring progress and reviewing as necessary."

4 Review: -

- "Reviewing performance when the changes have been 'bedded in'
- Identifying and rectifying anything which may have caused the organisation to fall short of its target
- Communicating the results of changes implemented to the organisation and the benchmarking partner
- Considering benchmarking again to continue the improvement process"

Learning activity 19.4

Search the internet for examples of benchmarking models that are used in the public sector. Note where they follow a similar process to that outlined above.

It is important to note that for benchmarking to be successful, it requires efficient and accurate performance evaluation and performance management as previously discussed.

A good example for public sector organisation benchmarking can be found between the NHS Estates and the Defence Estates Organisation (which began in 1999); where co-operation over improving management of the public sectors money assigned to property facilitated mutual learning and led to effective benchmarking between the two organisations. This is not just through results but in analysis of the benchmarking process and measures of performance. Because of the nature of the public sector, benchmarking in many areas including procurement should be easier than it otherwise would be in the private sector as demonstrated in the above example.

19

Summary

This study session has sought to build upon the previous study session by taking the models discussed and providing a greater degree of consideration in terms of their relevance to the evaluation of performance. By addressing the strengths and weaknesses identified using such models you may find yourself able to better manage improvement of performance. This requires consideration of the strengths and weaknesses of the models themselves through the understanding that the content must be relevant to the contextual setting of the procurement organisation.

Although this is an excellent tool in itself, you will find that such analysis is of greater value when compared with similar procurement functions conducted by other organisations through benchmarking exercises.

Revision Question

Critically assess the nature of procurement performance evaluation and indicate a means by which a procurement organisation could determine whether it is performing well or not.

Feedback

Feedback on learning activity 19.1

'Read the first chapter of How to Eat an Elephant. Note the comments in respect of process step improvements.'

You will find this book an easy one to read and follow. The early parts of the book identify and discuss key parts of the approach to quality improvement and they are based upon processes and undertaking them a step at a time.

Feedback on self assessment question 19.1

'Draw the basic construct of a simple system showing input, process and output. This is important because it is the basis of consideration of process evaluation.'

Diagram 19.2 Simple system – process diagram

Simple system - a Process diagram

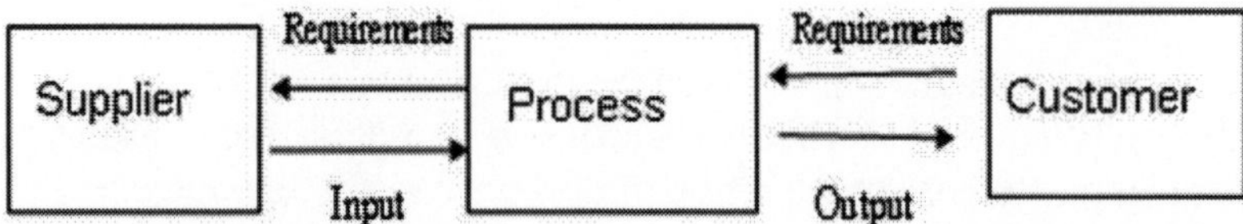

Above is an example of a simple system diagram. You will note that there is impute from a supplier who could be internal or external; and there is output to a customer who could be internal or external. Either way both the supplier and the customer are stakeholders. This is the underlying concept of a supply chain or quality chain within a procurement context.

Feedback on learning activity 19.2

'Go to the CIPFA website for their 'Introduction to Lean Thinking,' CIPFA 2006, Performance Improvement Network. Examine the views on Lean in Public Sector services.'

You will have found valuable insights in the paper that indicate how processes can be improved and that this can enable enhanced outcomes. What is important is that this excellent paper puts the concept of lean thinking into the context of the public sector. It provides clear approaches that should be considered for application within the procurement environment.

Feedback on self assessment question 19.2

'Go to the OGC website and look at the Procurement Excellence Pilot, the Procurement Excellence Model and the Procurement Excellence Guide.

Why do you think that there are three of these – why not just one?'

The differences between the three PEM's have been identified in the previous study session. You may recall that the first, the *Procurement Excellence Pilot*, contains questions that can be answered quantitatively, whilst the *Procurement Excellence Guide* provides details of the type of issues that questions should address, and therefore how they should be developed. The *Local Authority Procurement Excellence Guide* takes the format of the *Procurement Excellence Pilot*, asking questions which are relevant to the context of local authorities.

It is necessary to have more than one because of the depth and breath to which the PEM can be taken. Different documents provide different levels of detail depending on the requirements of the public sector organisation and the resources it has available (i.e. in terms of time, money, manpower, or requirement to develop its own detailed PEM).

Learning activity 19.3

'What do you think is the difference between qualitative and quantitative data in the context of procurement performance evaluation? Does it make a difference to the perspective of stakeholders or the governance of the procurement activity?'

There may be a perception on the part of users of the evaluation that quantitative data may be more believable because it is perceived as being 'precise'; on the other hand qualitative data may be perceived as being 'imprecise'. This may be because the former appears as hard data, whilst the latter is regarded as soft data. Some may see hard data as scientific, therefore accurate; whilst soft data is subjective and open to different interpretations.

However, you must bear in mind that quantitative schemes such as the *procurement excellence pilot*, where response may be arbitrarily allocated to a number may not result in a consistent, unified response. Similarly qualitative data is by its nature may provide varied interpretations of the same event. In both cases response is individual to the respondent, who may have a vastly different view to others within the same environment.

In short, wither approach is valuable but you must be aware of the limitations of generalising results.

Self assessment question 19.3

'The OGC guide on 'Improving Performance- project evaluation and benchmarking' in Construction provides an interesting insight into a specific area that could be applicable in a range of public sector procurement organisations. Read and note key points in respect of performance and identifying areas for improvement.'

This guide is invaluable as it highlights a number of areas that you may be able to utilise and which you should be able to identify in your answer. Although it is set in a construction context many of the issues raised apply to other public sector procurement environments. You will note for example the points on KPI's, requirements for project evaluation and reviews. In particular it will provide you with a performance management framework commencing with a key objective and ultimately ending with a review and evaluation.

Diagram 19.2 Performance management cycle

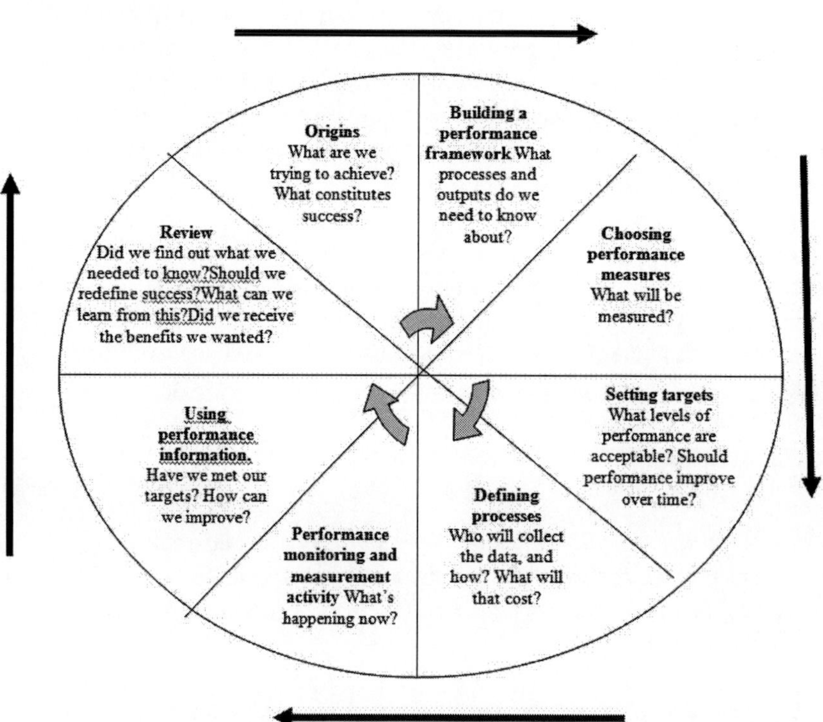

This figure shows performance management as a cycle of activities proceeding from a consideration of strategic aims through performance management and on to the review stage. While this cycle indicates the order in which some activities will be undertaken, in practice they may not be successive stages but iterative loops; for examples, the stage of performance monitoring and measuring is an ongoing process.

Feedback on learning activity 19.4

'Search the internet for examples of benchmarking models that are used in the public sector. Note where they follow a similar process to that outlined above.'

19

After searching on the internet you should be aware that there are a vast number of benchmarking models which have been produced and are in use in public sector organisations to assess their procurement activity. Keeping on the topic of construction raised through the OGC document; the following is a list of some organisations who have produced models currently in use:

- Clients' Charter –www.clientsuccess.org/home.html
- Design Quality Indicators – www.constructingexcellence.org.uk// resources/az/view.jspid=290
- CBI Probe – www.cbi.org.uk
- Probe (Post-Occupancy Review of Buildings and their their Engineering) – www.usablebuildings.co.uk
- BRE Digest – www.bree.co.uk
- Inside UK Enterprise – www.accountingweb.co.uk/vertical_ network/icke.html

Feedback to revision question

'Critically assess the nature of procurement performance evaluation and indicate a means by which a procurement organisation could determine whether it is performing well or not.'

It would be useful to set the scene by putting the whole issue of performance measurement into context. In this respect the following from Geert Bouckaert and Wouter van Dooren (2003, p.129) will assist:

CASE EXAMPLE 10.1 - THE MOVE TO BEST VALUE IN THE UK

"The new direction of performance management in the United Kingdom is well illustrated by the current local government modernization programme, many elements of which have acted as pilots for the modernization programme in the health services and other parts of government. The first part of this programme, the 'Best Value' initiative, was introduced in local government in 1997 to replace the much-hated CCT legislation, first as a pilot imitative, then as a statutory duty, from 1 April 2000.

In practice, Best Value means (DETR, 1999a):

- Every part of the council's budget must be reviewed at least once every five years.
- Every review must apply the '4Cs' methodology to the service or the cross-cutting issue, which consists of the following steps:
    - **C**hallenge the need for the service and the way it is carried out
    - **C**onsult with all relevant stakeholders
    - **C**ompare the performance of the service with other providers
    - **C**ompete – test the competitiveness of the service
- As a minimum level of comparison, each authority has to compare its performance with other comparable authorities against each of the 'best Value performance indicators' (of which there are around one hundred in the case of the largest local authorities). These indicators include some which measure inputs, volume of activity, volume of output,

19

productivity levels, unit costs, number of users, percentage of school children passing exams at 16 and 18, user satisfaction levels, reliability levels, numbers of complaints and so on – in other words, the whole spectrum from inputs to outcomes and from efficiency to quality.

- Each local authority must publish a plan to improve its performance significantly. Initially, these plans had to ensure that, within five years, each service would reach the performance level which the upper quartile of authorities achieved in 2000. (In 2002, this was amended to give more emphasis to 'stretch targets' agreed by each local authority with government departments across a range of priority issues)."

Having set the context you should then detail the importance of measuring performance generally and them subsequently managing the results. You should be able to discuss the various models discussed in this study session. Having done this you will need to identify benchmarking as the means of comparing your organisation with others. Any subsequent disparity could then be managed in accord with the results (for example, action to overcome deficiencies or building upon existing strengths).

Suggested Further Reading

Geert Bouckaert,; Wouter.van Dooren, , (2003), 'Performance Management and Management in Public Sector Organizations'

James P., Womack, Daniel T. Jones, (2005), "Lean consumption", Harvard Business Review, Vol. 83 No.3

James P., Womack, Daniel T. Jones; Daniel. Roos, (2007)., The Machine that Changed the World.

James P., Womack, Daniel T. Jones (2003)., Lean Thinking: Banish Waste and Create Wealth in Your Corporation

McCarron, Brendon., 2003, Introduction to "Lean Thinking" [Online] CIPFA., Available at: http://www.cipfanetworks.net/fileupload/upload/Lean_briefing1912007311331.pdf

19

Study Session 20

"Develop and apply a process with internal and external stakeholders, which incorporates their feedback on the performance of a procurement organisation"

Introduction

This final study session brings together many of the areas, topics and issues that you will have considered during the course of study for the Unit. It does so through a case study (differing with the approaches adopted in all of the preceding study sessions in the Unit), and asks pertinent questions which encourage you to develop answers in line with the intended learning outcomes for the session.

Session Learning Objectives

After completing this session you should be able to:

- assess stakeholder views of procurement performance
- distinguish between more influential / significant and less influential / significant stakeholder views and react accordingly.
- engage with stakeholders who are critical of procurement to understand their views and improve performance

Unit content coverage

This study session covers part of the following topic from the official CIPS unit content documents: *Critically evaluate methods and processes of performance evaluation of procurement* and specifically: *Develop and apply a process with internal and external stakeholders, which incorporates their feedback on the performance of a procurement organisation.*

Prior Knowledge

Prior to this study session you should have completed study sessions 1; 2; 3; 4; 5; 6; 7; 8; 9; 10; 11; 12; 13; 14; 15; 16; 17; 18; 19.

Timing

You should take about 3-4 hrs to read and complete this section, including learning activities, self assessment questions, the suggested further reading and the revision question.

Case Study - Milestone Payment Introduction:

Assume that you are the Integrated Project Team Leader (IPTL) for an anti-tank missile programme that is in the Demonstration phase of the CADMID cycle. In this role you are responsible for all procurement activities involved in the procurement process of that particulate project. As you should be aware, the CADMID cycle is the life cycle of a procurement project within the MOD. It is based upon British Standard which covers such asset procurement projects requiring the development of:

- a **Concept** of what is required;
- an **Assessment** of whether it is feasible;
- the **Demonstration** of whatever is being procured to ensure that it meets requirements;
- the **Manufacture** of the asset(s)/equipment
- and the **In service** delivery of the asset/equipment where it is to be used.
- until eventually the asset or equipment is subject of **Disposal**.

Situation:

A missile firing trial has recently been completed and the contractor has therefore submitted a milestone payment claim that relates to successful completion of the firing. You have the following reports (listed below) from your team members and other stakeholders. You now have to decide how to proceed. There are also some other communications concerning the recent missile firing, which you may wish to take into account. There are three questions below the reports that will help you find a solution.

Additional information:

You should be aware that the integrated project team that you lead includes a range of personal directly under your control. There are also a wide range of personal from within the MOD but not under your functional control, who also work with you and from whom you receive advice and guidance. In addition there are representatives of the prime contractor with whom there is a contractual arrangement, and also a number of sub contractor who supply the prime contractor but upon whom many of the technical aspects of the missile. These are all stakeholders who may need to be considered.

Reports from Team Members (Stakeholders or stakeholders' representatives):

Commercial Manager - The contract states that the milestone payment will be made on successful completion of prototype missile firing, including launch, guidance phase and warhead detonation. I understand that the firing was not successful, so the payment should not be made. We need to avoid condoning performance that is below the contract requirements, as it sets a precedent from which it will be difficult to recover. The trials plan is a contractual document, but has lower priority than the contract which includes the milestone statement given above.

Contractor's Programme Team Leader - The milestone criteria was successfully achieved, the missile launched successfully, guidance phase took the missile to the target and the warhead detonated. It is recognised that the warhead failed to have the expected effect on the target, but this has been proven in previous warhead trials. We recognise that we do need to demonstrate missile firing in accordance with the trial plan and are willing to do so after the milestone payment has been made. My team have been working very hard in difficult circumstances to achieve this milestone and acceptance would boost morale.

Member of Parliament for the constituency in which the contractor has its main manufacturing facility – I am writing to advise you of my concern having heard that you are withholding payment to this renowned British company, which has an excellent record for providing a quality product and service to our armed forces. I will expect you to confirm to me that this payment is now being made otherwise I will have to take the matter direct to the Minister of Defence, whom as I believe you are aware, is a personal friend of mine. I await your response.

Systems Engineer - All of the success criteria defined in the trial plan were achieved, except the requirement for the warhead to penetrate a 0.6 metre steel plate. The penetration was 0.5 metre and telemetry recorded considerable oscillation of the missile as it approached the target, which may be the cause of the failure. Previous warhead trials proved the warhead in a static test, but not in flight conditions. I recommend that the firing trial be repeated to prove the warhead in flight conditions and to comply with the trials plan.

Finance Officer - This milestone payment is £30M and has already been delayed by six months, which has adversely impacted on the accuracy of our Forecast of Outturn (FOO). If it is not paid this month, our end of year spend will be 5.3% below our forecast and we would fall outside the department target of ±5%. Our group leader has already expressed concern about underspend, which then undermines the credibility of our budgeting.

Requirements Manager - We need to remember that our soldiers are expected to fire this missile within 500 metres of enemy tanks and that missile launch indicates their position to the enemy. Our soldiers need to have confidence in the weapons they use and missile firing trials like these are important in gaining user confidence prior to acceptance into service. We need to be able to provide the user with clear evidence that the firing trial has been successful.

Project Manager - The missile firing trail is the only remaining activity before design freeze can be achieved and has already been delayed by four months. The production programme has been on hold for two months and any further delay adds to this, which impacts directly on acceptance into service.

Quality Assurance - We are concerned about the validity of this trial as some of the telemetry equipment was out of calibration and wind conditions exceeded the system specification. Wind conditions were very strong throughout the five days range time available and during the firing the wind was recorded at 92 miles per hour, which exceeded the system specification requirement of 85 miles per hour. Although we advised against it, the contractor decided to proceed, expressing confidence that the system would cope with the conditions.

Senior Manager from another supplier, (not the Prime Contractor on this project, but actually a subcontractor to the missile manufacturer in this particular procurement) - I was pleased that the testing of the missile was completed on time. I trust that this means that you will now allow greater freedom for our organisation to concentrate our production activity on the other key MoD project where we are the Prime contractor. We need the resources that are currently spending valuable development time with your project and the prime contractor for that. Hence with immediate effect we will refocus our production efforts to the other major MOD project, which I am sure you are aware, is extremely important given the deteriorating security situation in the region where that equipment is likely to be operating.

Secretary to the local Parish Council – I am contacting you at the behest of the Parish Councillors who have expressed concern about the noise created when ever a missile is tested fired from your site which is within the Parish Boundaries. The councillors are of the view that this could be moved to other sites that you company owns which are not near to the sort of peaceful cottages which we represent. Perhaps we could arrange a meeting to discuss this matter?

Questions:

1. What factors should the IPTL take into consideration when making the decision on the milestone payment?

2. What should the IPTL aim to achieve?

3. What options does the IPTL have and how should the IPTL proceed?

Feedback on case study 'Milestone Payment'

This Case Study is not real, in that it does not represent a specific procurement project, however, it does bring out many of the issues that stakeholders might raise in respect of a procurement project within the public sector.

You may wish to tackle this on your own or in cohort with others. You are likely to produce a range of findings and there is no one right answer. A debate around the relative merits of proposed solutions would help explore session learning objectives. The overall point is that stakeholders will take a view on procurement performance; you will need to be able to distinguish between more influential/significant stakeholders than less influential/significant stakeholders. And these will be different depending upon differing scenarios; you should recognise that there will be a need to engage with stakeholders, especially those who are critical of performance in order to understand their views and improve subsequently performance.

Some Possible Issues to consider in seeking a solution:

In order for you as IPTL to come to a solution to the case study a major focus should be upon stakeholder analysis and prioritisation. This is due to the number of stakeholders and differing views involved. Some stakeholders will need to be given a greater priority than others depending on the degree to which they can influence the procurement project. You should have undertaken a stakeholder mapping exercise, followed by analysis and an engagement strategy. However, assuming that this was not sufficiently undertaken you should now consider whether such as set of activities will assist you in identifying the key stakeholders.

1. Factors:

There are many stakeholder factors which the IPTL leader may wish to take into account. Listed below are some examples. It is important to note that some may require a greater emphasis than others depending on the stakeholder.

- Commercial/legal
- Technical
- Operational/user attitude
- Financial
- Motivation of contractor
- Schedule/programme
- Human elements/motivation of contractor's team
- Team unity – team members feel that due account was taken of their views
- Communication

2. Aim to achieve

The aim of the IPTL should be to ensure successful progression of the project. As IPTL you will have to manage those stakeholders who have issues which cannot be immediately resolved due to their low priority. As such you will have to engage in a degree of conflict resolution with the relevant stakeholders. There are many issues of concern to each of the stakeholders, for example the noise complaint by the secretary to the local parish council. Though this may be a relevant CSR concern, given the stage of the procurement project, prioritisation should be given to determining whether the project is able to move onto the next stage of the cycle. This will require resolution of the dispute between the commercial manager; systems engineer and the contractors programme team leader, regarding whether or not the firing was successfully completed within acceptable limits. This will require clarifying the initial measures of success which should have been agreed upon when contracting for the prototype development.

3. Options:

- Accept that milestone test was satisfactory and make full payment.
- Do not accept that the milestone test was satisfactory, and do not make payment.
- Accept that some of the milestone had been achieved and make a partial payment - say 50% or 66%.

The IPTL to negotiate to ensure:

- The trial is repeated and trials plan satisfied.
- Contractor continues with production at their risk.
- Pay some but not all of the £30M
- None of the stakeholders feel that their view has not been given appropriate consideration (effective stakeholder communication)

Learning Points:

- Team members, as key stakeholders, will provide advice from their own point
of view.
- No stakeholder offered a balanced view of the factors that need to be taken
into consideration.
- The IPTL needs to take account of all stakeholder issues, to enable an objective conclusion.
- Human elements like team unity and morale are as important as the hard factors like legal and technical, and are applicable to both internal and external stakeholders.
- Although a single well instrumented trial took place, there are several different interpretations of what happened.
- The IPLT can only establish a mutually acceptable solution by negotiation and discussion, e.g. ask the Finance Officer if a partial payment would bring underspend within the 5% limit.
- The milestone payment over-specified the success criteria and by stating "detonation" weaken the position of the customer. It would have been better to state "successful completion of prototype missile firing in accordance with the trails plan" to avoid ambiguity.

Summary

Having addressed the case study questions, you should be aware that this is not an extensive examination. It does however provide an excellent insight into practical scenarios where you will need to develop and apply a process with internal and external stakeholders which effectively incorporates their feedback on the procurement organisations performance. For example, you may wish to consider additional factors such as:

- What are the communication processes by which feedback can be received from internal and external stakeholders
- Do processes exist through which feedback can be incorporated into the procurement, particularly at the demonstration phase being discussed
- Context a procurement; this case study is set within and MOD context. Other public sector organisations may use a different procurement processes which are not necessarily life cycle based. Nevertheless, the basic stakeholder engagement strategies may still apply in order to improve performance

Hence, this study session has provided an opportunity to assess stakeholder views of particular areas of procurement performance. In doing so it provided you with the opportunity to distinguish between those stakeholders who have greater influence than others. It also provided you with the opportunity to consider the best way of engaging with stakeholders and when this is best undertaken.

References and Bibliography

Companies Act 2006. (c.46). London: HMSO

Freedom of Legislation Act 2000 (c.36) London: HMSO

The Data Protection Act 1998 (c.29) London: HMSO

The Environmental Information Regulations 2004 (No. 3391) London: HMSO

Public Sector Information Regulation 2005 (No. 1515) London: HMSO

Local Government Act 1999 (c. 27) London: HMSO

Modern Local Government: In Touch with the People [Cm 4014, July 1998]

The Public Contracts Regulations 2006 (No.5) London: HMSO

Alcatel Austria v Bunderministerium für Wissenschaft und Verkehr., Case C-81/98 (European Court of Justice). Alcatel Austria and others (Rec 1999,p I-7671) (Judgment) C-81/98; [1999] EUECJ C-81/98).

Lettings International Limited v London Borough of Newham [2008] EWHC 1583 (QB)

www.publicservice.co.uk, 2008, Councils were in on the con, says bidder [Online] Publicservice.co.uk, Available at: http://www.publicservice.co.uk/news_story.asp?id=5740&topic=PFI%20and%20partnerships [Accessed 23 April 2008]

12Manage.n.d. Assessing who or what really counts. Explanation of stakeholder analysis.[online] (Updated 28 Aug 2008). Available at: http://www.12manage.com/methods_stakeholder_analysis.html [Accessed 24 April 2008]

Algert, N.E., and Watson, K. 2002. Conflict management: introductions for individuals and organizations. Bryan, TX: The Centre for Change and Conflict Resolution

Alford, John,. 2001. 'The Implications of 'publicness' for strategic management theory' in Johnson, Gerry; Scholes, Kevan (eds), Exploring Public Sector Strategy. Dorchester, UK: Pearson Education Ltd. Ch. 1

American Society for Quality., n.d., Glossery., [Online] Available at: http://www.asq.org/glossary/q.html [Accessed Accessed 11 April 2008]

Andriof, J., Waddock, S., Husted, B., Rahman, S.S. (eds.), 2002, Unfolding Stakeholder Thinking, Greenleaf Publishing: Sheffield, UK

Argandona, 1998

Aquatron Breathing Air Systems v Strathclyde Fire Board [2007] CSOH 185 Available at: http://www.bailii.org/scot/cases/ScotCS/2007/CSOH_185.html [Accessed: 09 May 2008]

Baily, Peter; Farmer, David; Jessop, David; Jones, David; Crocker, Barry., 2008, Procurement, Principles and Management., 10th ed., Hampshire, UK: Pearson Education

Bellamy, Christine., 2003, 'Moving to E-Government: The Role of ICT's in the Public Sector' in Bovaird, Tony; Loffler, Elke (eds), Public Management and Governance. London: Routledge, pp.113-126

Bichard, Sir Michael., 2006, Centre for Excellence in Leadership – December 1 2006: Sir Michael Bichard's Speaking Notes., [Online] Centre for Excellence., Available at: http://www.centreforexcellence.org.uk/UsersDoc/Seminar%20Three%20-%20SirMichaelBichardsNotes.pdf [Accessed 15 May 2008]

Bichta, Constantina; Corporate Social Responsibility: A Role in Government Policy and Regulation [Online] University of Bath School of Management. Available at: http://bedsatbath.co.uk/cri/pubpdf/Research_Reports/16_Bichta.pdf [Accessed 15 May 2008]

Boaz, Annette; Nutlley, Sandra., 2003, 'Evidence-Based Policy and Practice' in Bovaird, Tony; Loffler, Elke (eds), Public Management and Governance. London: Routledge, pp. 225-236

Bovaird, Tony, 2003 'Strategic Management in Public Sector Organisations' in Bovaird, Tony; Loffler, Elke (eds), Public Management and Governance. London: Routledge, pp.55-74

Bovaird, Tony; Loffler, Elke., 2003, 'The Changing Context of Public Policy' in Bovaird, Tony; Loffler, Elke (eds), Public Management and Governance. London: Routledge, pp.13-24

Bovaird, Tony; Loffler, Elke., 2003, 'Understanding Public Management and Governance' in Bovaird, Tony; Loffler, Elke (eds), Public Management and Governance. London: Routledge, pp.3-11

Bovaird, Tony; Loffler, Elke., 2003, 'Quality Management in Public Sector Organizations' in Bovaird, Tony; Loffler, Elke (eds), Public Management and Governance. London: Routledge, pp.137-148

Bouckaert, Geert; van Dooren, Wouter., 2003, 'Performance Management and Management in Public Sector Organizations' in Bovaird, Tony; Loffler, Elke (eds), Public Management and Governance. London: Routledge, pp.127-136

British Bankers Association., 2008, The Business Banking Code., [Online] BBA., Available at: http://www.bba.org.uk/content/1/c6/01/31/27/Business_Code_2008.pdf [Accessed 29 May 2009]

Broussine, Mike. 2003., 'Public Leadership' in Bovaird, Tony; Loffler, Elke (eds), Public Management and Governance. London: Routledge, pp. 175-188

Brooks, Richard., 2007., Turn and Turn Again., [Online] CIPFA., Available at: http://www.cipfa.org.uk/publicfinance/features_details.cfm?news_id=30125 [Accessed 03 September 2008]

Brown, Des., 2008, Secretary of State's Policy Statement on Saftey, Health, Enviromental Protection and Sustainable Development, [Online] Ministry of Defence, Available at: http://www.mod.uk/DefenceInternet/AboutDefence/CorporatePublications/PolicyStrategyandPlanning/SecretaryOfStatesPolicyStatementOnHealthSafetyEnvironmentalProtection.htm [Accessed 02 October 2008]

Buttler, Richard; Gill, Jaz. 2001, 'Formation and Control of Public-Private Partnerships: A Stakeholder Approach' in Johnson, Gerry; Scholes, Kevan (eds), Exploring Public Sector Strategy. Dorchester, UK: Pearson Education Ltd., Ch. 11

Cabinet Office, 1998, NHS Procurement Review, [Online] Cabinet Office. Available at: http://www.hcsu.org.uk/index.php?option=com_docman&task=doc_download&gid=454 [Accessed 23 May 2008]

CBI; QinetiQ. 2006. Innovation and Public Procurement: A New Approach to Stimulating Innovation [Online] CBI/QinetiQ. Available at: http://www.cbi.org.uk/pdf/innovationbrief1006.pdf [Accessed 29 May 2008]

Central England Procurement Partnership, 2006, Description: About CEPP [Online] CEPP. Available at: http://www.cepp.org.uk/description.html [Accessed 10 May 2008]

Centre for Effective Dispute Resolution, 2006., Press Release 25 May 2006: 'Conflicts Costs Business £33 Billion Every Year', [Online] CEDR, Available at: http://www.cedr.com/index.php?location=/news/archive/20060525_77.htm¶m=releases [Accessed 02 September 2008]

Chadwick, Tom. 2002 'Purchasing in the higher education sector' In Day, M (Eds.), Gower Handbook of Purchasing Management (3rd Edition) Aldershot: Gower. pp. 329-342

Chan, James L., 2003, 'Changing Roles of Public Financial Management' in Bovaird, Tony; Loffler, Elke (eds), Public Management and Governance. London: Routledge, pp.101-112

CIPFA, n.d., The CIPFA Financial Management Model, [Online] CIPFA, Accessed: http://www.cipfa-fm-model.org.uk/ [Accessed 08 August 2008]

Clarke, John., 2003, 'Security Through Inspection and Audit: Policies, Structures and Processes' in Bovaird, Tony; Loffler, Elke (eds), Public Management and Governance. London: Routledge, pp.149-160

Clarkson Centre for Business Ethics, 1999

Commission of European Communities., 2003, Commission Recommendation of 06/05/2003 Concerning the Definition of Micro, Small and Medium Sized Enterprises., [Online] European Commmission., Available at: http://ec.europa.eu/enterprise/enterprise_policy/sme_definition/decision_sme_en.pdf [Accessed 09 August 2008]

Cornwall County Council, 2005, Corporate Procurement Strategy 2005-2008 [Online] Cornwall County Council, Available at: http://www.cornwall.gov.uk/media/pdf/b/l/Corporate_Procurement_Strategy.pdf [Accessed 10 August 2008]

Cranfield University School of Management, 2008., Doughty Centre for Corporate Responsibility., [Online] Cranfied University., Available at: http://www.som.cranfield.ac.uk/som/research/centres/ccr/sources.asp [Accessed 30 August 2008]

Crosby, Philip., 1983., Quality is Free: The Art of Making Quality Certain., New York: McGraw-Hill.

Davis, Howard. 2003, 'Ethics and Standards of Conduct' in Bovaird, Tony; Loffler, Elke (eds), Public Management and Governance. London: Routledge, pp. 213-224

Drucker, Peter F., 2007., Innovation and Entrepreneurship, 2nd Rev ed., Oxford: Elsevier Ltd

Collier, Nardine; Fishwick, Frank; Johnson, Gerry (eds), 2001, 'The Process of Strategy Development in the Public Sector' in Johnson, Gerry; Scholes, Kevan (eds), Exploring Public Sector Strategy. Dorchester, UK: Pearson Education Ltd. Ch. 2

Conflict Management Plus., 2008., Case Studies: Individual Case Studies – Conflict Management Skills [Online] Conflict Management Plus, Available at: http://www.conflictmanagementplus.com/case_studies/conflict_manag.htm [Accessed 22 July 2008]

Cousins, P. D. 2002. 'A conceptual model for managing long-term inter-organizational relationships.' European Journal of Purchasing and Supply Management 8: 71–82.

District of Easington Corporate Procurement Manager., 2006., Adoption of the National SME Concordat., [Online] District of Easington., http://www.easington.gov.uk/images/SME%20Concordatreviewrepor_tcm4-8016.pdf [Accessed 10 May 2008]

Department for Business Enterprise and Regulatory Reform., 2007, Enterprise Directorate: Small and Medium Enterprise Statistics for the UK and Regions., [Online] (Updated 02 October 2008) BERR. Available at: http://stats.berr.gov.uk/ed/sme/ [Accessed 03 July 2008]

Department for Business Enterprise and Regulatory Reform, 2008, UK Government Response to the European Commissions Consultation [Online] BERR, http://www.berr.gov.uk/files/file45778.doc [Accessed 07 May 2008]

Department for Communities and Local Government, 2007, Developing the Local Government Services Market: Working Paper on Local Authority Shared Services, London: DCLG Publications

Department for Communities and Local Government, 2006, Rethinking Service Delivery: Volume Three – Shared Service and Public/Public Partnerships, London: DCLG Publications

Department for the Environment, Food and Rural Affairs., 2005., Schools calls time on old style lunches - North Cerney Primary School, [Online] Available at: http://www.defra.gov.uk/farm/policy/sustain/procurement/casestudies/northcerney.htm [Accessed 10 July 2008]

Department of Health, 2004, Choosing Health: Making Healthier Choices Easier, [Online] DH. Available from: http://www.dh.gov.uk/en/Publicationsandstatistics/Publications/PublicationsPolicyAndGuidance/DH_4094550?IdcService=GET_FILE&dID=2344&Rendition=Web [Accessed 07 July 2008]

Department of Trade and Industry., 2004, A Government Action Plan for Small Businesses, [Online] BERR, Available at: http://www.berr.gov.uk/files/file39767.pdf [Accessed 19 September]

Donaldson and Preston (1995)

European Foundation for Quality Management., n.d., EFQM Membership., [Online] EFQM., Available at: http://www.efqm.org/uploads/membership%20application%20and%20contract.pdf [Accessed 04 May 2008]

European Foundation for Quality Management., n.d., Introducing Excellence., [Online] EFQM., Available at: http://www.efqm.org/uploads/introducing_english.pdf [Accessed 02 June 2008]

European Foundation for Quality Management., n.d., The EFQM Excellence Model., [Online] EFQM., Available at: http://www.efqm.org/Default.aspx?tabid=35 [Accessed 19 July 2008]
Emmett, Stuart. 2005. Supply Chain Management in 90 Minutes., Gloucester: Management Books

Engle, P., 1997. The social organization of innovation: a focus on stakeholder interaction. Amsterdam, Netherlands: Royal Tropical Institute

Erridge, Andrew. 2003. 'Contracting for Public Services: Competition and Partnership' in Bovaird, Tony; Loffler, Elke (eds), Public Management and Governance. London: Routledge, pp.89-100

Erridige, Andrew., 2007., Machinery of Government. Lincolnshire: The Chartered Institute of Purchasing and Supply

Eversheds, 2007., Briefing note 69/2007 - A successful damages claim under the procurement regulations [Online] Eversheds, Available at: https://www.eversheds.com/uk/home/articles/index.page?ArticleID=templatedata%5CEversheds%5Carticles%5Cdata%5Cen%5CLocal_government%5CLocal_Government_briefing_note_69_2007 [Accessed 16 September 2008]

Forbes, Tom., 2001, 'Devolution and Control Within the UK Public Sector: National Health Service Trusts', in Johnson, Gerry; Scholes, Kevan (eds), Exploring Public Sector Strategy. Dorchester, UK: Pearson Education Ltd., Ch. 16

Freer, Steve., 2002., Keeping Pace with the Changing Role of the Public Sector Accountant., [Online] CIPFA., Available at: http://www.cipfa.org.uk/international//download/pres_sf_2002.doc [Accessed 29 April 2008]

Fox, Tom; Ward, Helina; Howard, Bruce., 2002, Public Sector Roles in Strengthening Corporate Social Responsibility: A Baseline Study [Online] The World Bank, Available at: http://info.worldbank.org/etools/docs/library/57491/Public%20Sector%20Roles%20in%20Strengthening%20Corporate%20Social%20Responsibility%20-%20A%20Baseline%20Study.pdf [Accessed 15 May 2008]

Frederick, 1998

Freeman, Edward R., 1984. Strategic Management: a Stakeholder Approach. Boston: Pitman

Freeman, R.; Gilbert, D., Jr. 1987, Managing Stakeholder Relations. In S. Prakhash; C. Falbe, ed. Business and Society: Dimensions of Conflict and Cooperation. Toronto: Lexington Books. pp.397-422

Frooman, J. 1999. 'Stakeholder influence strategies'. Academy of Management Review. Vol. 24, 191-205.

The Foundation Coalition (2001), How might you select your conflict management style? [Online] (Updated October 14 2008), The Foundation Coalition., Available at: http://www.foundationcoalition.org/home/keycomponents/teams/conflict1f.html [Accessed 13 June 2008]

Gershon, Peter., 1999, Tackling the Improvement of Public Sector Procurement, London: TSO

Gershon, Sir Peter., 2004, Releasing Resources to the Front Line: Independent Review of Public Sector Efficiency., London: TSO

Gibbons, Michael. 2007, Better Dispute Resolution: A Review of Employment Dispute Resolution in Great Britain [Online] Department for Business Enterprise and Regulatory Reform. Available at: http://www.berr.gov.uk/files/file38516.pdf [Accessed 24 July 2008]

Gillbert, John., 2004., How to Eat and Elephant: A Slice by Slice Guide to Total Quality Management (3rd ed.)., Liverpool: Liverpool Business Publishing

Goleman, Daniel., 1998, Working With Emotional Intelligence,. New York: Bantham Books.

Goodall, Niel., 2004, Best Practice for Public Sector I.T. Projects, [Online] Tescom, Available at: http://tescom-intl.com/site/en/tescom.asp?pi=61&doc_id=2005 [Accessed 17 June 2008]

Grimble, R; Wellard, K. 1996. Stakeholder methologies in natural resource management: a review of principles, contexts, experiences and opportunites. Paper presented at the ODA NRSP Socioeconomic Methologies Workshop, 29-30 Apr, 1996, London, UK

Harrington, Barbara; Mcloughin, Kevin; Riddell, Duncan (eds), 2001, 'Business Process Re-Engineering in the Public Sector: A Case Study of the Contributions Agency' in Johnson, Gerry; Scholes, Kevan (eds), 2001, Exploring Public Sector Strategy. Dorchester, UK: Pearson Education Ltd., Ch. 15

Hampshire County Council., 2008., Contract Standing Order Procedures – The Constitution: Part 3., [Online] (Updated 14 April 2008) Hampshire County Council. Available at: http://www3.hants.gov.uk/constitution/part3/part3_f.htm [Accessed 12 August 2008]

Herbert, David. 2001, 'Clinical Governance' in Johnson, Gerry; Scholes, Kevan (eds), Exploring Public Sector Strategy. Dorchester, UK: Pearson Education Ltd. Ch. 7

Hill, Sandra. 2001, 'Public Sector Partnerships and public/Voluntary Sector Partnerships: The Scottish Experience' in Johnson, Gerry; Scholes, Kevan (eds), Exploring Public Sector Strategy. Dorchester, UK: Pearson Education Ltd., Ch. 12

HM Government., 2005, Securing the Future: The UK Government Sustainable Development Strategy, (Cm. 6467) London: HMSO

HM Treasury., 2003., Managing the Risk of Fraud: A Guide for Managers,. [Online] HM Treasury., Available at: http://64.233.183.104/search?q=cache:oNfbAOIHKNUJ:www.hm-treasury.gov.uk/media/2/8/Managing_the_risk_fraud.pdf+A+risk-based+approach+enables+organisations+to+target+their+resources,+both+for+improving+controls+and+for+pro-active&hl=en&ct=clnk&cd=1&gl=uk [Accessed 28 April 2008]

HM Treasury., 2007., Managing Public Money., London: TSO

HM Treasury., 2002., Opportunity and Security for All: Investigating in an Enterprising, Fairer Britain – New Public Spending Plans 2003-2006., [Online] HM Treasury., Available at: http://62.164.176.164/3080.htm [Accessed 13 July 2008]

HM Treasury. 2007. Transforming Government Procurement. London: TSO

Improvement and Development Agency, 2003, Sustainability and Local Government Improvement [Online] I&DeA., Available at: http://www.idea.gov.uk/idk/aio/1701515 [Accessed 16 June 2008]

Improvement and Development Agency, 2003, Local Government Sustainable Procurement Strategy [Online] I&DeA., Available at: http://www.idea.gov.uk/idk/aio/7643299 [Accessed 16 June 2008]

Improvement Network., n.d., Financial Management: What is it About?. [Online] Idea., Available at: http://www.idea.gov.uk/imp/core/page.do?pageId=1006639 [Accessed 19 August 2008]

Johnson, Gerry., 2001, 'Mapping and Re-Mapping Organisational Culture: A Local Government Example; in Johnson, Gerry; Scholes, Kevan (eds), 2001, Exploring Public Sector Strategy. Dorchester, UK: Pearson Education Ltd., Ch. 17

Jørgensen; Bank, Helle; Pruzan-Jørgensen, Michael P.; Jungk, Margaret; and Cramer, Aron., 2003. Strengthening Implementation of Corporate Social Responsibility in Global Supply Chains. World Bank and International Finance Corporation: Washington, D.C.

Johnson, G. & Scholes, K. 2001. Exploring Corporate Strategy (2nd ed.). London: Prentice Hall.

Juran, Joseph M., 1992., Juran on Quality by Design: The New Steps for Planning Quality into Goods and Services., New York: NY Free Press

Kano, Noriaki, 1984. "Attractive quality and must-be quality". The Journal of the Japanese Society for Quality Control (14:2), 39-48.

Kaplan, Robert S.; Norton, David P., 1992., "The Balanced Scorecard: Measures That Drive Performance," Harvard Business Review (January-February 1992), 71-79

Kepplinger, Gary L., 2008., Decision., [Online] GAO., Available at http://www.gao.gov/decisions/bidpro/311344.pdf [Assessed 18 August 2008]
Kraljic, P., 1983. 'Purchasing must become supply management'. Harvard Business Review 61 (5), 109–117.

Lancaster University Management School. 2005 Case Study of Successful Complex IT Projects [online] Lancaster University. Available at: http://bcs.org/upload/pdf/casestudy.pdf [Accessed 17 September 2008]
Lock

Leeds Council Procurement Unit, 2008, Contracts' Procedure Rules, [online] Leeds Council, Available at: http://www.leeds.gov.uk/files/Internet2007/2008/25/contract%20procedure%20rules%20-%20may%202008.pdf [Accessed 01 May 2008]
Local Government Task Force., 2006., Top Ten Tips for a Successful Procurement Process [Online] BPI Solutions., Available at: http://www.bipsolutions.com/pdf/tentoptips.pdf [Accessed 02 June 2008]

Loffler, Elke, 2003,. 'Governance and Government: Networking with External Stakeholders' in Bovaird, Tony; Loffler, Elke (eds), Public Management and Governance. London: Routledge, pp.163-174

Long, N. 1992. 'From paradigm to lost paradigm regained?' In N.Long; A.Long ed. Battlefields of Knowledge: the Interlocking of Theory and Practice in Social Research and Development. London, UK: Routledge, pp.16-43

Macbeth, D.K. (2002). Managing a portfolio of supplier relationships. In Day, M (Eds.), Gower Handbook of Purchasing Management (3rd Edition) Aldershot: Gower. pp. 51-62

Maclay, Murry & Spenc LLP., 2008., Procurement Update: Spring 2008., [Online] MMS., Available at: http://emailinfo.mms.co.uk/go.asp?/mPOTCN8/bMMS001 [Accessed 06 August 2008]

Marshall, Richard M., n.d. What's So Bad About Conflict? [Online] Devx.

Available at: http://careerlink.devx.com/articles/hc0002/hc0002.asp. [Accessed 16 July 2008]

Martin, Steve. 2003, 'Engaging With Citizens and Other Stakeholders' in Bovaird, Tony; Loffler, Elke (eds), Public Management and Governance. London: Routledge, pp.189-202

Maylor, Harvey., 2003., Project Management (3rd edition)., Essex: Financial Times/ Prentice Hall

McCarron, Brendon., 2003, Introduction to "Lean Thinking" [Online] CIPFA., Available at: http://www.cipfanetworks.net/fileupload/upload/Lean_briefing1912007311331.pdf [Accessed 11 April 2008]

Mendelow, A. 1991. 'Stakeholder Mapping', Proceedings of the Second International Conference of Information Systems, Cambridge, MA
Ministry of Defence., 2005., Ministry of Defence Annual Reports and Accounts 2005-06., (Hc. 1394) London: TSO

Ministry of Defence, 2007, Ministry of Defence Plan 2007., [Online] MOD Available at : http://www.mod.uk/NR/rdonlyres/A5810AB5-6CDB-4B97-A8CF-976D3B9676B4/0/defence_plan2007.pdf [Accessed....]

Ministry of Defence., 2005., Defence Industrial Strategy: Defence White Paper., (Cm 6697) London: HMSO [Accessed 20 September 2008]

Moor, David., n.d, Cases in Defence Acquisition (in preparation)

Murray, Gordan., n.d. ...In the Spotlight: Scrutinising Strategic Procurement. [Online] I&DeA., Available at: http://www.idea.gov.uk/idk/aio/1701470 [Accessed 18 August 2008]

Murry, James., 2006., Report Labels Public Sector IT Chiefs "Reckless"., [Online] IT Week,. Available at: http://www.computing.co.uk/itweek/news/2164899/report-labels-public-sector.htm [Accessed 14 May 2008]

Nabarro, 2008, Controlling Conflict: The Management and Avoidence of Disputes. Nabarro [online] Available at: http://www.nabarro.com/Downloads/Controlling%20conflict.pdf [Accessed 19 May 2008]

National Audit Office., 2005, Ministry of Defence - Driving the Successful Delivery of Major Defence Projects: Effective Project Control is a Key Factor in Successful Projects, [Online] NAO. Available at: http://www.nao.org.uk/publications/nao_reports/05-06/050630es.pdf [Accessed 22 August 2008]

National Audit Office., 2006. Ministry of Defence: Major Project Reports 2006, London: TSO

National Computing Centre. N.d. Managing Conflict in the e-world. [online] NCC. Available at: http://www.nccmembership.co.uk/pooled/articles/BF_WEBART/view.asp?Q=BF_WEBART_113245 [Accessed 25 August 2008]

National Health Service, 2005, SMEs – Capturing Information on Our Contract Management System., [Online] NHS,. Available at: http://www.pasa.nhs.uk/environrpt/2005/purchasing/smes.htm [Accessed14 August 2008]

National Health Service, 2008. Leicestershire and Rutland NHS Procurement Partnership [Online] NHS. Available at: http://www.leicsprocurement.nhs.uk/ [Accessed 11 May 2008]

Nolan, Lord Michael., 1995., Standards in Public Life: First Report of the Committee on Standards in Public Life., Volume 1: Report., (Cm. 2850-I) London: HSMO

Office of the Deputy Prime Minister., 2003., National Procurement Strategy For Local Government. [Online] ODPM., Available at: http://www.rce.gov.uk/rce/aio/10209 [Accessed 17 September 2008]

Office of the Deputy Prime Minister. 2005. An Organisational Development Resource Document for Local Government, London: ODPM Publications

Office of Government Commerce., n.d., Communications Strategy., [Online] OGC, Available at: http://www.ogc.gov.uk/documentation_and_templates_communications_strategy_.asp [Accessed 09 July 2008]

Office of Government Commerce., n.d., The Government Procurement Code of Good Practice: For Customers and Suppliers. [Online] OGC., Available at: http://www.ogc.gov.uk/documents/cp0080_Gov_Procurement_Code_Good_Practice.pdf [Accessed 15 May 2008]

Office of Government Commerce. n.d. Procurement Capability Reviews [online] OGC. Available at: http://www.ogc.gov.uk/ogc_-_transforming_government_procurement_procurement_capability_reviews.asp [Accessed 15 May 2008]

Office of Government Commerce. n.d. Stakeholder Issues (Stakeholder Map) [online] OGC. Available at: http://www.ogc.gov.uk/documentation_and_templates_stakeholder_issues_stakeholder_map.asp [Accessed 06 April 2008]

Office of Government Commerce, n.d. Tendering for Public Contracts: A Guide for Small Businesses [Online] Supply2.gov.uk., Available at: http://www.supply2.gov.uk/pdfs/file39469.pdf [Accessed 17 June 2008]

Office of Government Commerce. 2008. By and Make a Difference: How to Address Social Issues in Public Procurement., [Online] OGC, Available at: http://www.ogc.gov.uk/documents/Social_Issues_in_Public_Procurement.pdf [Accessed 15 May 2008]

Office of Government Commerce. 2005. Smaller Supplier…Better Value? The Value of Money that Small Firms Can Offer., [Online] OGC, Available at: http://www.ogc.gov.uk/documents/Small_Supplier_Better_Value.pdf [Accessed 18 March 2008]

Office of Government Commerce, 2006, Supply Chain Management Wizard [Online] OGC., Available at: http://www.ogc.gov.uk/documents/SupplyChainWizard.pdf [Accessed 06 April 2008]

Office of Government Commerce. 2004. Managing Risks with Delivery Partners [Online] OGC. Available at: http://www.ogc.gov.uk/documents/cp0013.pdf [Accessed 26 May 2008]

Office of Government Commerce. 2006. Category Management Toolkit: Stakeholder Management Plan. [online] OGC. Available at: http://www.ogc.gov.uk/documents/Stakeholder_Management_Plan.pdf [Accessed 02 August 2009]

Office of Government Commerce., 2003, OGC Report to the Chancellor of the Exchequer: Increasing Competition and Improving Long-Term Capacity Planning in the Government Market Place, [Online] OGC., Available at: http://www.ogc.gov.uk/documents/report_to_Chancellor.pdf [Accessed 16 May 2008]

Office of Government Commerce, 2007. OGC Gateway Review [online] (updated 04 August 2008) OGC, Available at: http://www.ogc.gov.uk/ppm_documents_ogc_gateway.asp [Accessed 16 May 2008]

Office of Government Commerce, 1999, The Procurement Excellence Pilot., [Online] OGC., Available at: http://www.ogc.gov.uk/documents/Procurement_Excellence_Pilot.pdf [Accessed 16 May 2008]

Office of Government Commerce., n.d., Procurement Excellence Model., [Online] (Updated 2008/06/03) OGC., Available at: http://www.ogc.gov.uk/procurement_documents_procurement_excellence_model_publications_guidance.asp [Accessed 16 May 2008]

Office of Government Commerce., n.d., Resources for All., [Online] (Updated 2008/10/01) OGC., Available at: http://www.ogc.gov.uk/Resource_Toolkit_resources_for_all.asp [Accessed 19 September 2008]

Office of Government Commerce., 2007., Improving Performance: Project Evaluation and Benchmarking – Achieving Excellence in Construction Procurement Guide [Online] OGC, Available at: http://www.ogc.gov.uk/documents/CP0068AEGuide8.pdf [Accessed 20 May 2008]

Patton, Rob. N.d. Keeping Conflict Constructive, [online] Open University. Available at: http://www.open2.net/moneyandmanagement/management_organisation/keeping_conflict_constructive.html [Accessed 30 August 2008]

Pajunen, Kalle; Näsi Juha. 2004. Stakeholder Management as a Play. In The Proceedings of e-Business Research Forum 2004. Tampre, Finland: Tampere University of Technology, pp. 520-533

Pembroke County Council., n.d., Procurement Strategy: 2006 – 2011., [Online] Pembroke County Council, Available at: www.pembrokeshire.gov.uk/objview.asp?Language=&object_id=2684 [Accessed 02 May 2008]

Prince, Les; Puffitt, Ray., 2001., 'The Maslin Multi-Dimensional Matrix: A New Tool to Aid Strategic Decision Making in the Public Sector' in Johnson, Gerry; Scholes, Kevan (eds), Exploring Public Sector Strategy. Dorchester, UK: Pearson Education Ltd, Ch. 8

Quality Scotland., n.d. EFQM., [Online] Quality Scotland., Available at: http://www.qualityscotland.co.uk/efqm.asp [Accessed 13 April 2008]

Ramirez, Ricardo., 1999. 'Chapter 5: Stakeholder analysis and conflict management'. In Daniel Buckles ed. Cultivating Peace: Conflict and Collaboration in Natural Resource Management. Washington DC: International Development Research Centre. Ch.2

Raudsepp, Eugene., Hone Your Skills to Boost Your Career, [online] Available at: http://www.salesopedia.com/content/view/343/10479/ [Accessed 11 August 2008]

Reed (2002) ….. (Page 5)
Röling, N.; Wagemakers, M. ed. 1998. Facilitating Sustainable Agriculture: Participatory Learning and Active Management in times of Environmental Uncertainty. Cambridge, UK: Cambridge University Press

RR Donnelly. 2008. The Best Practice Indicators for Public Procurement in Scotland: Guidance [Online] The Scottish Government. Available at: http://www.scotland.gov.uk/Resource/Doc/225104/0060921.pdf [Accessed 12 May 2008]

Savage, G. T., Nix, T. W., Whitehead, C. J. & Blair, J. D. 1991. Strategies for assessing and managing organizational stakeholders. Academy of Management Executive. Vol. 5, 61-75.

SBAC. 2006. 21st Century Supply Chains (SC21) [Online] (Updated 5 Oct 2008) SBAC. Available at: http://www.sbac.co.uk/pages/80338686.asp [Accessed 09 May 2008]

Scholes, Kevan., 2001, 'Stakeholder Mapping: A Practical Tool for Public Sector Managers' in Johnson, Gerry; Scholes, Kevan (eds), Exploring Public Sector Strategy. Dorchester, UK: Pearson Education Ltd., Ch. 9

Scholes, Kevan., 2001, 'Strategy and Structures in the Public Sector' in Johnson, Gerry; Scholes, Kevan (eds), 2001, Exploring Public Sector Strategy. Dorchester, UK: Pearson Education Ltd., Ch. 13

Scottish Environmental Protection Agency. 2006. River Basin Planning Strategy for the Scotland River Basin District. [online] SEPA Available at: http://www.sepa.org.uk/pdf/wfd/rbmp/strategy/rbmp_strategy.pdf [Accessed 14 May 2008]

Simms, Sir Neville (ed.)., 2006, Procuring the Future – Sustainable Procurement National Action Plan: Recommendations from Sustainable Procurement Task Force [Online] Department for the Environment, Food and Rural Affairs. Available at: http://www.defra.gov.u k/sustainable/government/publications/procurement-action-plan/documents/full-document.pdf [Accessed 17 May 2008]

Supply2.gov.uk., 2008., Supply2.gov.uk: Supplier Route to Government [Online] Supply2.gov.uk., Available at: http://www.supply2.gov.uk/ [Accessed 16 April 2008]

Susskind, L.; Cruikshank, J. 1987. Breaking the Impass. New York: Basic Books

Sustainable Procurement Cupboard, n.d., Sustainable Procurement Cupboard Case Study: Local Authorities Standardise the Pre-Qualification Questionnaire (PQQ) in the East Midlands., [Online] Sustainable Procurement Cupboard., Available at: http://www.procurementcupboard.org/Files/Sustainable%20 Procurement%20Cupboard%20Case%20Study%20PQQv2.doc [Accessed 11June 1008]

The Better Regulation Task Force; Small Business Council., 2003., Government: Supporter or Customer?., [Online] BRTF., Available at: http:// www.ogc.gov.uk/better_regulation_task_force_smes___brtf_monitoring.asp [Accessed 19 June 2008]

The Foundation Coalition, n.d. Understanding Conflict and Conflict Management, [Online] The Foundation Coalition. Available at: http://www. foundationcoalition.org/publications/brochures/conflict.pdf [Accessed 19 April 2008]

The Glasgow Herald,. 2008., Glasgow hospital project to be 100% public funded,. [Online] The Glasgow Herald, Available at: http://www.theherald. co.uk/news/news/display.var.2216026.0.Glasgow_hospital_project_to_ be_100_public_funded.php [Accessed 24 July 2008]

The Highland Council. 2007. Contract Standing Orders. [Online] The Highland Council. Available at: http://www.highland.gov.uk/NR/ rdonlyres/00D39820-0874-44B4-82DD-D702B3A3F3D5/0/highlandcouncilco ntractstandingordersdecember2007final.pdf [Accessed 28 May 2008]

Thomas, Kenneth W.; Kilmann, Ralph H., 1974, Thomas-Kilmann Conflict MODE Instrument, Mountain View, CA: Xicom and CPP Inc.

University of Gloucestershire., 2006., Procurement Manual., [Online] The Enviromental Association for Universities and Colleges., Available at: http:// www.eauc.org.uk/file_uploads/uogpurchsection1_4issue1.pdf [Accessed 02 September 2008]

United Nations General Assembly., 1987., 42/187.Report of the World Commission on Environment and Development [A/RES/42/187] Available at: http://www.un.org/documents/ga/res/42/ares42-187.htm

Ward, Helina., 2004, Public Sector Roles in Strengthening Corporate Social Responsibility: Taking Stock, [Online] The World Bank ;International Finance Corporation., Available at: http://www.iied.org/pubs/pdfs/16014IIED.pdf [Accessed 15 May 2008]

West Midlands Police Authority, 2008, Terms of Reference: Finance and Resource Committee, [Online] West Midlands Police Authority. Available at: http://www.west-midlands-pa.gov.uk/terms_fas.asp [Accessed 09 May 2008]

Womack, James P.; Jones, Daniel T., 2003., Lean Thinking: Banish Waste and Create Wealth in Your Corporation, New York: Simon & Schuster

Womack, James P., Jones, Daniel T., 2005, "Lean consumption", Harvard Business Review, Vol. 83 No.3, pp.58-69.

Womack, James P.; Jones, Daniel T.; Roos, Daniel., 2007., The Machine that Changed the World., New York: Simon & Schuster

Wilkinson, Matthew., n.d. The Pilot OpenStrategy® for Sustainable Procurement in the North West - Final Project Report to Defra Sustainable Procurement Task Force Secretariat [Online] North West Regional Planning Technical Website Available at: http://www.nwrpb.org.uk/downloads/documents/aug_06/nwra_1156411980_Final_Project_Report_to_the_DE.pdf [Accessed 16 May 2008]

Wisniewski, Mik., 2001, 'Measuring Up to the Best: A Managers Guide to Benchmarking' in Johnson, Gerry; Scholes, Kevan (eds), Exploring Public Sector Strategy. Dorchester, UK: Pearson Education Ltd., Ch. 5